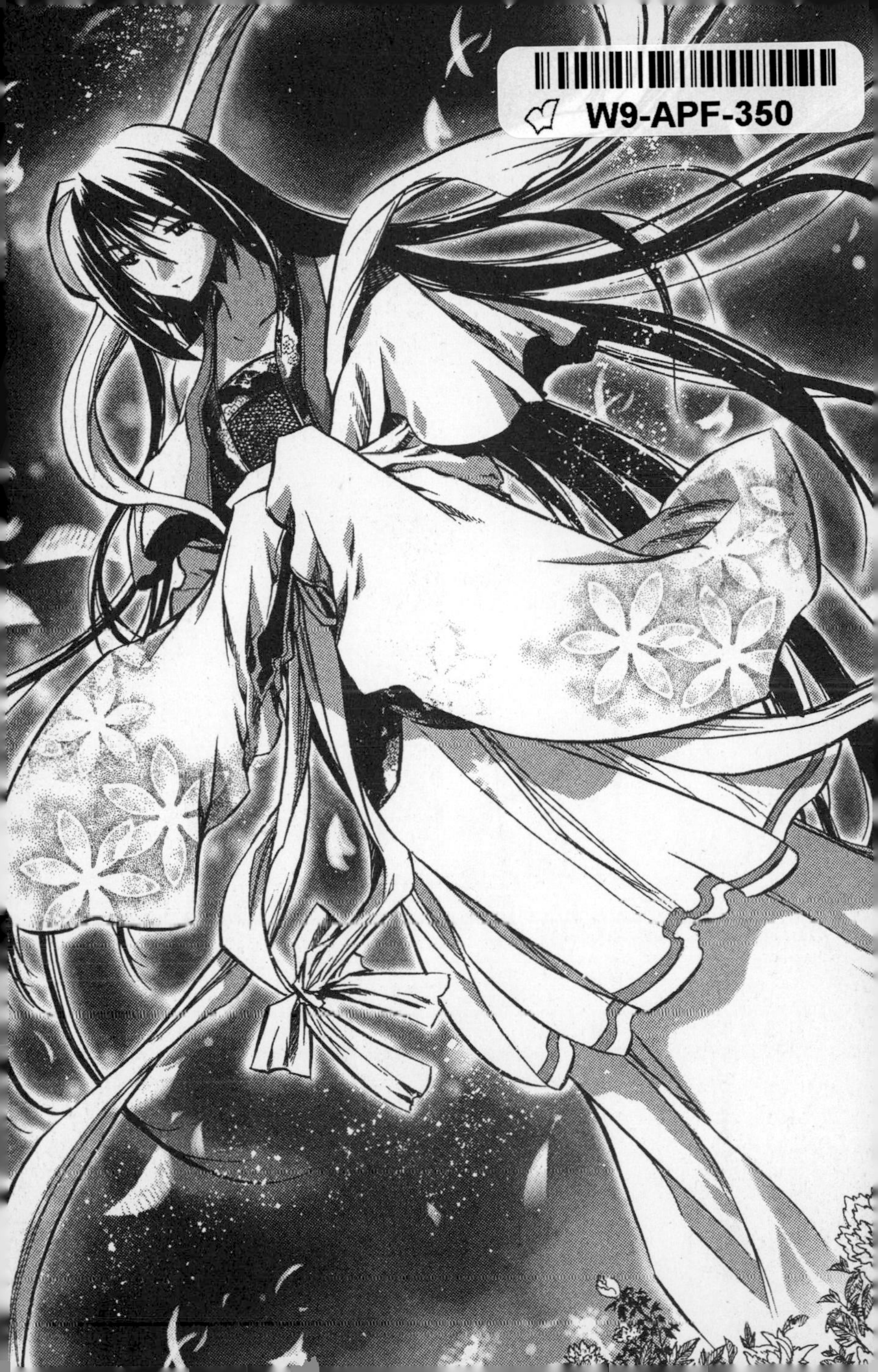

CHRONICLES OF THE CURSED SWORD

Volume 7

Story by
YEO BEOP-RYONG
Art by
PARK HUI-JIN

Los Angeles • Tokyo • London • Hamburg

Translator - Yongju Ryu
English Adaptation - Matt Varosky
Copy Editor - Aaron Sparrow
Retouch and Lettering - Abelardo Bigting
Cover Layout - Gary Shum
Graphic Designer - Vicente Rivera, Jr.

Editor - Bryce P. Coleman
Digital Imaging Manager - Chris Buford
Pre-Press Manager - Antonio DePietro
Production Managers - Jennifer Miller and Mutsumi Miyazaki
Art Director - Matt Alford
Managing Editor - Jill Freshney
VP of Production - Ron Klamert
President & C.O.O. - John Parker
Publisher & C.E.O. - Stuart Levy

E-mail: info@TOKYOPOP.com
Come visit us online at www.TOKYOPOP.com

A 🔊 TOKYOPOP® Manga

TOKYOPOP Inc.
5900 Wilshire Blvd. Suite 2000
Los Angeles, CA 90036

Chronicles of the Cursed Sword Vol. 7

ISBN: 1-59182-424-9

First TOKYOPOP printing: July 2004

10 9 8 7 6 5 4 3 2 1

Printed in the USA

Chronicles

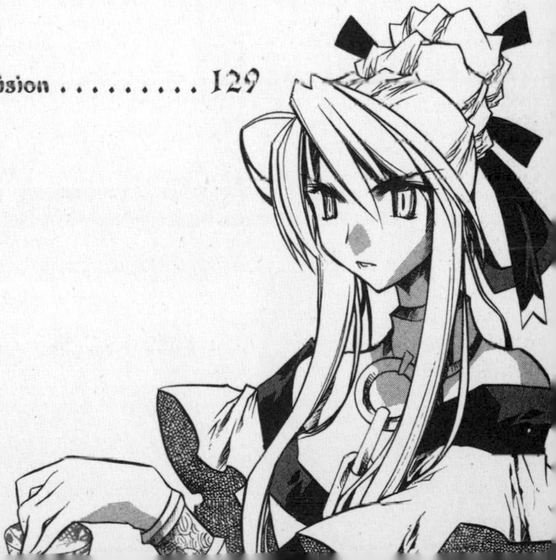

CHRONICLES OF THE CURSED SWORD

the cast of characters

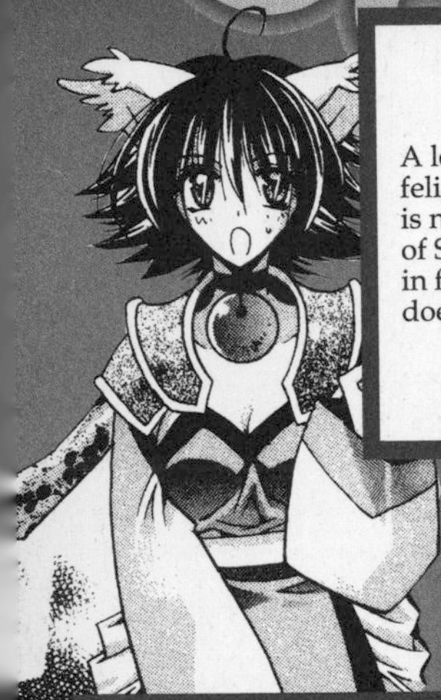

MINGLING

A lesser demon with feline qualities, Mingling is now the loyal follower of Shyao Lin. She lives in fear of Rey, who still doesn't trust her.

THE PASA SWORD

A living sword that hungers for demon blood. It grants its user incredible power, but at a great cost—it can take over the user's body and, in time, his soul.

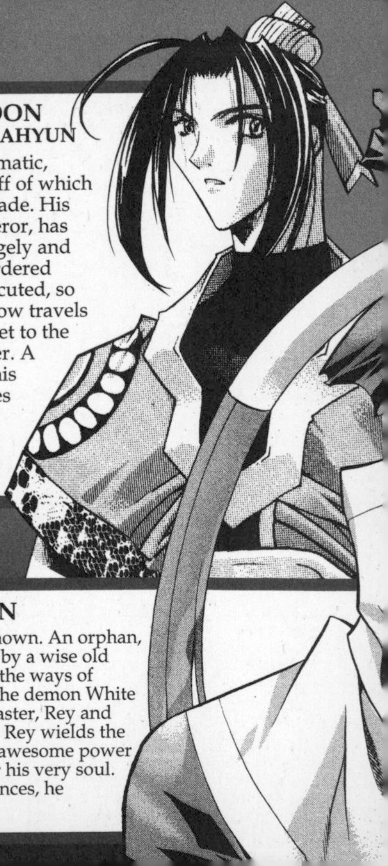

JARYOON
KING OF HAHYUN

Noble and charismatic, Jaryoon is the stuff of which great kings are made. His brother, the emperor, has been acting strangely and apparently has ordered Jaryoon to be executed, so the young king now travels to the capital to get to the heart of the matter. A great warrior in his own right, he does not have magical abilities and is unaccustomed to battling demons.

SHYAO LIN

A sorceress and Rey Yan's traveling companion. Shyao grew fond of Rey during their five years of study together with their master, and thinks of him as her little brother. She's Rey's conscience—his sole tie to humanity. She also seems quite enamored with the handsome Jaryoon.

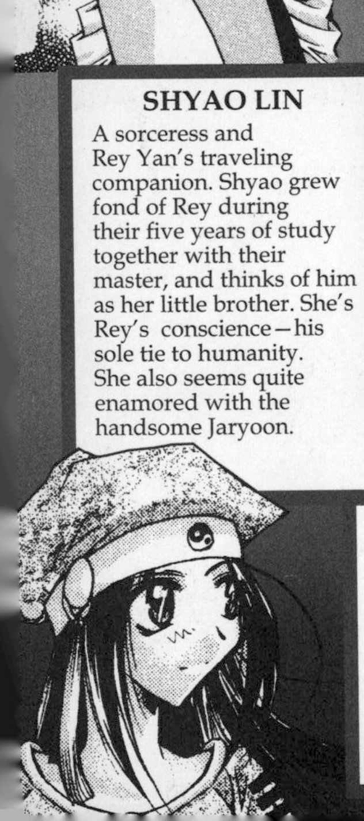

REY YAN

Rey's origins remain unknown. An orphan, he and Shyao were raised by a wise old man who trained them in the ways of combat and magic. After the demon White Tiger slaughtered their master, Rey and Shyao became wanderers. Rey wields the PaSa sword, a weapon of awesome power that threatens to take over his very soul. Under the right circumstances, he could be a hero.

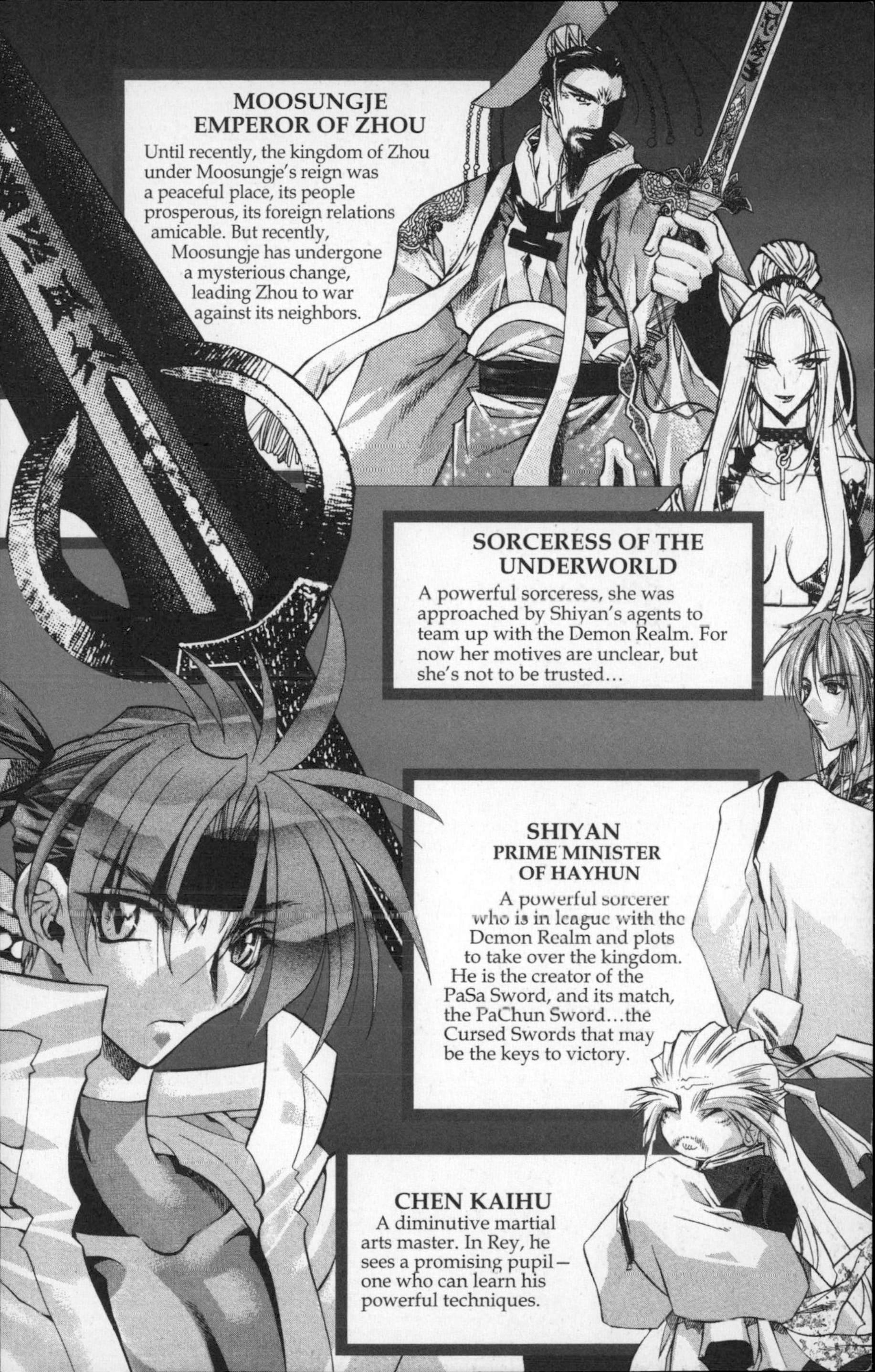

MOOSUNGJE
EMPEROR OF ZHOU

Until recently, the kingdom of Zhou under Moosungje's reign was a peaceful place, its people prosperous, its foreign relations amicable. But recently, Moosungje has undergone a mysterious change, leading Zhou to war against its neighbors.

SORCERESS OF THE UNDERWORLD

A powerful sorceress, she was approached by Shiyan's agents to team up with the Demon Realm. For now her motives are unclear, but she's not to be trusted...

SHIYAN
PRIME MINISTER OF HAYHUN

A powerful sorcerer who is in league with the Demon Realm and plots to take over the kingdom. He is the creator of the PaSa Sword, and its match, the PaChun Sword...the Cursed Swords that may be the keys to victory.

CHEN KAIHU

A diminutive martial arts master. In Rey, he sees a promising pupil—one who can learn his powerful techniques.

The story so far...

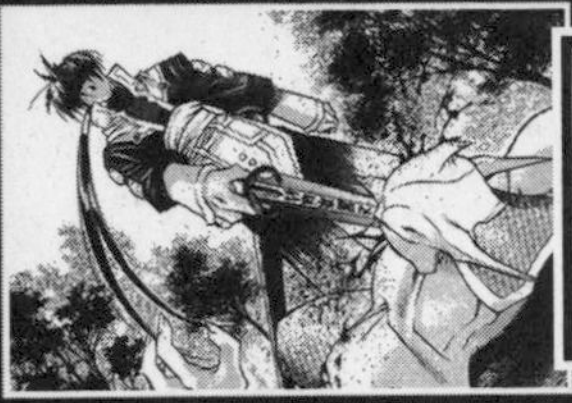

Rey Yan and Shyao Lin rescued Jaryoon using Rey's cursed PaSa sword.

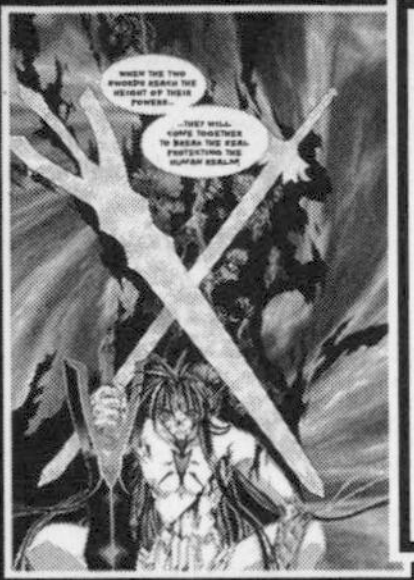
WHEN THE TWO SWORDS REACH THE HEIGHT OF THEIR POWERS...
...THEY WILL COME TOGETHER TO BREAK THE SEAL PROTECTING THE HUMAN REALM.

The demon possessing Rey conspires with the Sorceress of the Underworld to summon the Demon Emperor by combining the powers of the PaSa and PaChun swords.

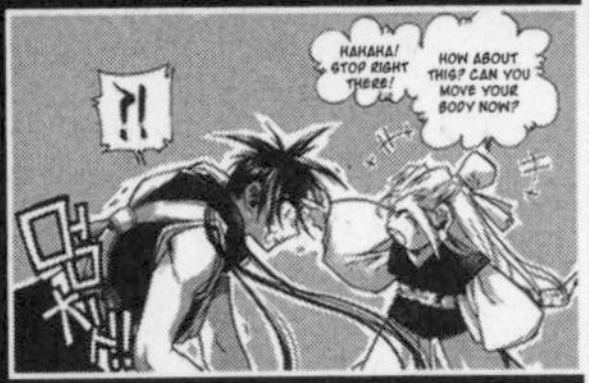
?!
HAHAHA! STOP RIGHT THERE!
HOW ABOUT THIS? CAN YOU MOVE YOUR BODY NOW?

Rey begins rigorous training with chen Kaihu—a diminuitive martial arts master with powerful techniques.

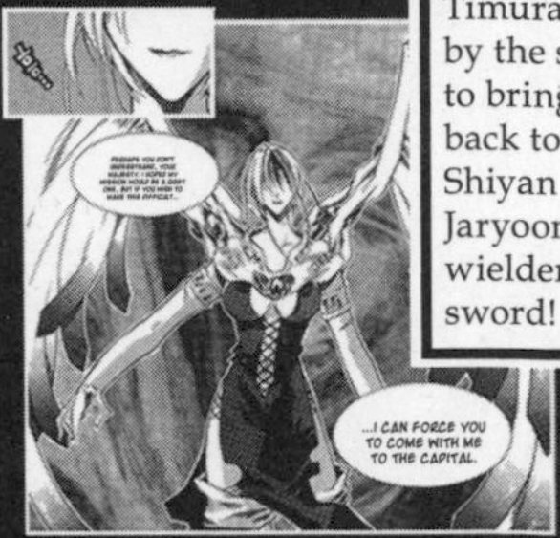
...I CAN FORCE YOU TO COME WITH ME TO THE CAPITAL.

Timura Oshu is sent by the sinister Shiyan to bring Jaryoon back to the capital. Shiyan has plans for Jaryoon—as the new wielder of the PaChun sword!

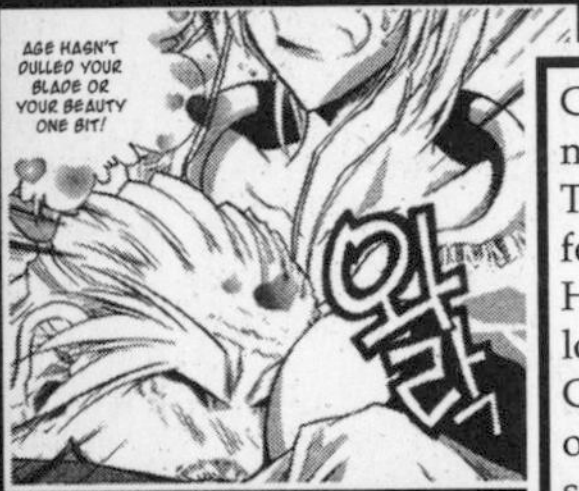
AGE HASN'T DULLED YOUR BLADE OR YOUR BEAUTY ONE BIT!

Chen Kaihu mistakes Timura Oshu for Lady Hwaren, his long-lost love. Could they be one and the same?

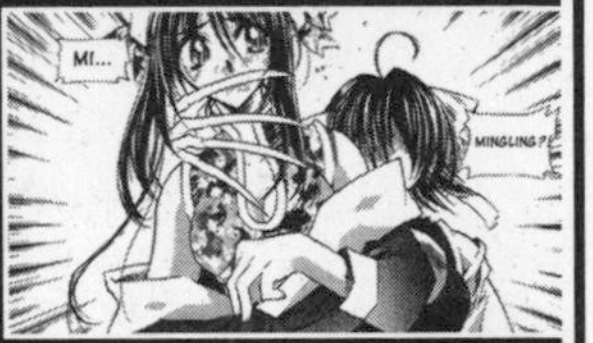
MI...
MINGLING?!

Timura Oshu possesses Mingling, using her to threaten Shyao's life. Given no choice, Jaryoon reluctantly accompanies Timura to the capital...

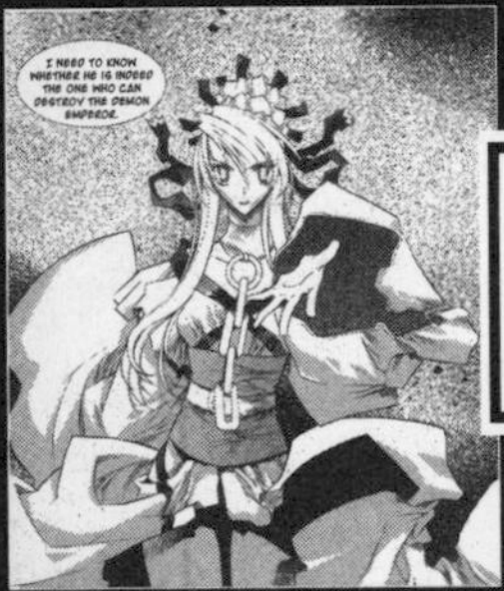
I NEED TO KNOW WHETHER HE IS INDEED THE ONE WHO CAN DESTROY THE DEMON EMPEROR.

The powerful woman warrior Hyacia tracks down Rey. She wants to test his mettle in order to determine if he's powerful enough to defeat the Demon Emperor.

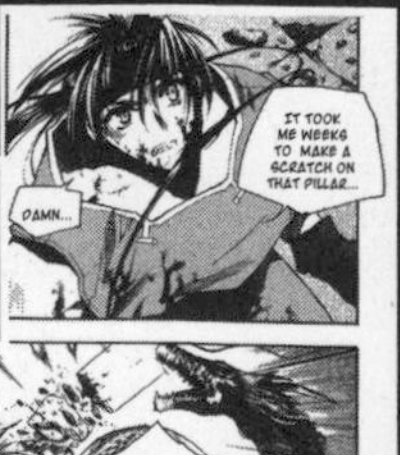
IT TOOK ME WEEKS TO MAKE A SCRATCH ON THAT PILLAR...
DAMN...

Rey battles Shouren—the Sorcerer of the Dark—whose true form is that of a dragon!

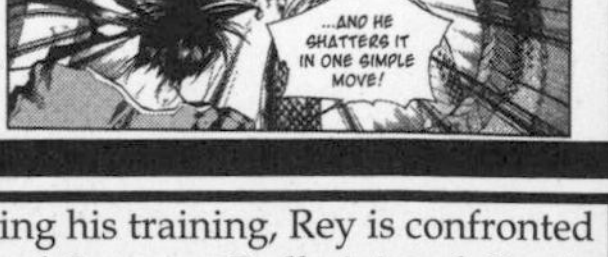
...AND HE SHATTERS IT IN ONE SIMPLE MOVE!

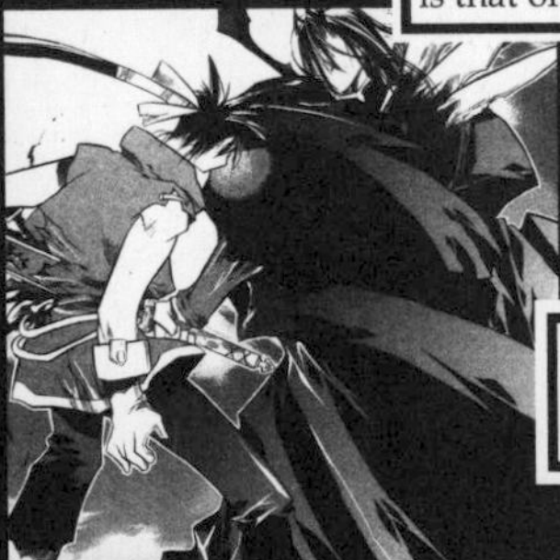

After completing his training, Rey is confronted by the possessed, Jaryoon. Badly injured, Rey is saved at the last moment by Hyacia...

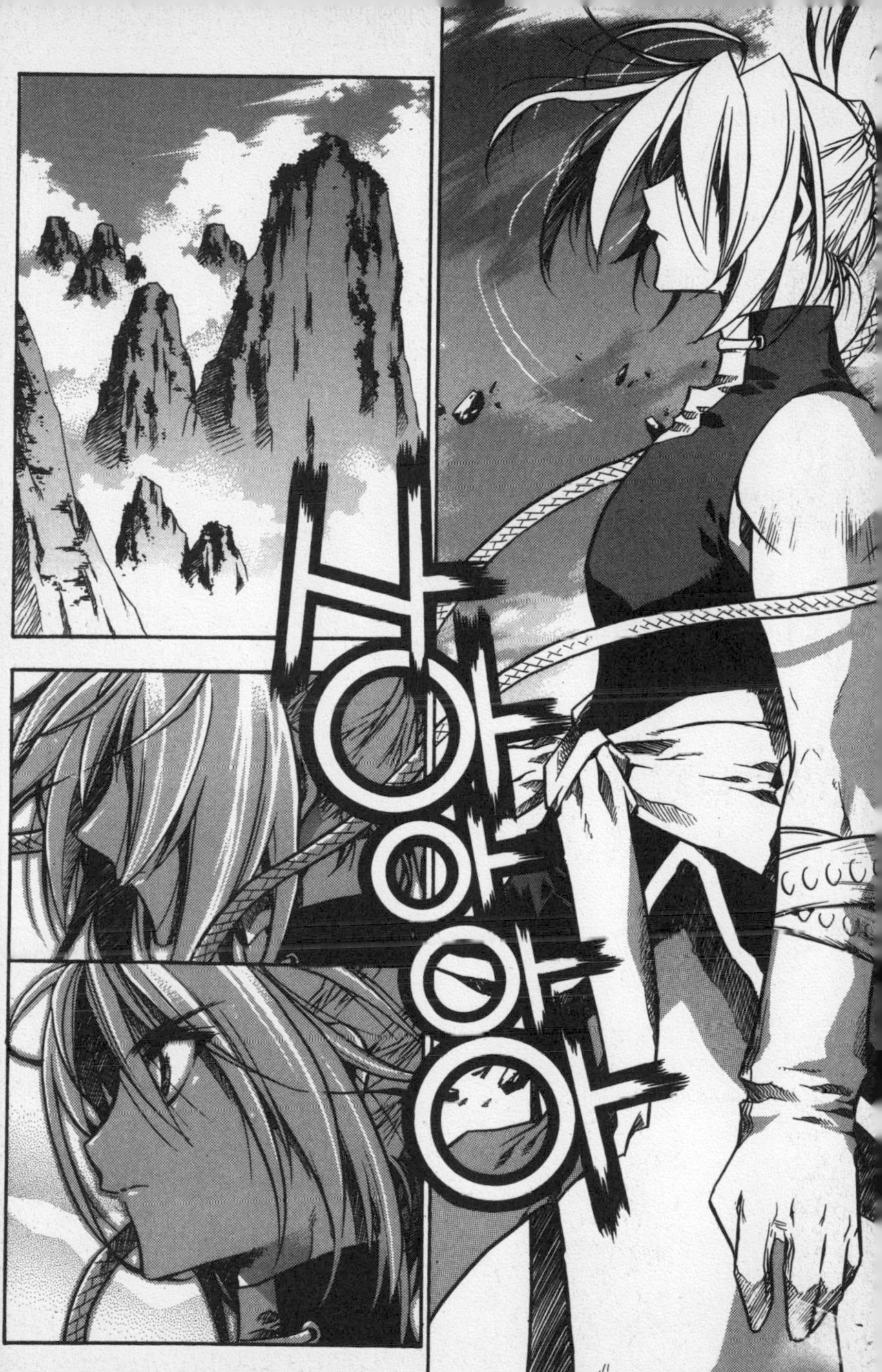

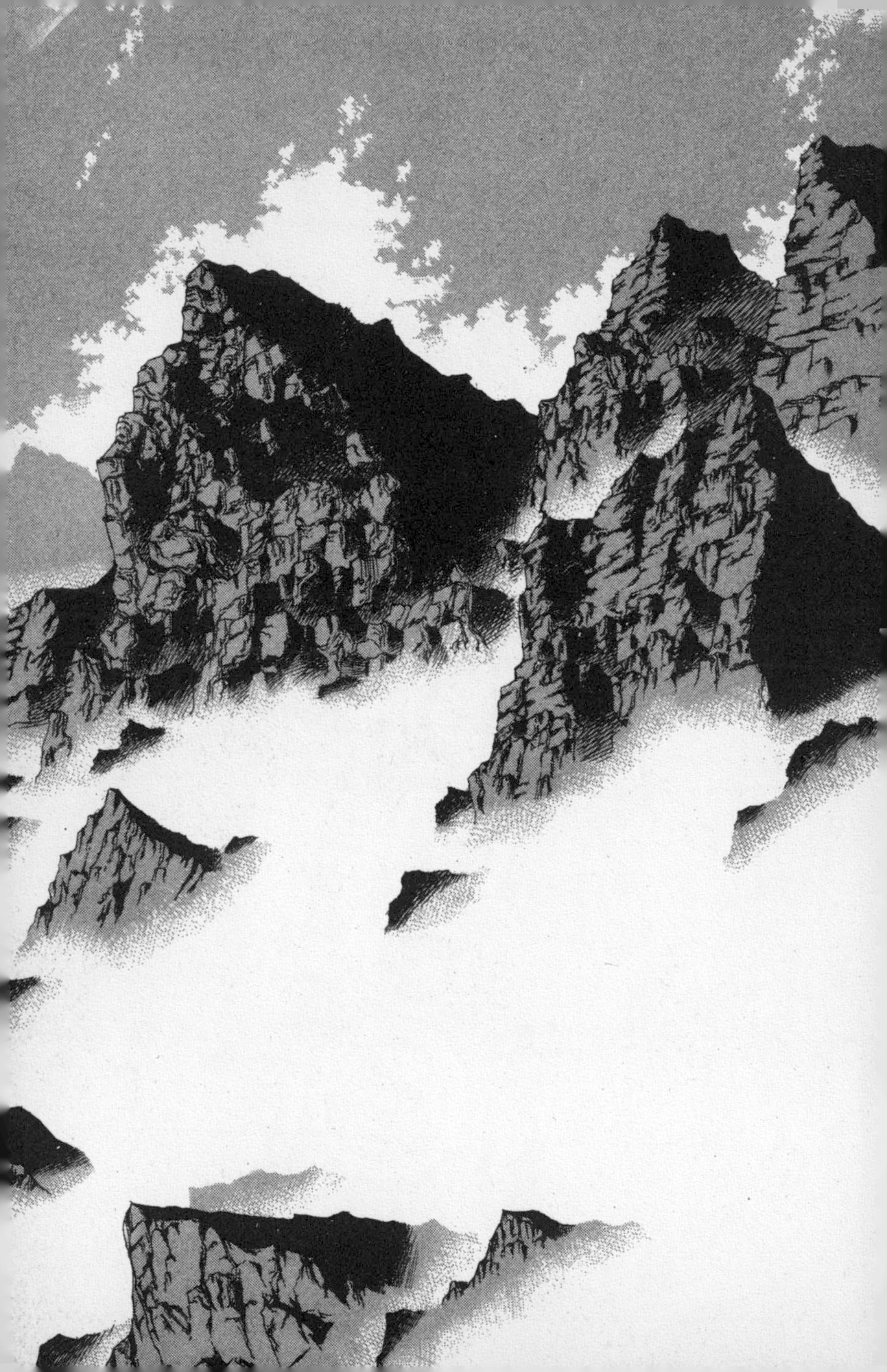

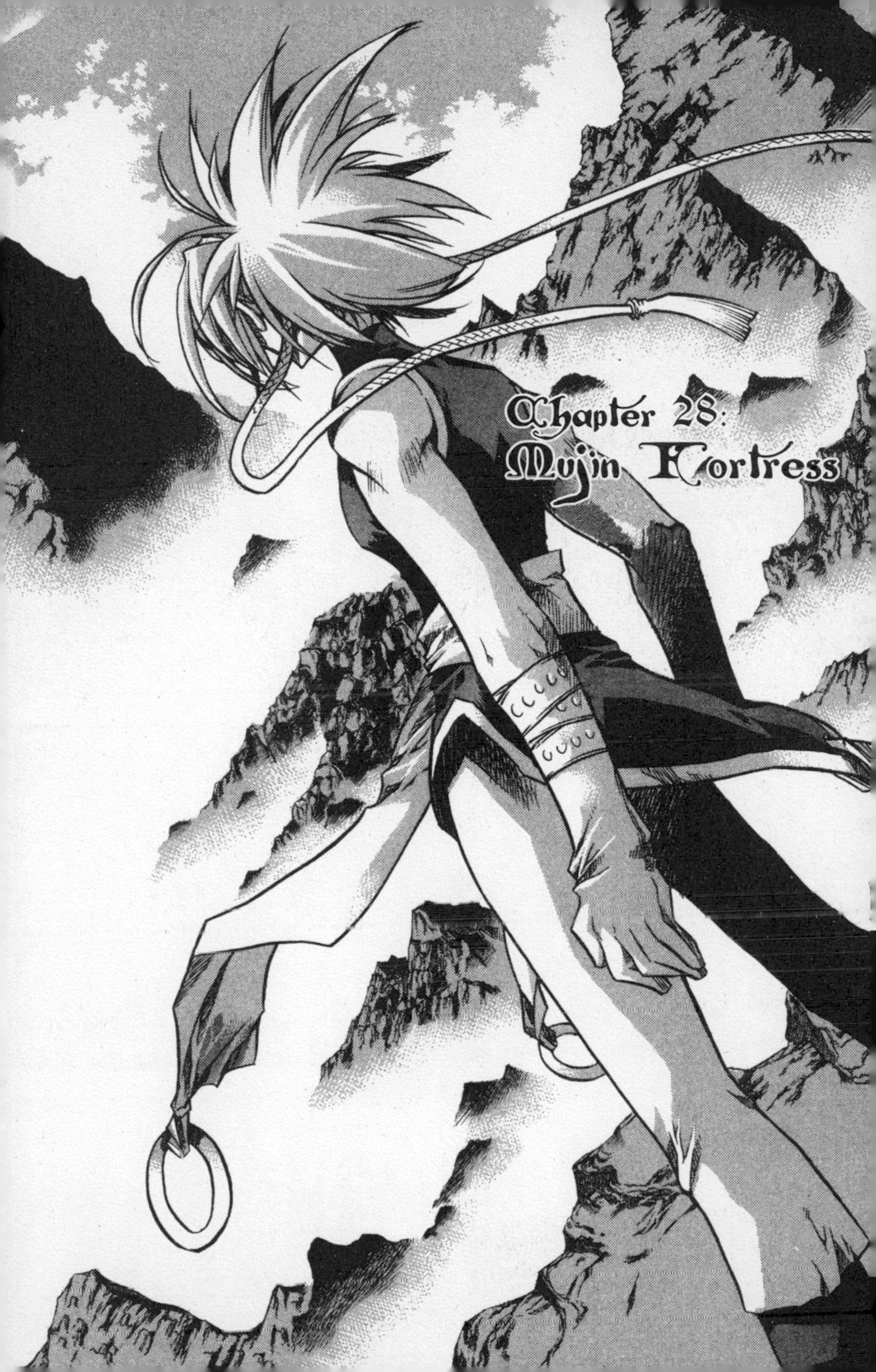
Chapter 28:
Mujin Fortress

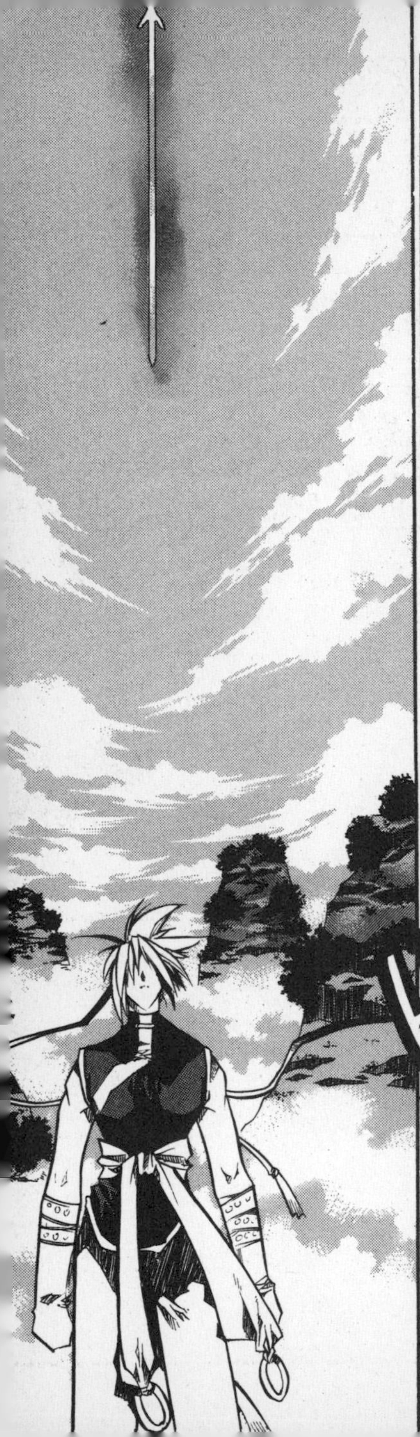
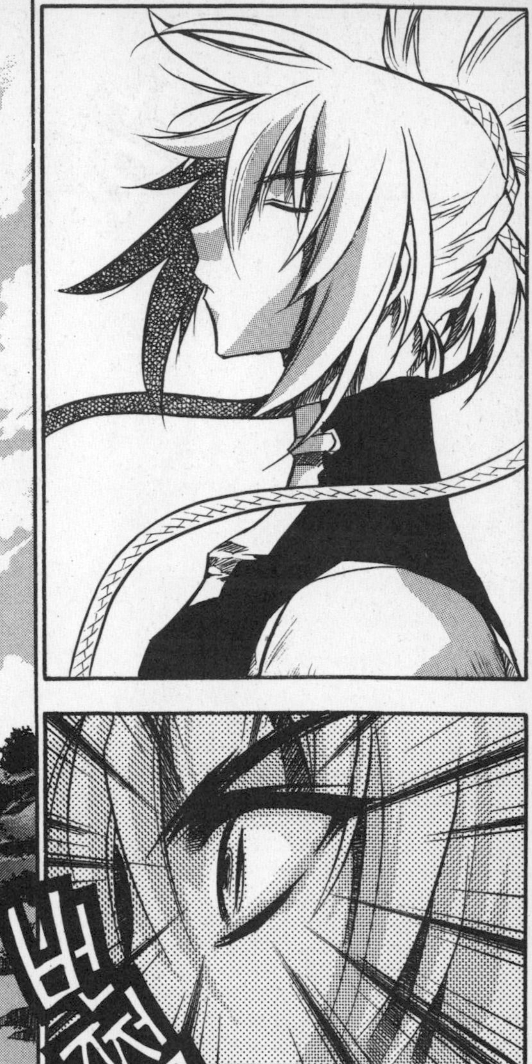
번쩍

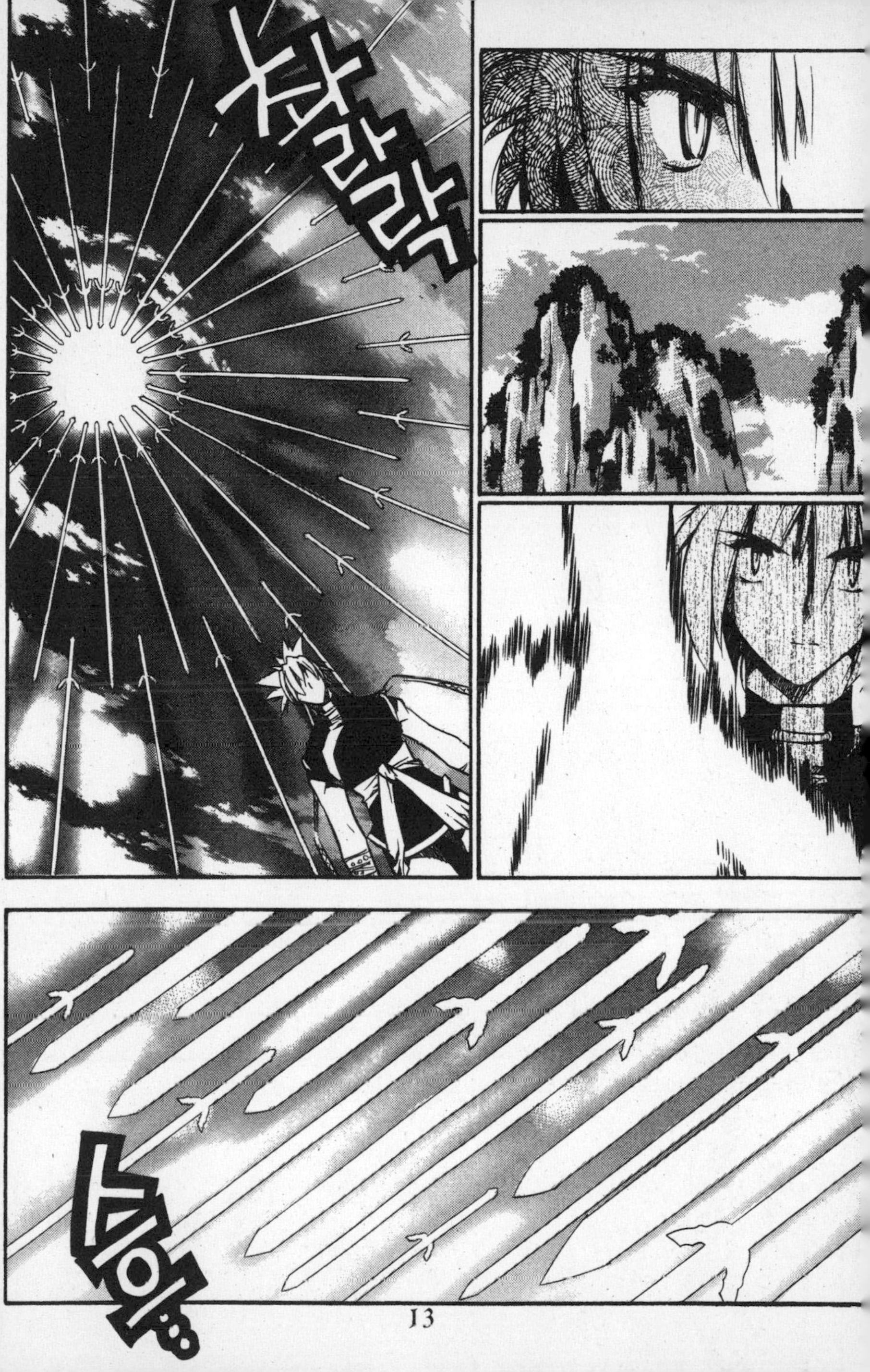
촤라락

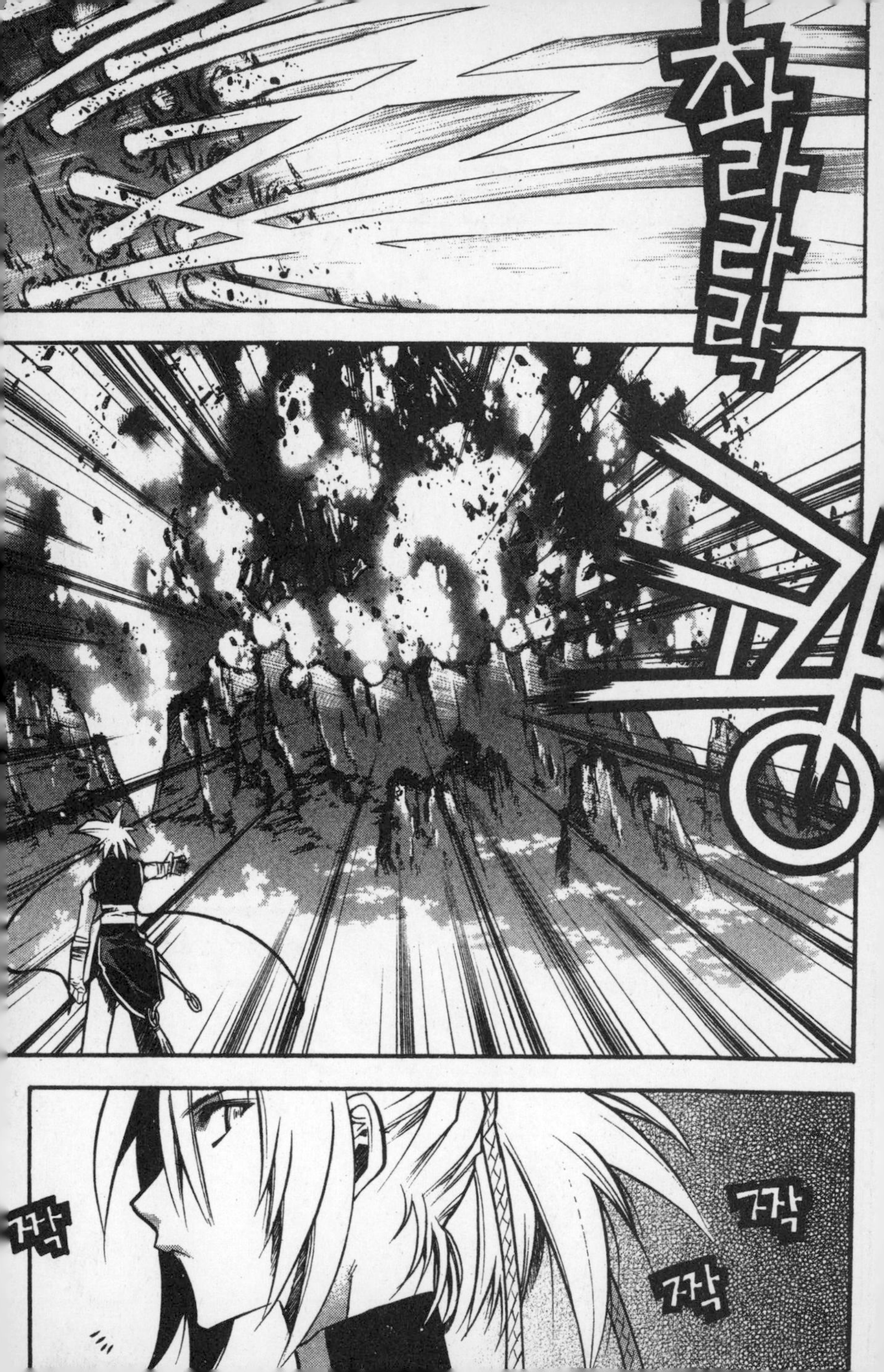

차라락
쾅
가각
가각
가각

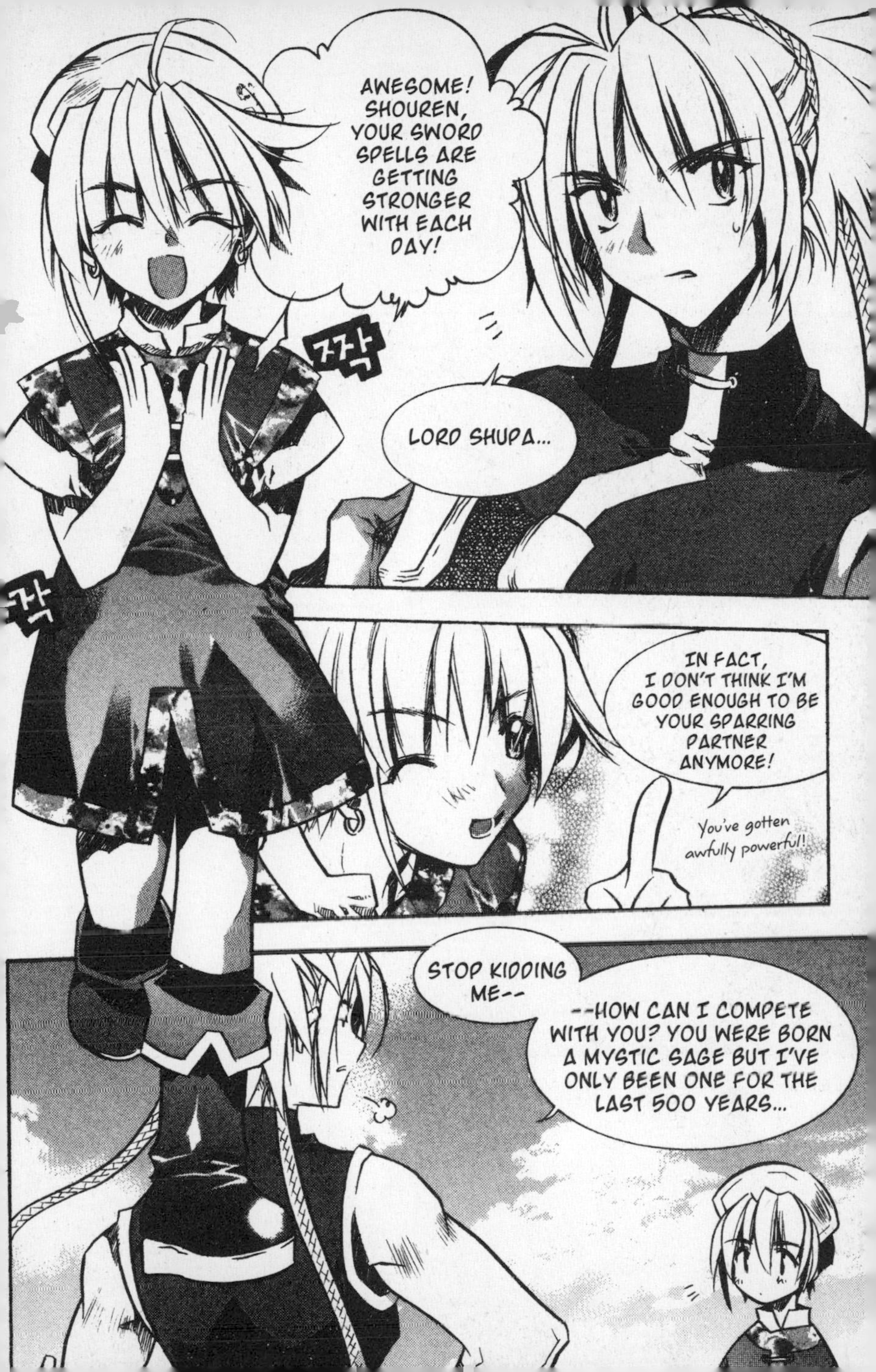
AWESOME! SHOUREN, YOUR SWORD SPELLS ARE GETTING STRONGER WITH EACH DAY!
짝
LORD SHUPA...
IN FACT, I DON'T THINK I'M GOOD ENOUGH TO BE YOUR SPARRING PARTNER ANYMORE!
You've gotten awfully powerful!
STOP KIDDING ME--
--HOW CAN I COMPETE WITH YOU? YOU WERE BORN A MYSTIC SAGE BUT I'VE ONLY BEEN ONE FOR THE LAST 500 YEARS...

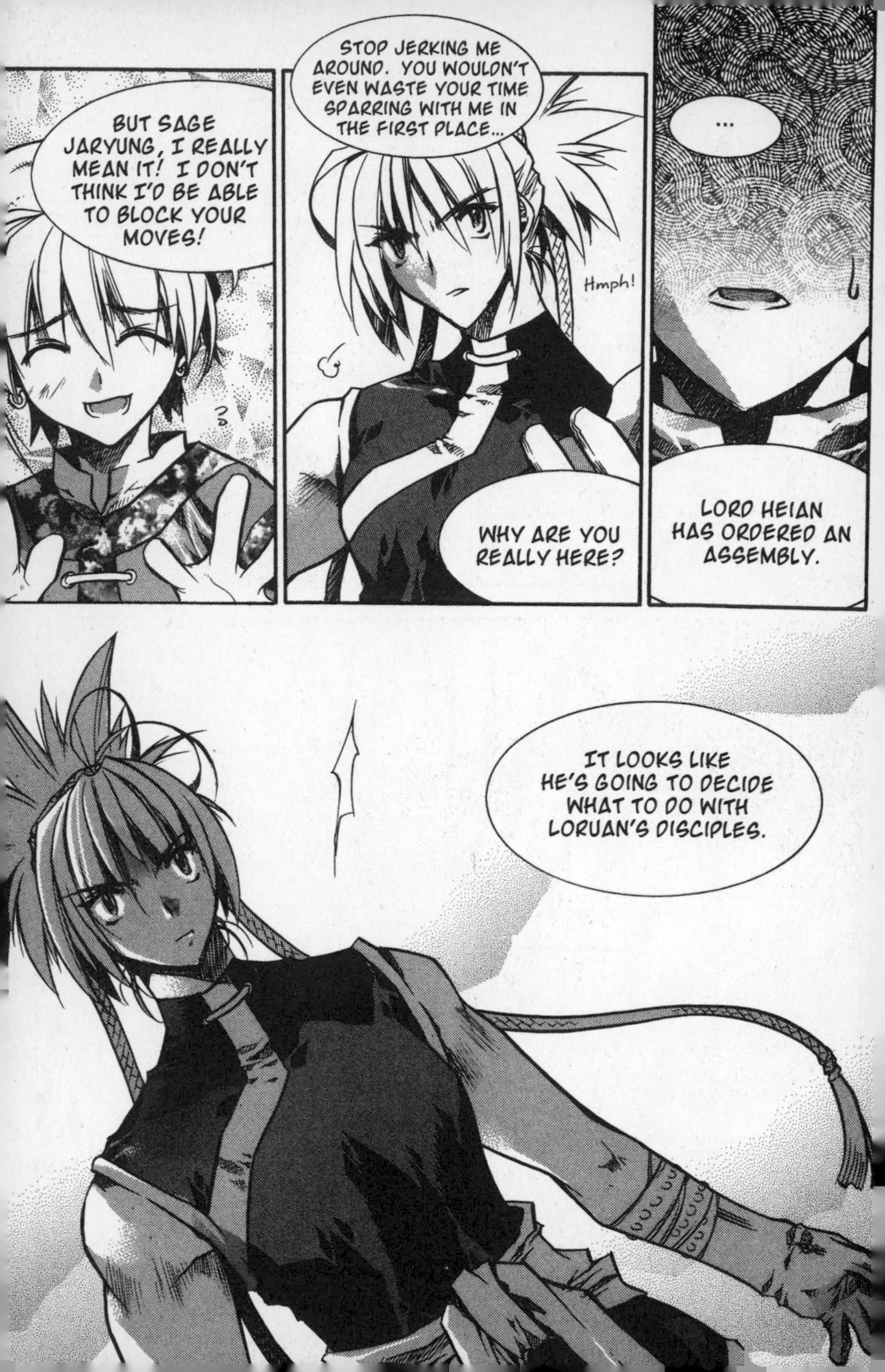
BUT SAGE JARYUNG, I REALLY MEAN IT! I DON'T THINK I'D BE ABLE TO BLOCK YOUR MOVES!
STOP JERKING ME AROUND. YOU WOULDN'T EVEN WASTE YOUR TIME SPARRING WITH ME IN THE FIRST PLACE...
Hmph!
WHY ARE YOU REALLY HERE?
...
LORD HEIAN HAS ORDERED AN ASSEMBLY.
IT LOOKS LIKE HE'S GOING TO DECIDE WHAT TO DO WITH LORUAN'S DISCIPLES.

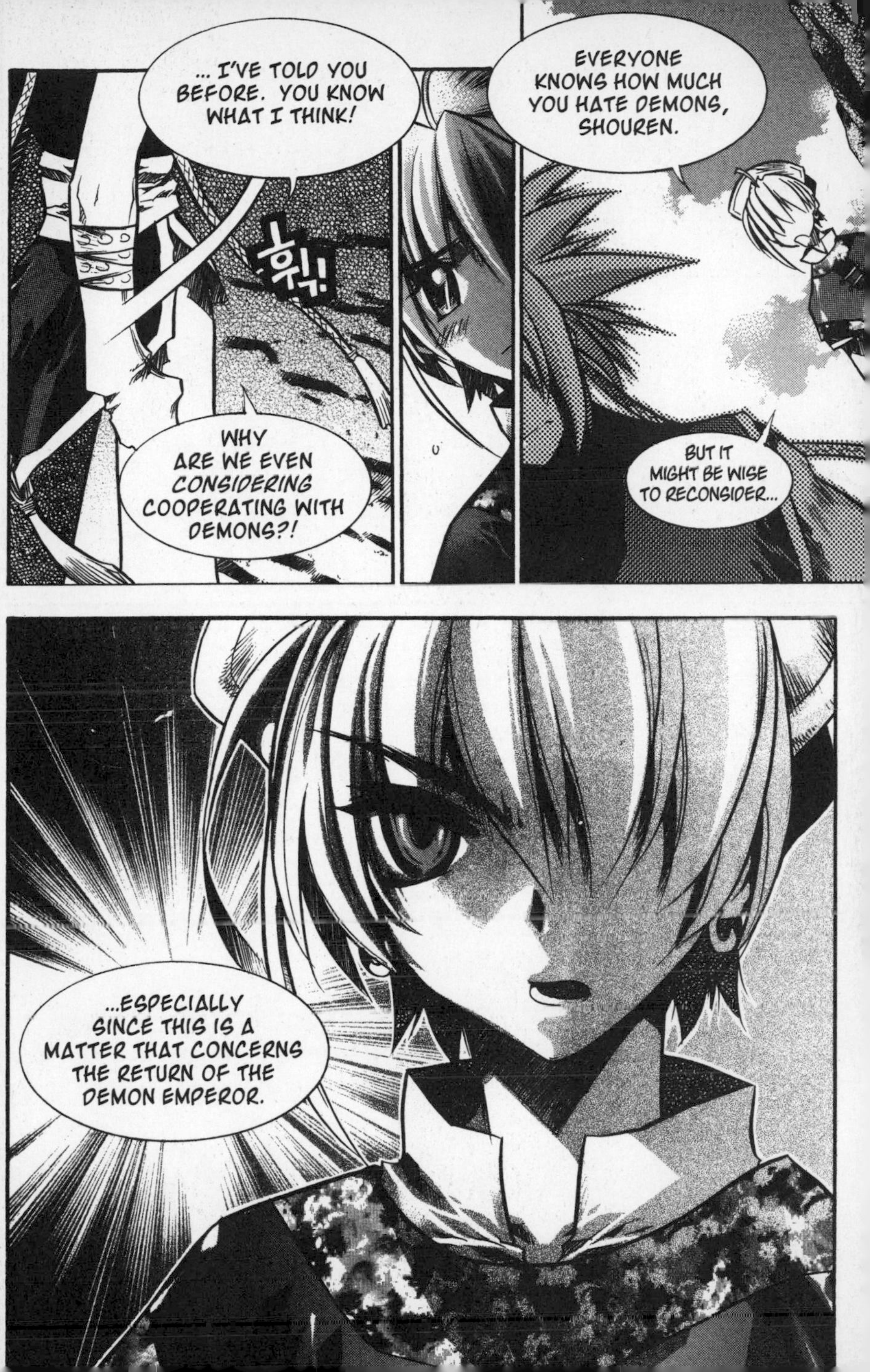
... I'VE TOLD YOU BEFORE. YOU KNOW WHAT I THINK!
휙!
WHY ARE WE EVEN CONSIDERING COOPERATING WITH DEMONS?!
EVERYONE KNOWS HOW MUCH YOU HATE DEMONS, SHOUREN.
BUT IT MIGHT BE WISE TO RECONSIDER...
...ESPECIALLY SINCE THIS IS A MATTER THAT CONCERNS THE RETURN OF THE DEMON EMPEROR.

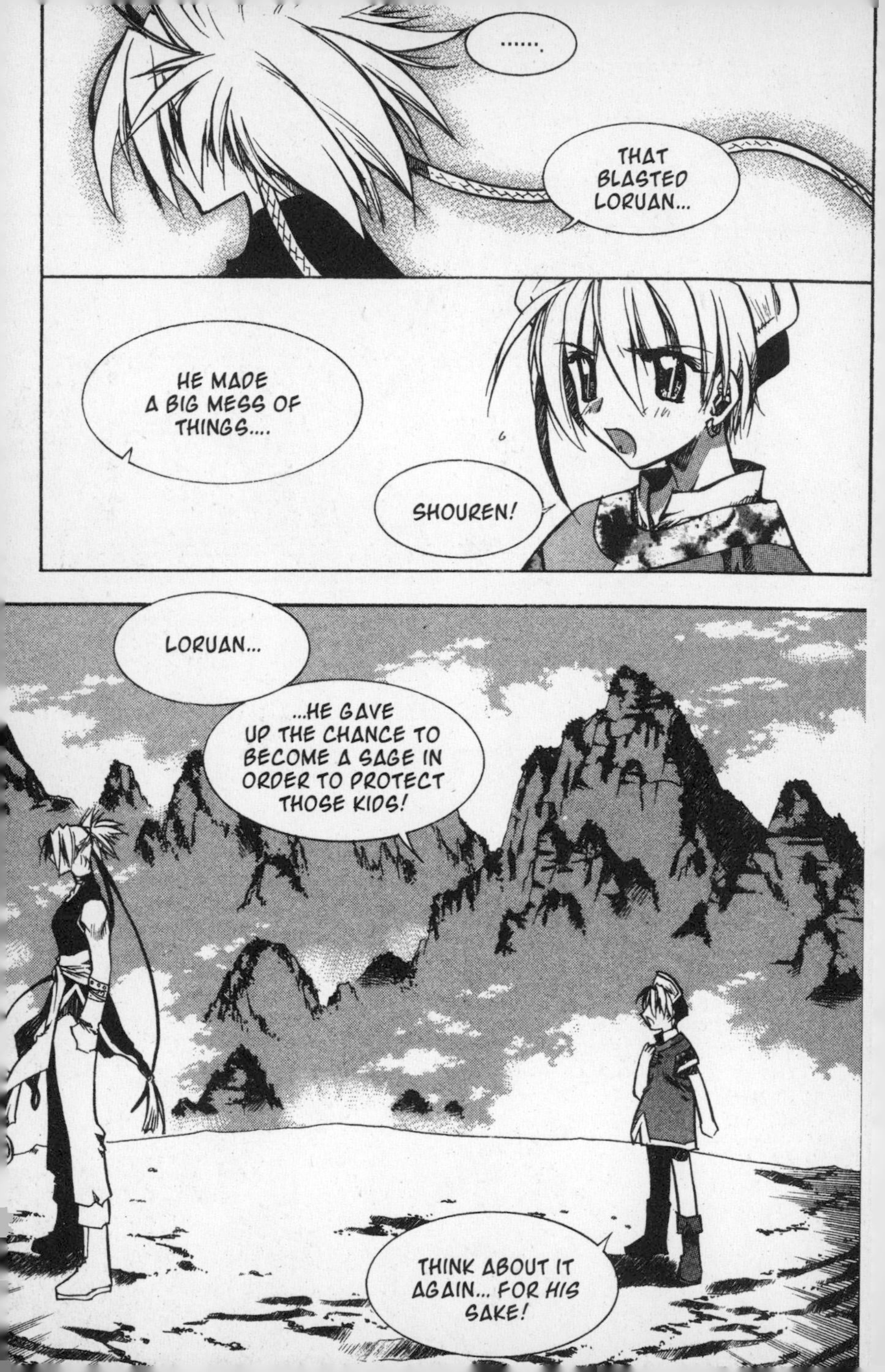

......
THAT BLASTED LORUAN...
HE MADE A BIG MESS OF THINGS....
SHOUREN!
LORUAN...
...HE GAVE UP THE CHANCE TO BECOME A SAGE IN ORDER TO PROTECT THOSE KIDS!
THINK ABOUT IT AGAIN... FOR HIS SAKE!

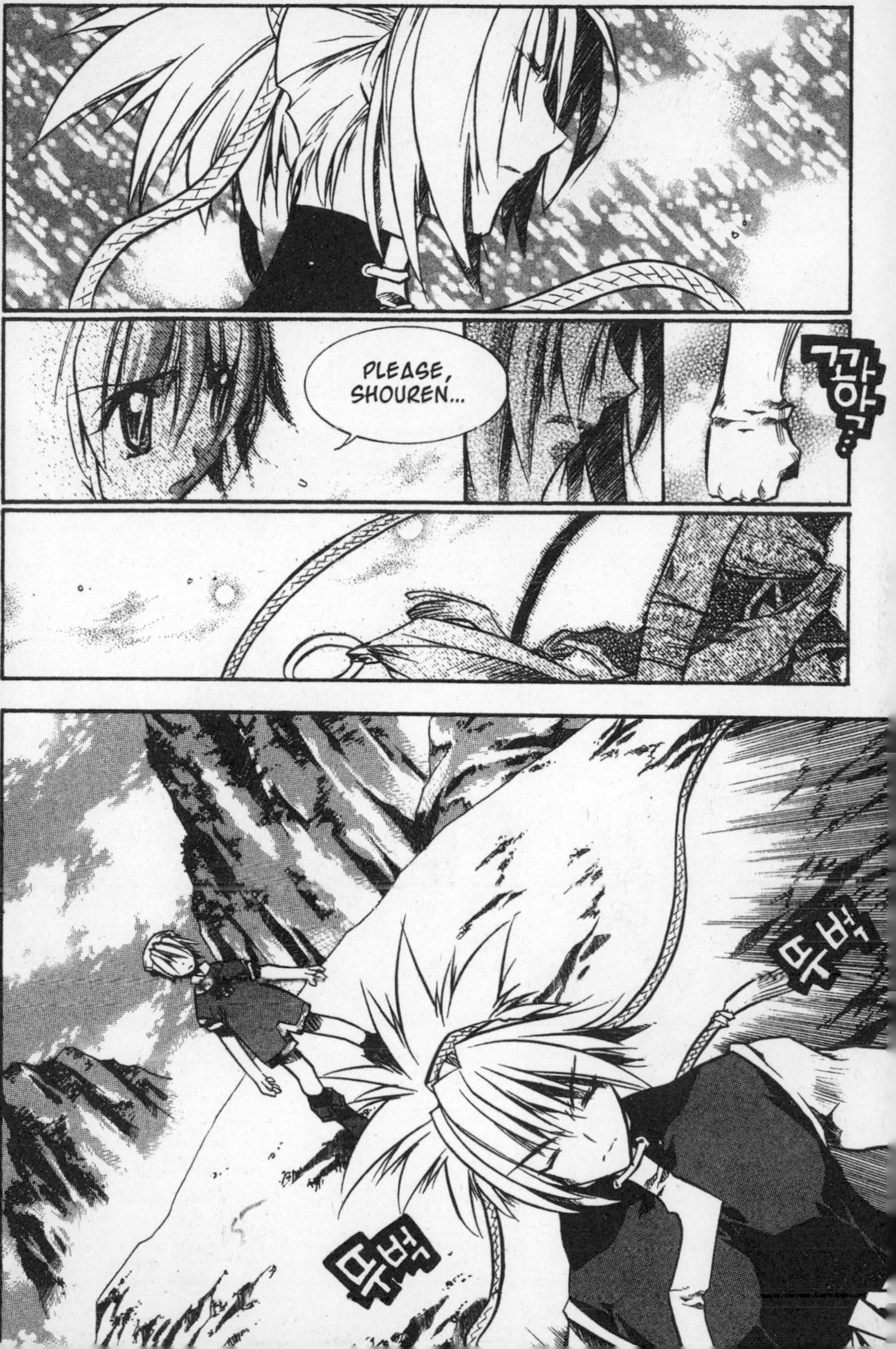
PLEASE, SHOUREN...
꽈악...
푸벅
푸벅

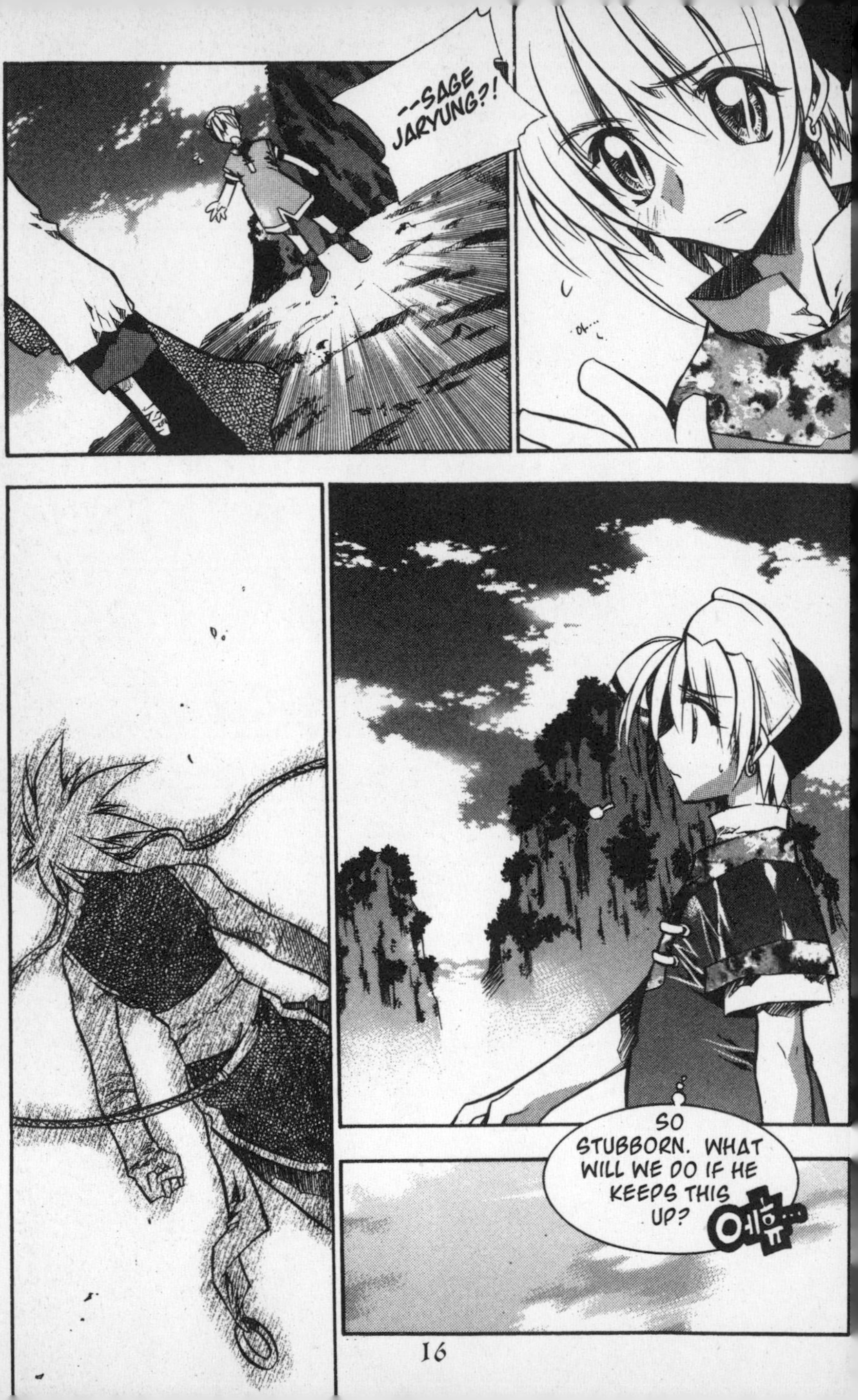
--SAGE JARYUNG?!
SO STUBBORN. WHAT WILL WE DO IF HE KEEPS THIS UP?
에휴...

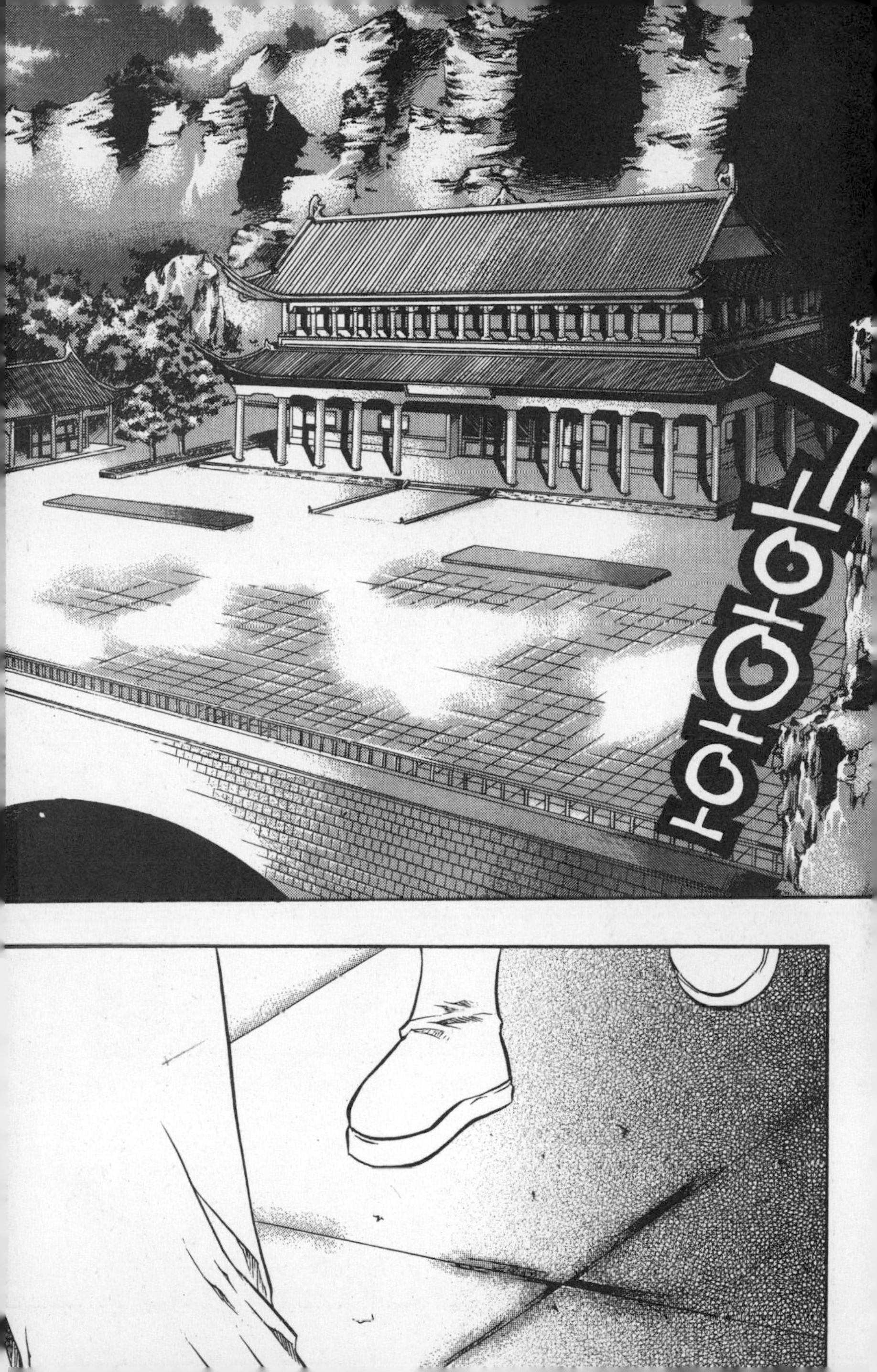
아아아악

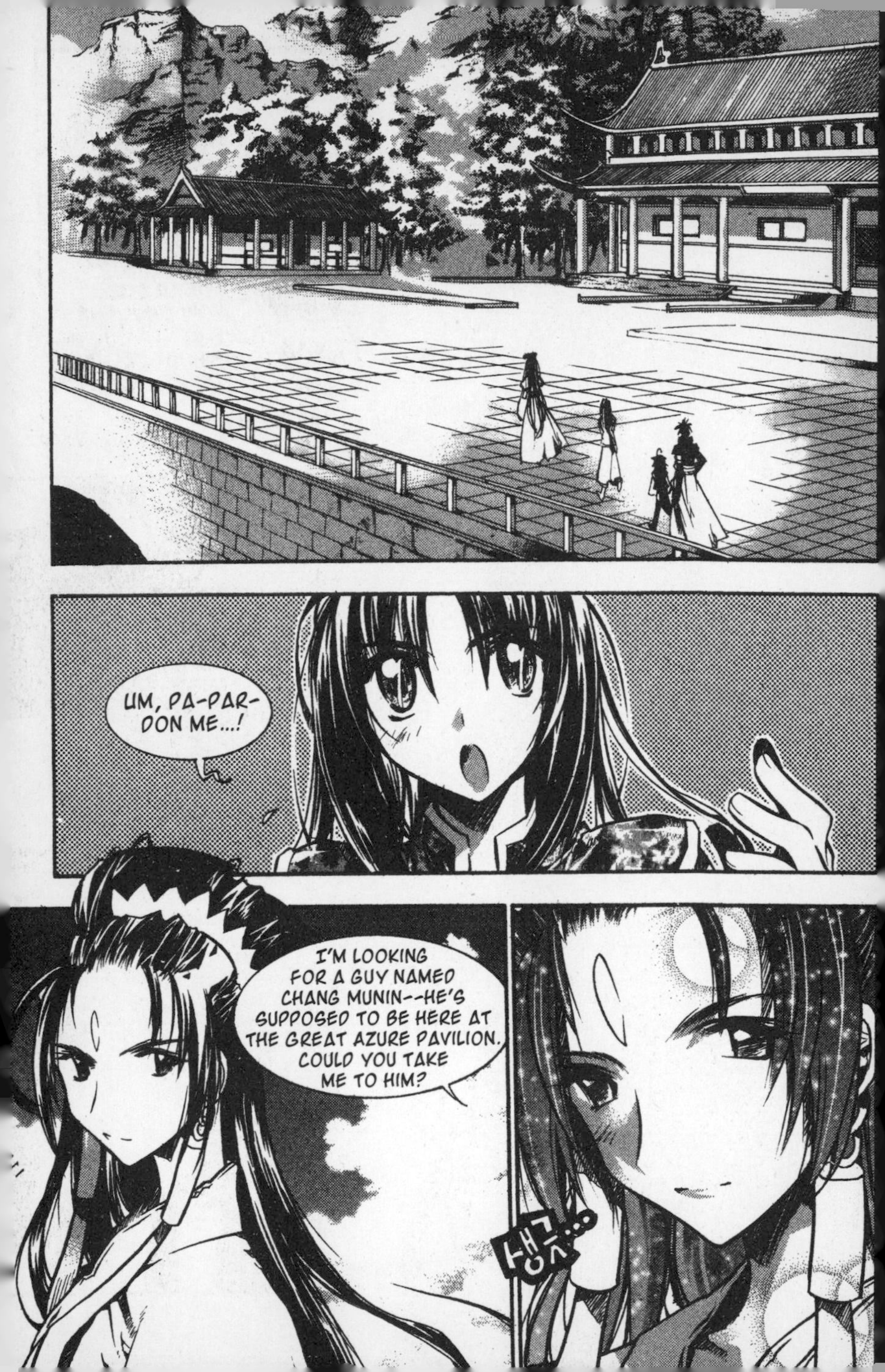
UM, PA-PAR-DON ME...!
I'M LOOKING FOR A GUY NAMED CHANG MUNIN--HE'S SUPPOSED TO BE HERE AT THE GREAT AZURE PAVILION. COULD YOU TAKE ME TO HIM?

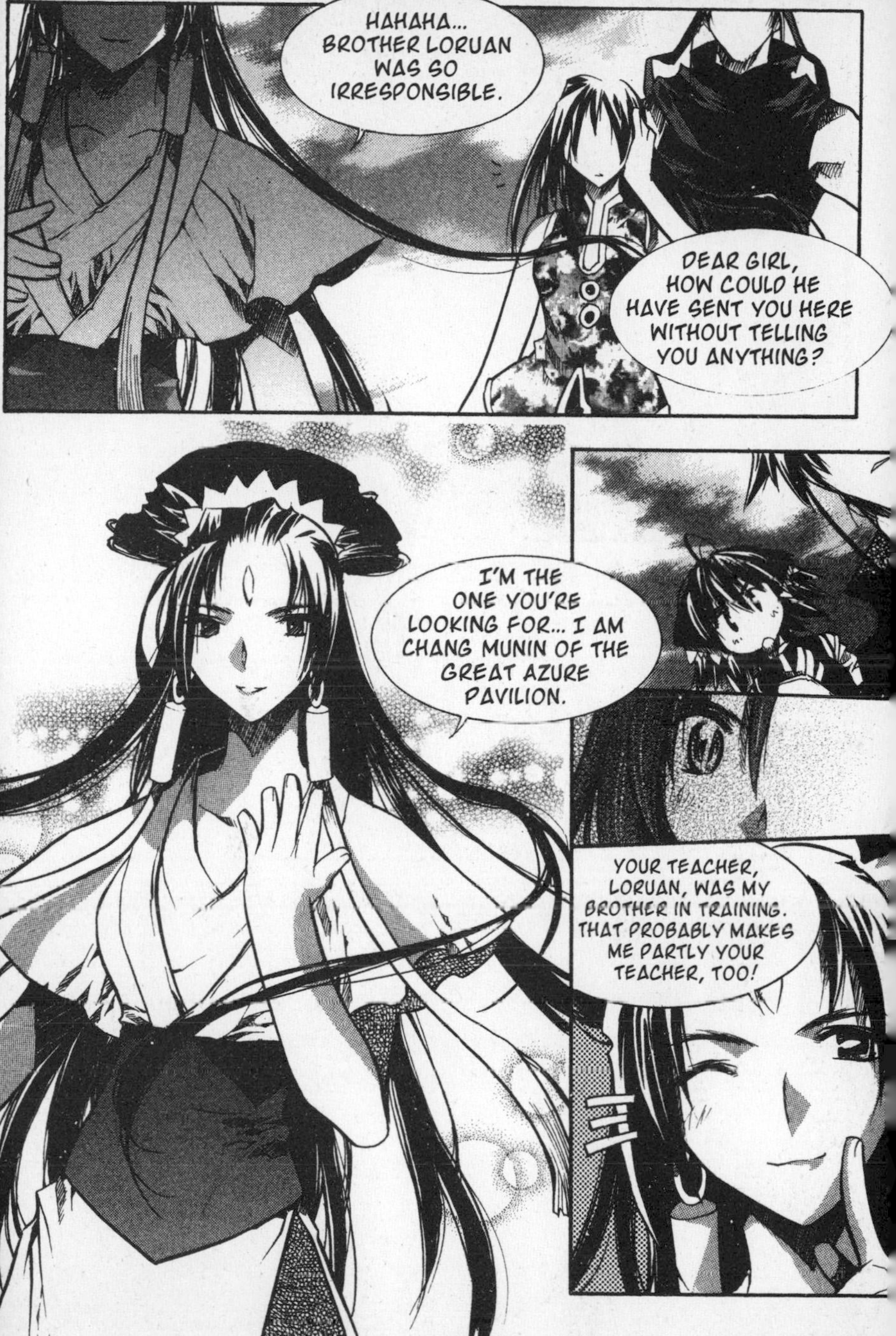
HAHAHA... BROTHER LORUAN WAS SO IRRESPONSIBLE.
DEAR GIRL, HOW COULD HE HAVE SENT YOU HERE WITHOUT TELLING YOU ANYTHING?
I'M THE ONE YOU'RE LOOKING FOR... I AM CHANG MUNIN OF THE GREAT AZURE PAVILION.
YOUR TEACHER, LORUAN, WAS MY BROTHER IN TRAINING. THAT PROBABLY MAKES ME PARTLY YOUR TEACHER, TOO!

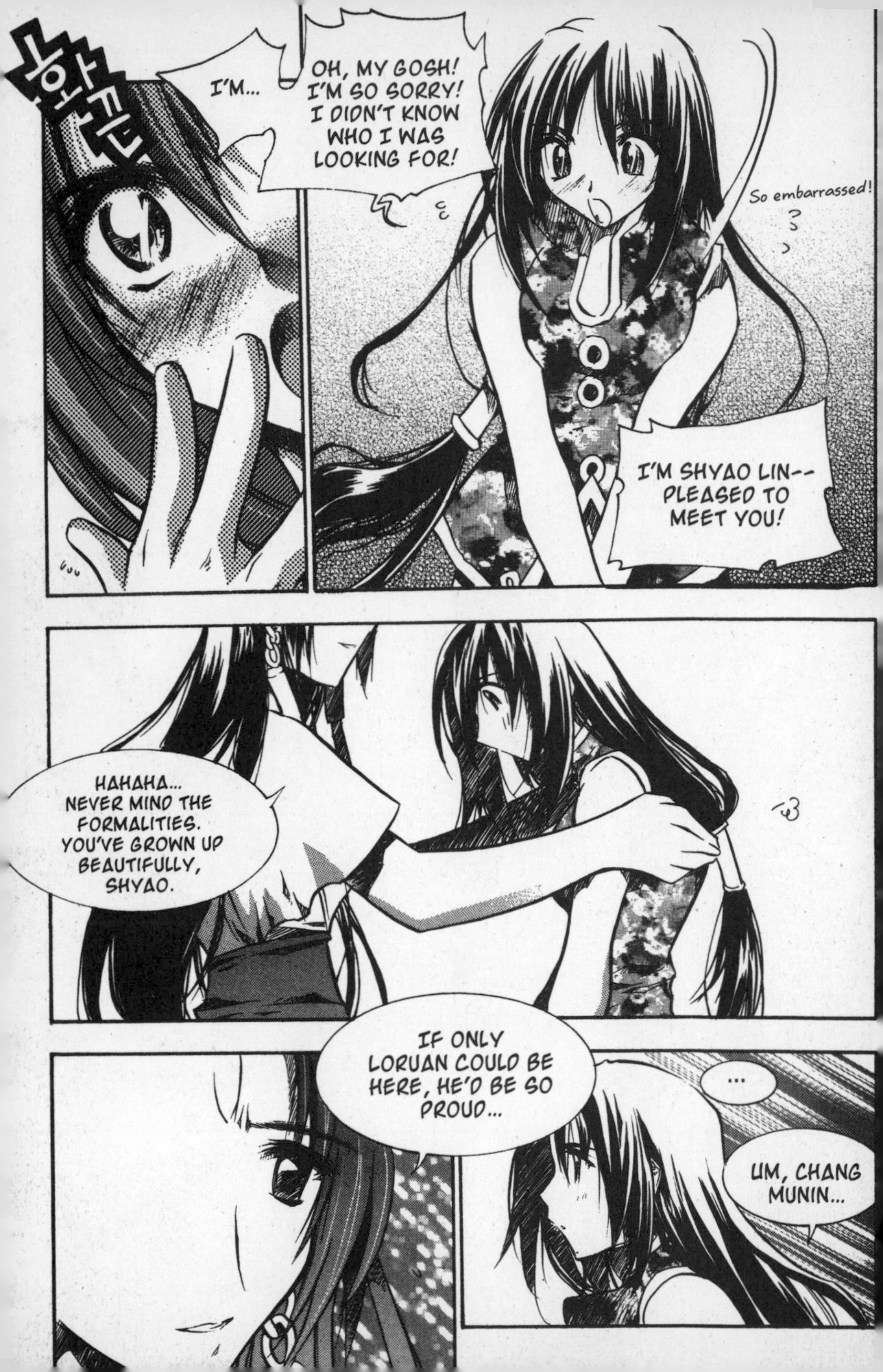
화끈
I'M...
OH, MY GOSH! I'M SO SORRY! I DIDN'T KNOW WHO I WAS LOOKING FOR!
So embarrassed!
I'M SHYAO LIN-- PLEASED TO MEET YOU!
HAHAHA... NEVER MIND THE FORMALITIES. YOU'VE GROWN UP BEAUTIFULLY, SHYAO.
IF ONLY LORUAN COULD BE HERE, HE'D BE SO PROUD...
...
UM, CHANG MUNIN...

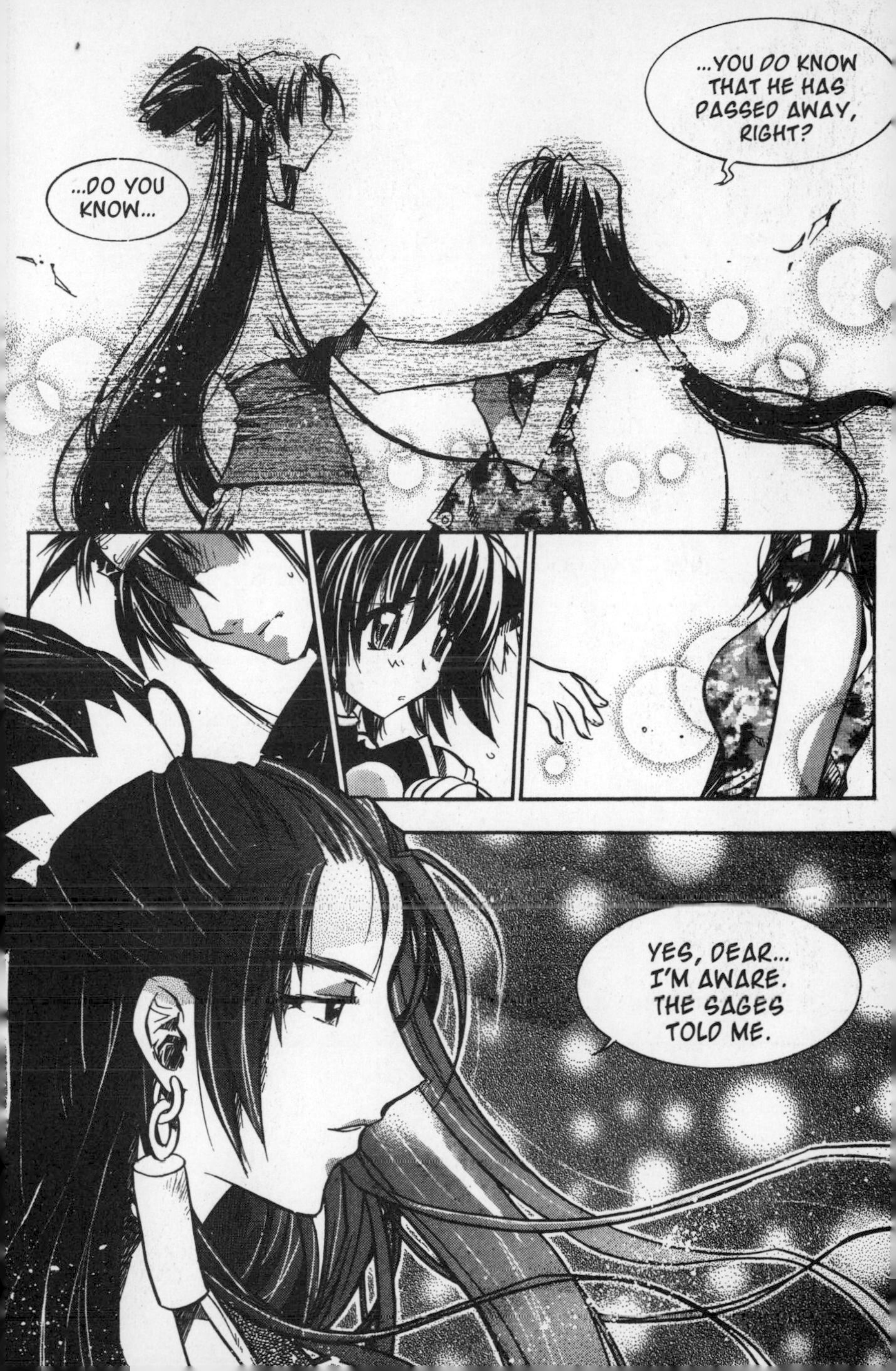
...DO YOU KNOW...
...YOU DO KNOW THAT HE HAS PASSED AWAY, RIGHT?
YES, DEAR... I'M AWARE. THE SAGES TOLD ME.

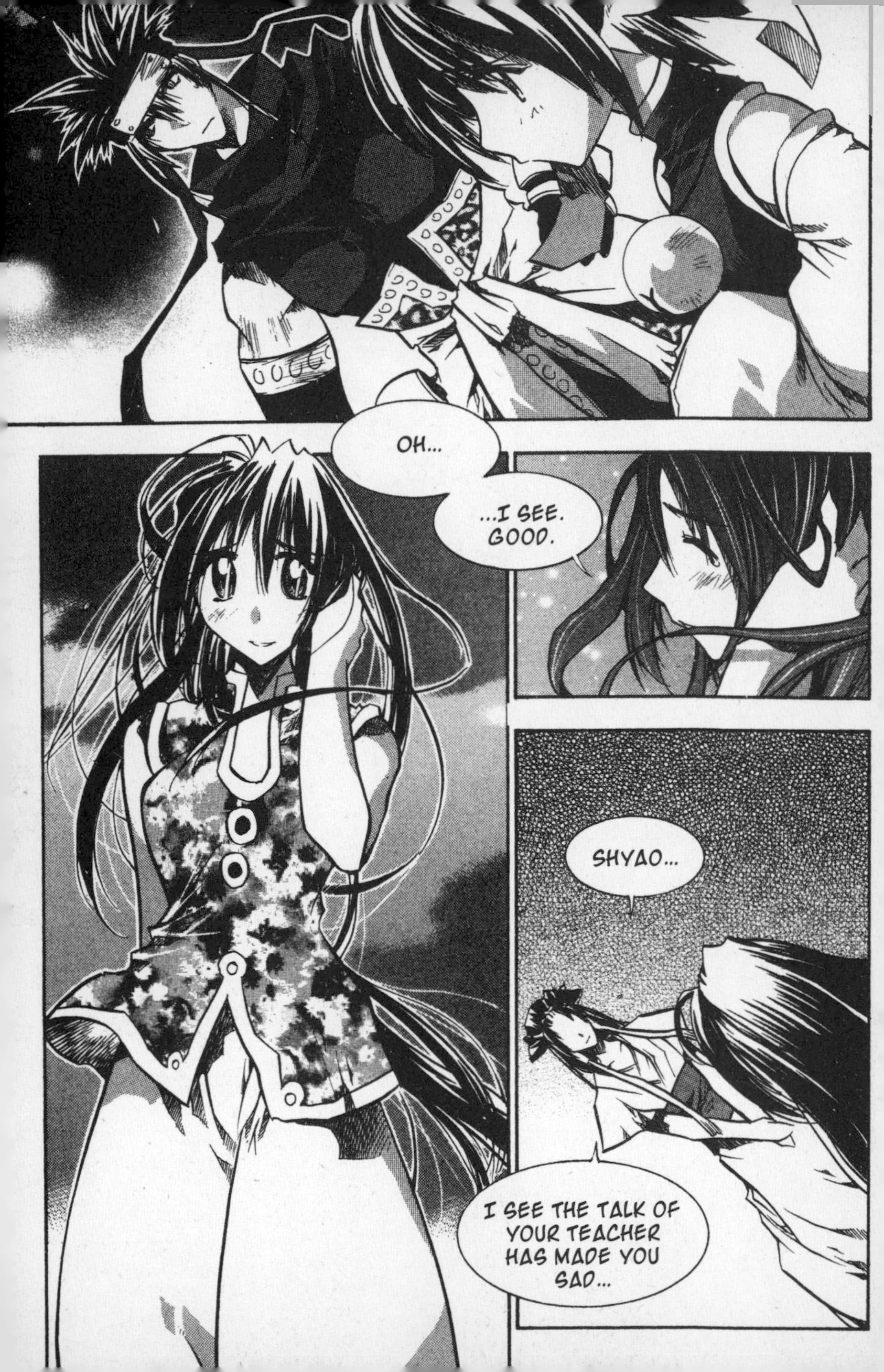
OH...
...I SEE. GOOD.
SHYAO...
I SEE THE TALK OF YOUR TEACHER HAS MADE YOU SAD...

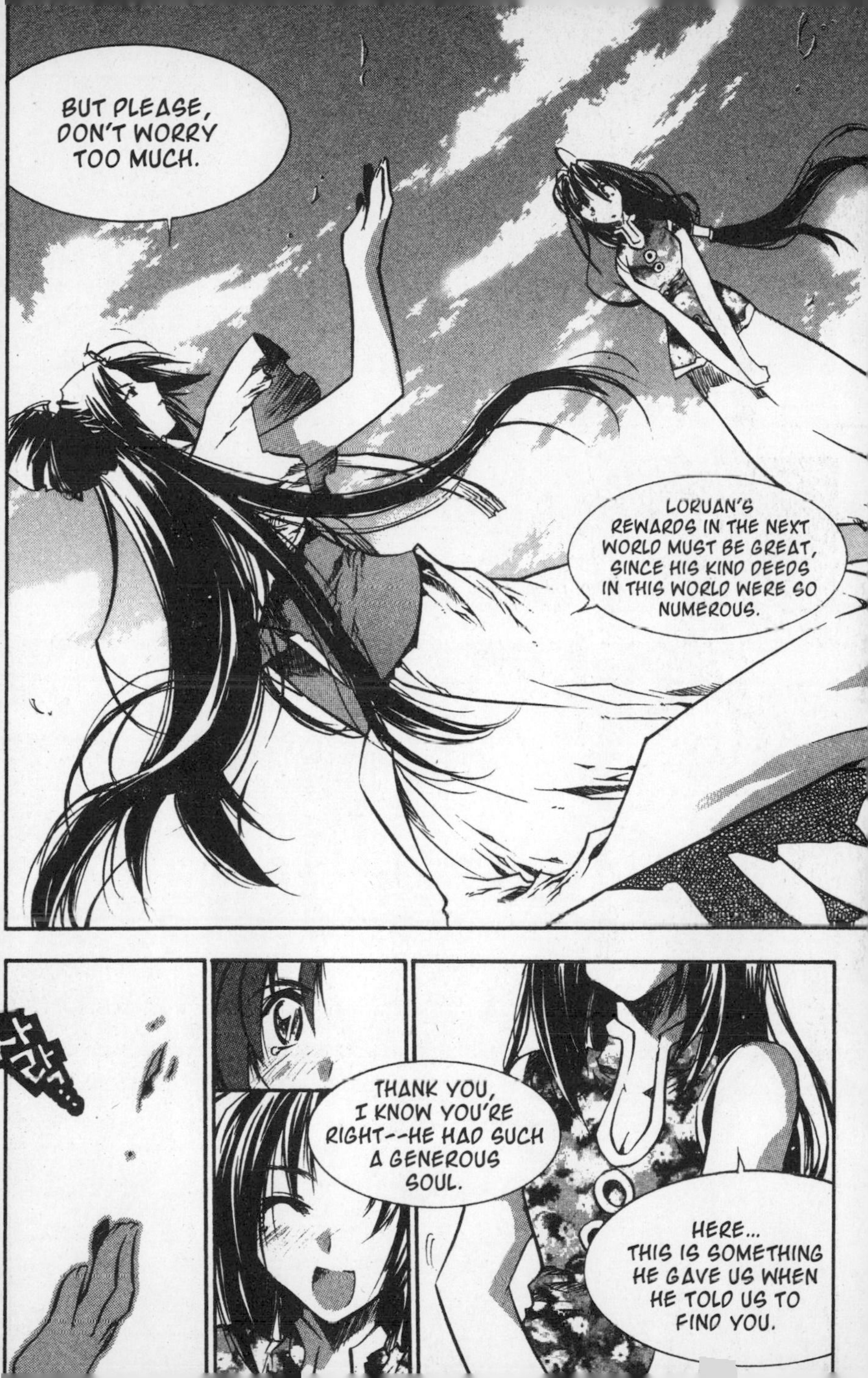
BUT PLEASE, DON'T WORRY TOO MUCH.
LORUAN'S REWARDS IN THE NEXT WORLD MUST BE GREAT, SINCE HIS KIND DEEDS IN THIS WORLD WERE SO NUMEROUS.
THANK YOU, I KNOW YOU'RE RIGHT--HE HAD SUCH A GENEROUS SOUL.
HERE... THIS IS SOMETHING HE GAVE US WHEN HE TOLD US TO FIND YOU.

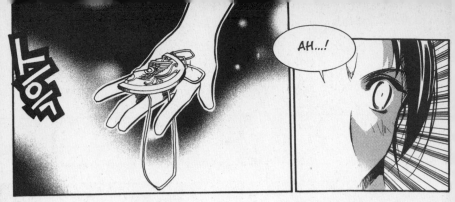

AH...!

I DIDN'T THINK....

...I'D EVER SEE THIS AGAIN!

OH, THAT MAN...

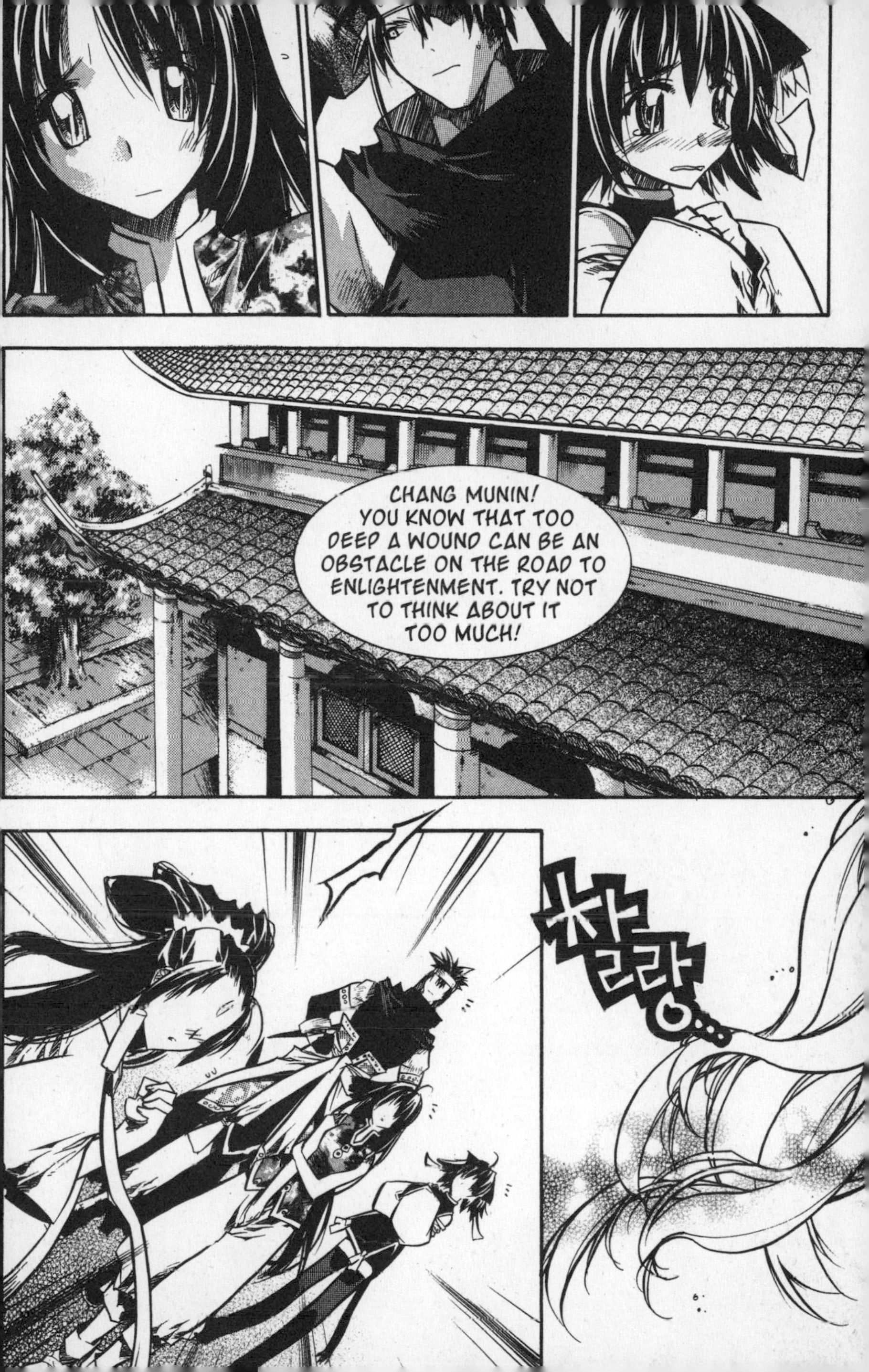
CHANG MUNIN! YOU KNOW THAT TOO DEEP A WOUND CAN BE AN OBSTACLE ON THE ROAD TO ENLIGHTENMENT. TRY NOT TO THINK ABOUT IT TOO MUCH!
차르랑...

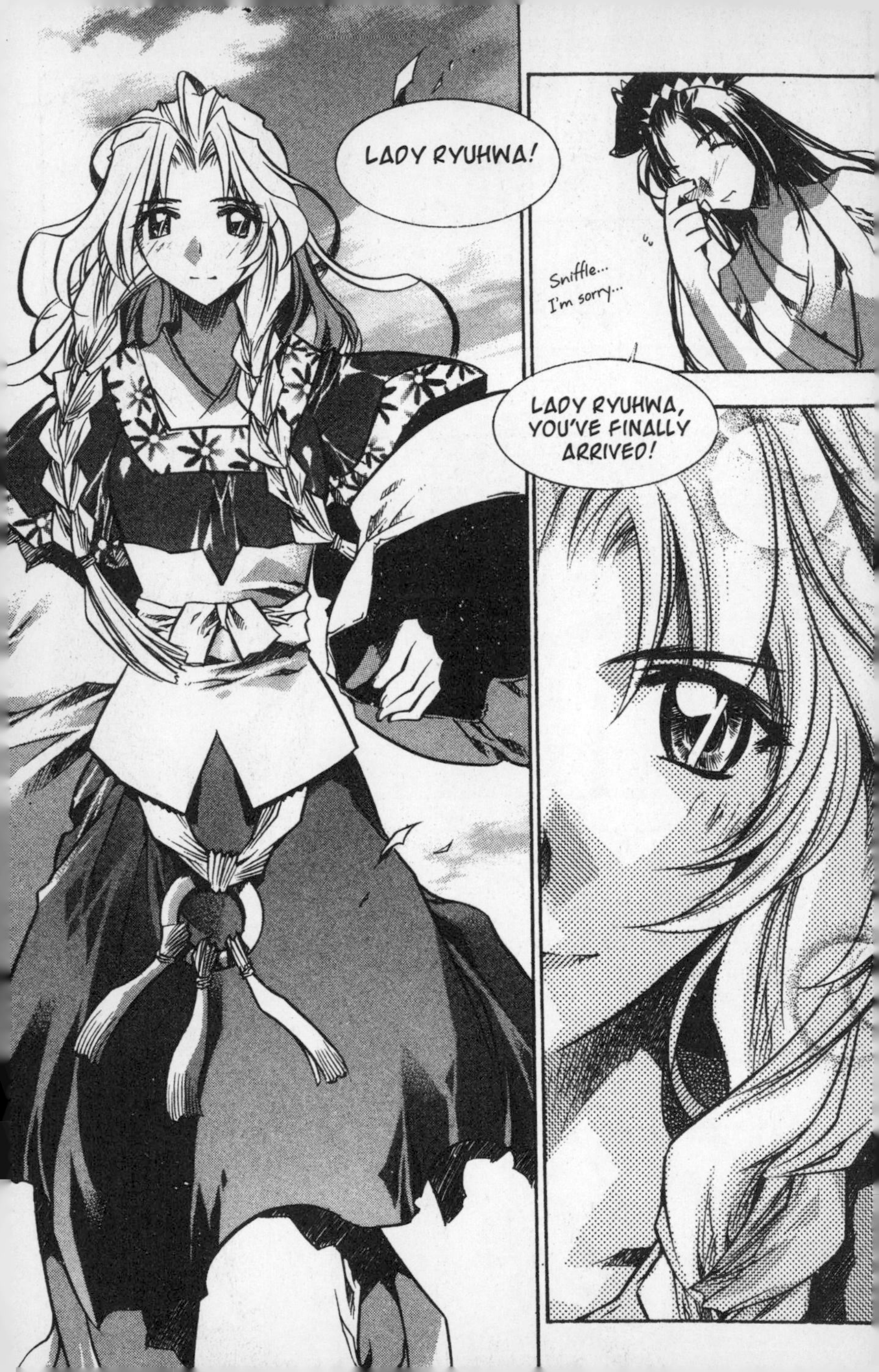
LADY RYUHWA!
Sniffle... I'm sorry...
LADY RYUHWA, YOU'VE FINALLY ARRIVED!

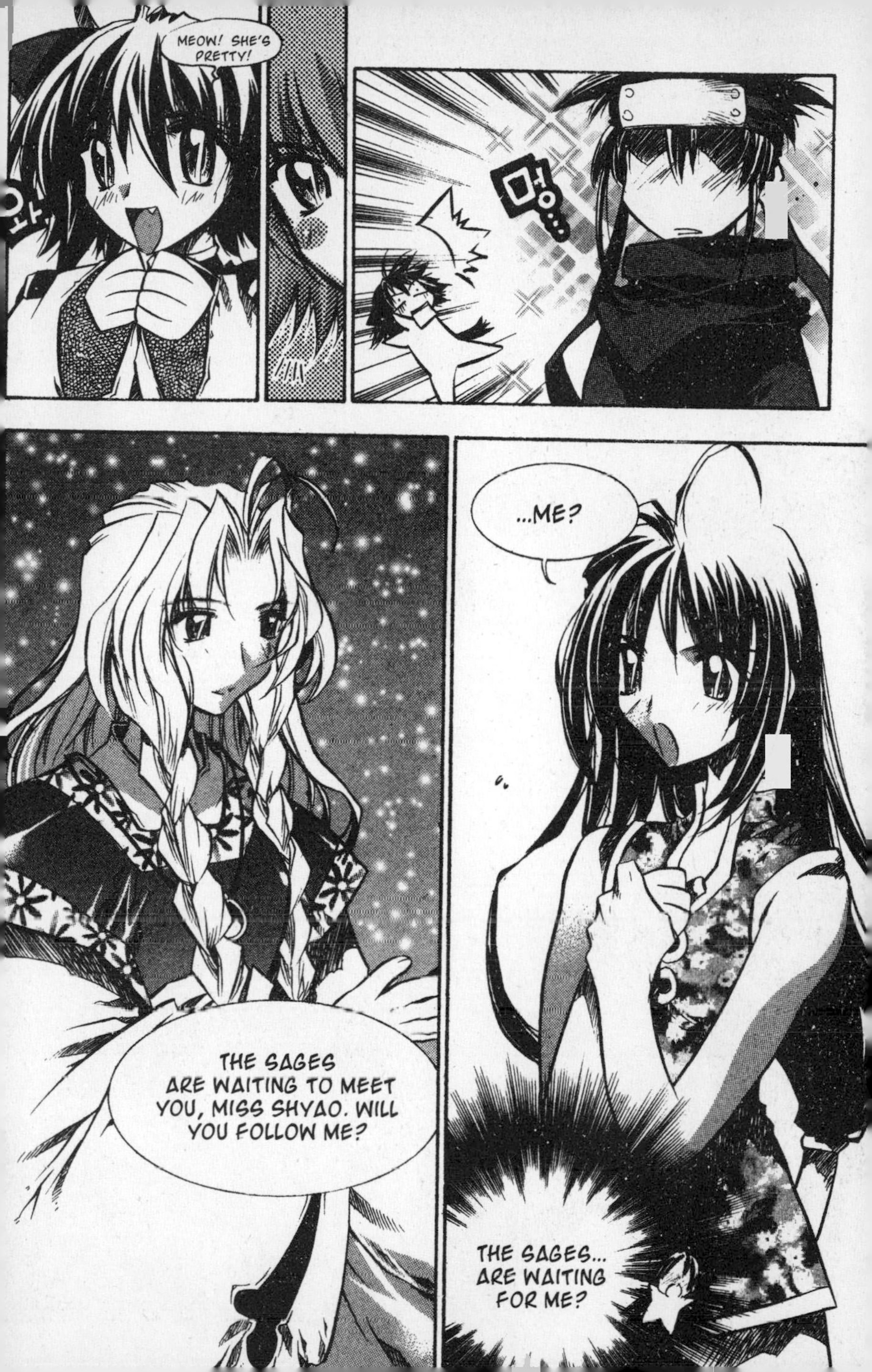
MEOW! SHE'S PRETTY!
THE SAGES ARE WAITING TO MEET YOU, MISS SHYAO. WILL YOU FOLLOW ME?
...ME?
THE SAGES... ARE WAITING FOR ME?

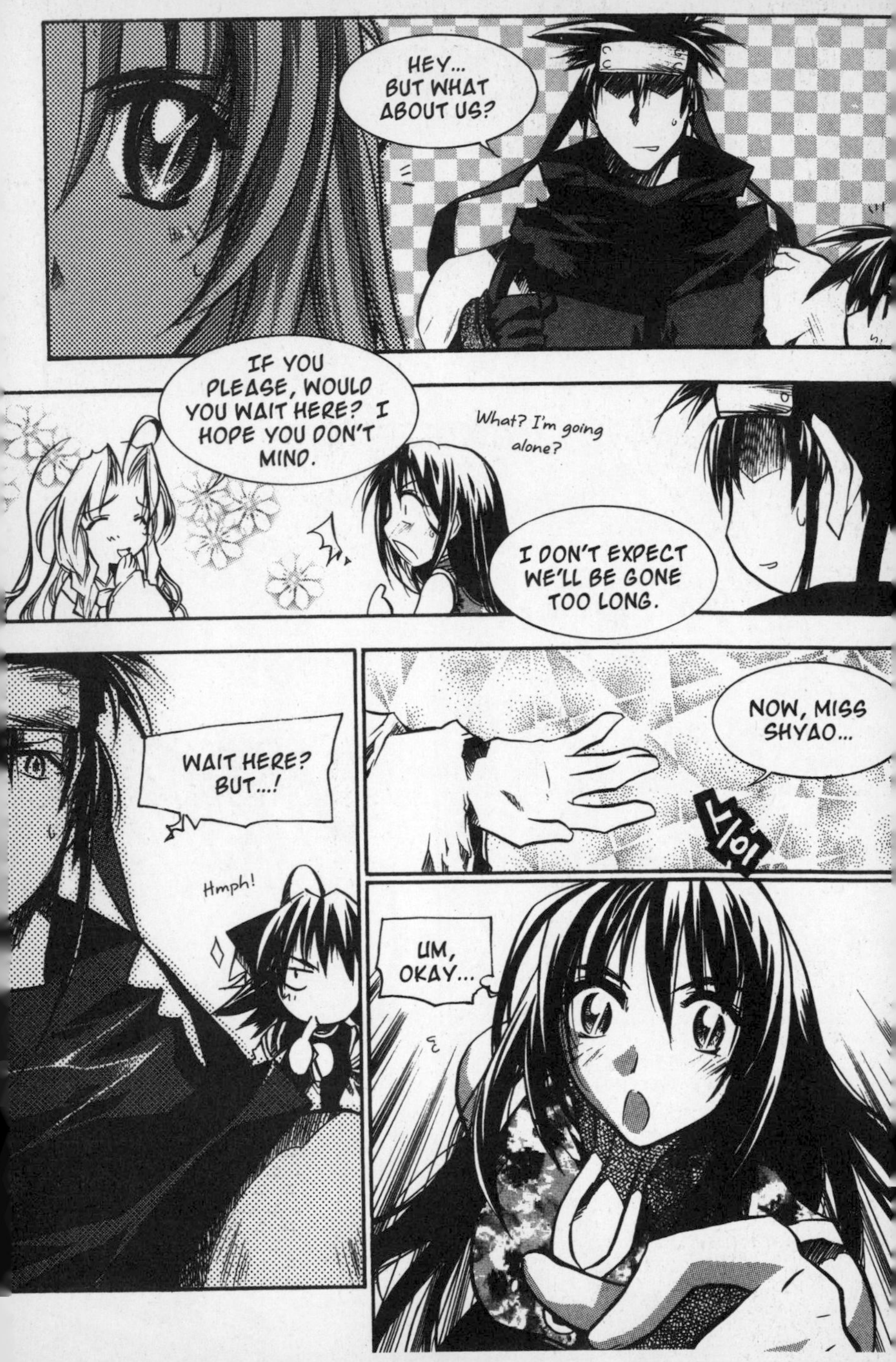
HEY...
BUT WHAT
ABOUT US?
IF YOU PLEASE, WOULD YOU WAIT HERE? I HOPE YOU DON'T MIND.
What? I'm going alone?
I DON'T EXPECT WE'LL BE GONE TOO LONG.
WAIT HERE? BUT...!
Hmph!
NOW, MISS SHYAO...
UM, OKAY...

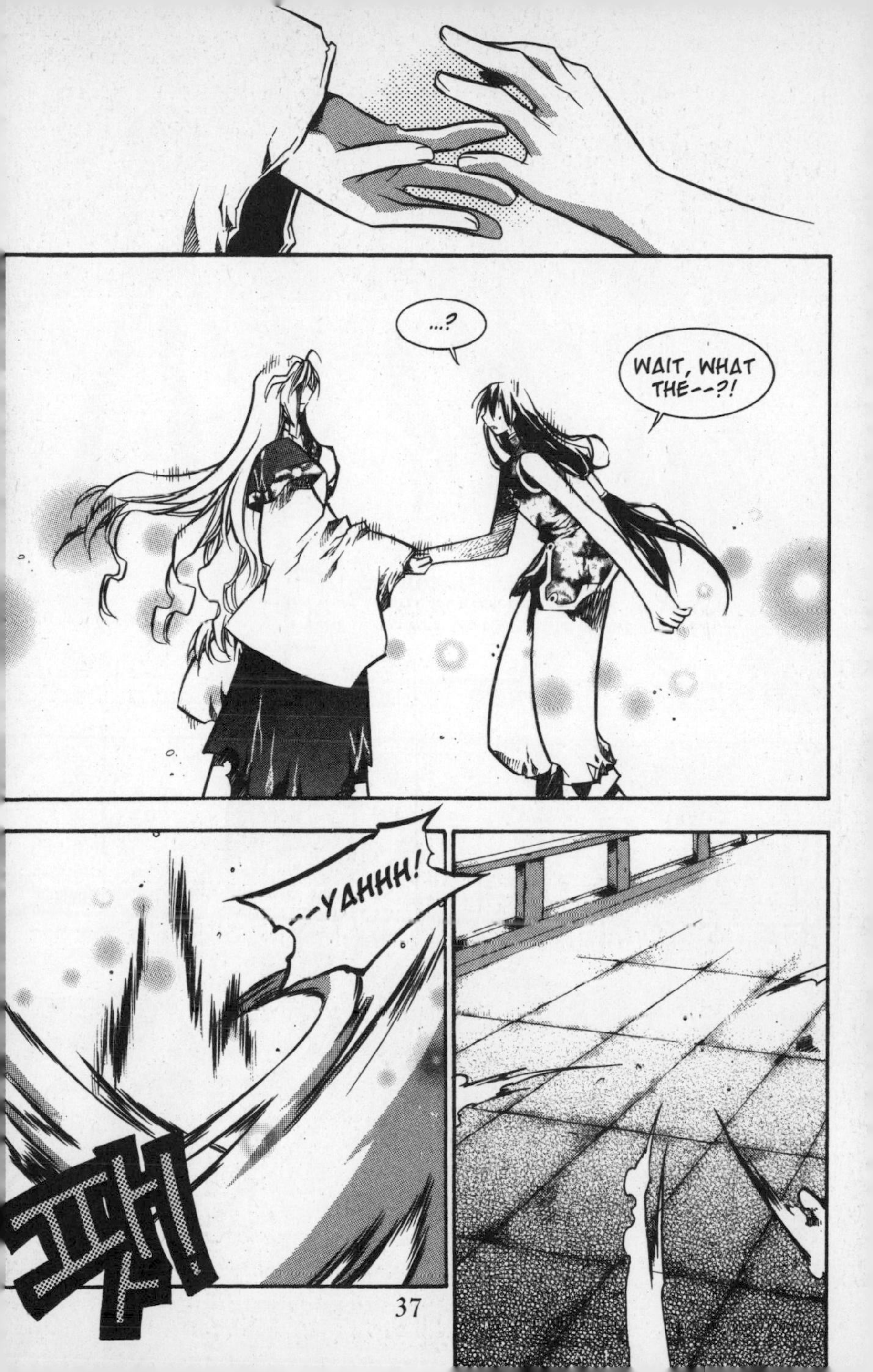
...?
WAIT, WHAT THE--?!
--YAHHH!

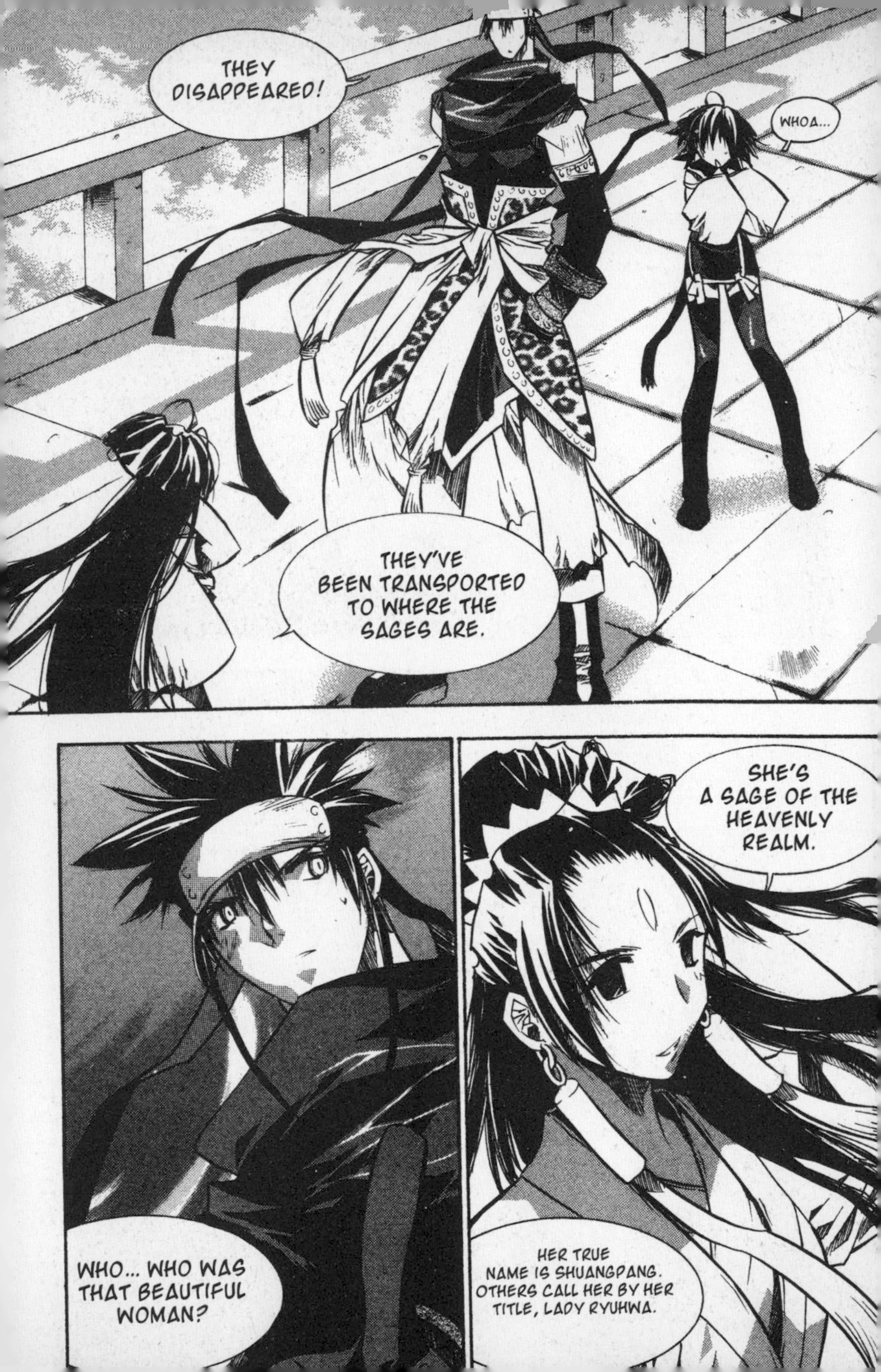
THEY DISAPPEARED!
WHOA...
THEY'VE BEEN TRANSPORTED TO WHERE THE SAGES ARE.
WHO... WHO WAS THAT BEAUTIFUL WOMAN?
SHE'S A SAGE OF THE HEAVENLY REALM.
HER TRUE NAME IS SHUANGPANG. OTHERS CALL HER BY HER TITLE, LADY RYUHWA.

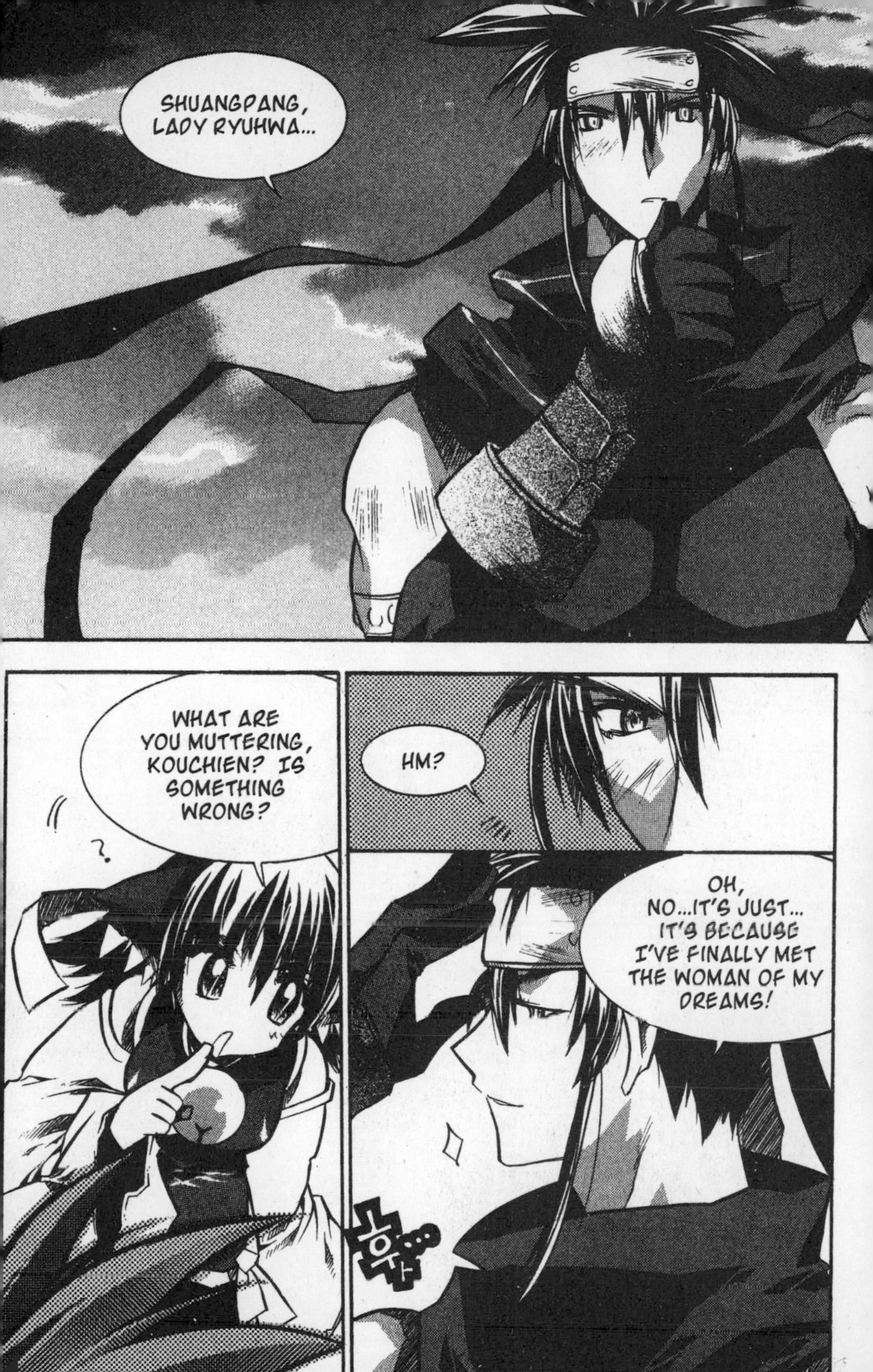
SHUANGPANG, LADY RYUHWA...
WHAT ARE YOU MUTTERING, KOUCHIEN? IS SOMETHING WRONG?
?
HM?
OH, NO...IT'S JUST... IT'S BECAUSE I'VE FINALLY MET THE WOMAN OF MY DREAMS!

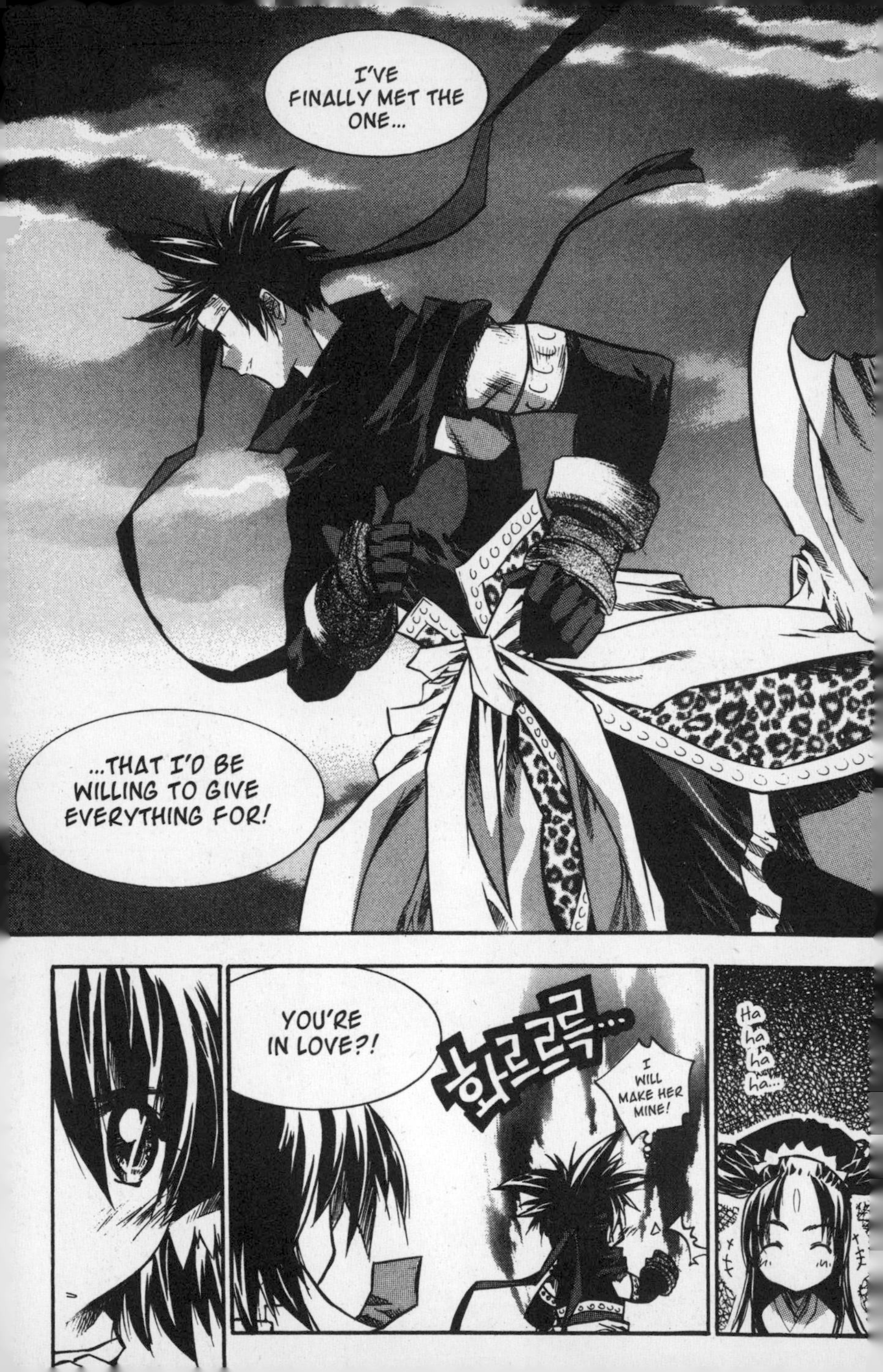
I'VE FINALLY MET THE ONE...
...THAT I'D BE WILLING TO GIVE EVERYTHING FOR!
YOU'RE IN LOVE?!
화르르륵...
I WILL MAKE HER MINE!
Ha ha ha ha...

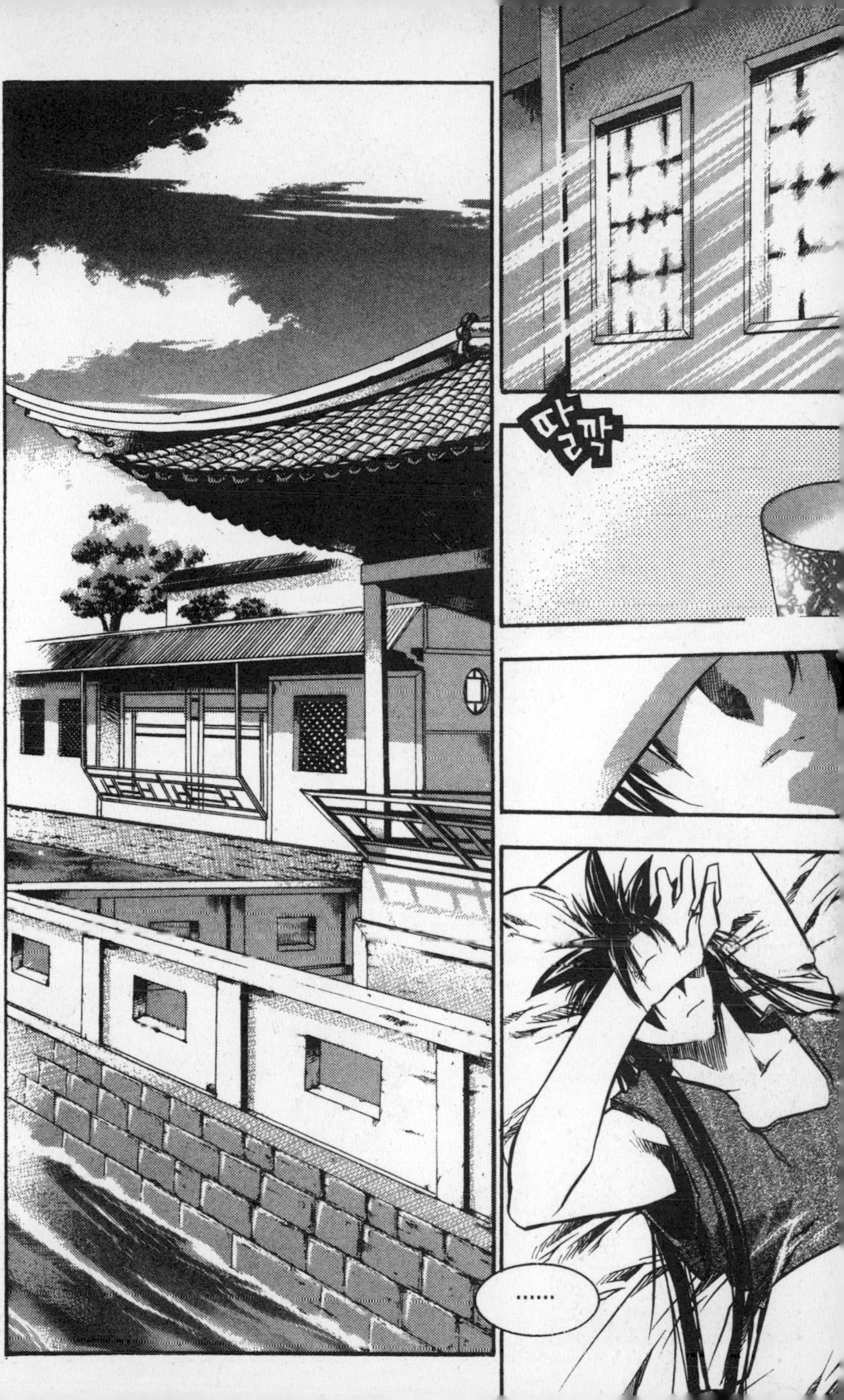
딸깍
......

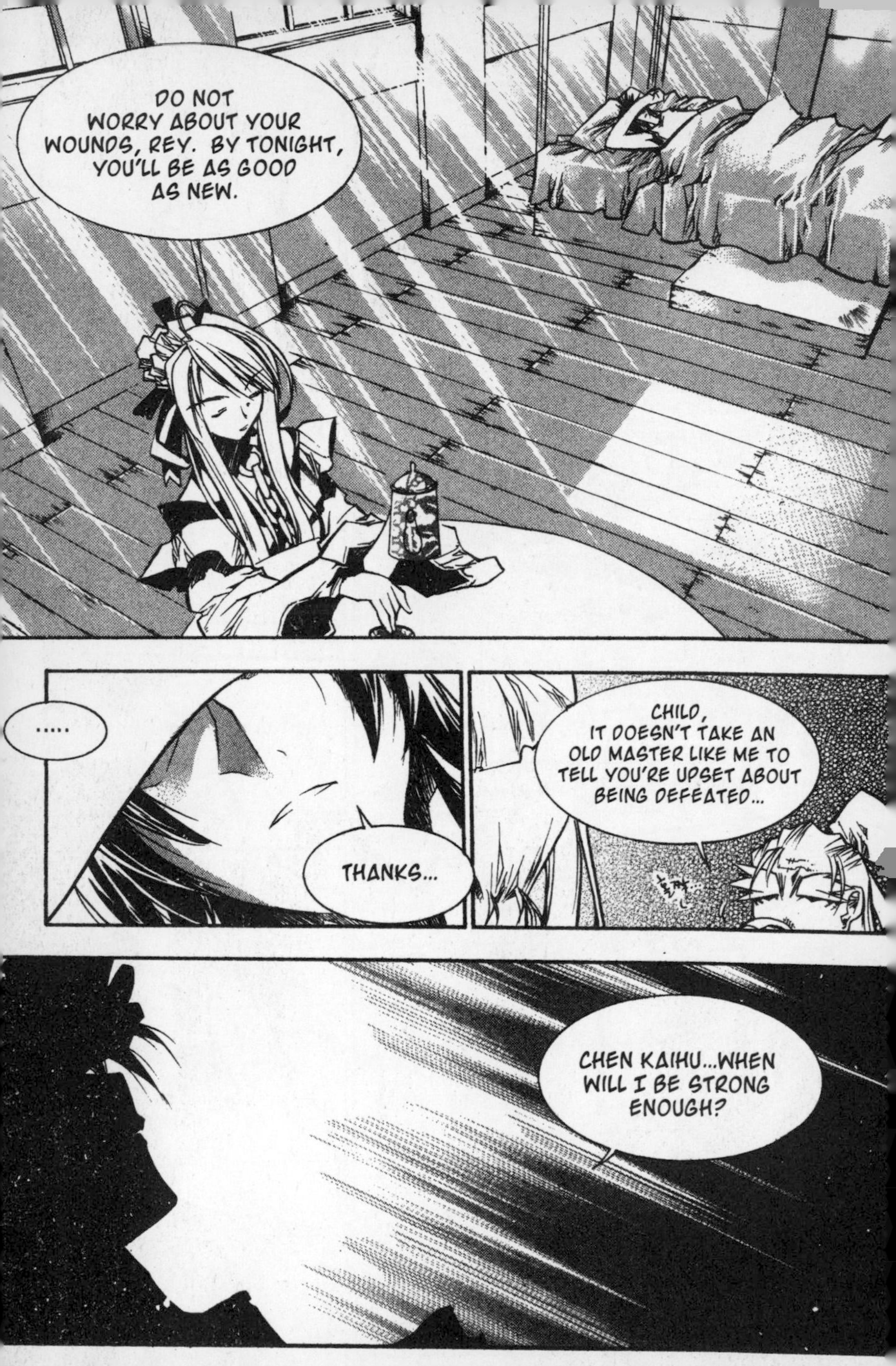
DO NOT WORRY ABOUT YOUR WOUNDS, REY. BY TONIGHT, YOU'LL BE AS GOOD AS NEW.
.....
THANKS...
CHILD, IT DOESN'T TAKE AN OLD MASTER LIKE ME TO TELL YOU'RE UPSET ABOUT BEING DEFEATED...
CHEN KAIHU...WHEN WILL I BE STRONG ENOUGH?

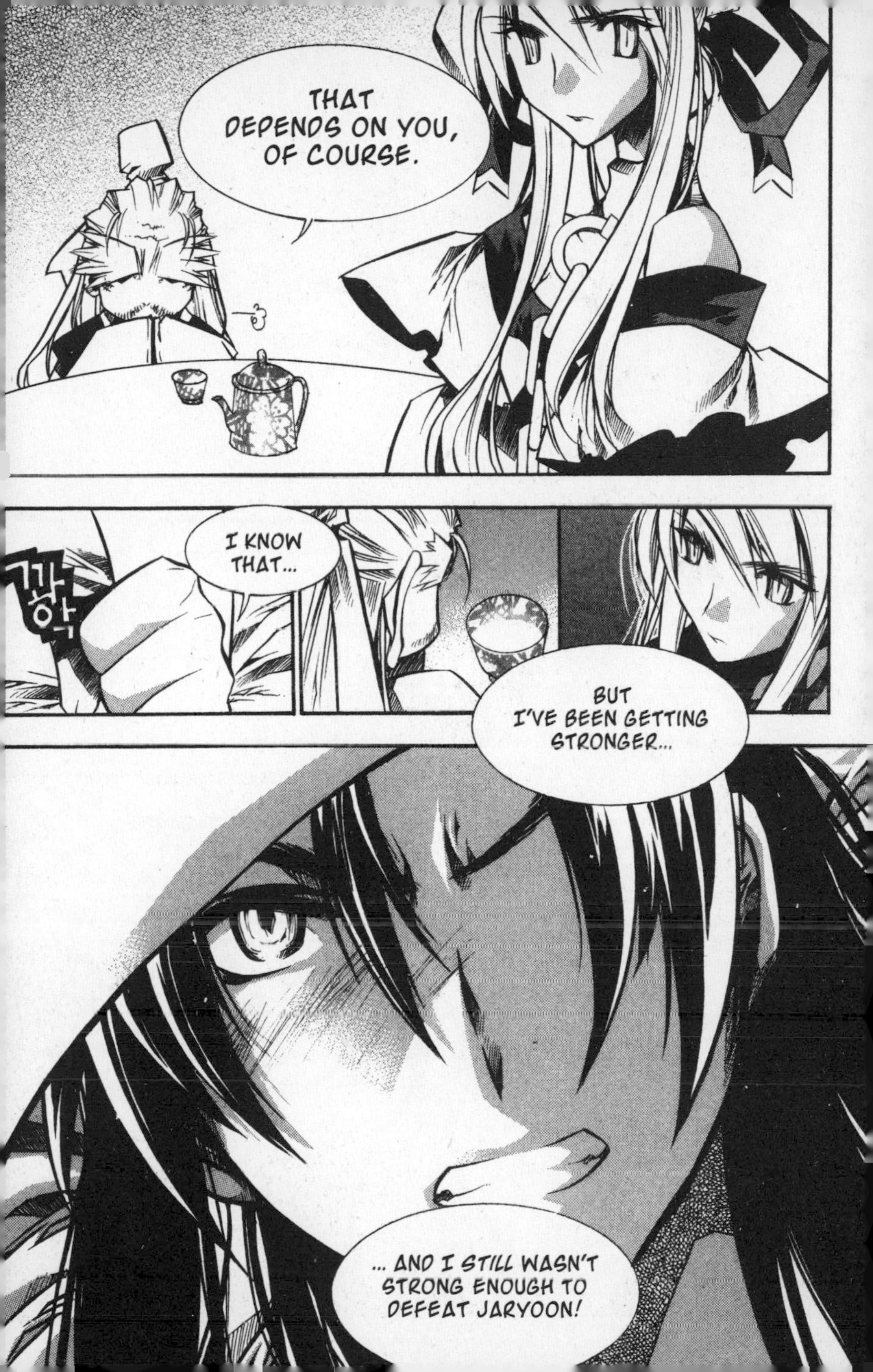
THAT DEPENDS ON YOU, OF COURSE.
꽈악
I KNOW THAT...
BUT I'VE BEEN GETTING STRONGER...
... AND I STILL WASN'T STRONG ENOUGH TO DEFEAT JARYOON!

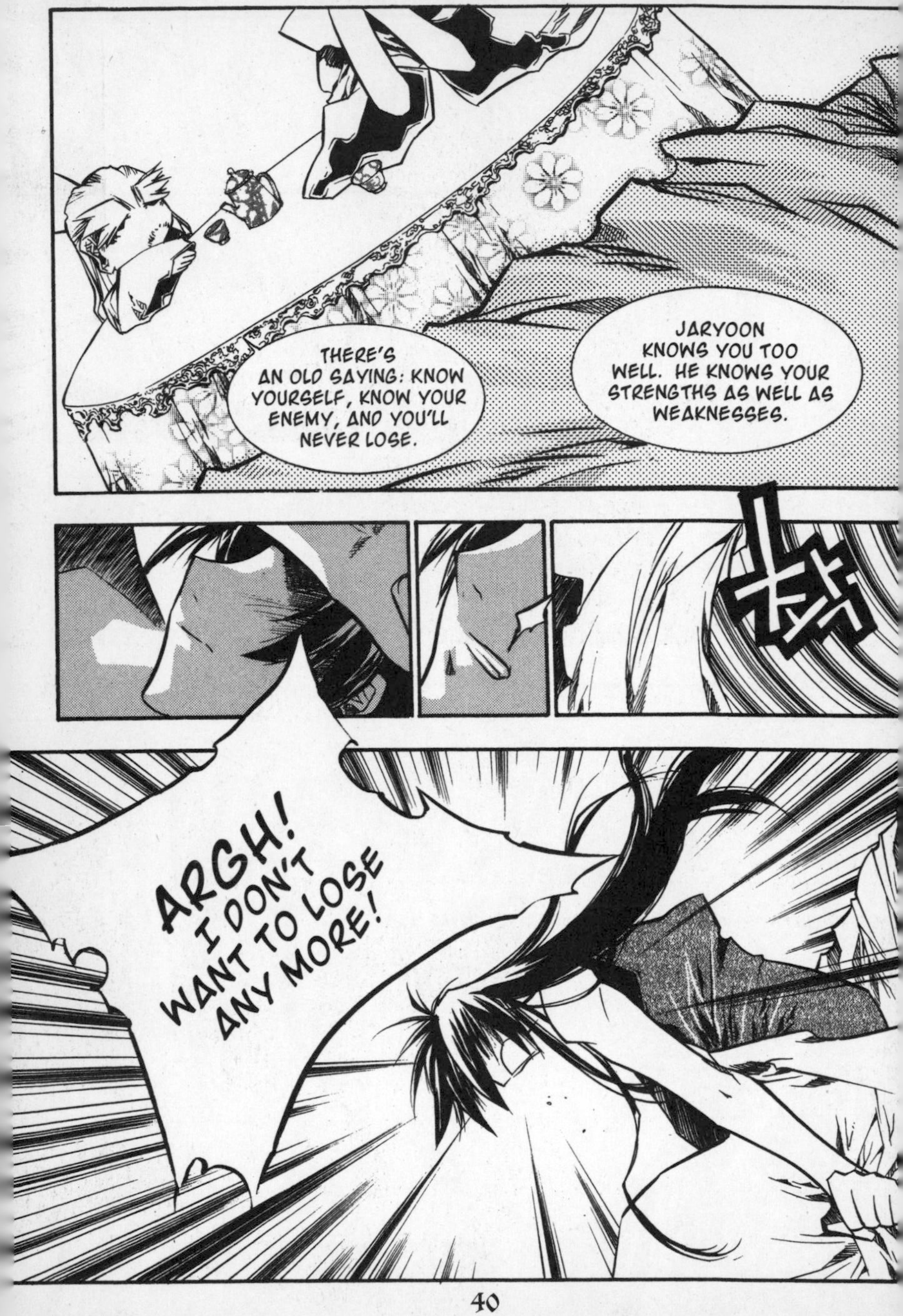
THERE'S AN OLD SAYING: KNOW YOURSELF, KNOW YOUR ENEMY, AND YOU'LL NEVER LOSE.
JARYOON KNOWS YOU TOO WELL. HE KNOWS YOUR STRENGTHS AS WELL AS WEAKNESSES.
ARGH! I DON'T WANT TO LOSE ANY MORE!

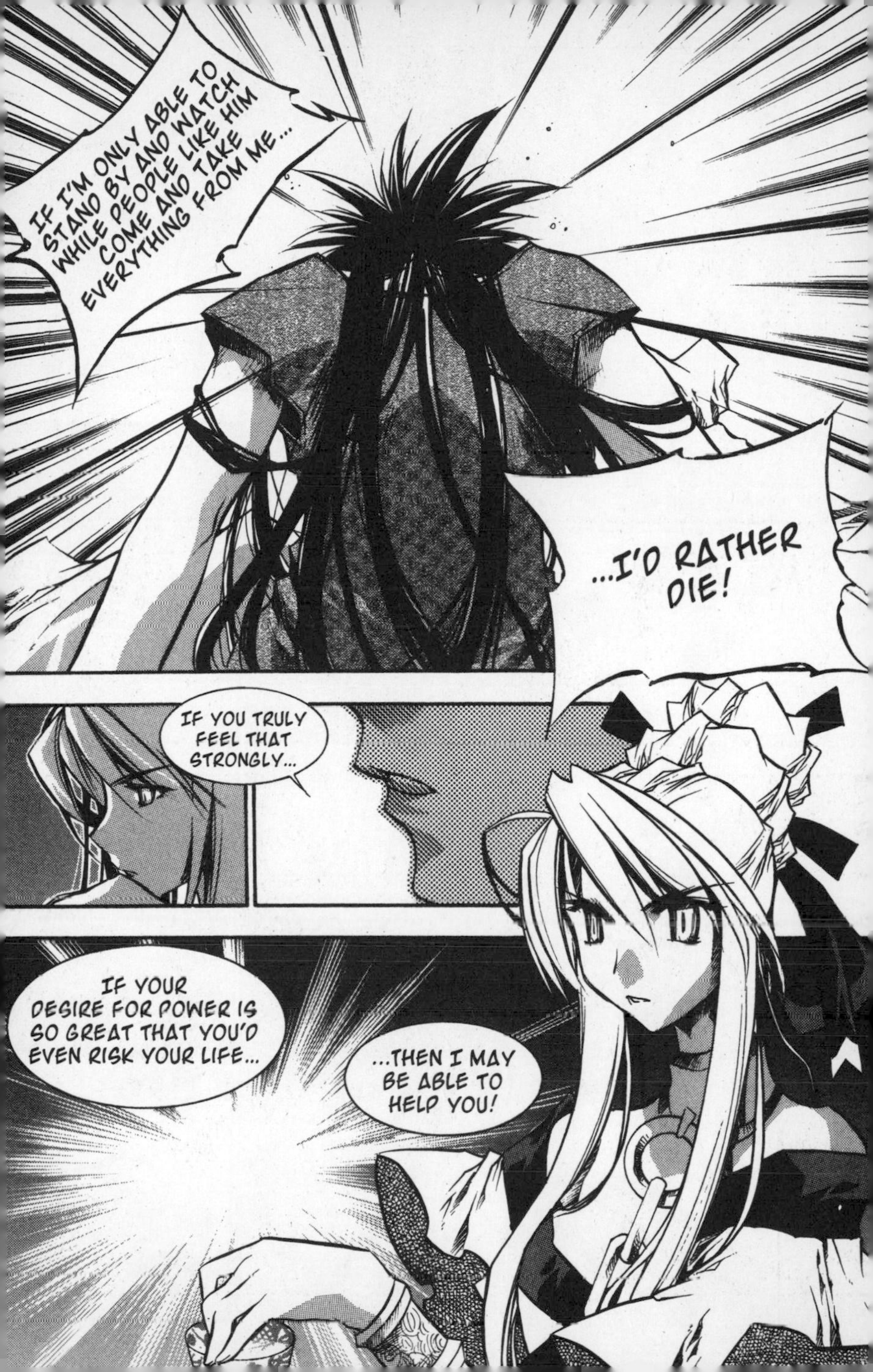
IF I'M ONLY ABLE TO STAND BY AND WATCH WHILE PEOPLE LIKE HIM COME AND TAKE EVERYTHING FROM ME...
...I'D RATHER DIE!
IF YOU TRULY FEEL THAT STRONGLY...
IF YOUR DESIRE FOR POWER IS SO GREAT THAT YOU'D EVEN RISK YOUR LIFE...
...THEN I MAY BE ABLE TO HELP YOU!

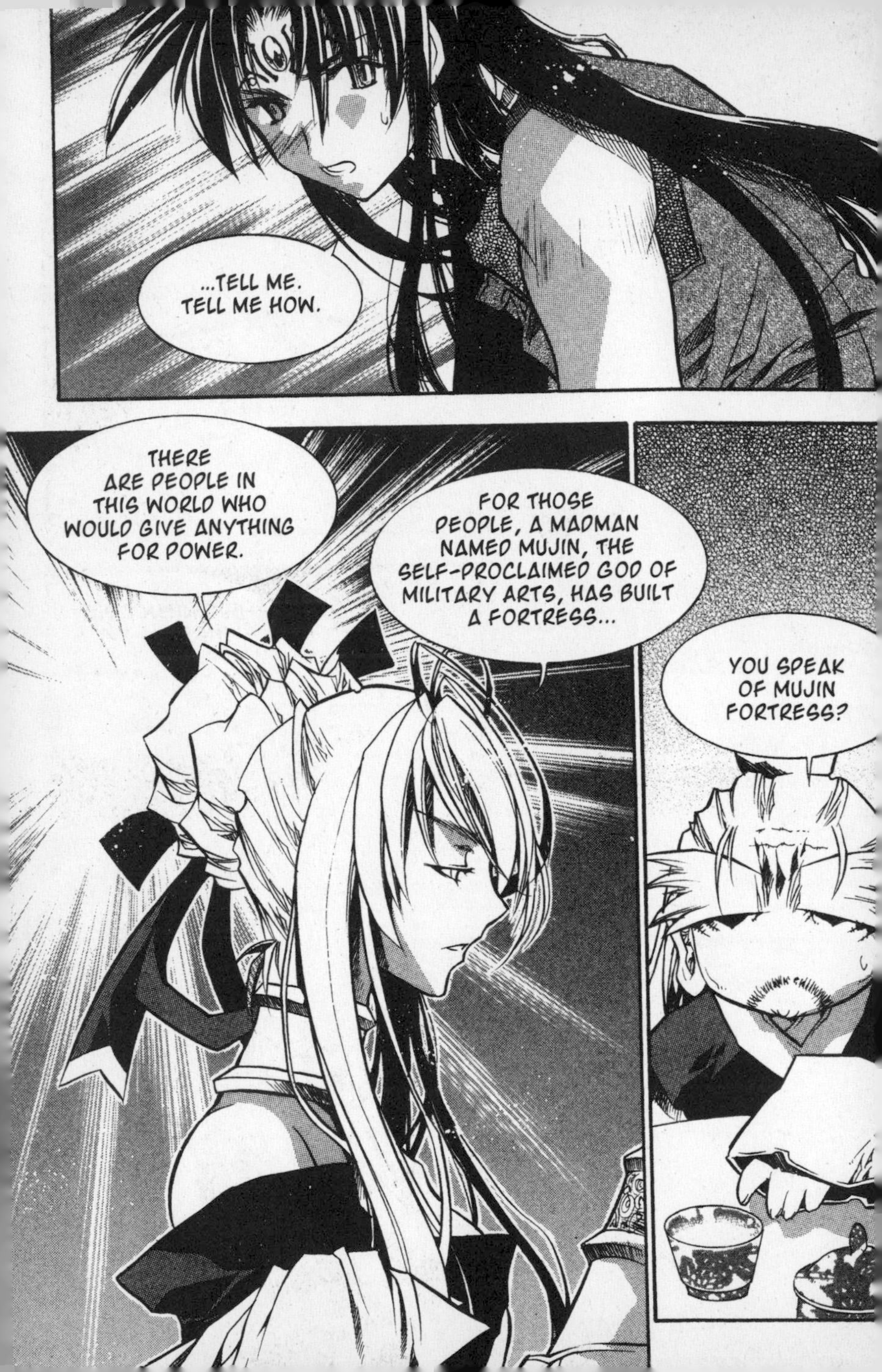
...TELL ME. TELL ME HOW.
THERE ARE PEOPLE IN THIS WORLD WHO WOULD GIVE ANYTHING FOR POWER.
FOR THOSE PEOPLE, A MADMAN NAMED MUJIN, THE SELF-PROCLAIMED GOD OF MILITARY ARTS, HAS BUILT A FORTRESS...
YOU SPEAK OF MUJIN FORTRESS?

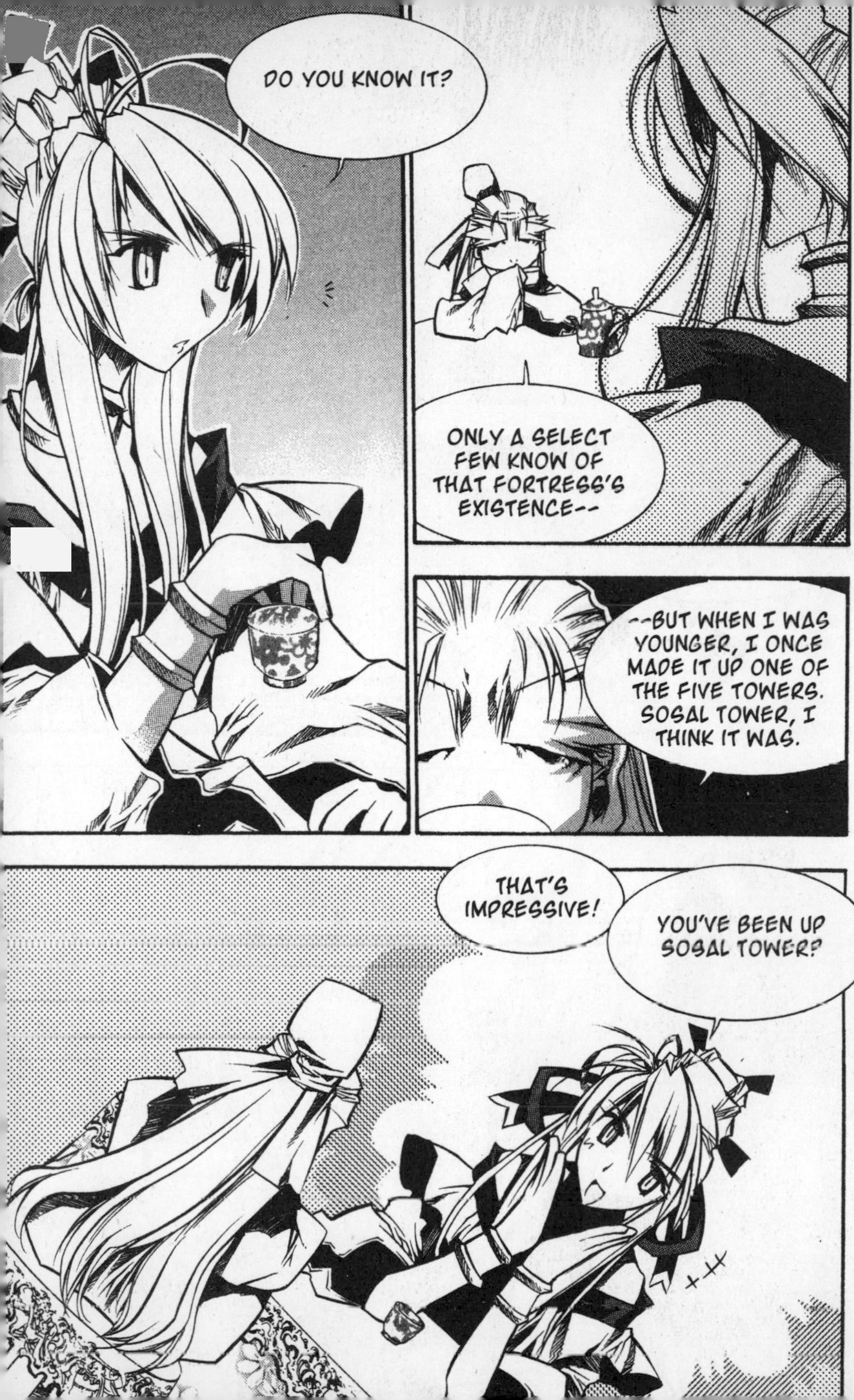
DO YOU KNOW IT?
ONLY A SELECT FEW KNOW OF THAT FORTRESS'S EXISTENCE--
--BUT WHEN I WAS YOUNGER, I ONCE MADE IT UP ONE OF THE FIVE TOWERS. SOSAL TOWER, I THINK IT WAS.
THAT'S IMPRESSIVE!
YOU'VE BEEN UP SOSAL TOWER?

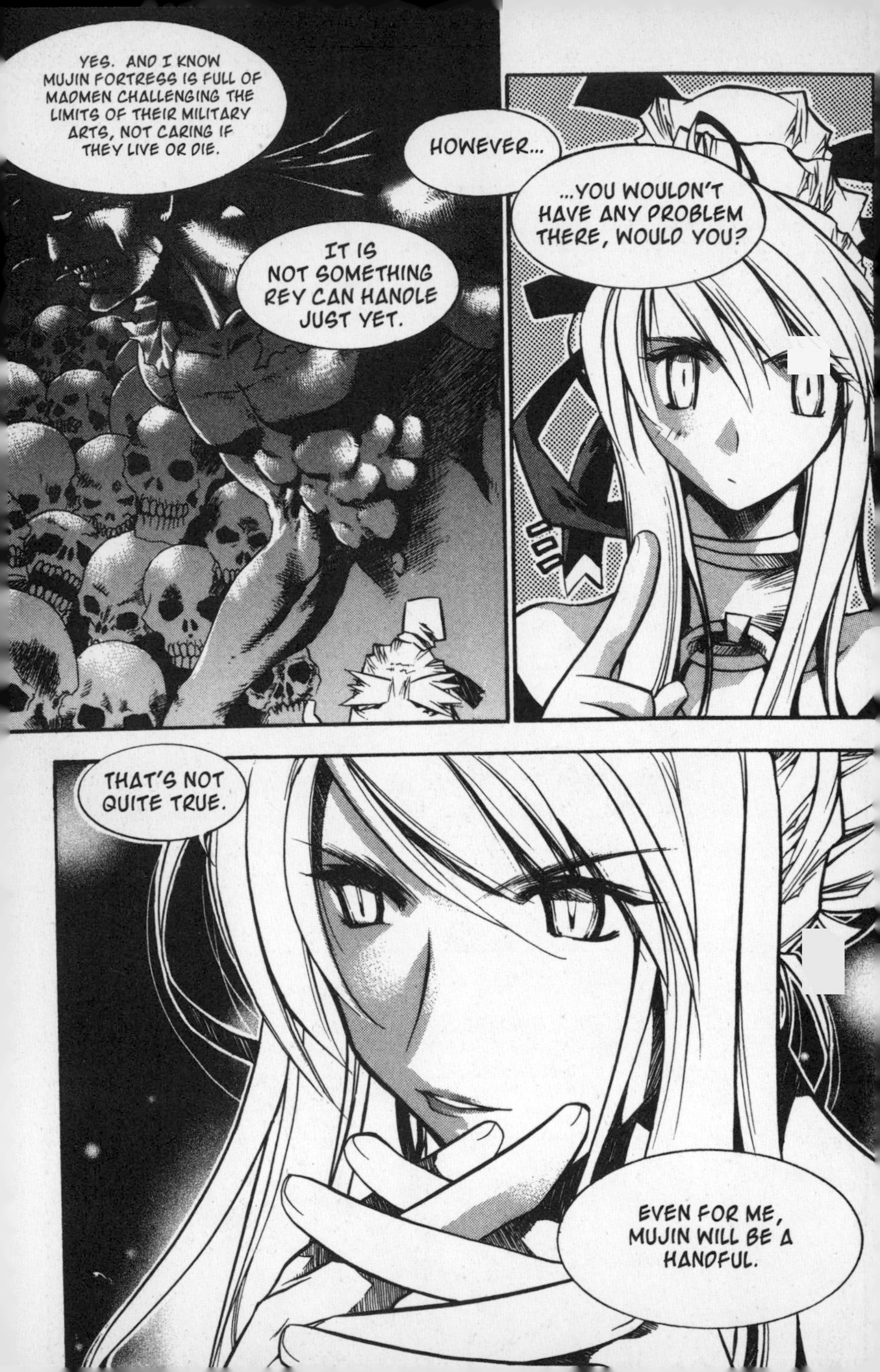
YES. AND I KNOW MUJIN FORTRESS IS FULL OF MADMEN CHALLENGING THE LIMITS OF THEIR MILITARY ARTS, NOT CARING IF THEY LIVE OR DIE.
IT IS NOT SOMETHING REY CAN HANDLE JUST YET.
HOWEVER...
...YOU WOULDN'T HAVE ANY PROBLEM THERE, WOULD YOU?
THAT'S NOT QUITE TRUE.
EVEN FOR ME, MUJIN WILL BE A HANDFUL.

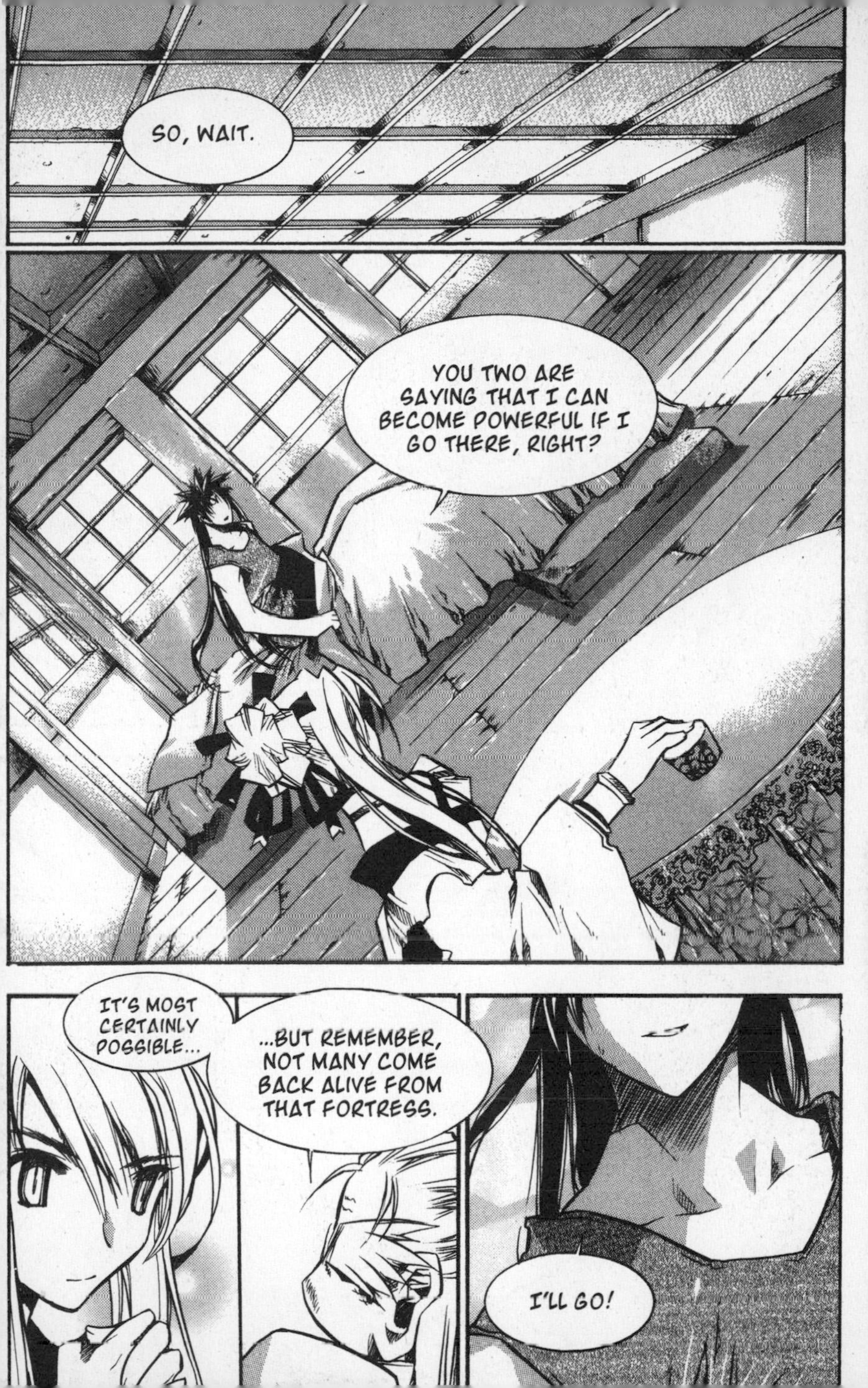
SO, WAIT.
YOU TWO ARE SAYING THAT I CAN BECOME POWERFUL IF I GO THERE, RIGHT?
IT'S MOST CERTAINLY POSSIBLE...
...BUT REMEMBER, NOT MANY COME BACK ALIVE FROM THAT FORTRESS.
I'LL GO!

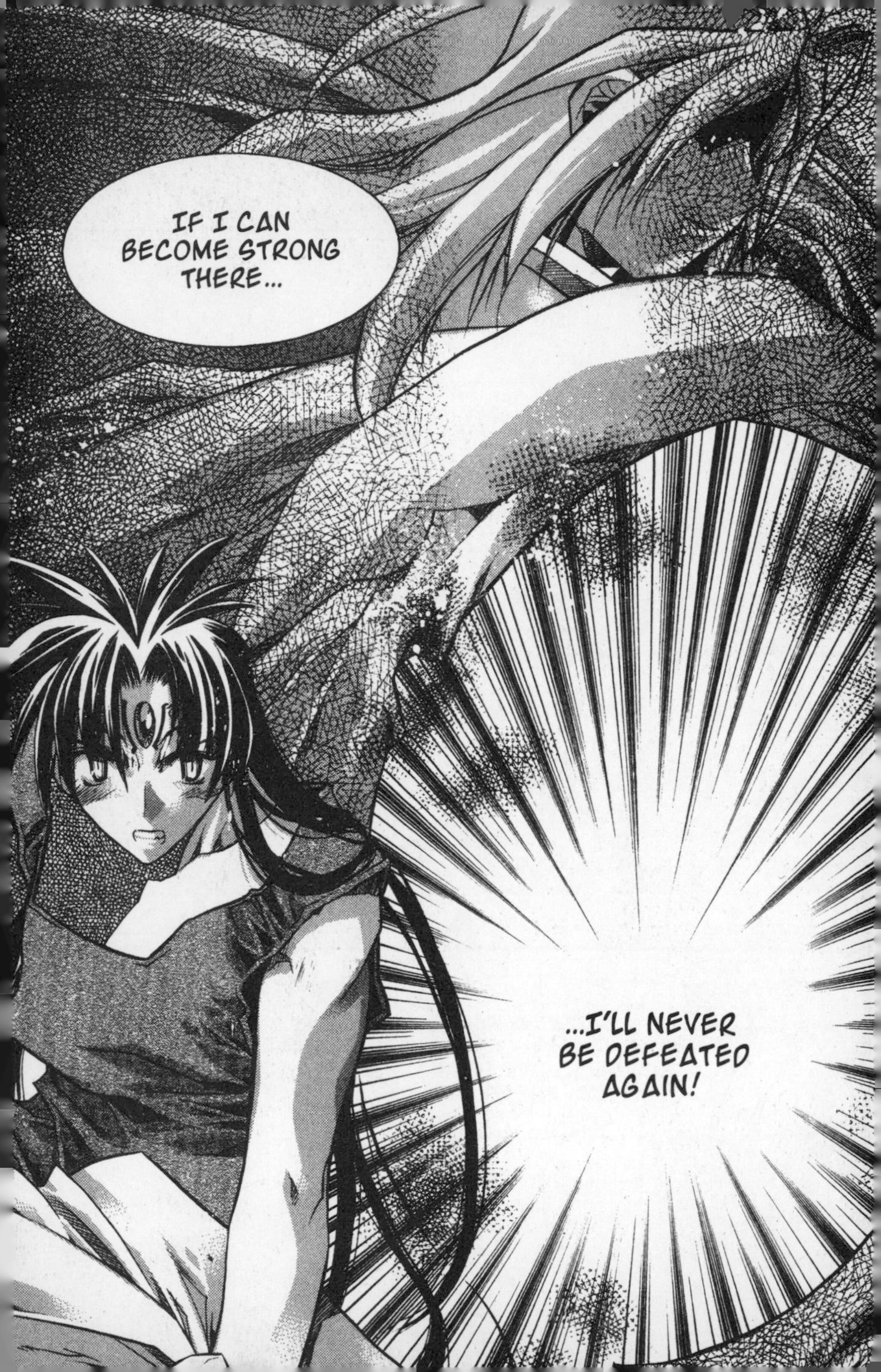
IF I CAN BECOME STRONG THERE...
...I'LL NEVER BE DEFEATED AGAIN!

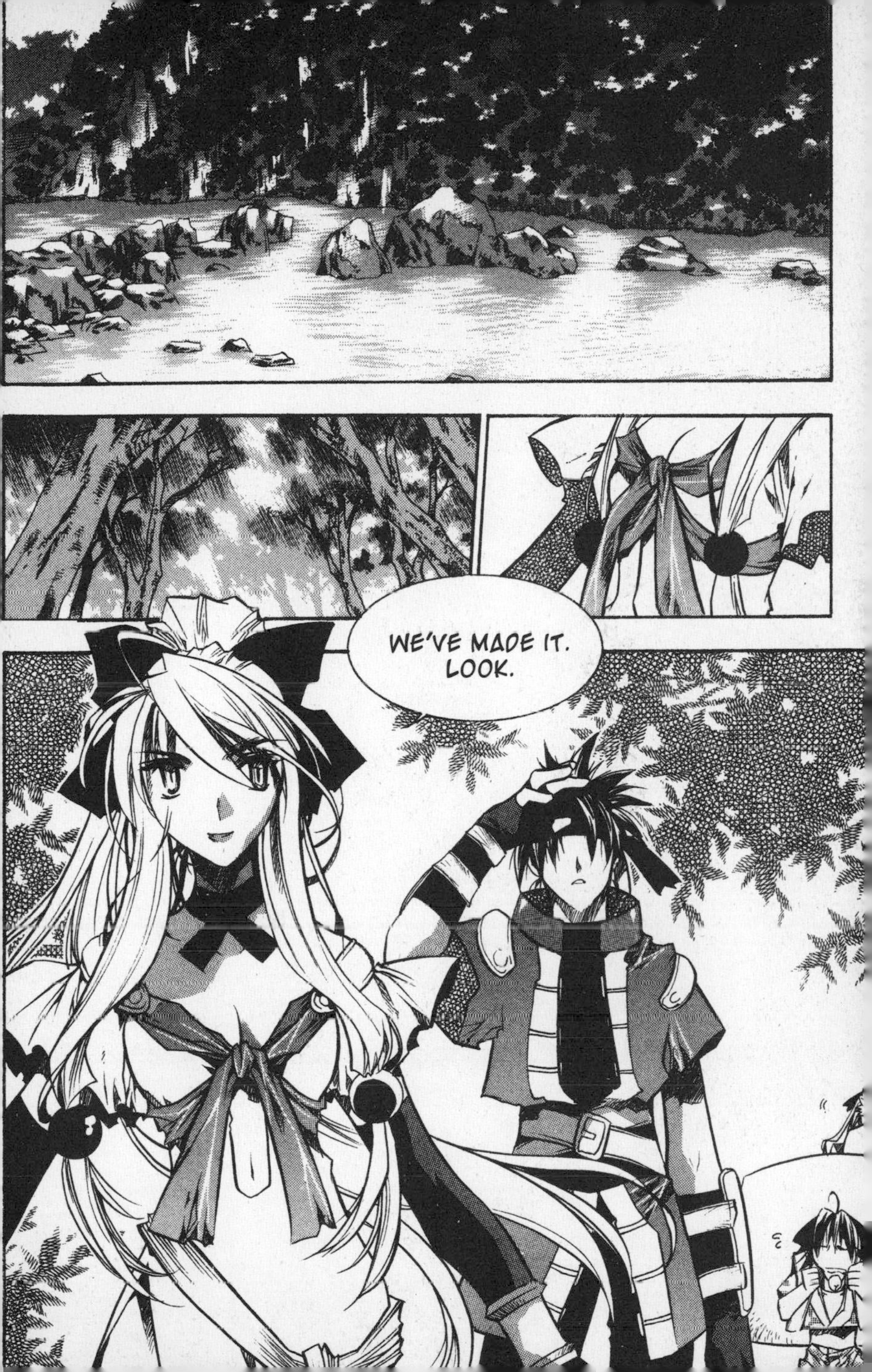
WE'VE MADE IT. LOOK.

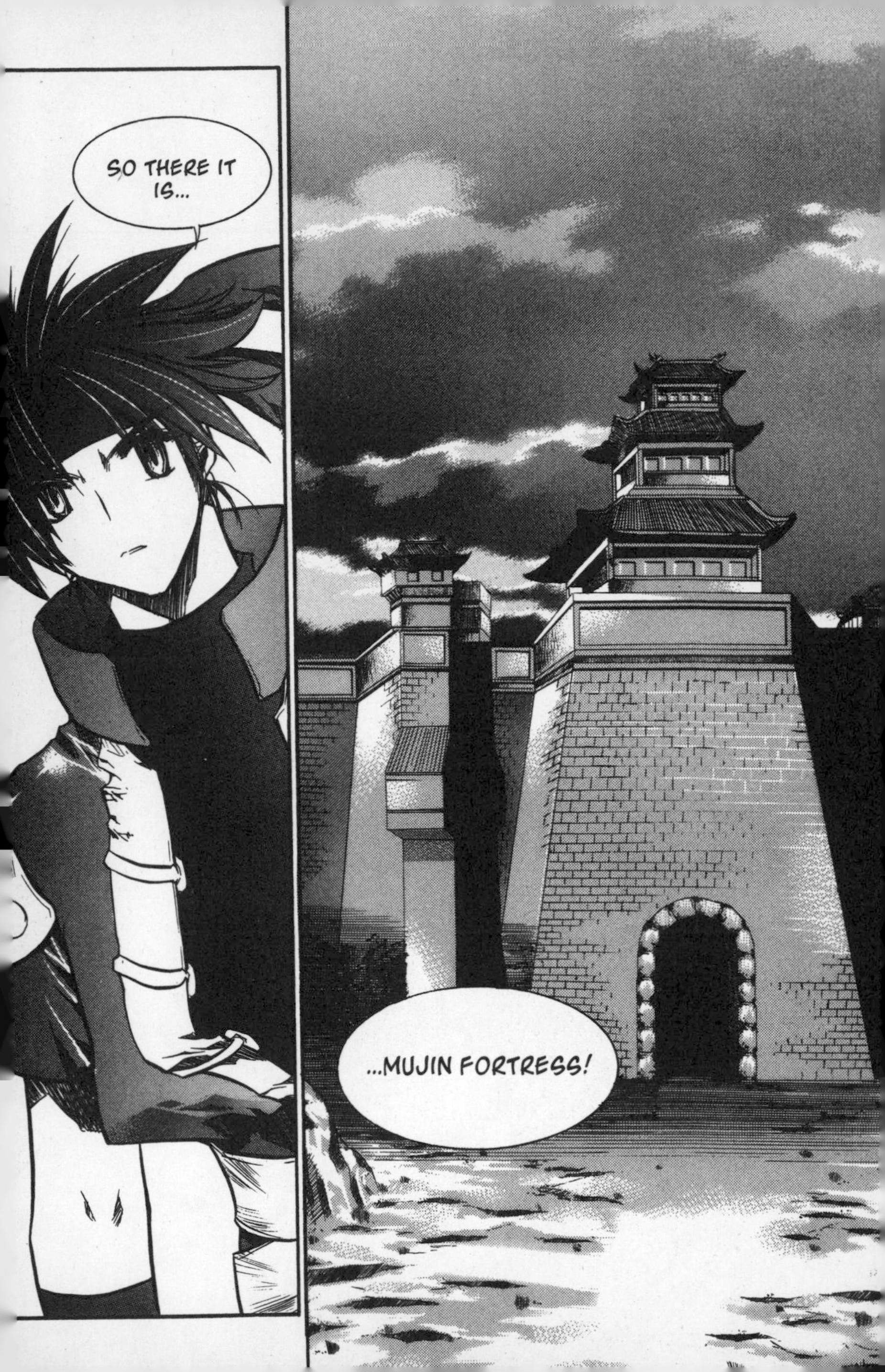
SO THERE IT IS...
...MUJIN FORTRESS!

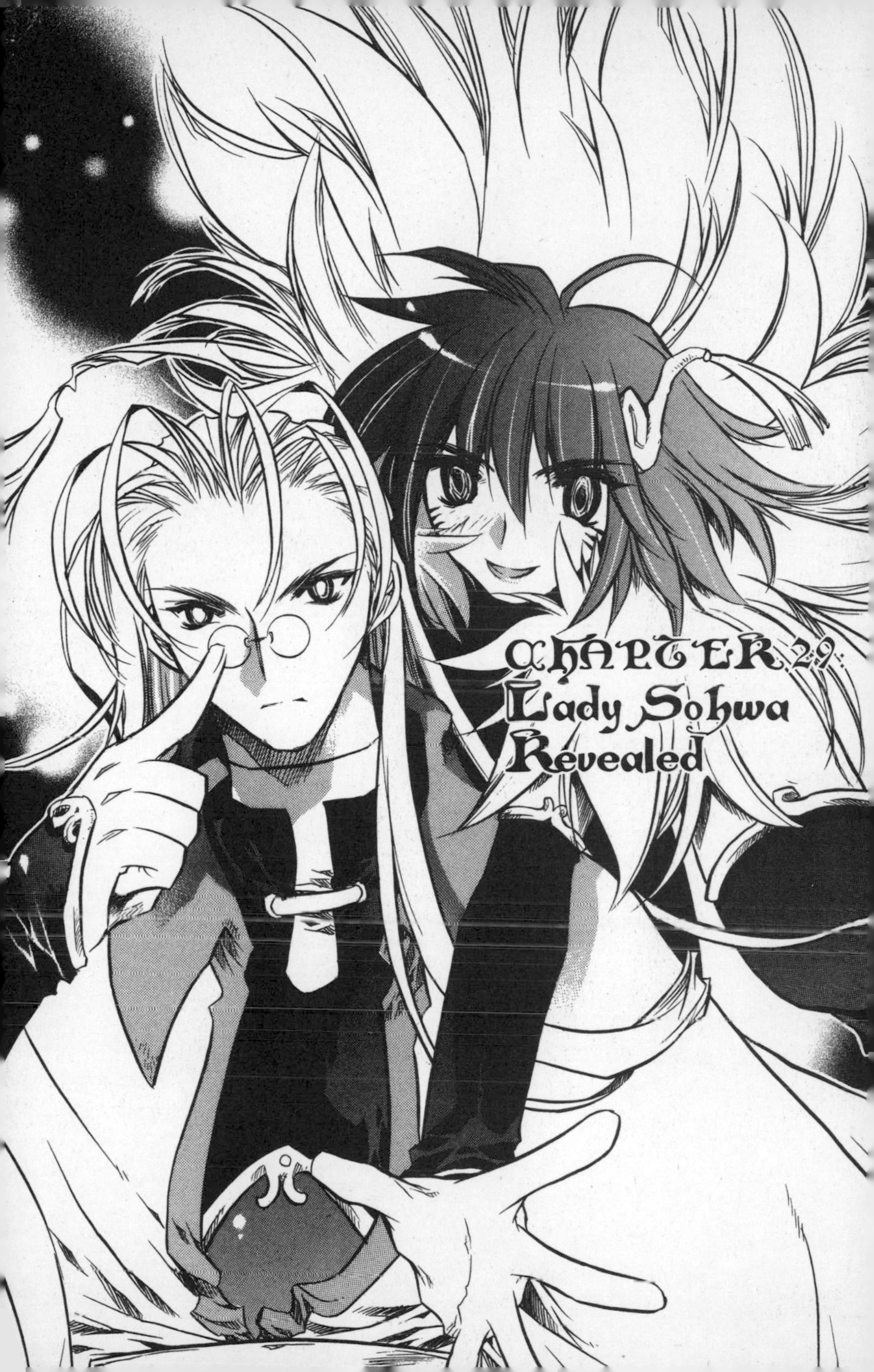
CHAPTER 29:
Lady Sohwa
Revealed

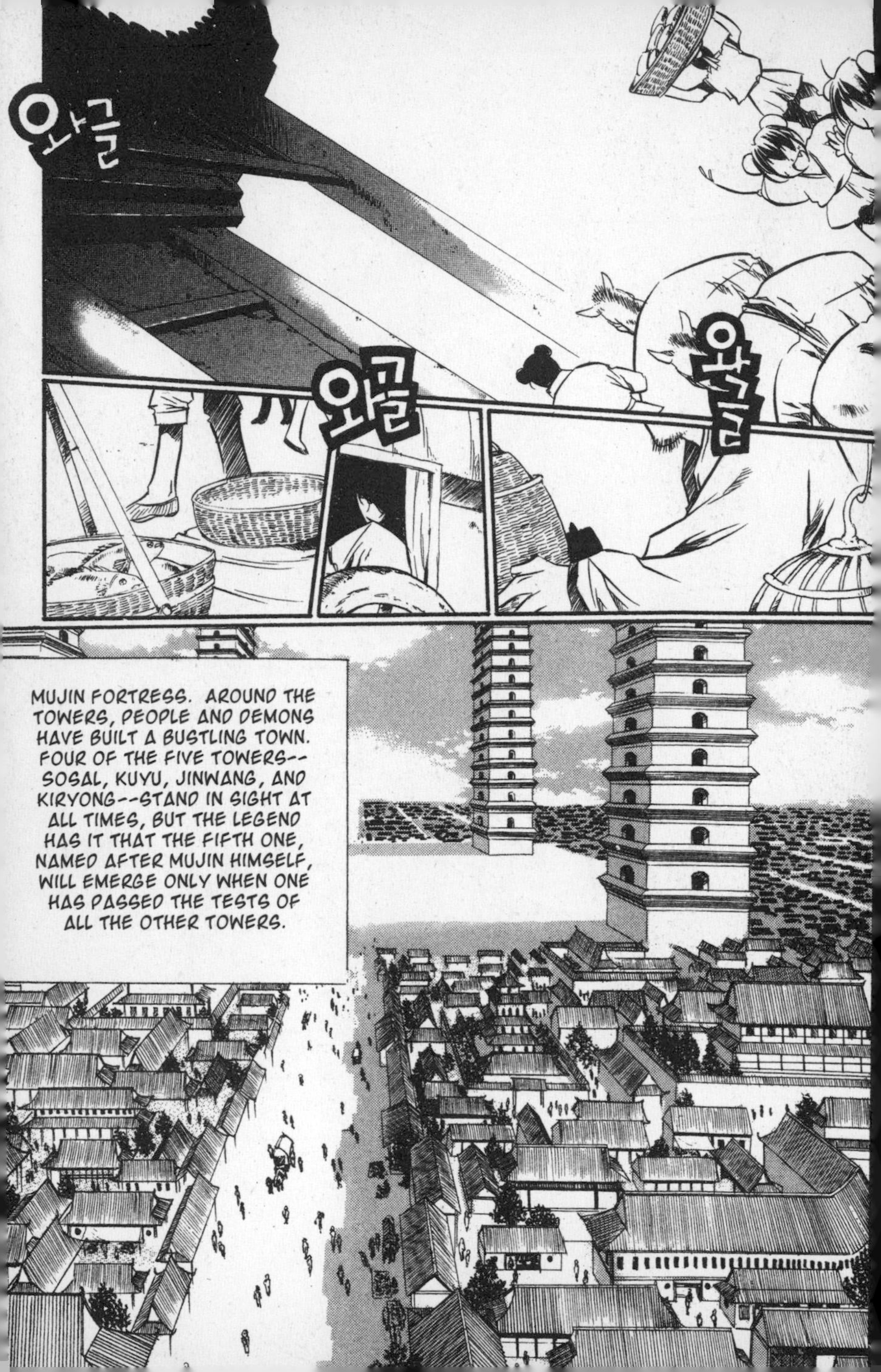
와글
와글
와글
MUJIN FORTRESS. AROUND THE TOWERS, PEOPLE AND DEMONS HAVE BUILT A BUSTLING TOWN. FOUR OF THE FIVE TOWERS--SOSAL, KUYU, JINWANG, AND KIRYONG--STAND IN SIGHT AT ALL TIMES, BUT THE LEGEND HAS IT THAT THE FIFTH ONE, NAMED AFTER MUJIN HIMSELF, WILL EMERGE ONLY WHEN ONE HAS PASSED THE TESTS OF ALL THE OTHER TOWERS.

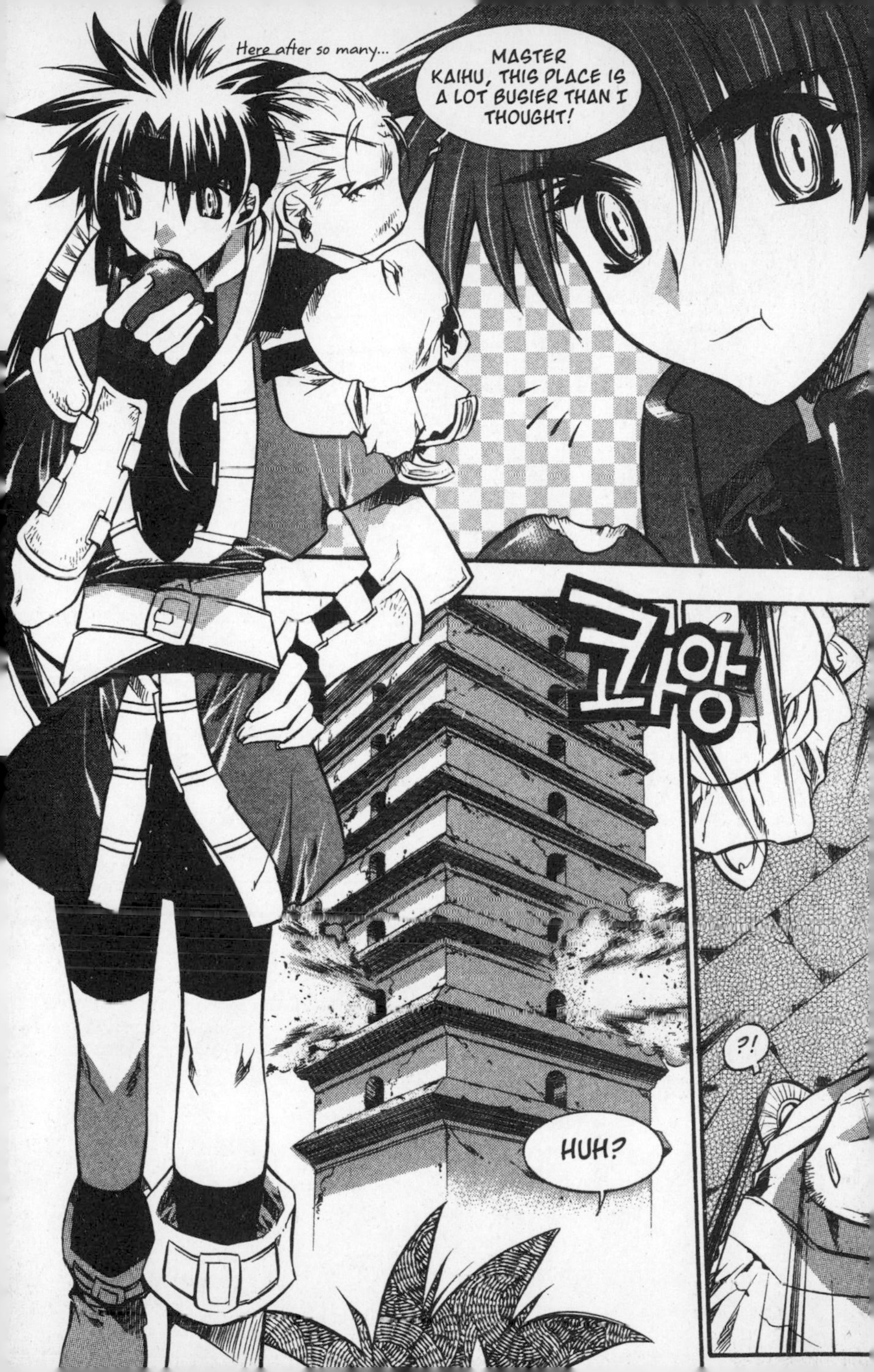
Here after so many...
MASTER KAIHU, THIS PLACE IS A LOT BUSIER THAN I THOUGHT!
콰앙
HUH?
?!

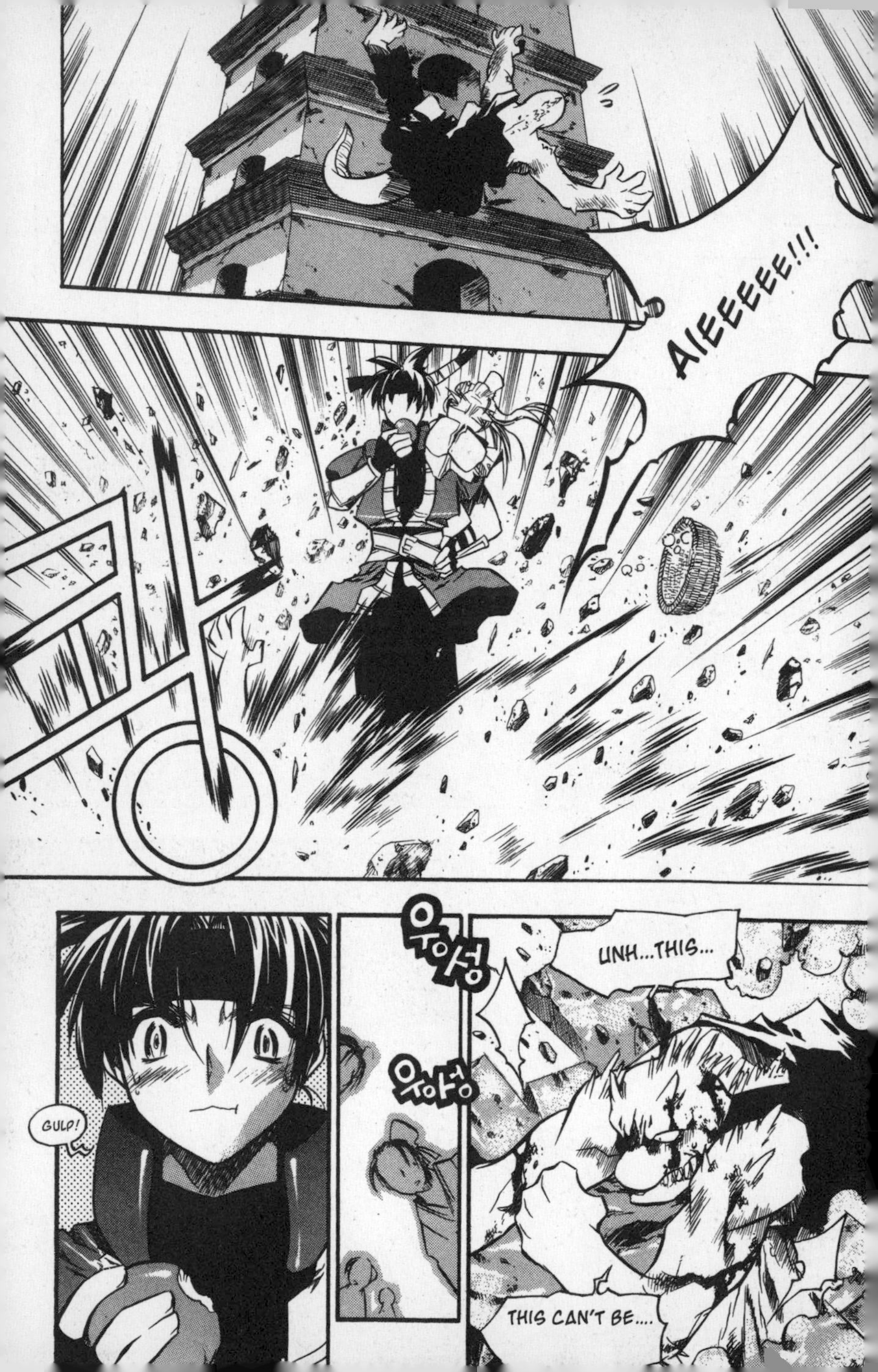
AIEEEEE!!!
GULP!
으앙
으앙
UNH...THIS...
THIS CAN'T BE....

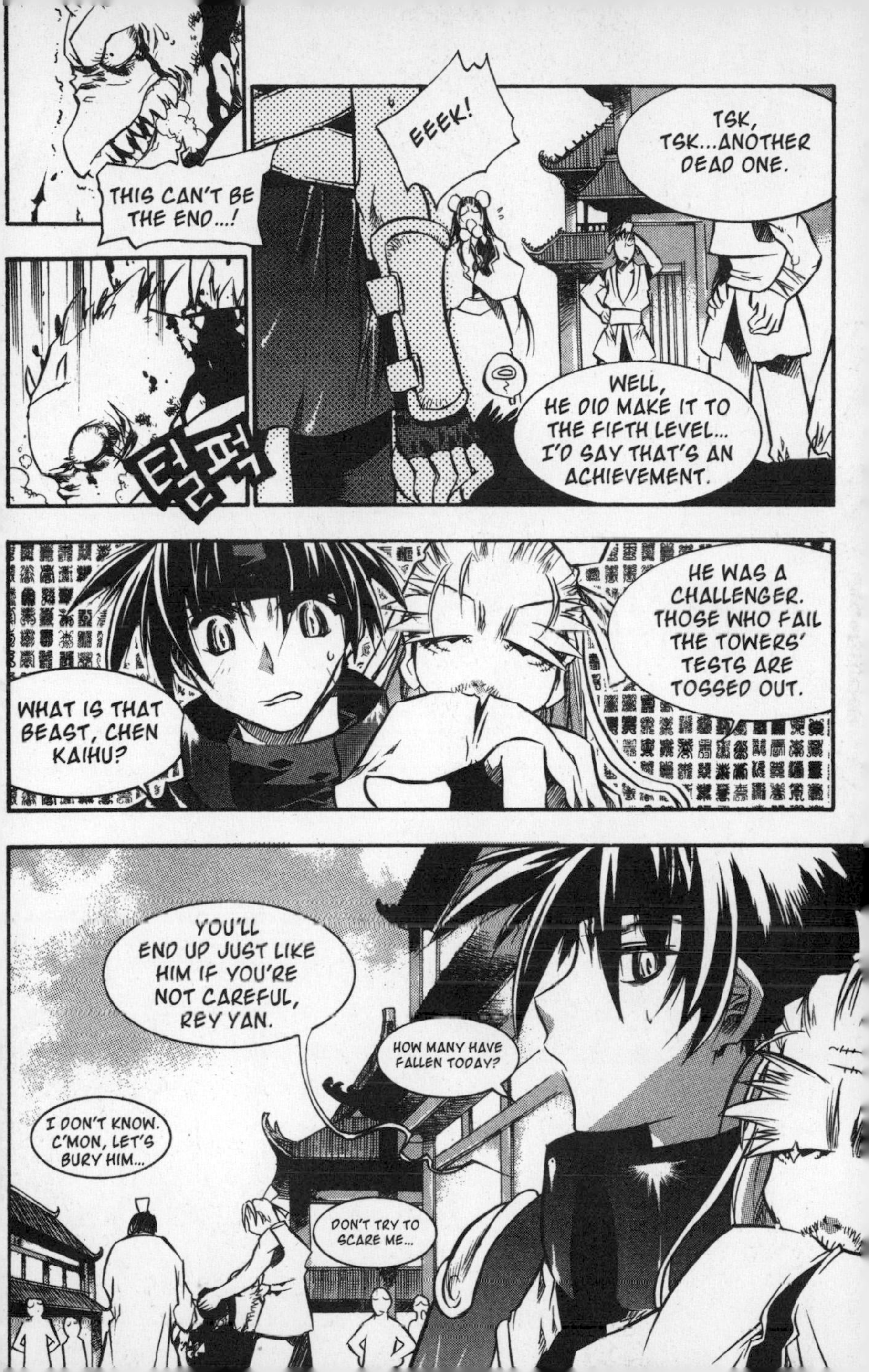
THIS CAN'T BE THE END...!
EEEK!
TSK, TSK...ANOTHER DEAD ONE.
WELL, HE DID MAKE IT TO THE FIFTH LEVEL... I'D SAY THAT'S AN ACHIEVEMENT.
WHAT IS THAT BEAST, CHEN KAIHU?
HE WAS A CHALLENGER. THOSE WHO FAIL THE TOWERS' TESTS ARE TOSSED OUT.
YOU'LL END UP JUST LIKE HIM IF YOU'RE NOT CAREFUL, REY YAN.
HOW MANY HAVE FALLEN TODAY?
I DON'T KNOW. C'MON, LET'S BURY HIM...
DON'T TRY TO SCARE ME...

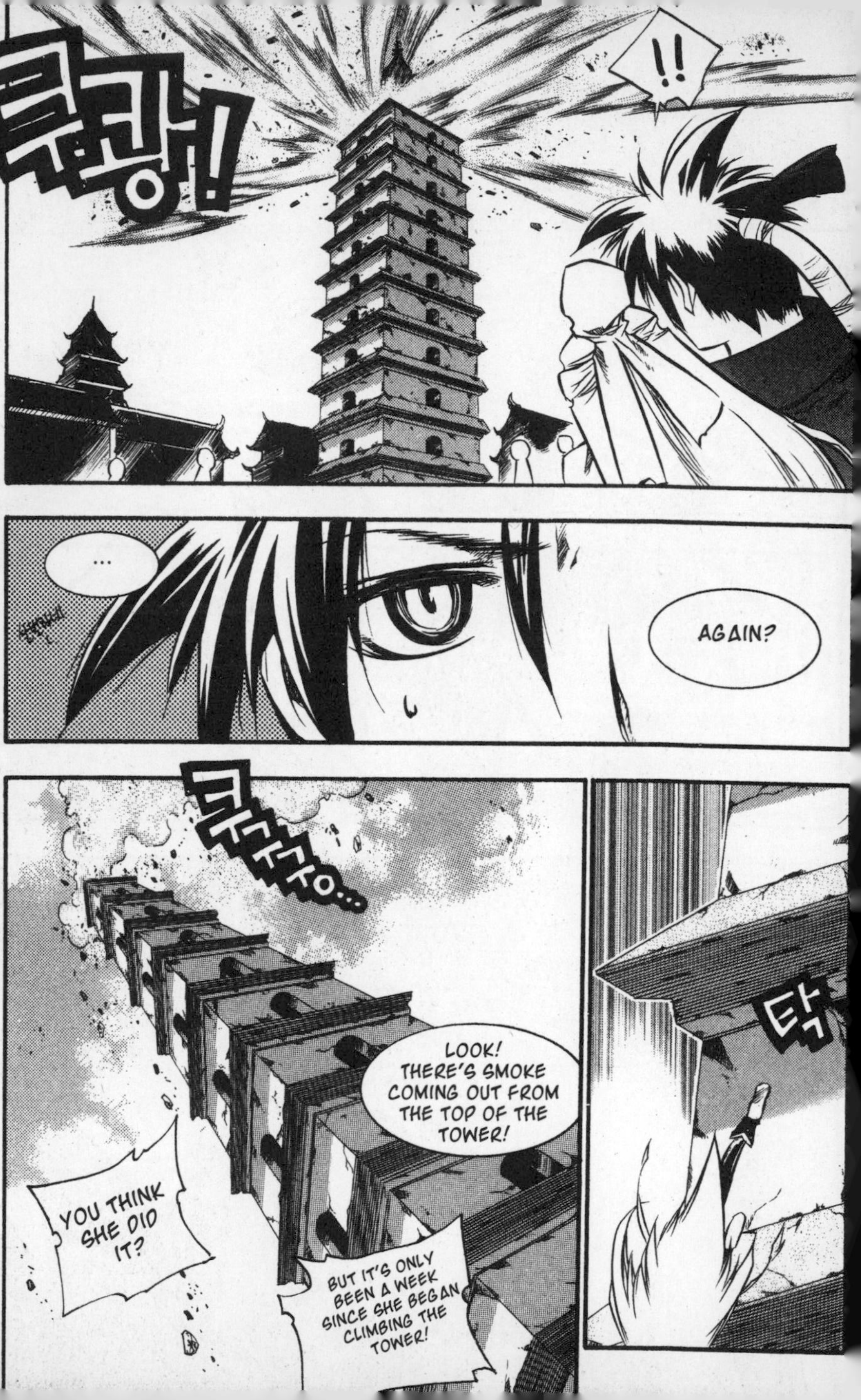
!!
...
AGAIN?
LOOK! THERE'S SMOKE COMING OUT FROM THE TOP OF THE TOWER!
YOU THINK SHE DID IT?
BUT IT'S ONLY BEEN A WEEK SINCE SHE BEGAN CLIMBING THE TOWER!
탁

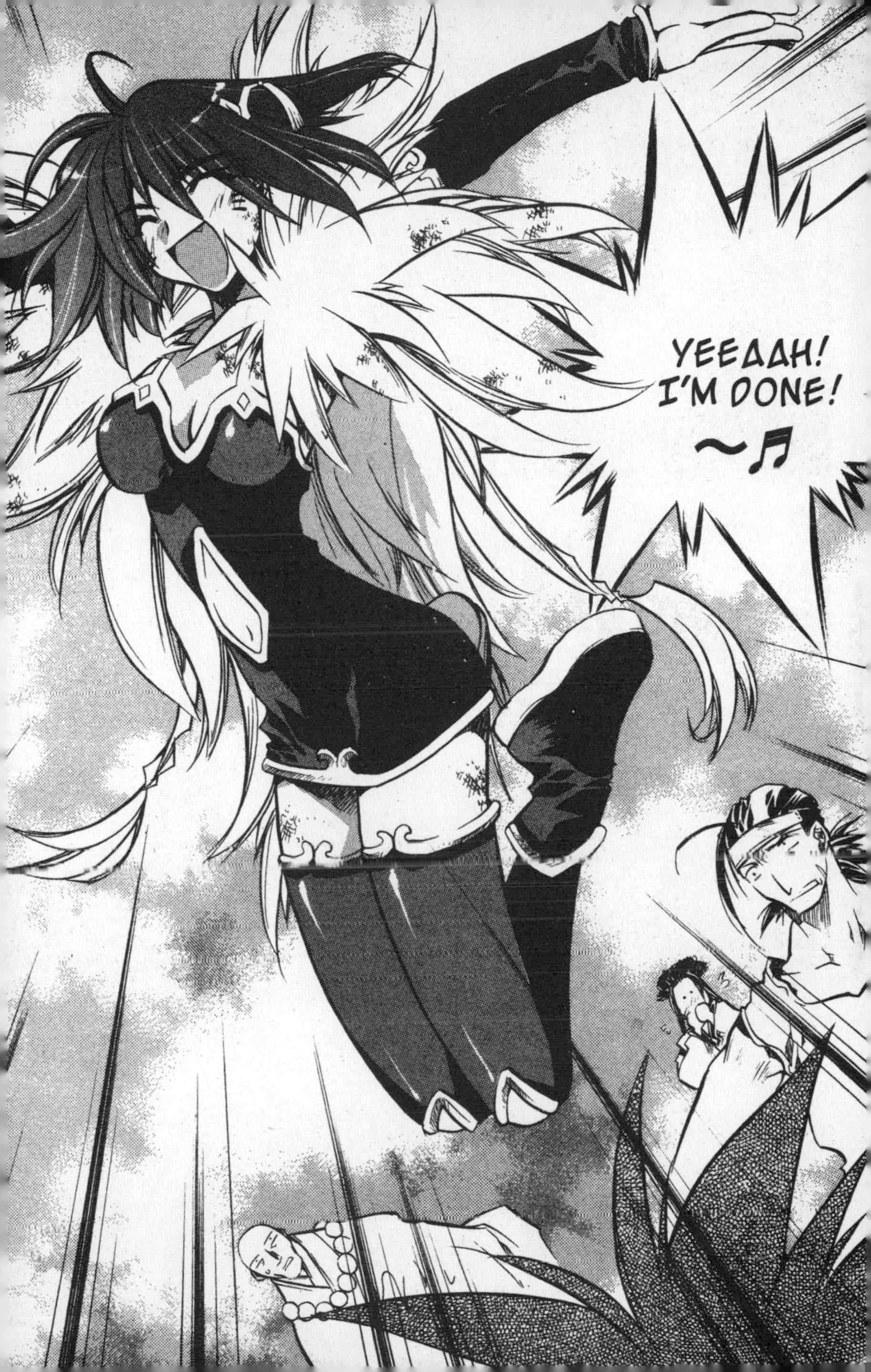
YEEAAH! I'M DONE! ~♫

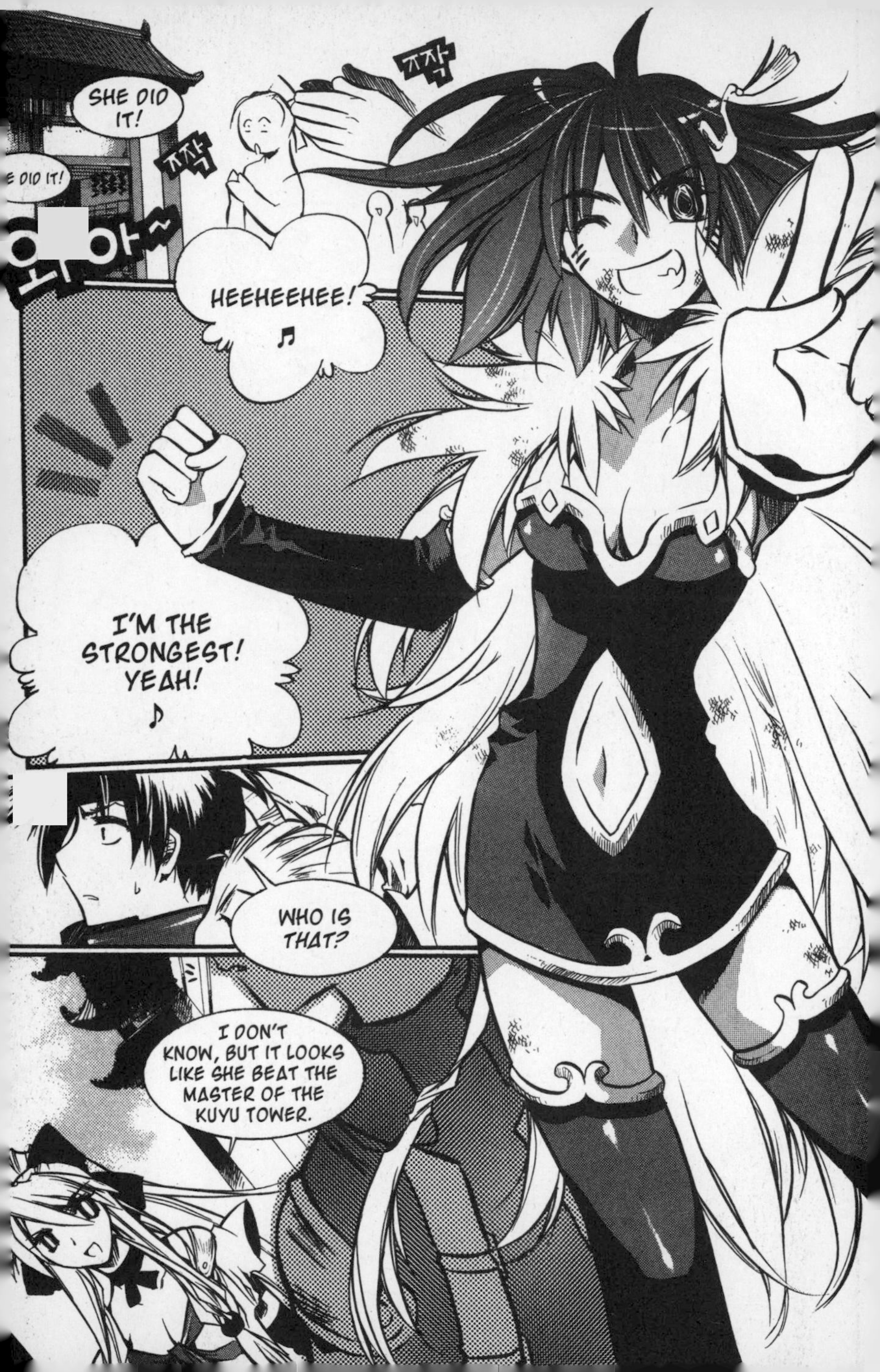
SHE DID IT!
E DID IT!
짝
짝
아~
HEEHEEHEE! ♫
I'M THE STRONGEST! YEAH! ♪
WHO IS THAT?
I DON'T KNOW, BUT IT LOOKS LIKE SHE BEAT THE MASTER OF THE KUYU TOWER.

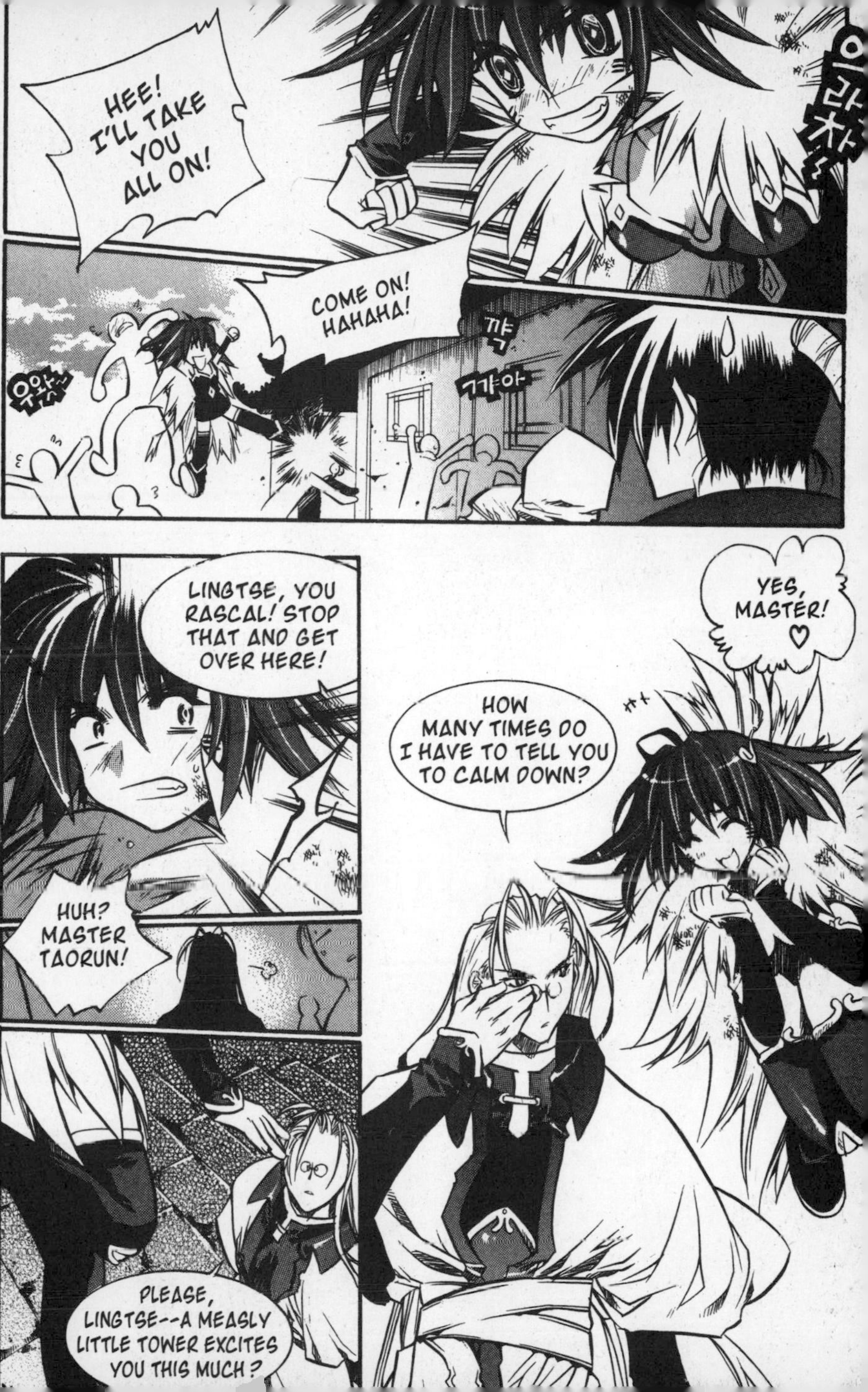
HEE! I'LL TAKE YOU ALL ON!
으랏차~
우왓~
COME ON! HAHAHA!
깍
LINGTSE, YOU RASCAL! STOP THAT AND GET OVER HERE!
HUH? MASTER TAORUN!
PLEASE, LINGTSE--A MEASLY LITTLE TOWER EXCITES YOU THIS MUCH?
HOW MANY TIMES DO I HAVE TO TELL YOU TO CALM DOWN?
YES, MASTER! ♡

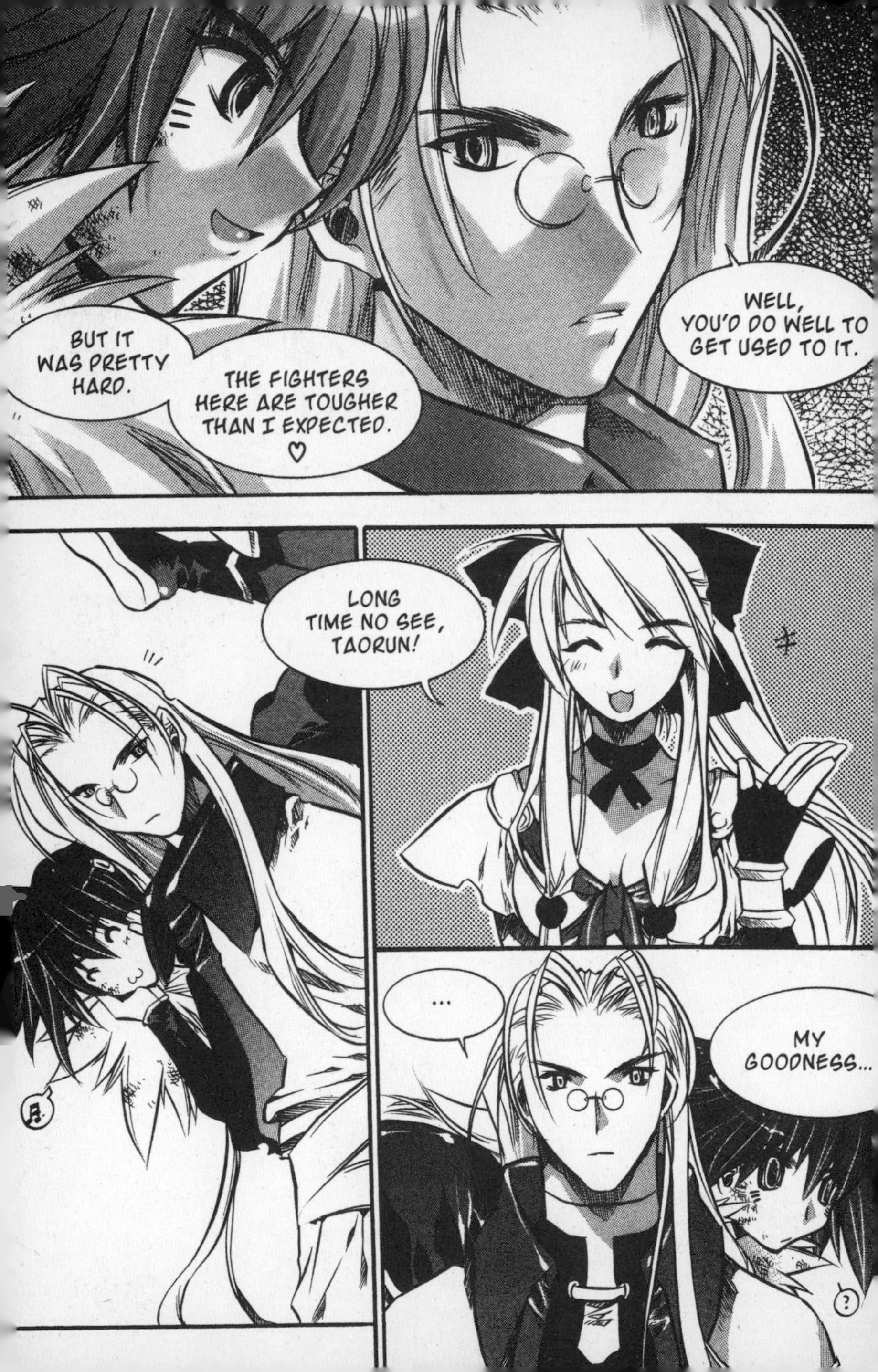
BUT IT WAS PRETTY HARD.
THE FIGHTERS HERE ARE TOUGHER THAN I EXPECTED. ♡
WELL, YOU'D DO WELL TO GET USED TO IT.
LONG TIME NO SEE, TAORUN!
...
MY GOODNESS...

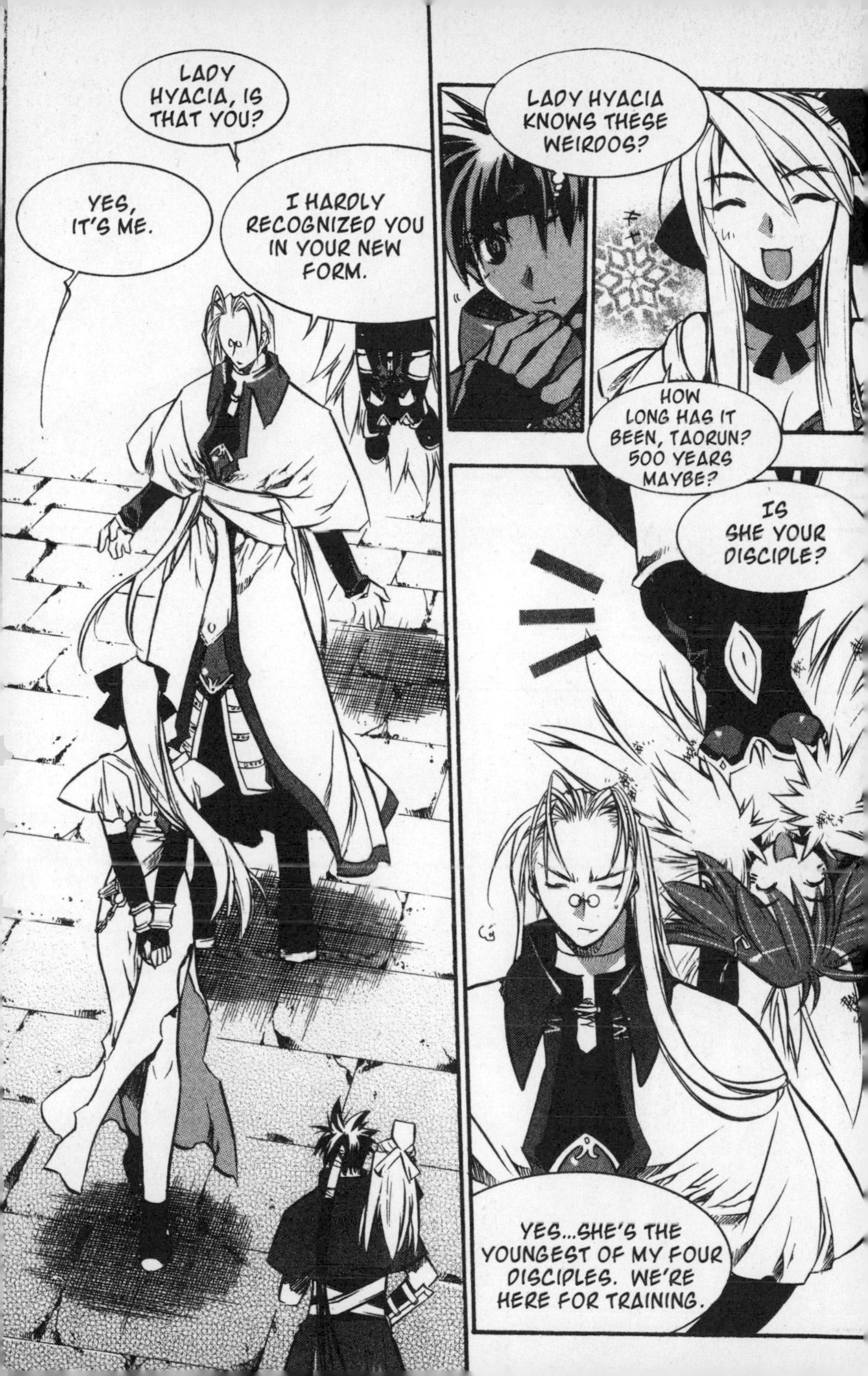
LADY HYACIA, IS THAT YOU?
YES, IT'S ME.
I HARDLY RECOGNIZED YOU IN YOUR NEW FORM.
LADY HYACIA KNOWS THESE WEIRDOS?
HOW LONG HAS IT BEEN, TAORUN? 500 YEARS MAYBE?
IS SHE YOUR DISCIPLE?
YES...SHE'S THE YOUNGEST OF MY FOUR DISCIPLES. WE'RE HERE FOR TRAINING.

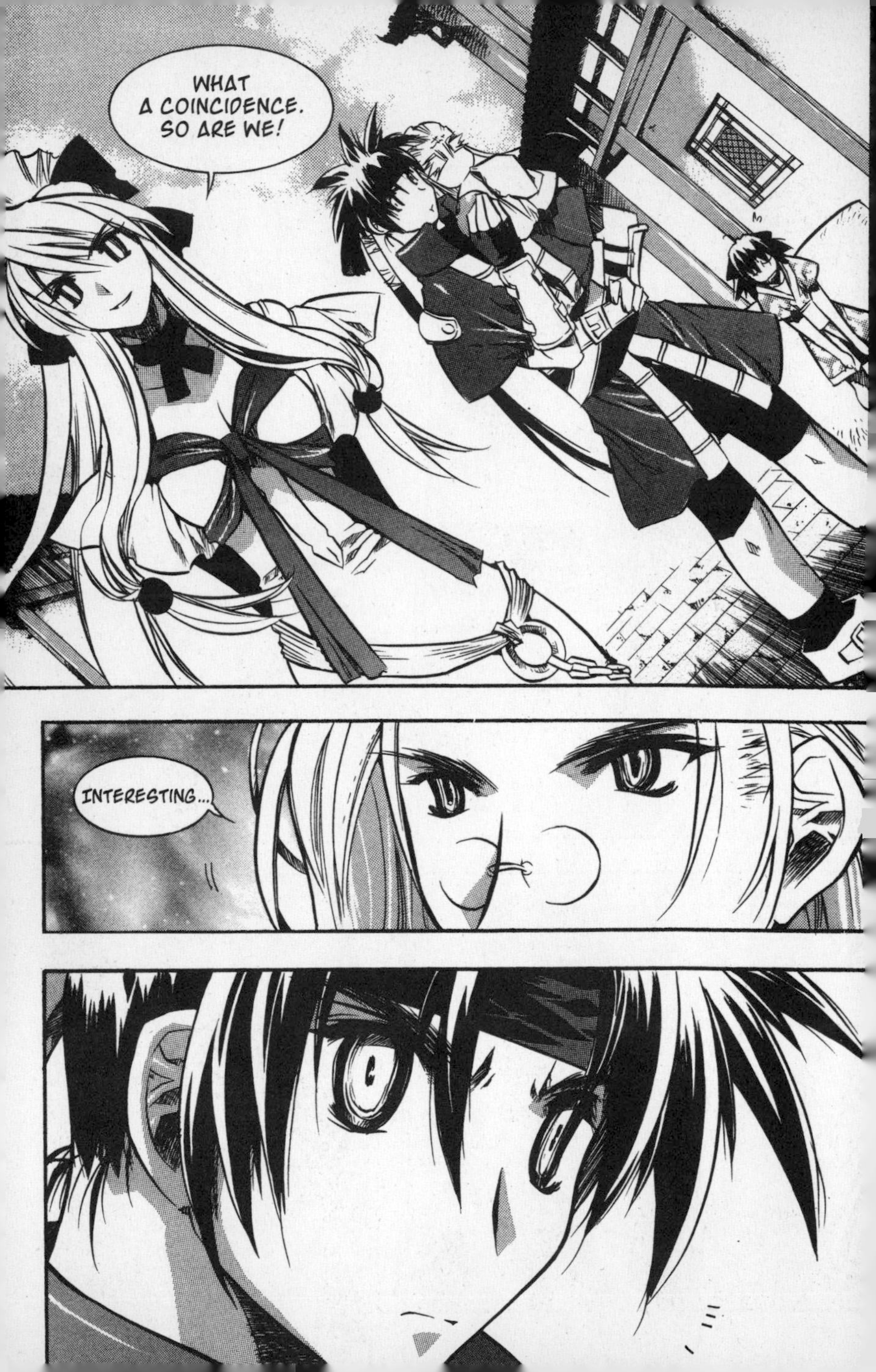
WHAT A COINCIDENCE. SO ARE WE!
INTERESTING...

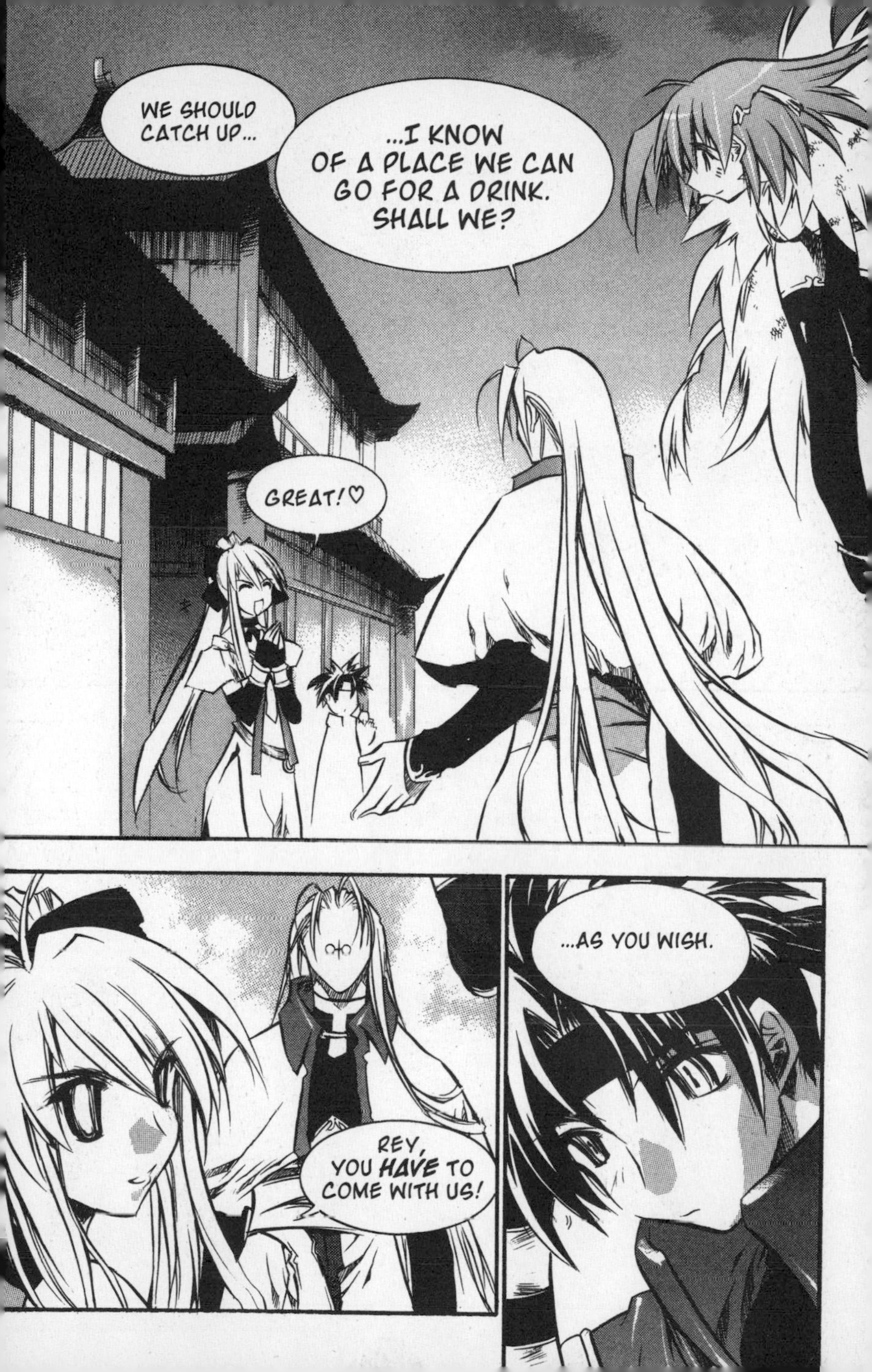
WE SHOULD CATCH UP...
...I KNOW OF A PLACE WE CAN GO FOR A DRINK. SHALL WE?
GREAT!♡
REY, YOU **HAVE** TO COME WITH US!
...AS YOU WISH.

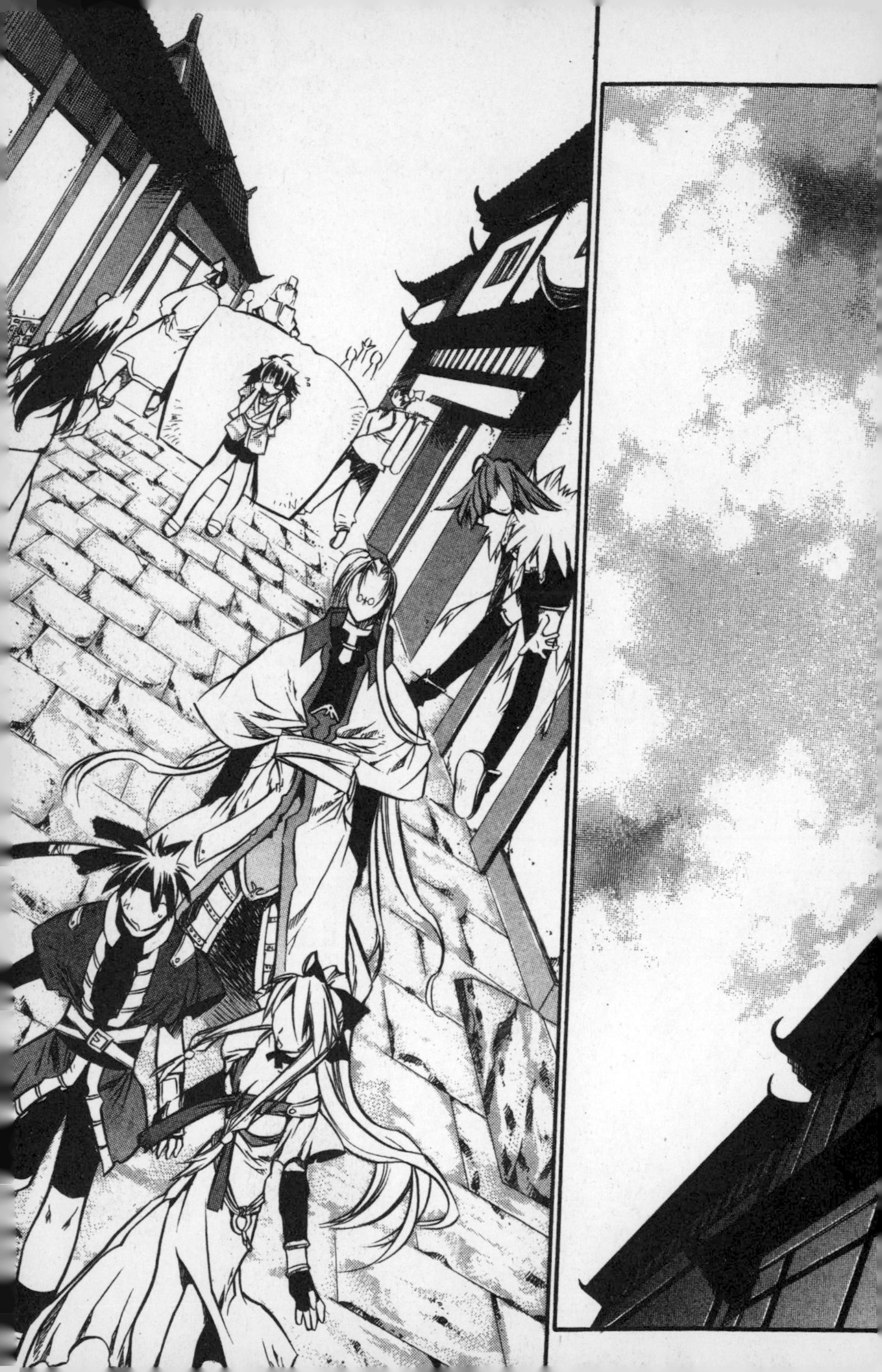

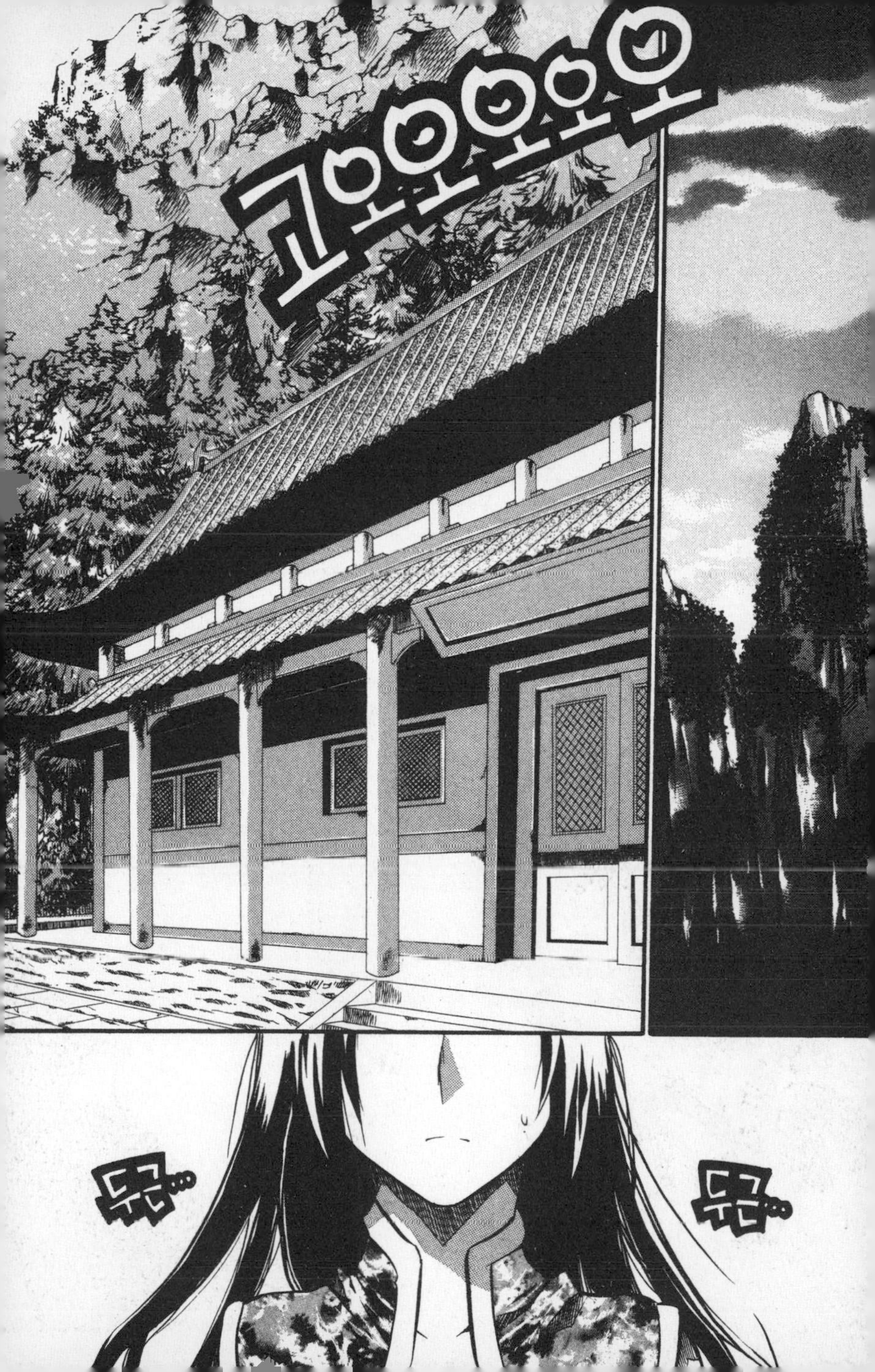
고오오오오오
두근...
두근...

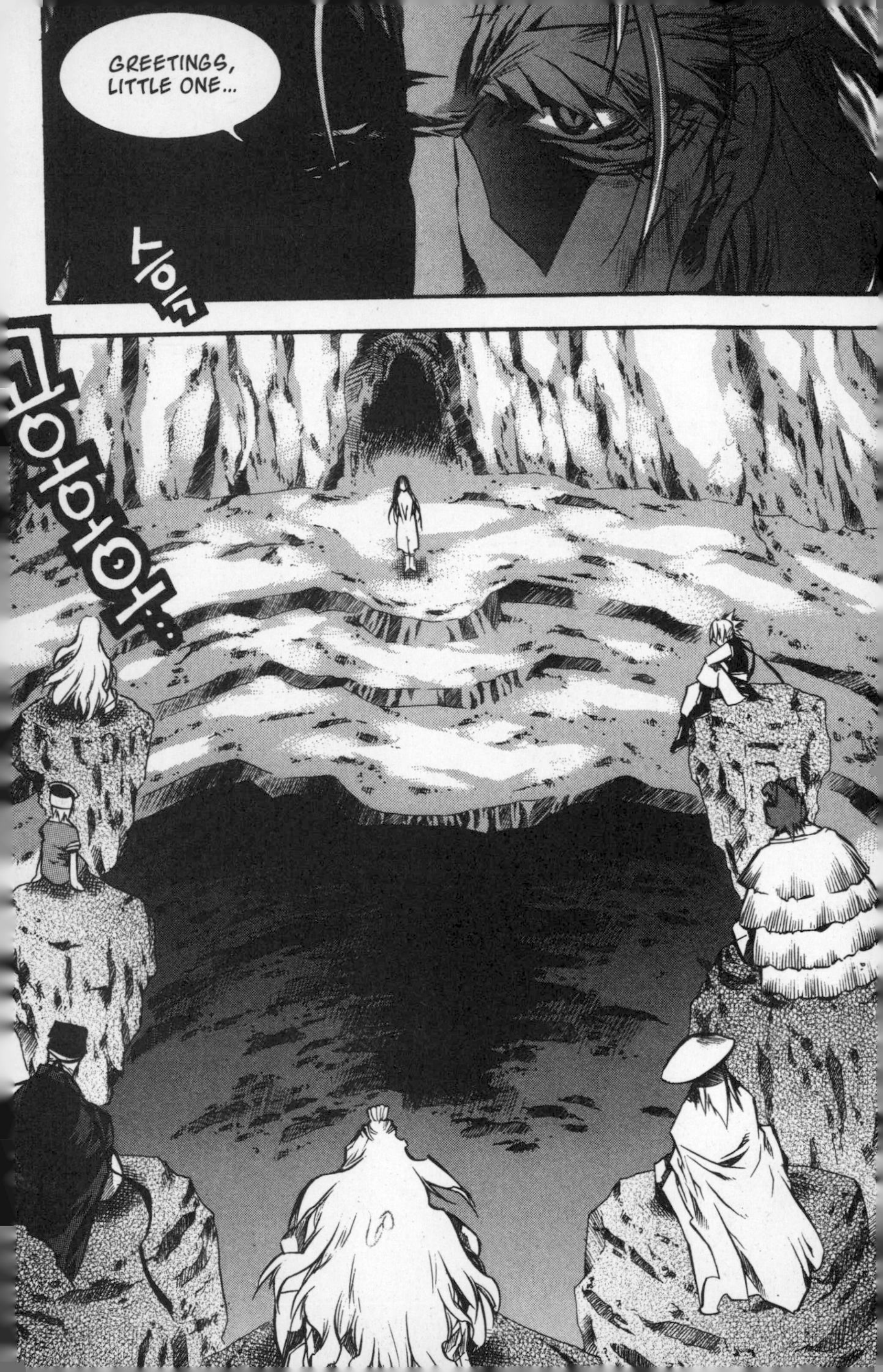
GREETINGS, LITTLE ONE...

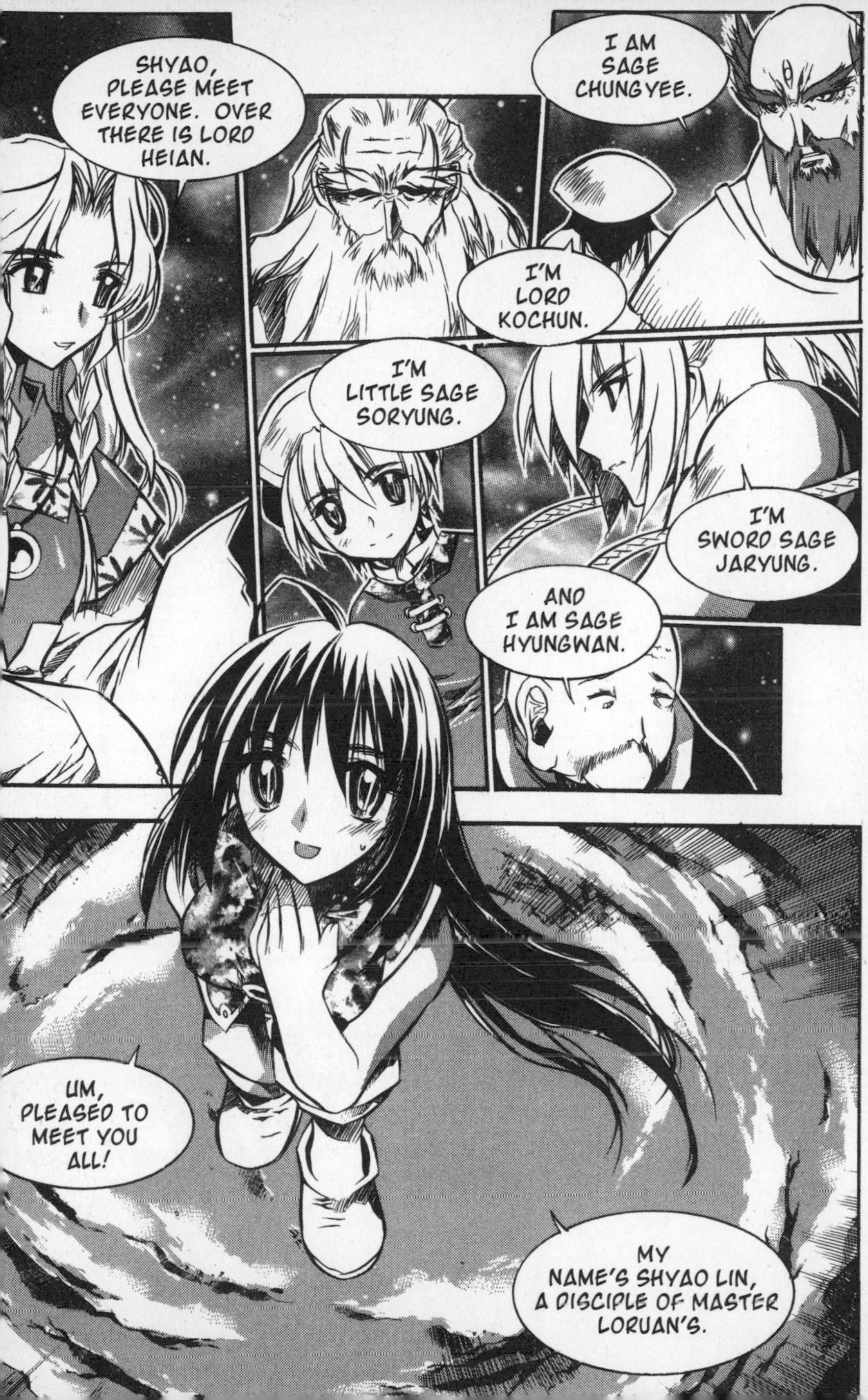
SHYAO, PLEASE MEET EVERYONE. OVER THERE IS LORD HEIAN.
I AM SAGE CHUNGYEE.
I'M LORD KOCHUN.
I'M LITTLE SAGE SORYUNG.
I'M SWORD SAGE JARYUNG.
AND I AM SAGE HYUNGWAN.
UM, PLEASED TO MEET YOU ALL!
MY NAME'S SHYAO LIN, A DISCIPLE OF MASTER LORUAN'S.

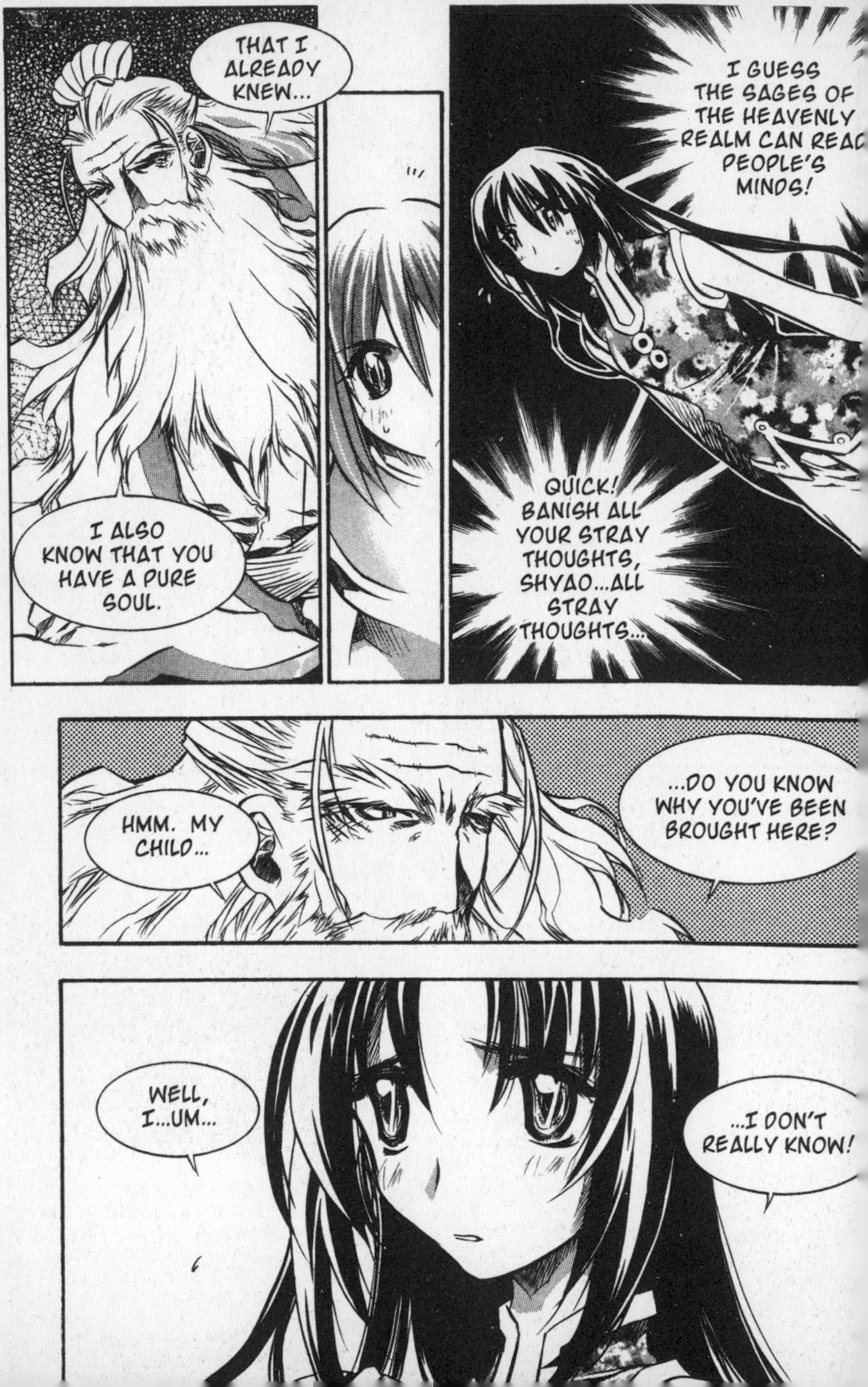
THAT I ALREADY KNEW...
I ALSO KNOW THAT YOU HAVE A PURE SOUL.
I GUESS THE SAGES OF THE HEAVENLY REALM CAN READ PEOPLE'S MINDS!
QUICK! BANISH ALL YOUR STRAY THOUGHTS, SHYAO...ALL STRAY THOUGHTS...
HMM. MY CHILD...
...DO YOU KNOW WHY YOU'VE BEEN BROUGHT HERE?
WELL, I...UM...
...I DON'T REALLY KNOW!

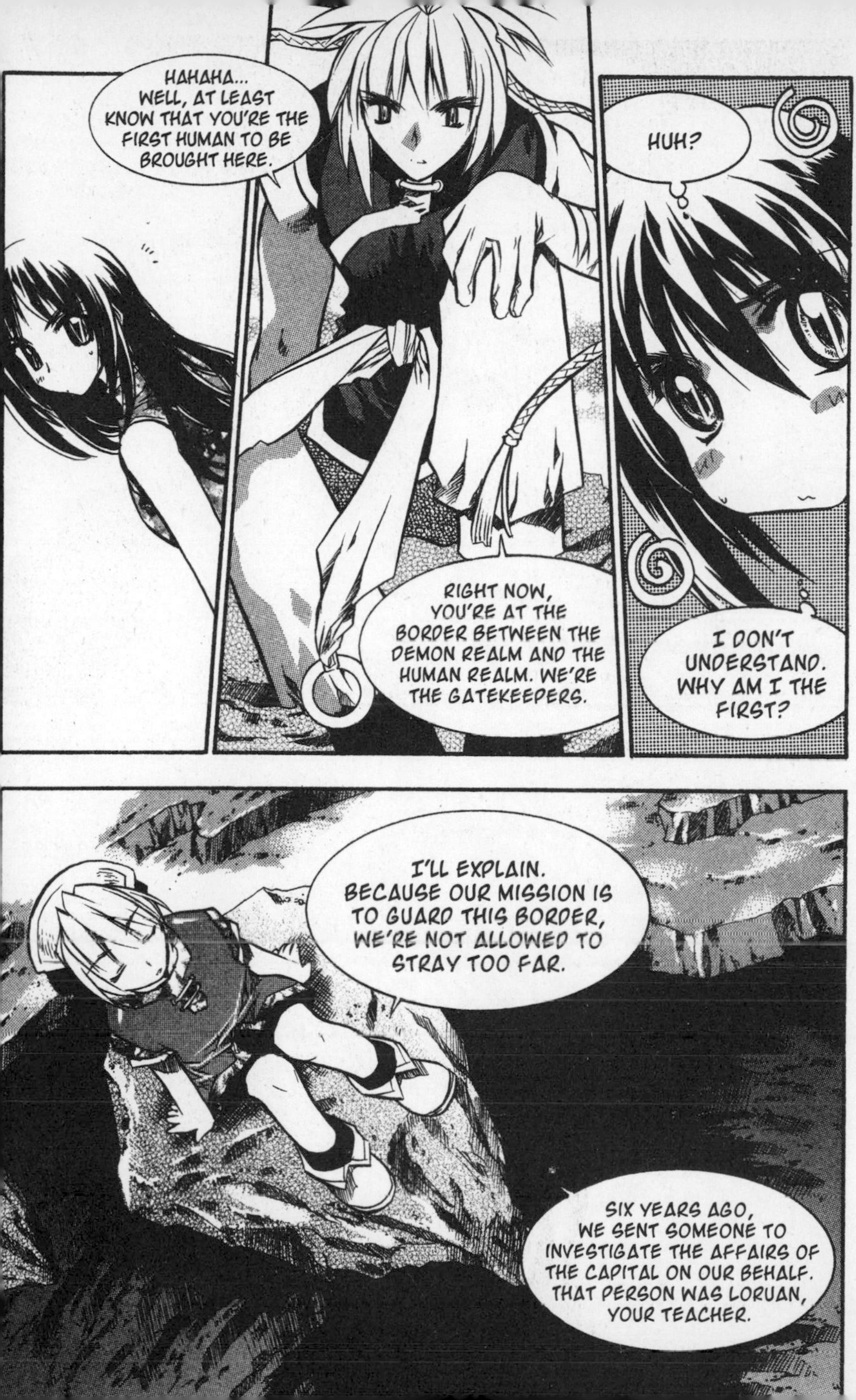
HAHAHA... WELL, AT LEAST KNOW THAT YOU'RE THE FIRST HUMAN TO BE BROUGHT HERE.
RIGHT NOW, YOU'RE AT THE BORDER BETWEEN THE DEMON REALM AND THE HUMAN REALM. WE'RE THE GATEKEEPERS.
HUH?
I DON'T UNDERSTAND. WHY AM I THE FIRST?
I'LL EXPLAIN. BECAUSE OUR MISSION IS TO GUARD THIS BORDER, WE'RE NOT ALLOWED TO STRAY TOO FAR.
SIX YEARS AGO, WE SENT SOMEONE TO INVESTIGATE THE AFFAIRS OF THE CAPITAL ON OUR BEHALF. THAT PERSON WAS LORUAN, YOUR TEACHER.

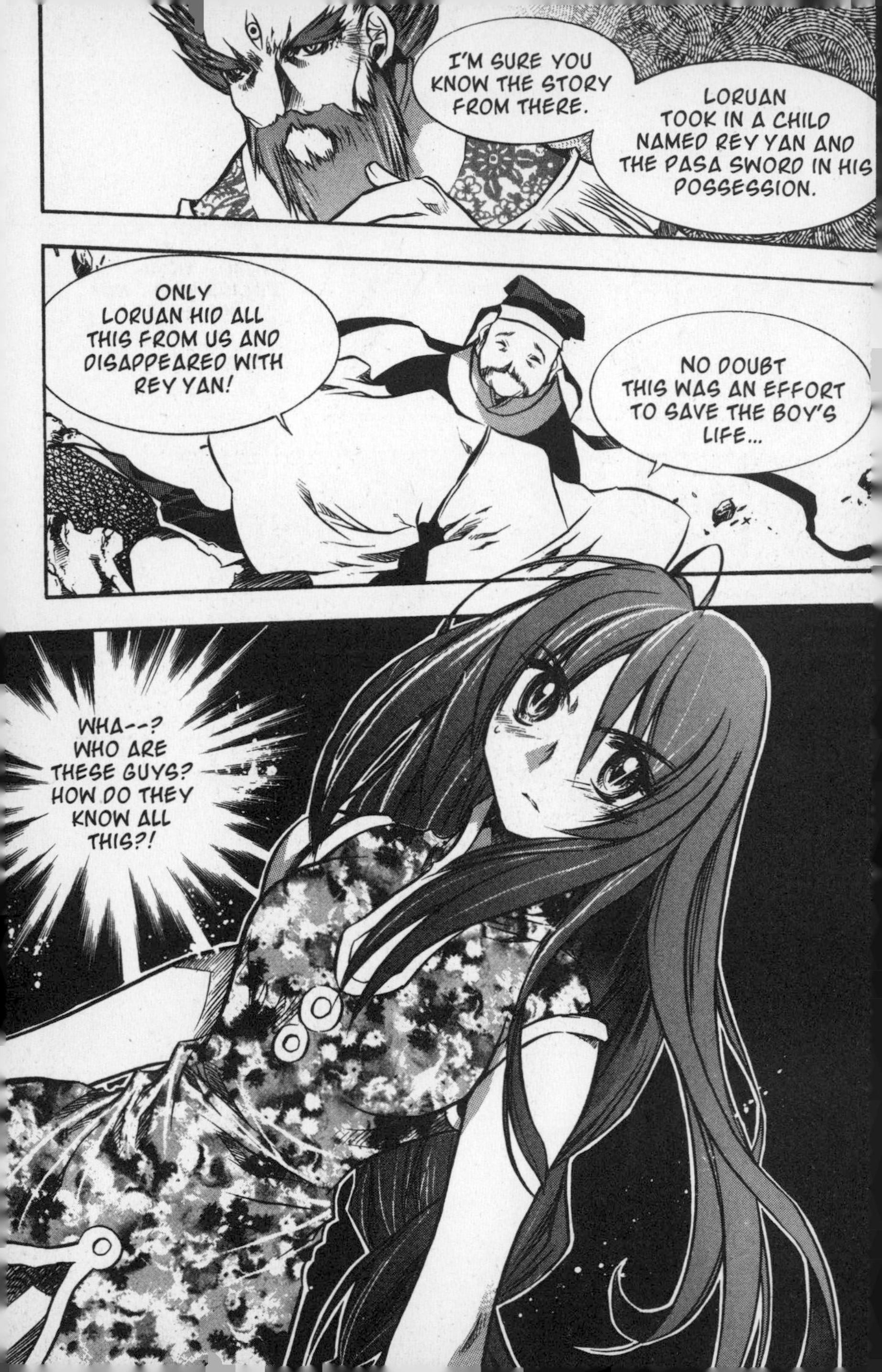
I'M SURE YOU KNOW THE STORY FROM THERE.
LORUAN TOOK IN A CHILD NAMED REY YAN AND THE PASA SWORD IN HIS POSSESSION.
ONLY LORUAN HID ALL THIS FROM US AND DISAPPEARED WITH REY YAN!
NO DOUBT THIS WAS AN EFFORT TO SAVE THE BOY'S LIFE...
WHA--? WHO ARE THESE GUYS? HOW DO THEY KNOW ALL THIS?!

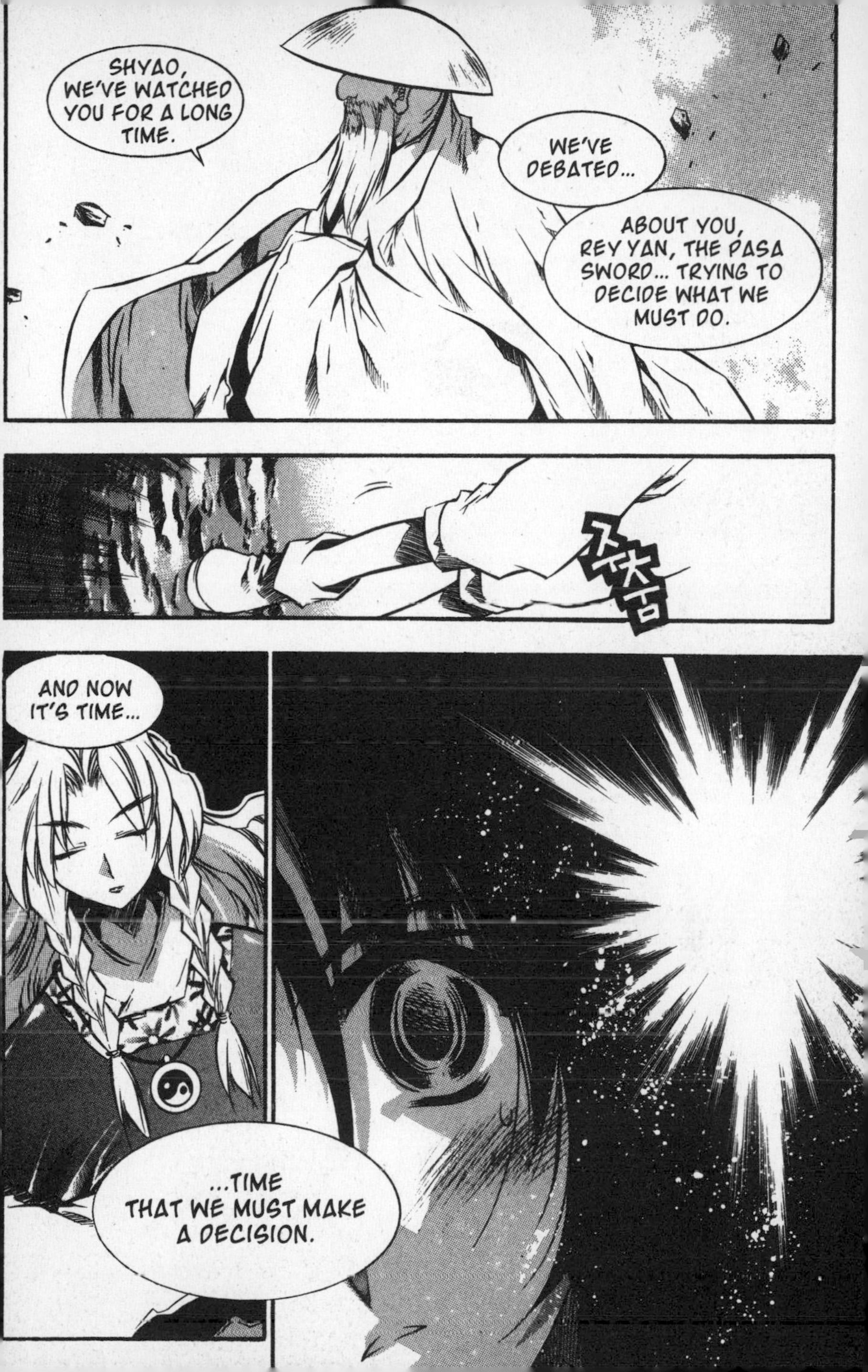
SHYAO, WE'VE WATCHED YOU FOR A LONG TIME.
WE'VE DEBATED...
ABOUT YOU, REY YAN, THE PASA SWORD... TRYING TO DECIDE WHAT WE MUST DO.
AND NOW IT'S TIME...
...TIME THAT WE MUST MAKE A DECISION.

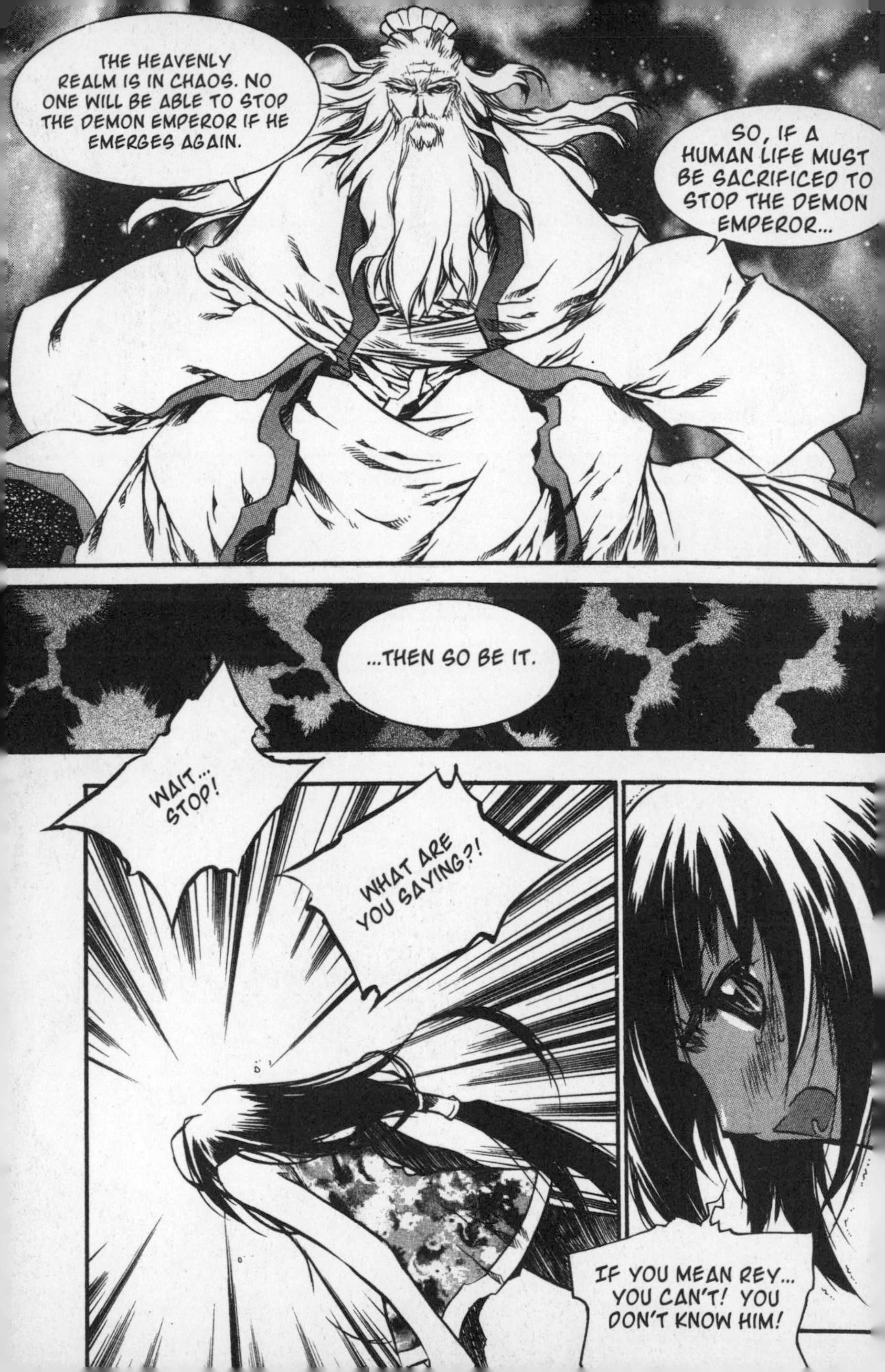
THE HEAVENLY REALM IS IN CHAOS. NO ONE WILL BE ABLE TO STOP THE DEMON EMPEROR IF HE EMERGES AGAIN.
SO, IF A HUMAN LIFE MUST BE SACRIFICED TO STOP THE DEMON EMPEROR...
...THEN SO BE IT.
WAIT... STOP!
WHAT ARE YOU SAYING?!
IF YOU MEAN REY... YOU CAN'T! YOU DON'T KNOW HIM!

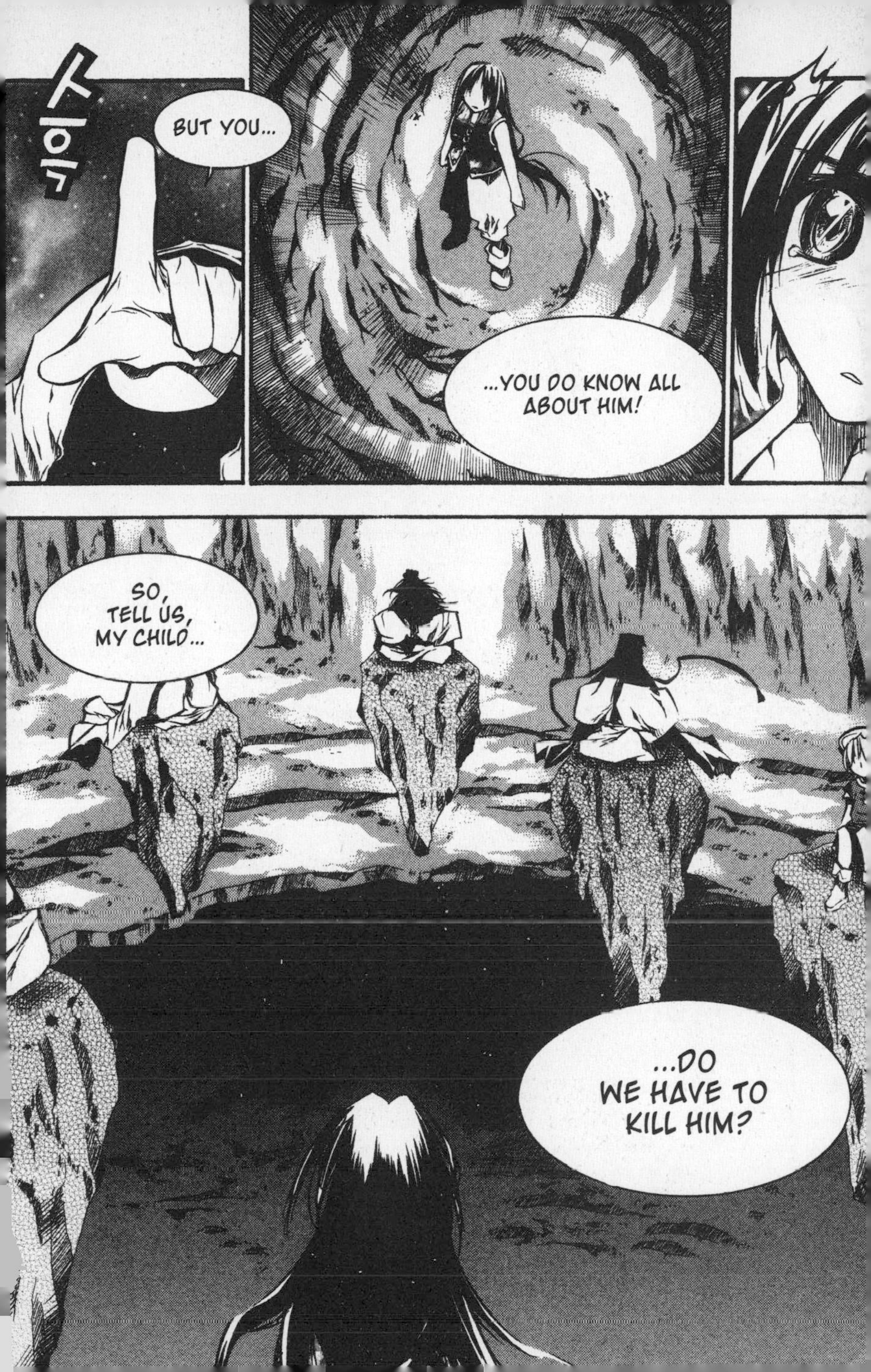
BUT YOU...
...YOU DO KNOW ALL ABOUT HIM!
SO, TELL US, MY CHILD...
...DO WE HAVE TO KILL HIM?

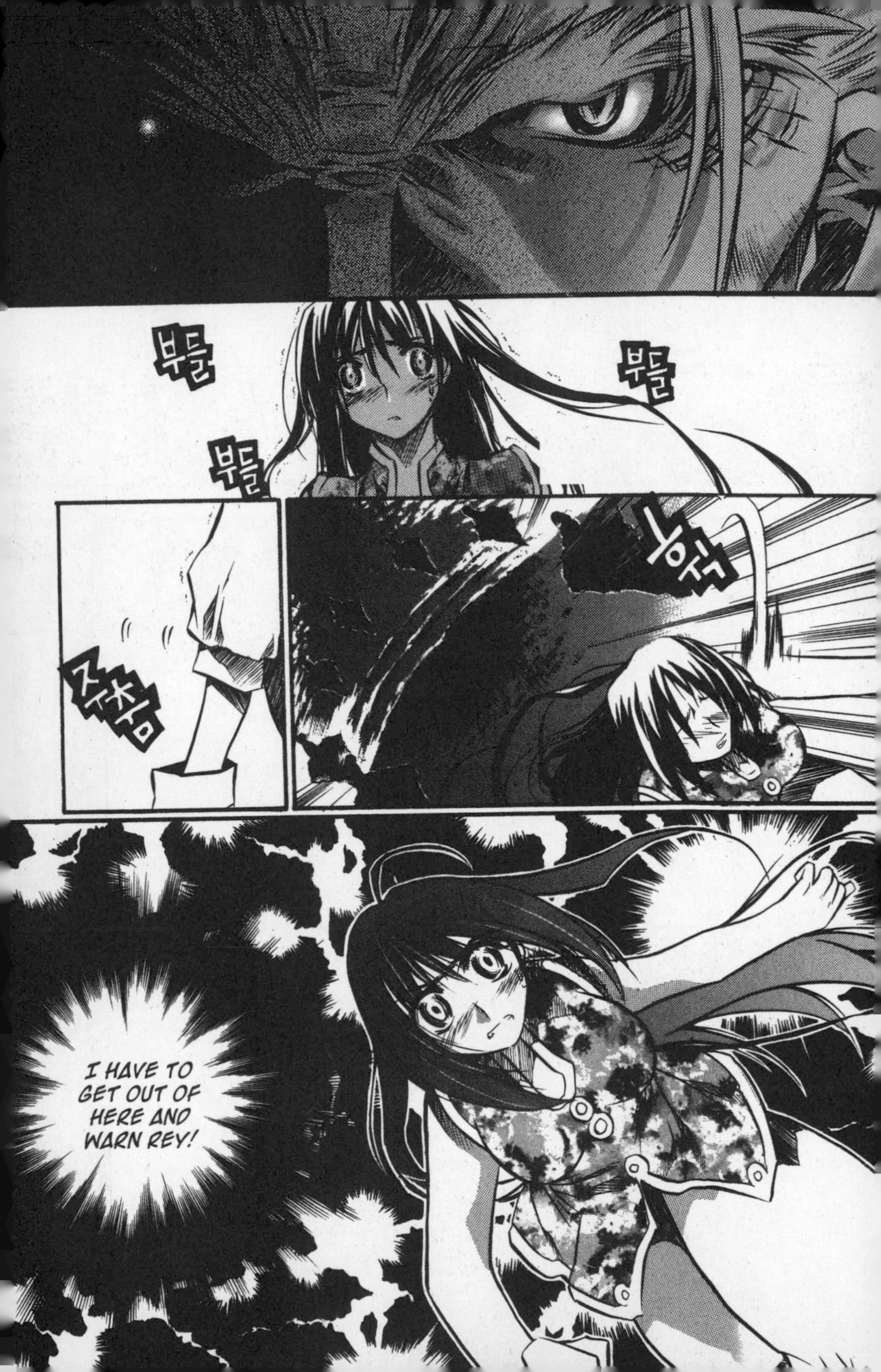
부들
부들
부들
주춤
I HAVE TO GET OUT OF HERE AND WARN REY!

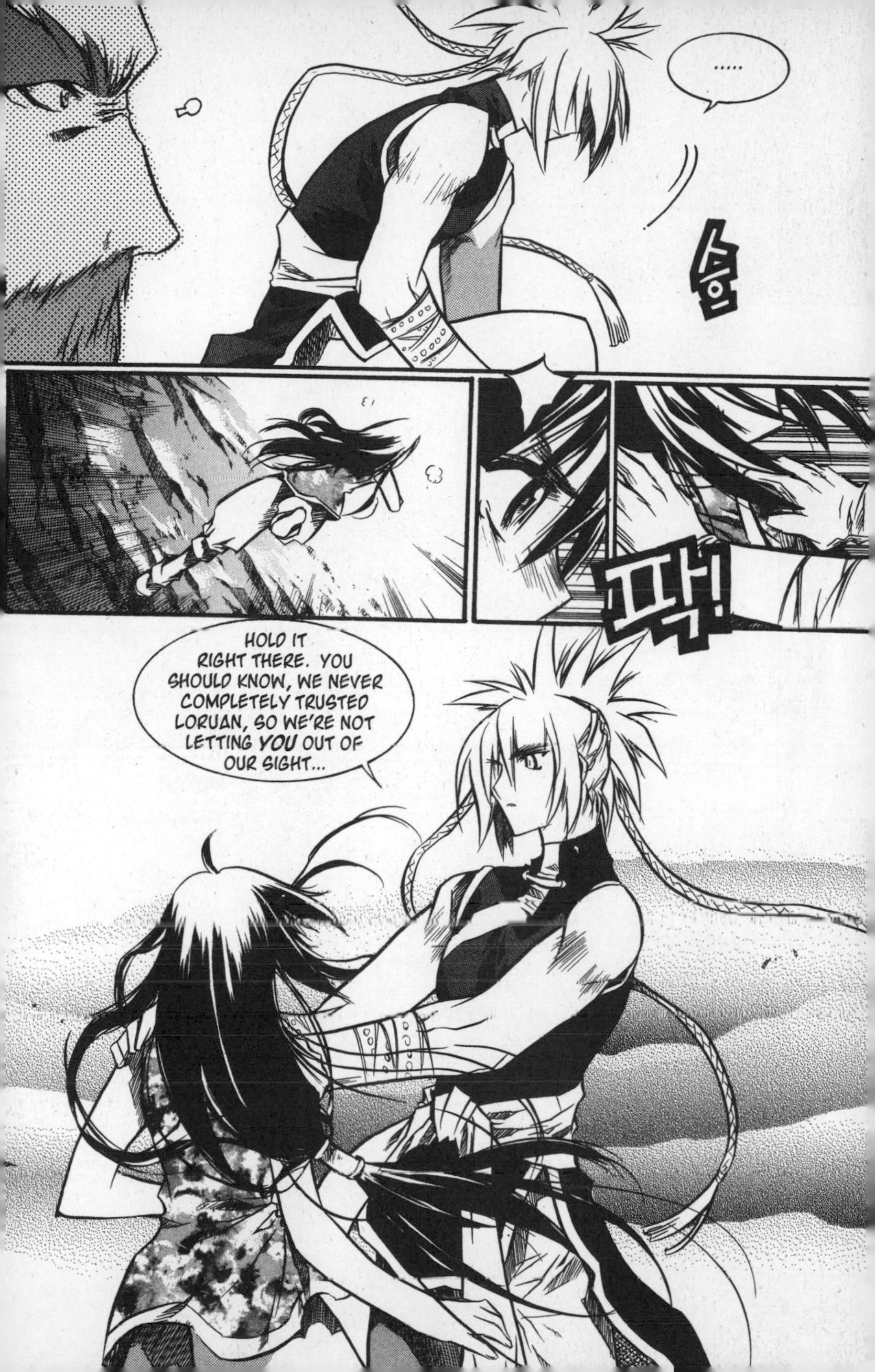
.....
슝
파악!
HOLD IT RIGHT THERE. YOU SHOULD KNOW, WE NEVER COMPLETELY TRUSTED LORUAN, SO WE'RE NOT LETTING *YOU* OUT OF OUR SIGHT...

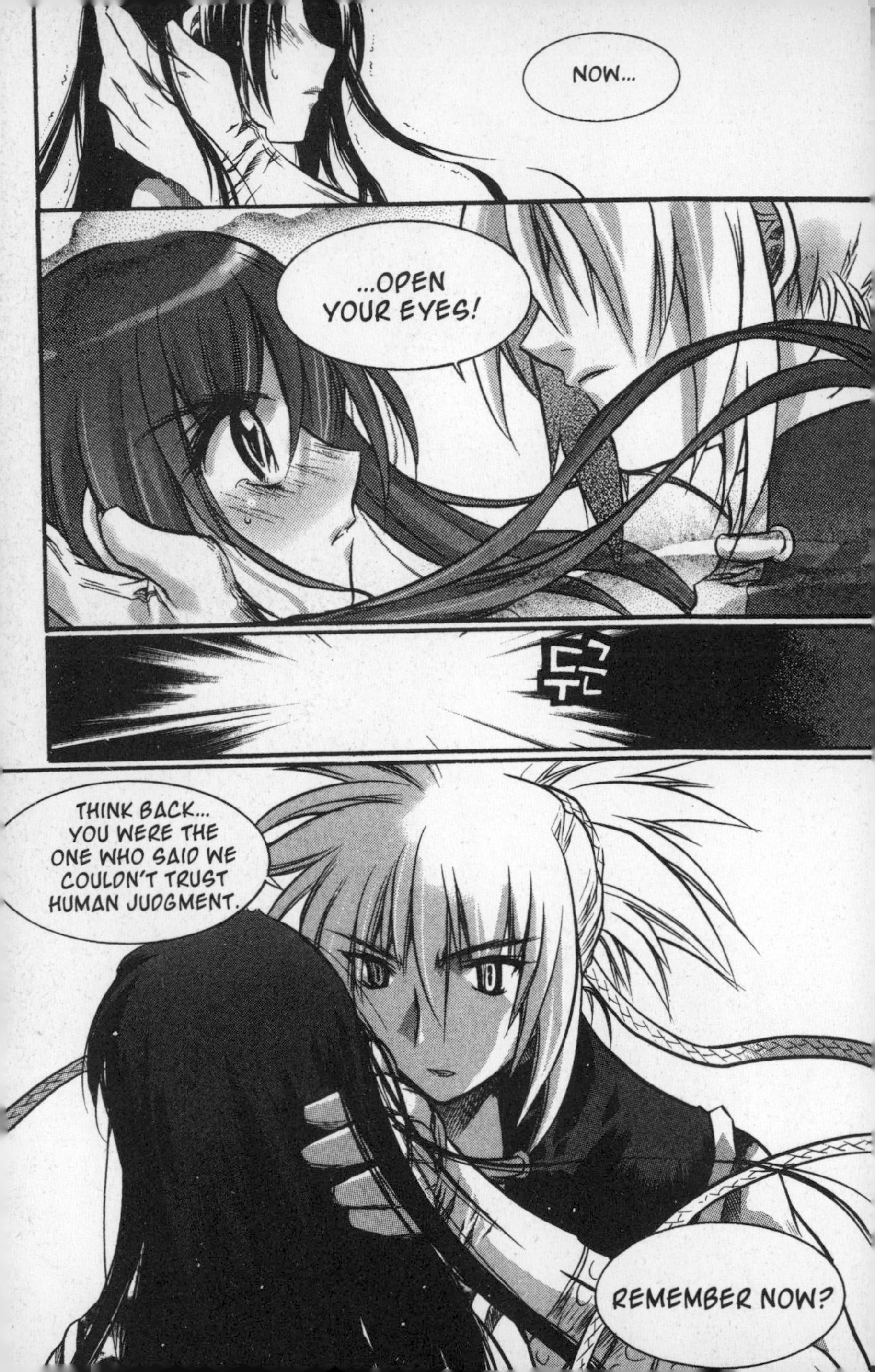
NOW...
...OPEN YOUR EYES!
THINK BACK... YOU WERE THE ONE WHO SAID WE COULDN'T TRUST HUMAN JUDGMENT.
REMEMBER NOW?

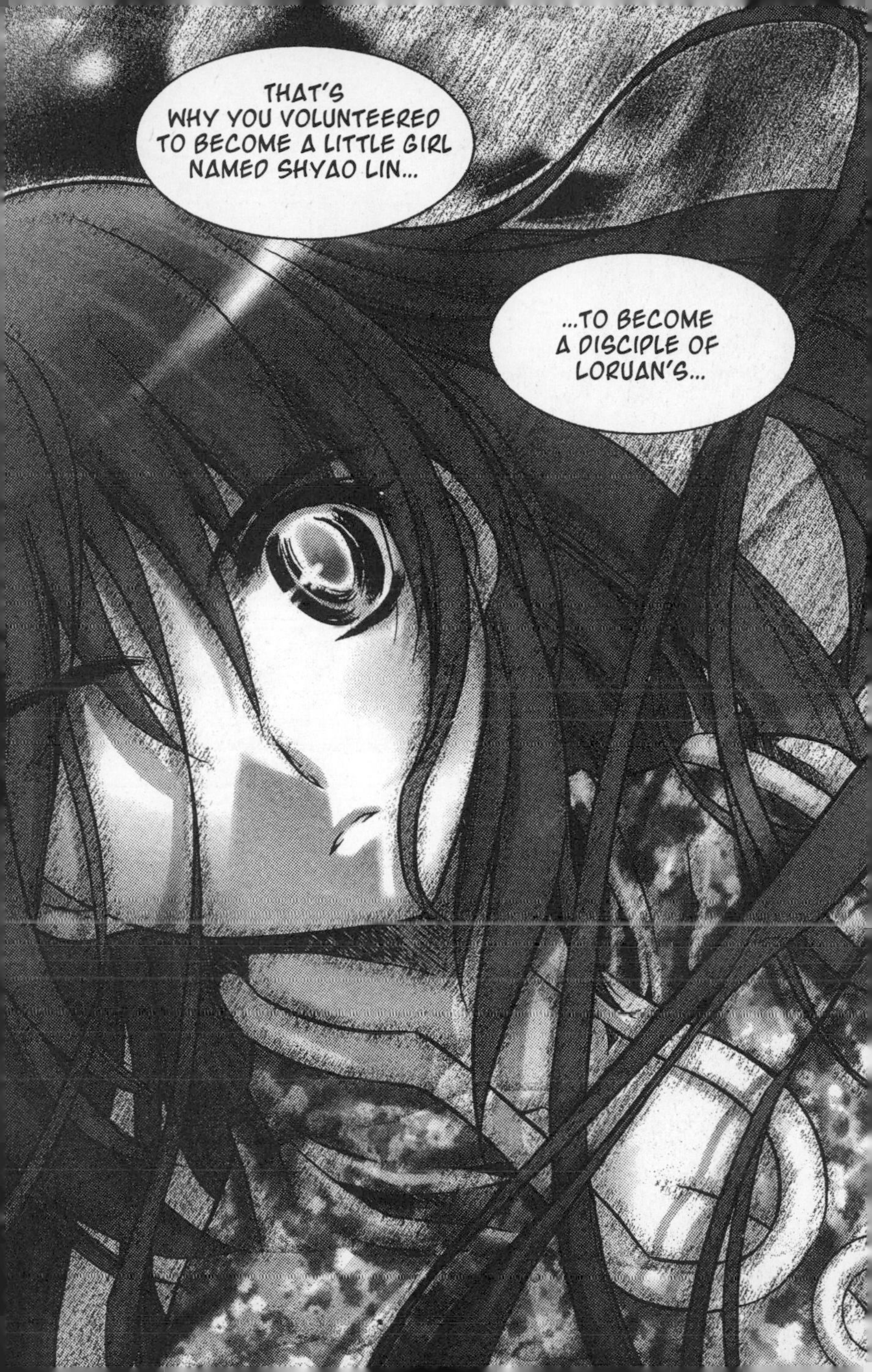
THAT'S WHY YOU VOLUNTEERED TO BECOME A LITTLE GIRL NAMED SHYAO LIN...
...TO BECOME A DISCIPLE OF LORUAN'S...

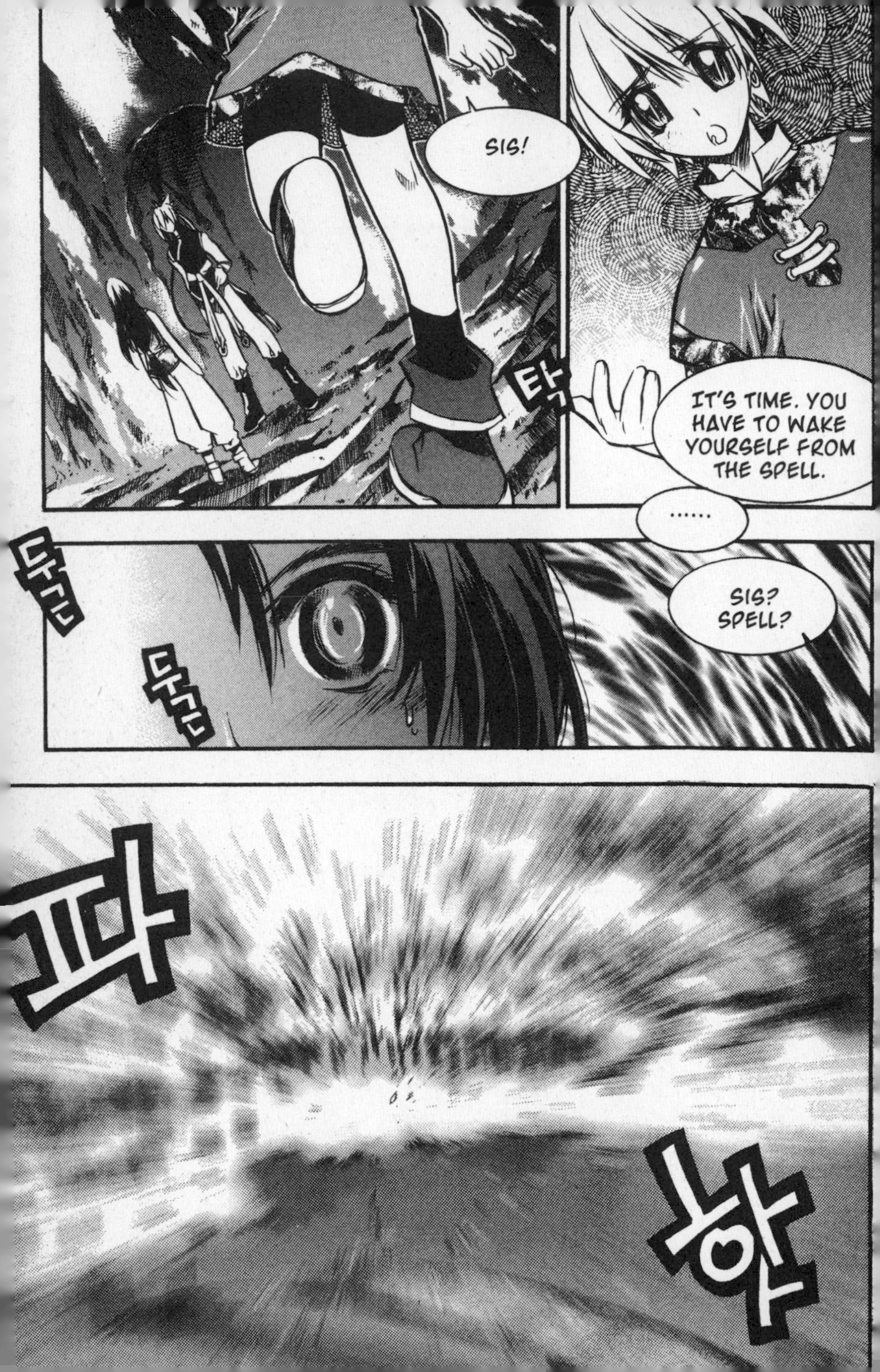
SIS!
탁
IT'S TIME. YOU HAVE TO WAKE YOURSELF FROM THE SPELL.
......
SIS? SPELL?

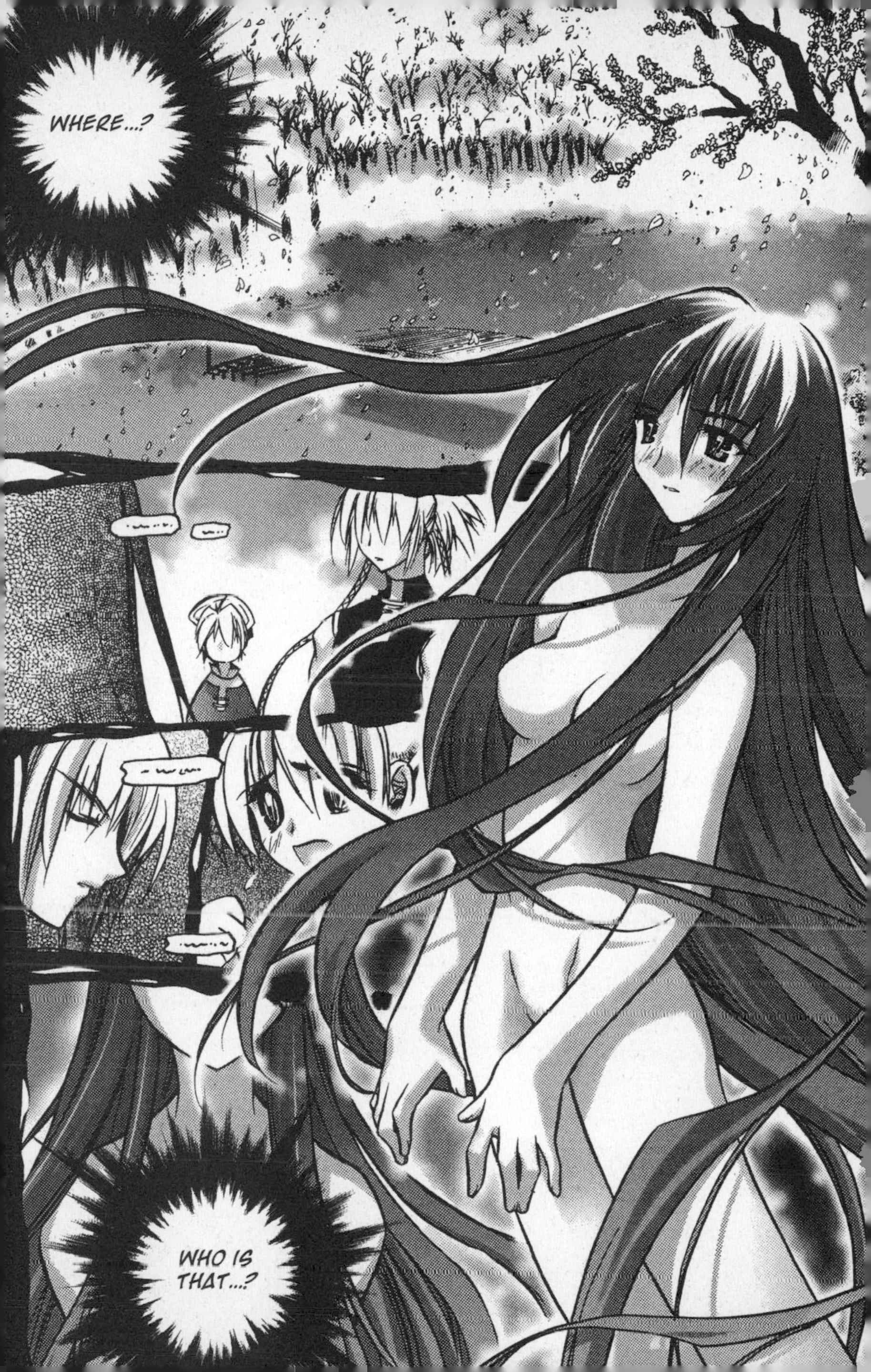

WHERE...?
WHO IS THAT...?

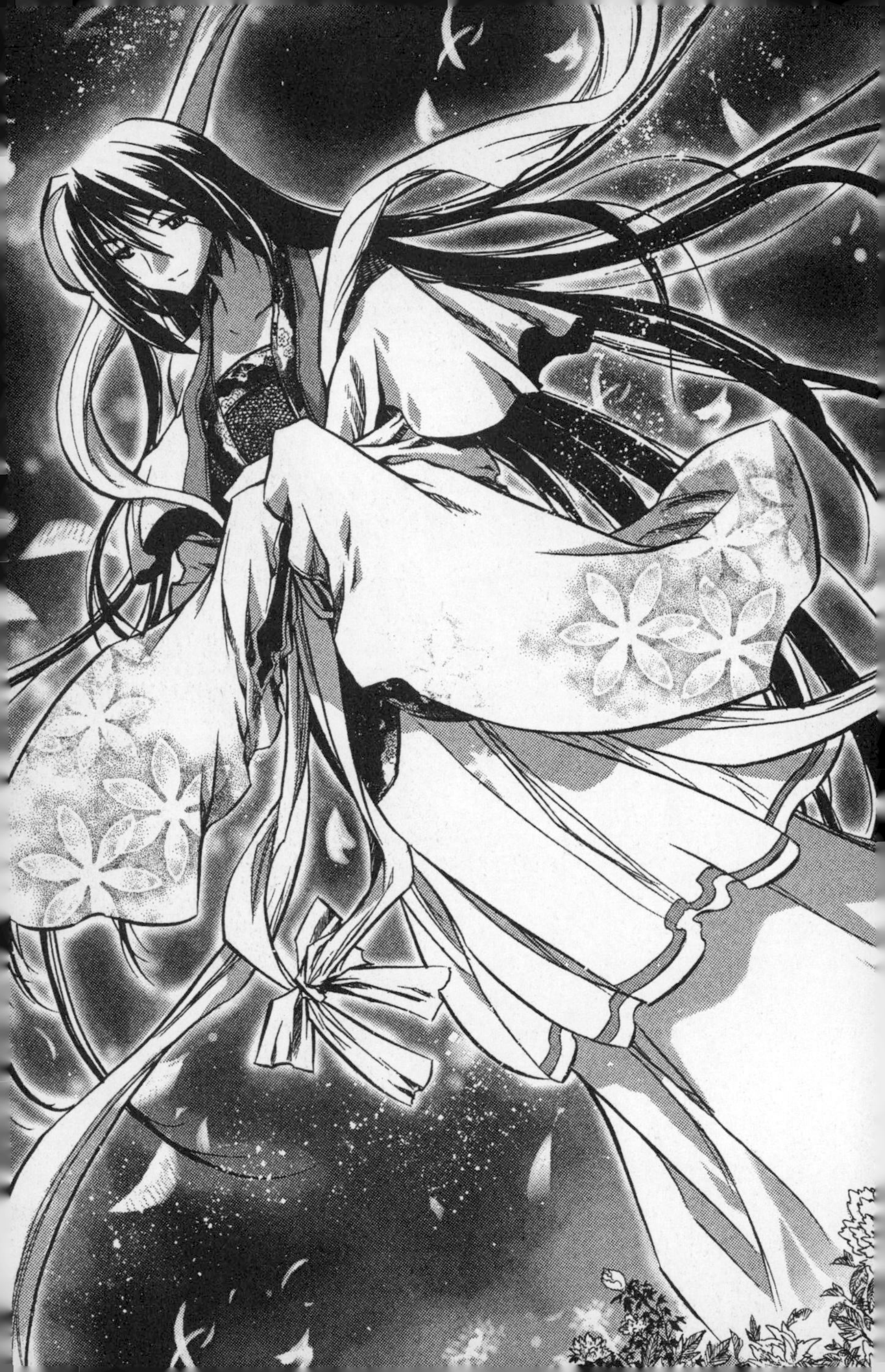

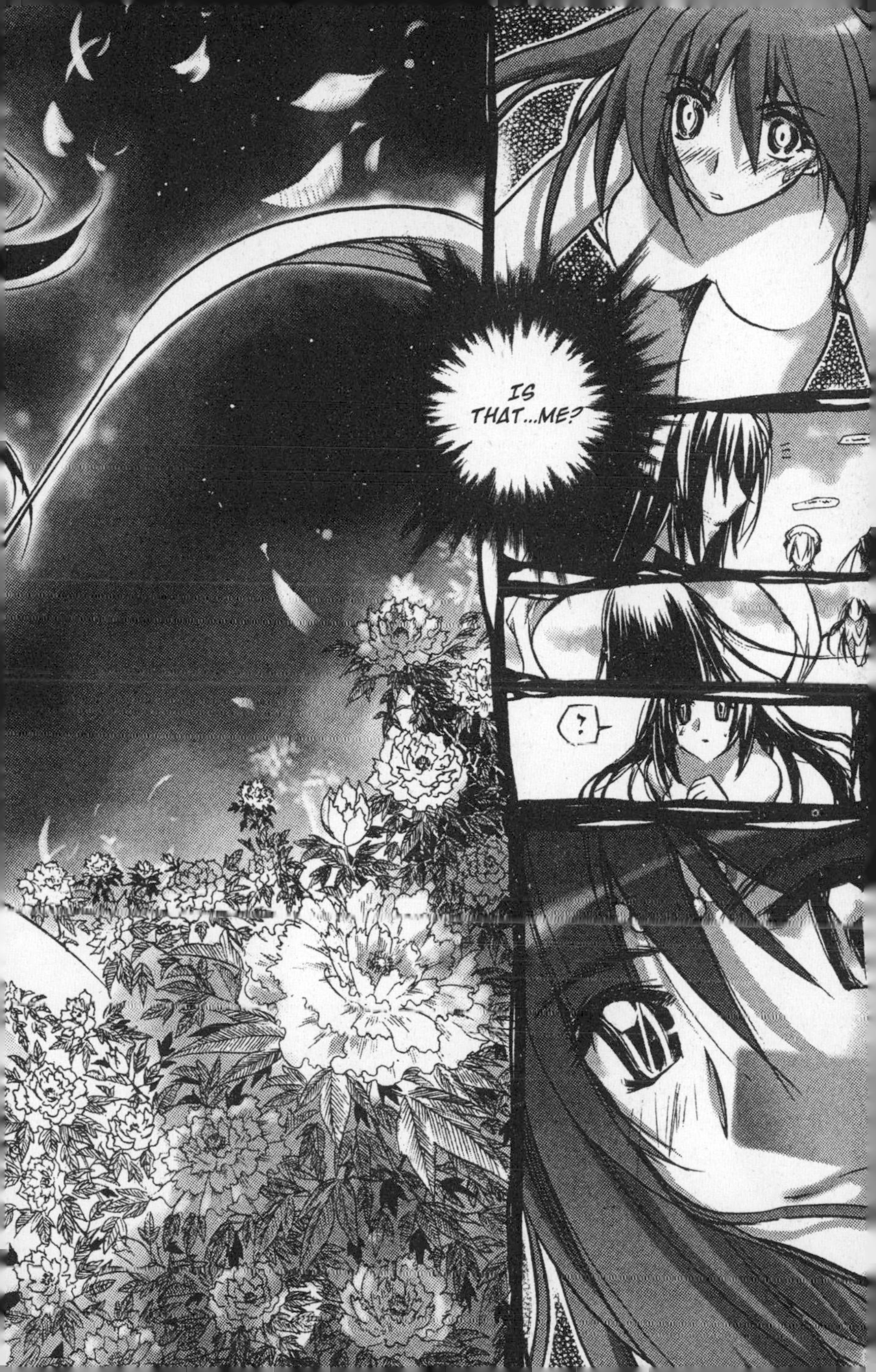
IS THAT...ME?
?

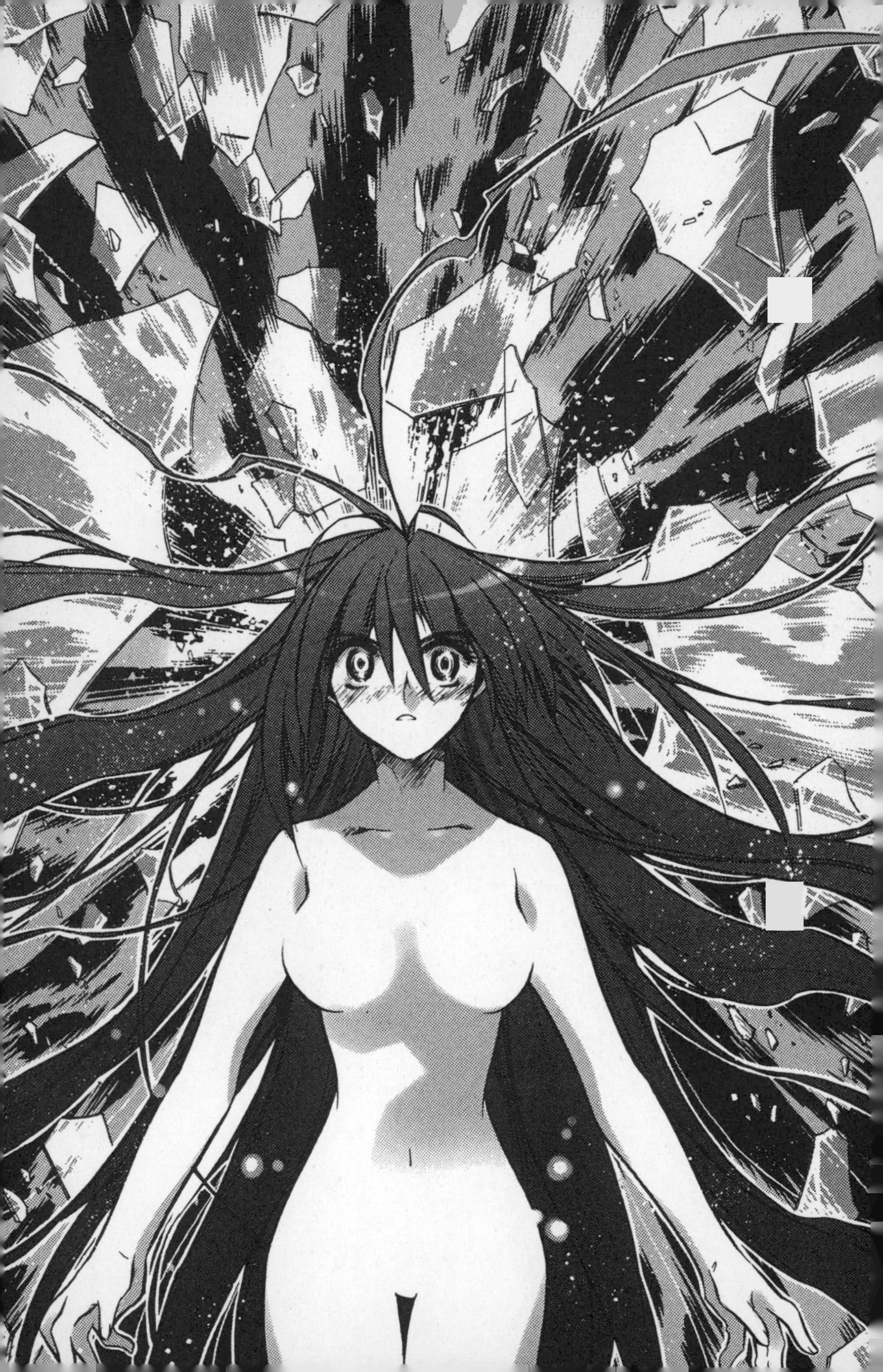

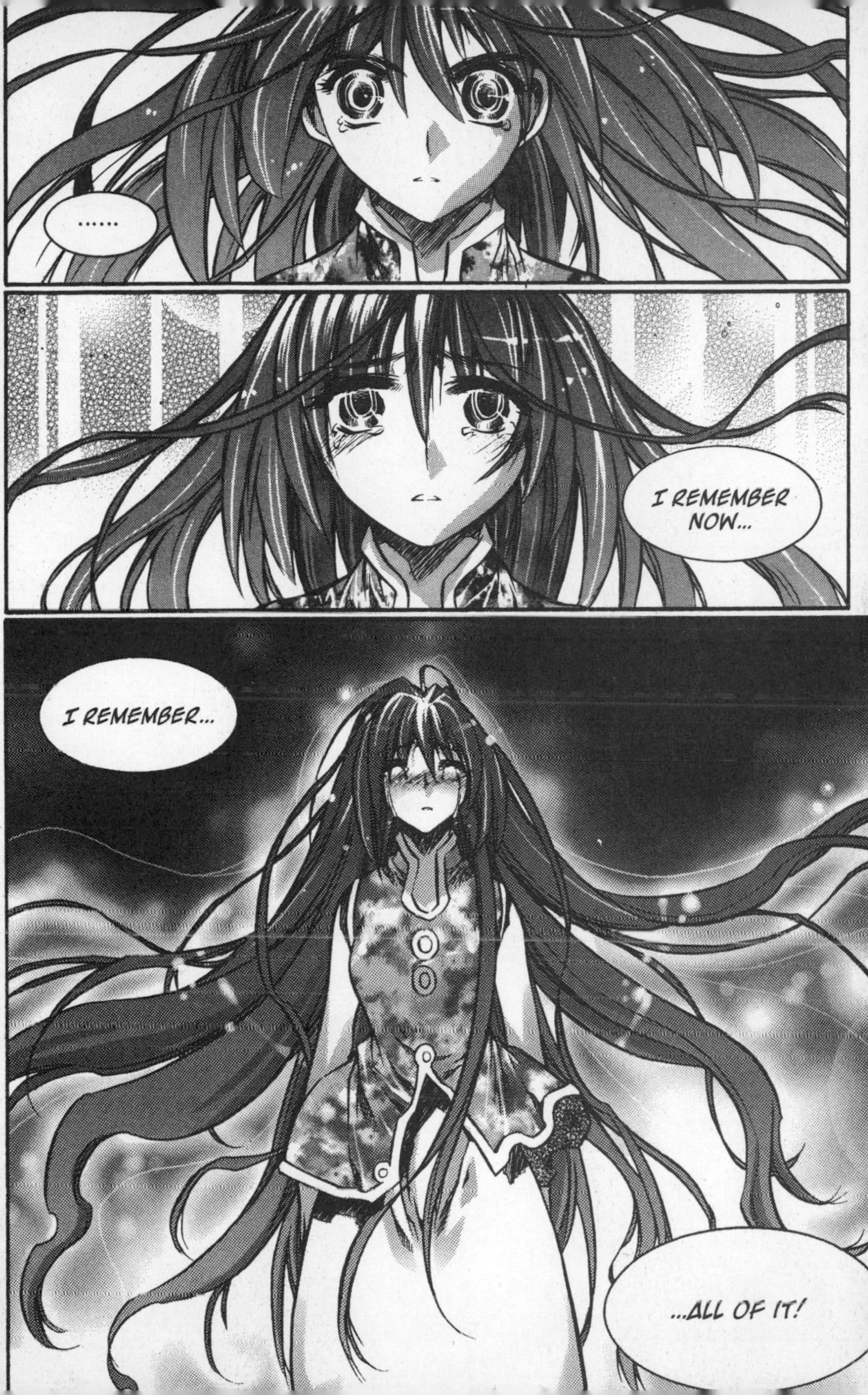
......
I REMEMBER NOW...
I REMEMBER...
...ALL OF IT!

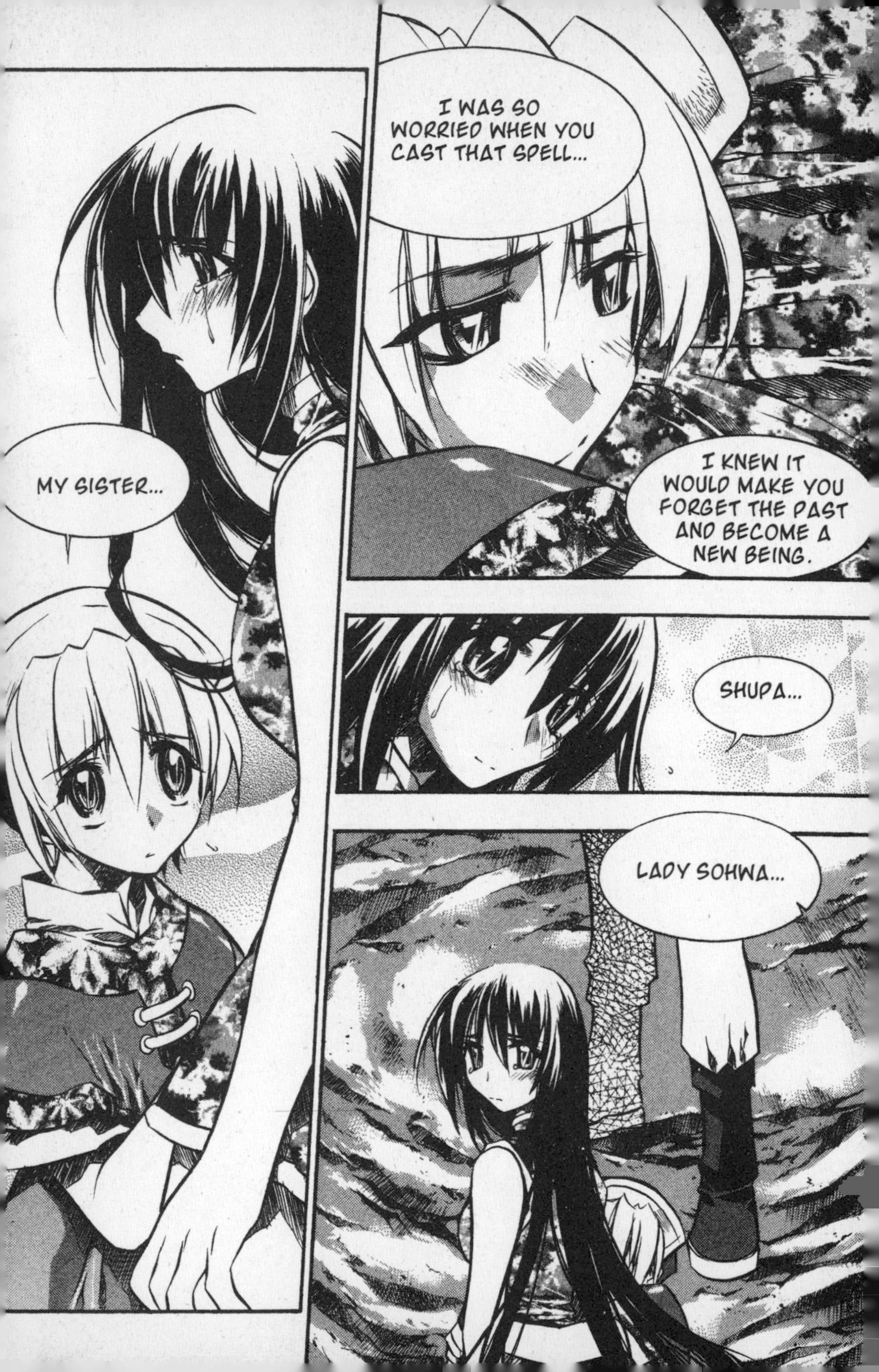
MY SISTER...
I WAS SO WORRIED WHEN YOU CAST THAT SPELL...
I KNEW IT WOULD MAKE YOU FORGET THE PAST AND BECOME A NEW BEING.
SHUPA...
LADY SOHWA...

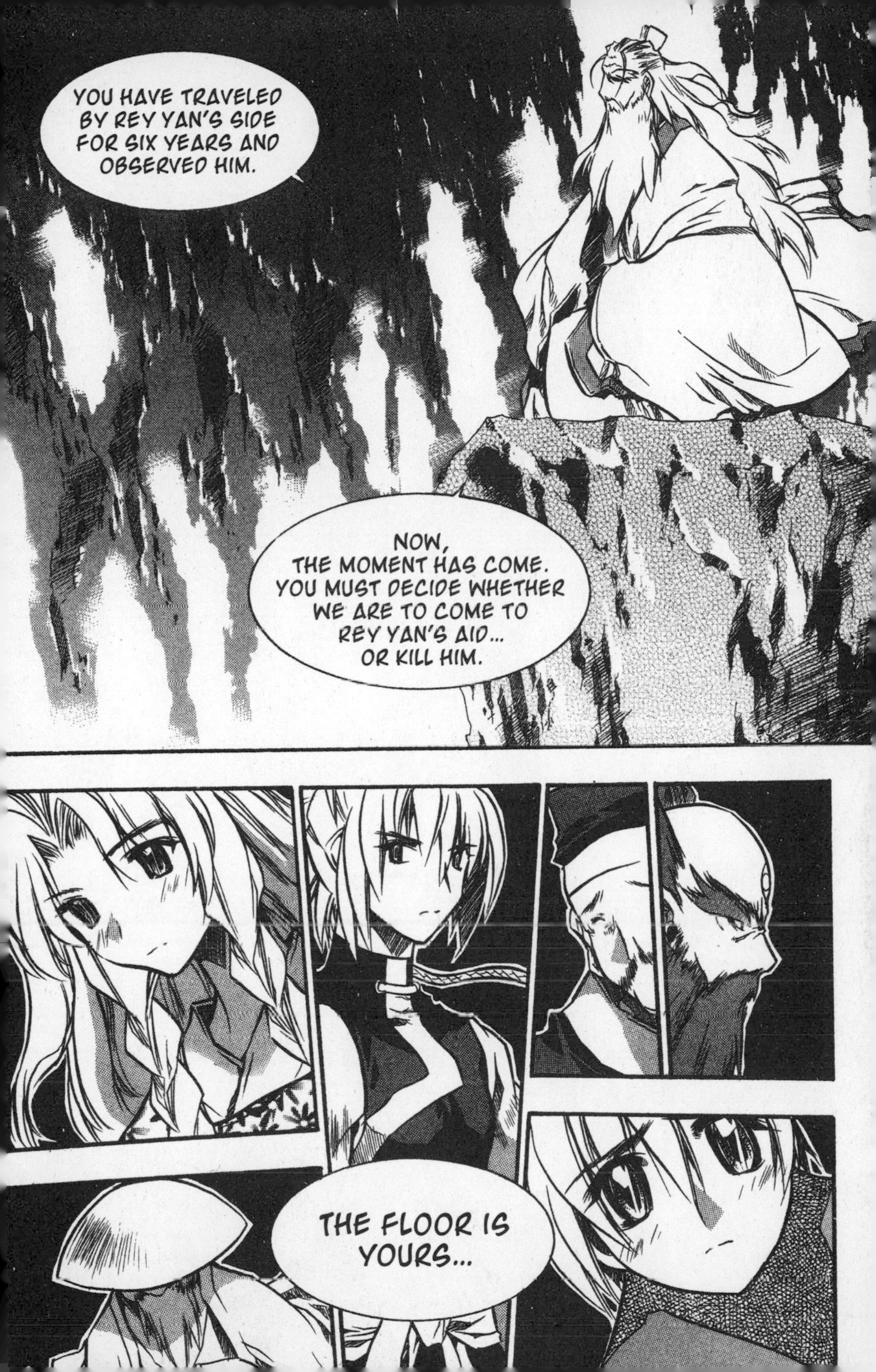
YOU HAVE TRAVELED BY REY YAN'S SIDE FOR SIX YEARS AND OBSERVED HIM.
NOW, THE MOMENT HAS COME. YOU MUST DECIDE WHETHER WE ARE TO COME TO REY YAN'S AID... OR KILL HIM.
THE FLOOR IS YOURS...

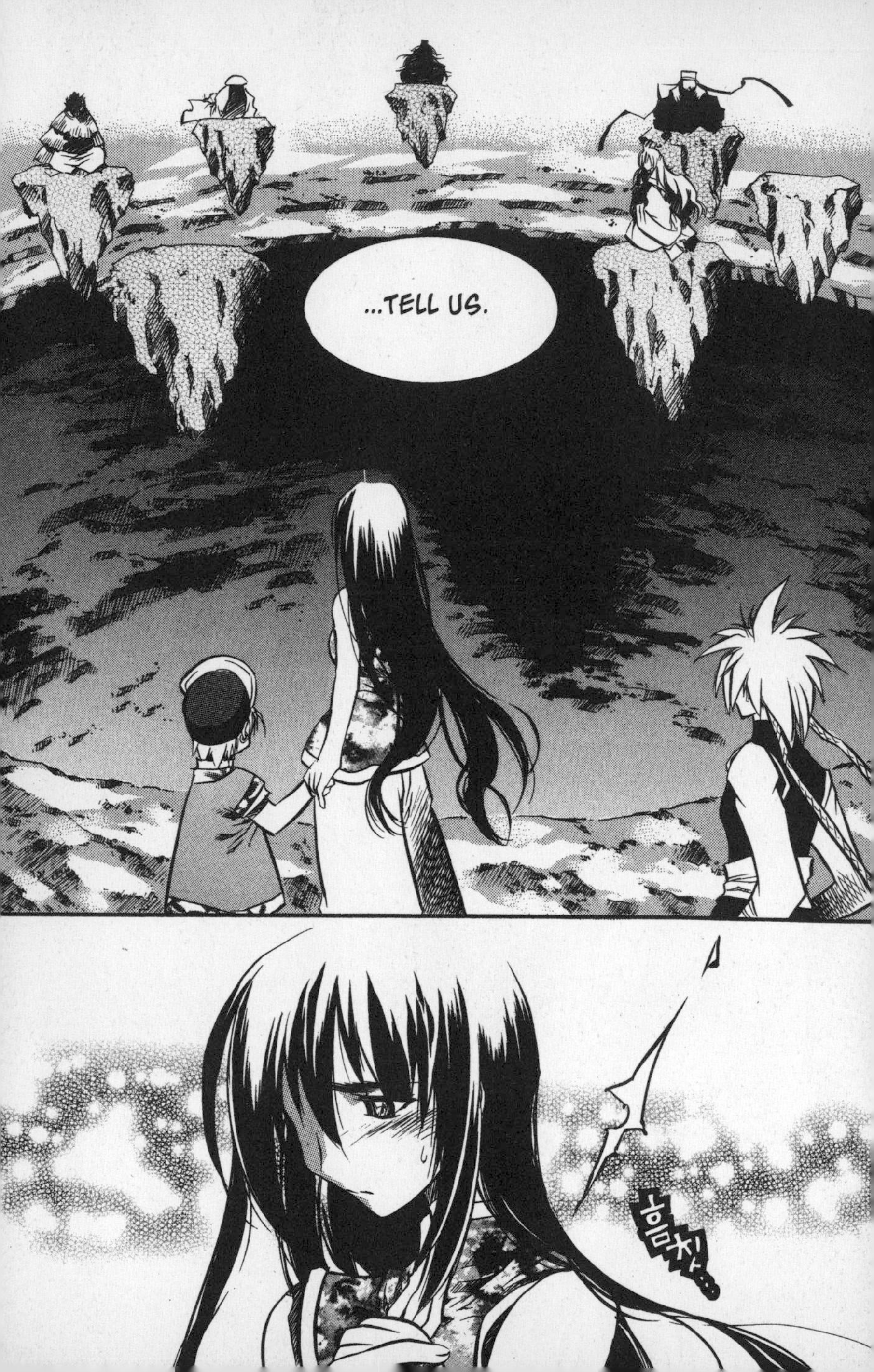
...TELL US.
흠칫...

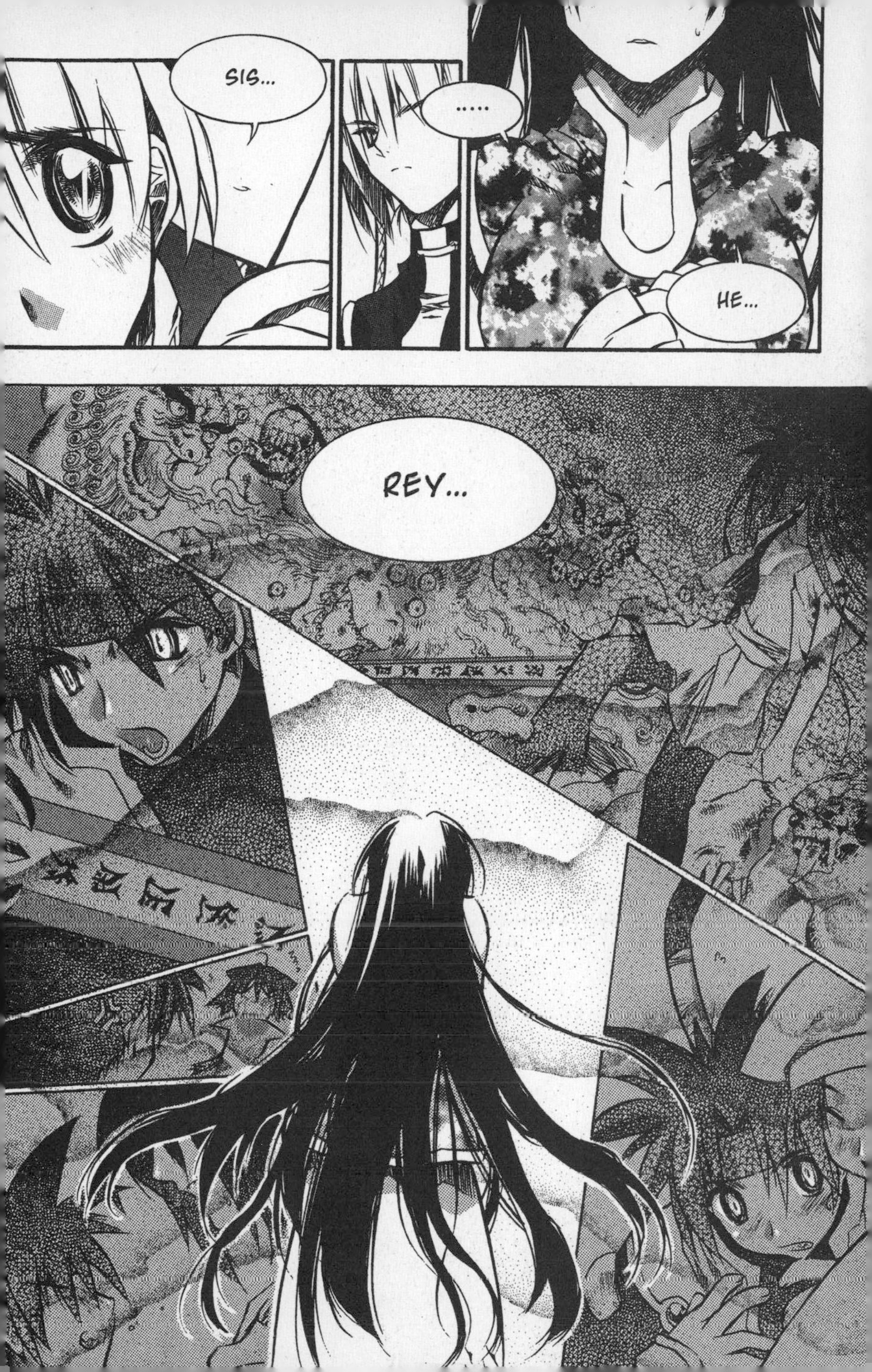
SIS...
......
HE...
REY...

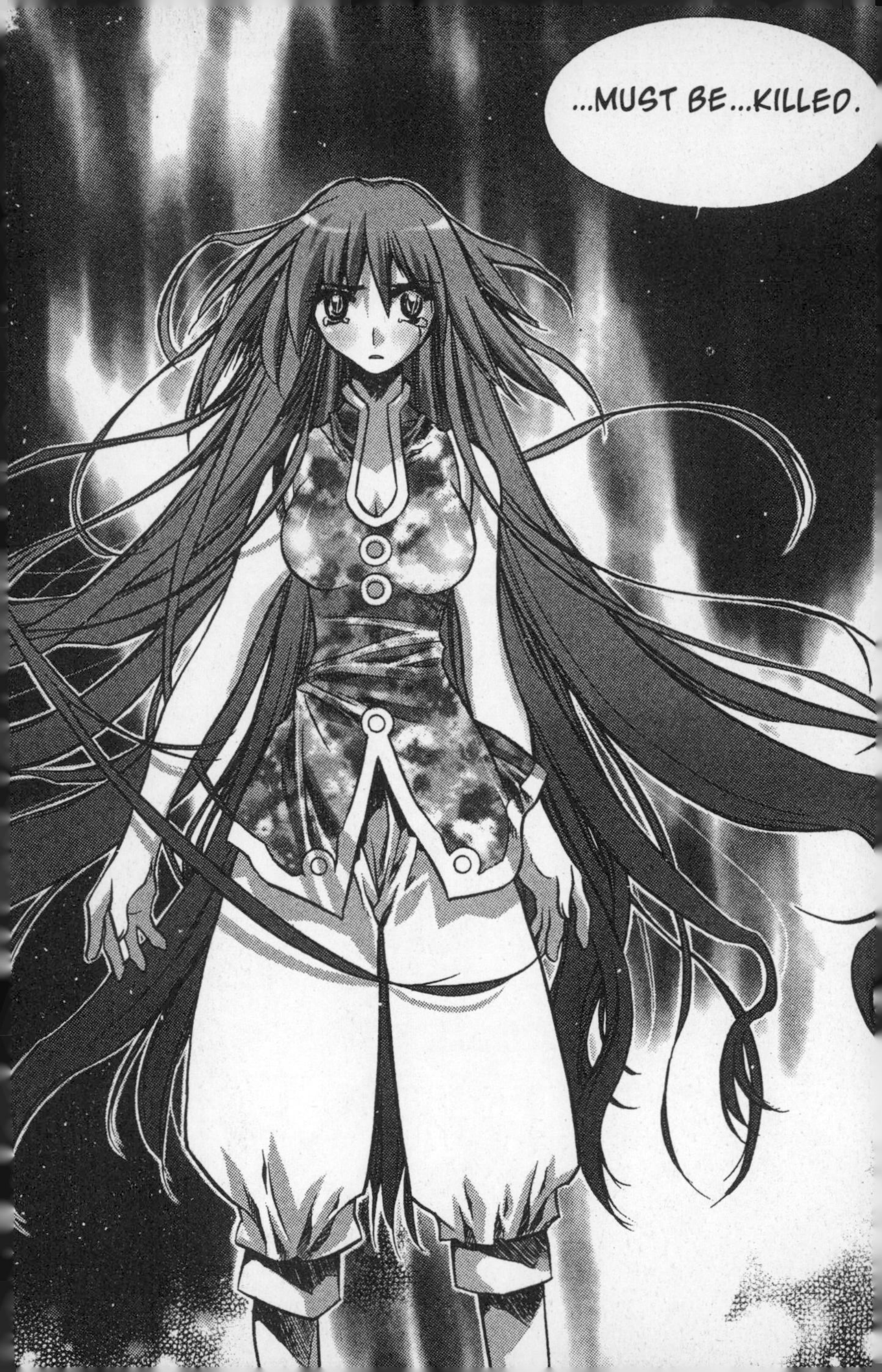
...MUST BE...KILLED.

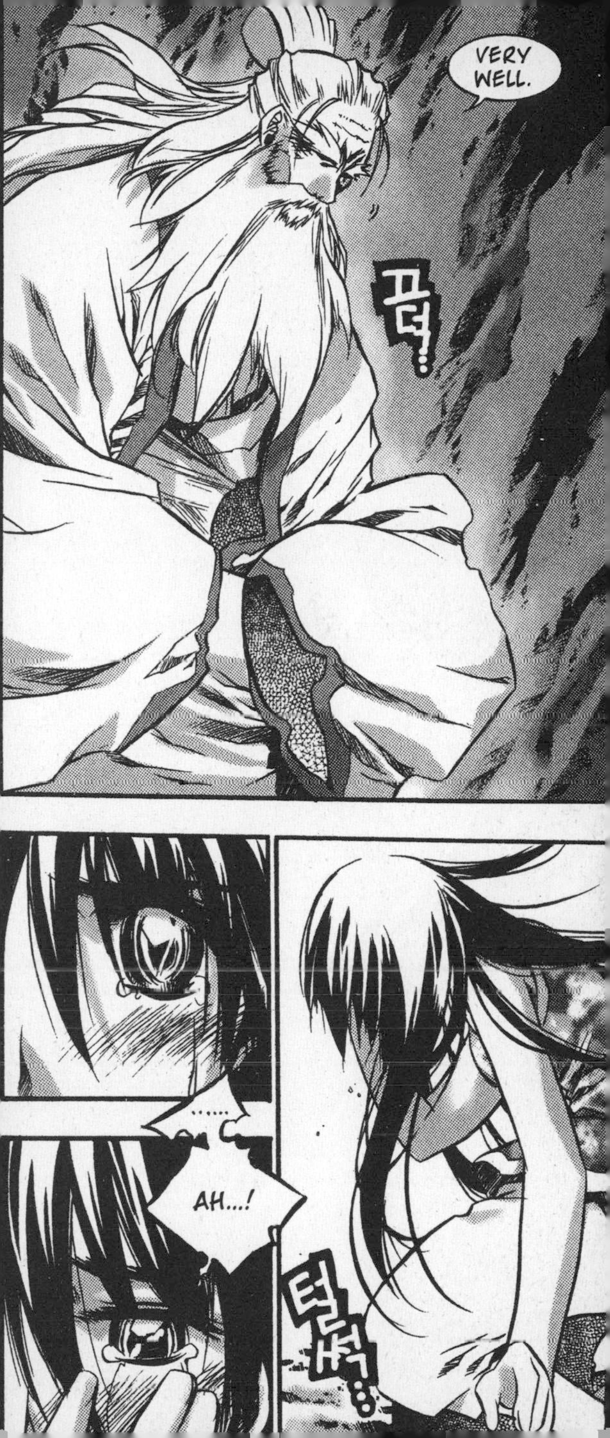
VERY WELL.
끄덕!
......
AH...!
털썩..

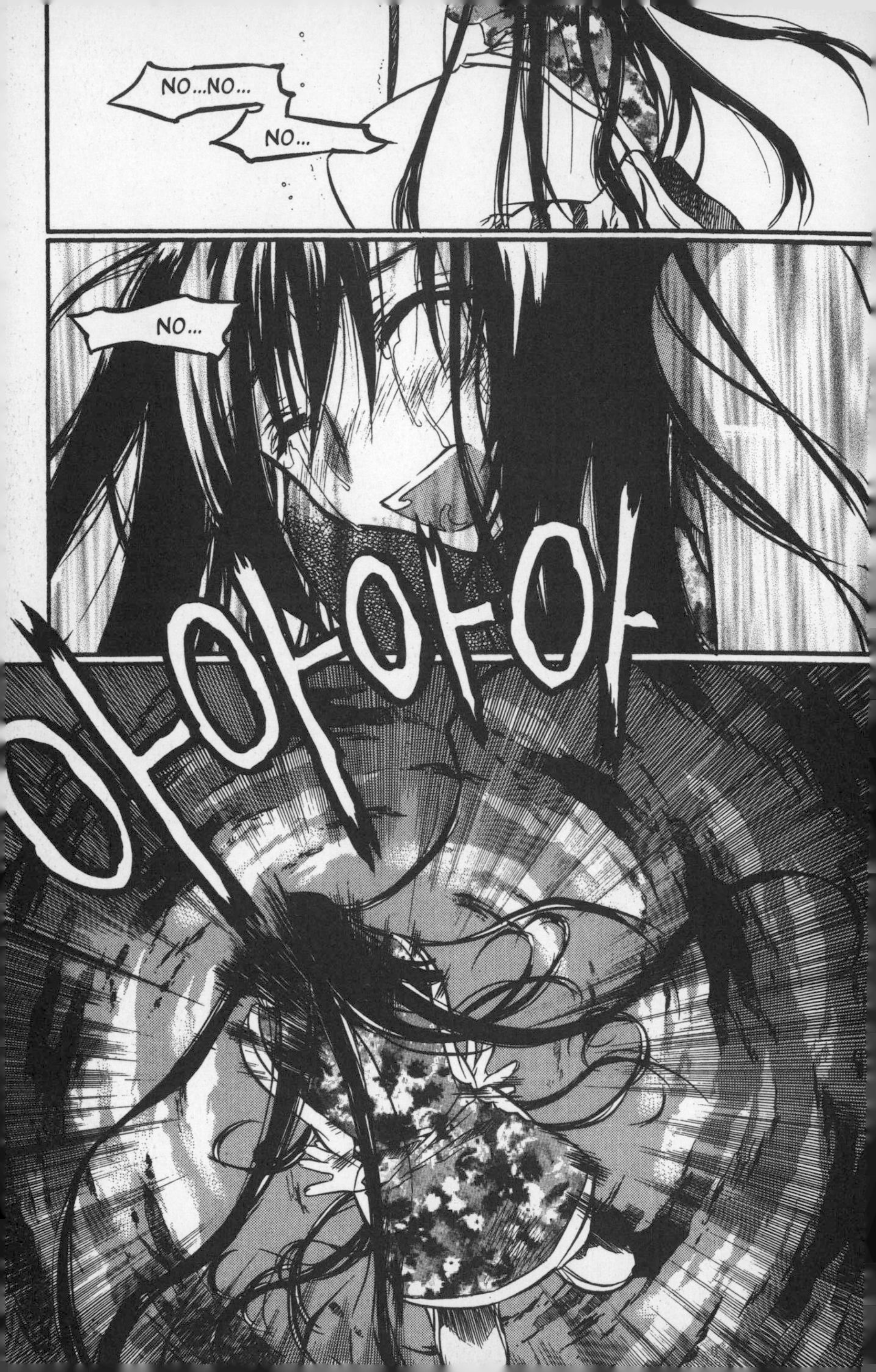
NO...NO...
NO...
NO...

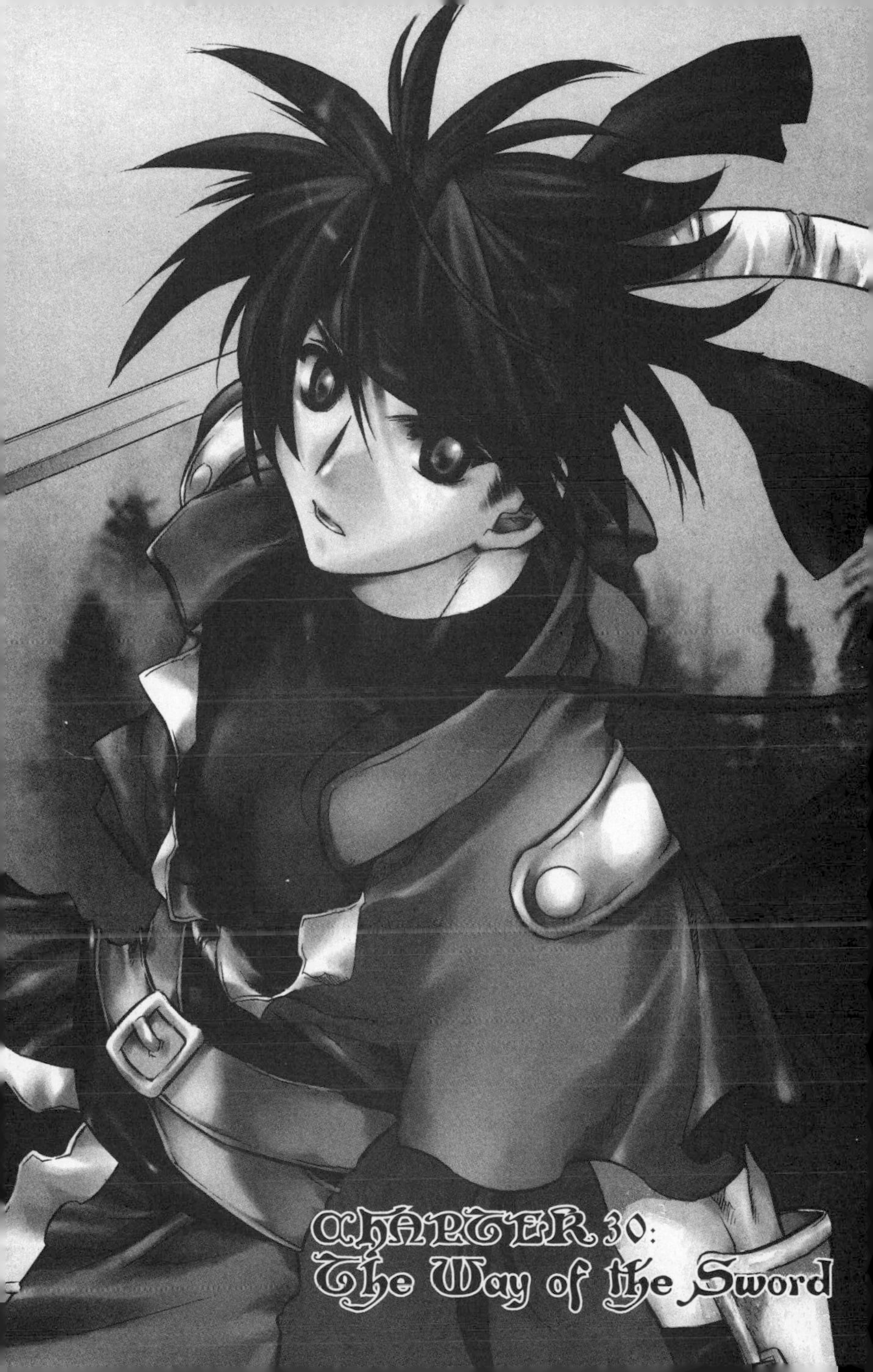
CHAPTER 30:
The Way of the Sword

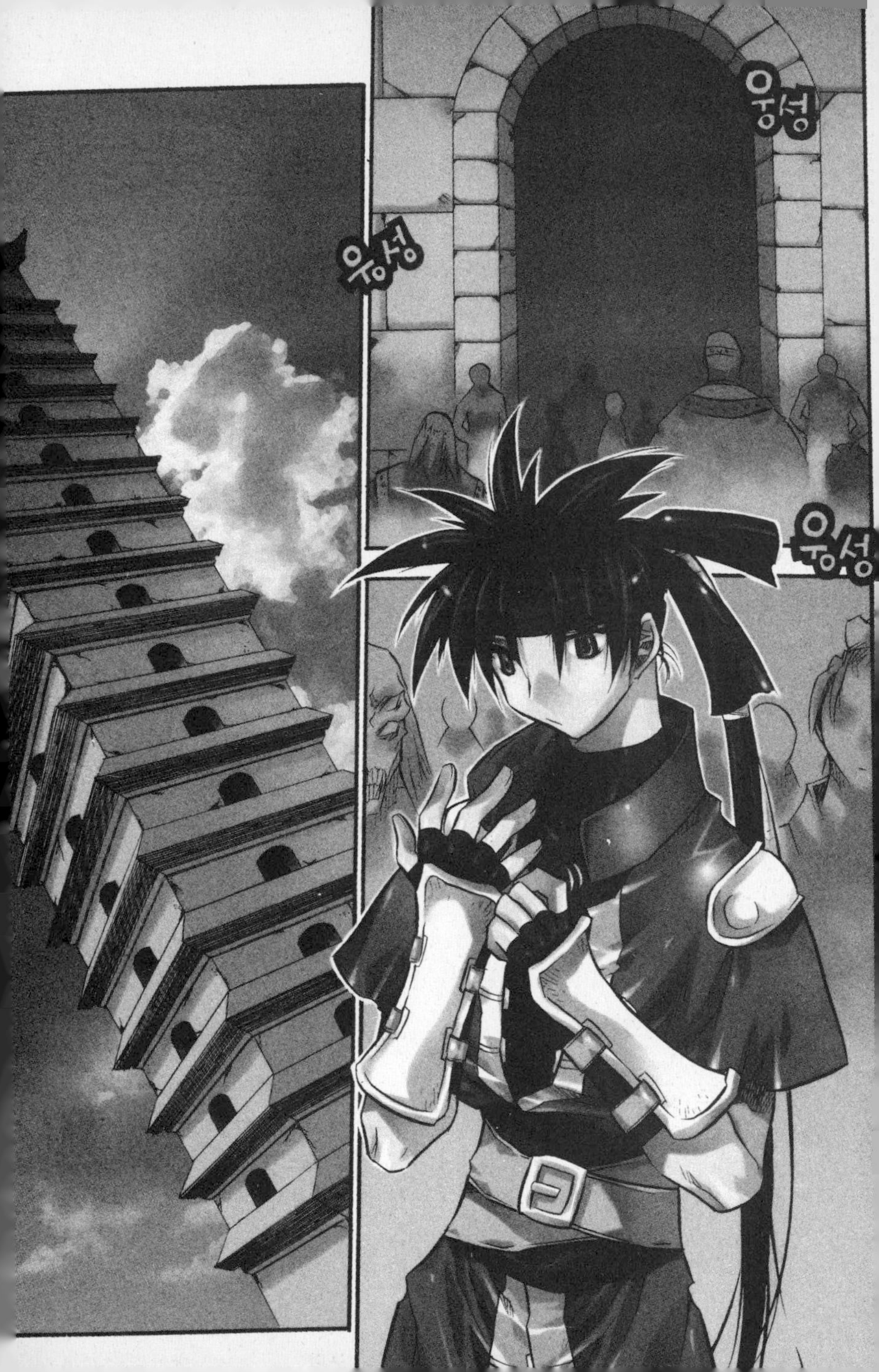
웅성
웅성
웅성

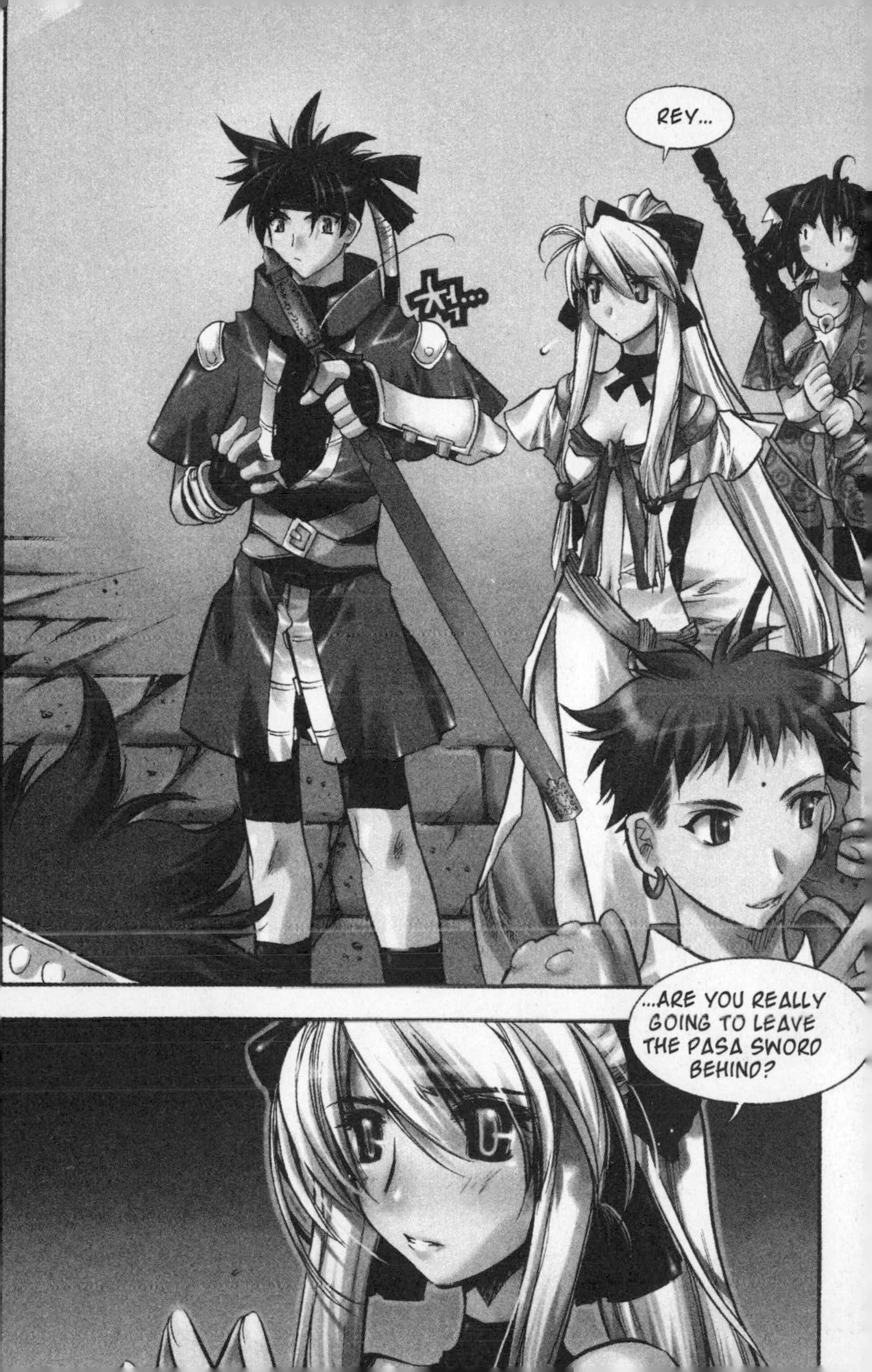
REY...
척...
...ARE YOU REALLY GOING TO LEAVE THE PASA SWORD BEHIND?

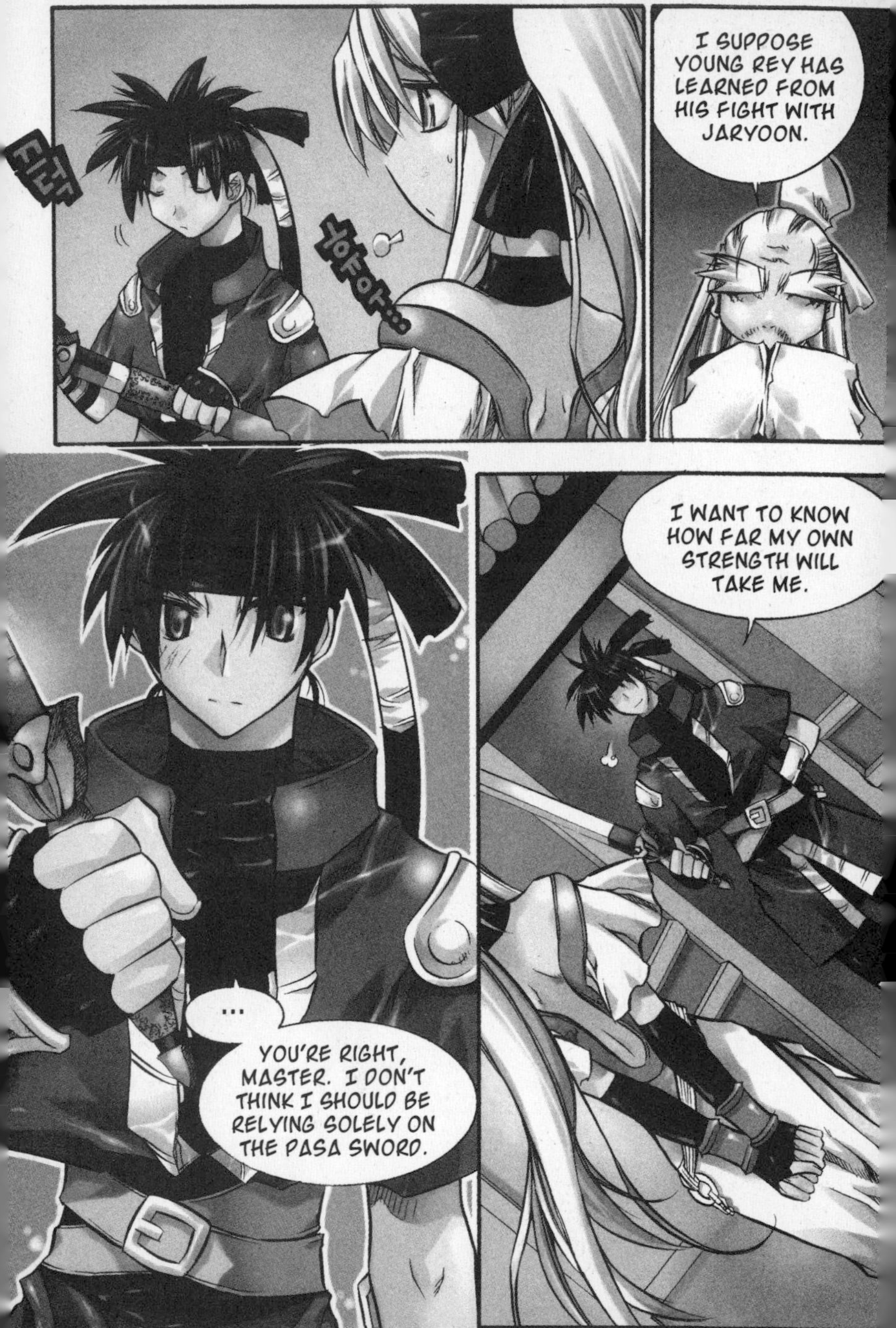
I SUPPOSE YOUNG REY HAS LEARNED FROM HIS FIGHT WITH JARYOON.
...
YOU'RE RIGHT, MASTER. I DON'T THINK I SHOULD BE RELYING SOLELY ON THE PASA SWORD.
I WANT TO KNOW HOW FAR MY OWN STRENGTH WILL TAKE ME.

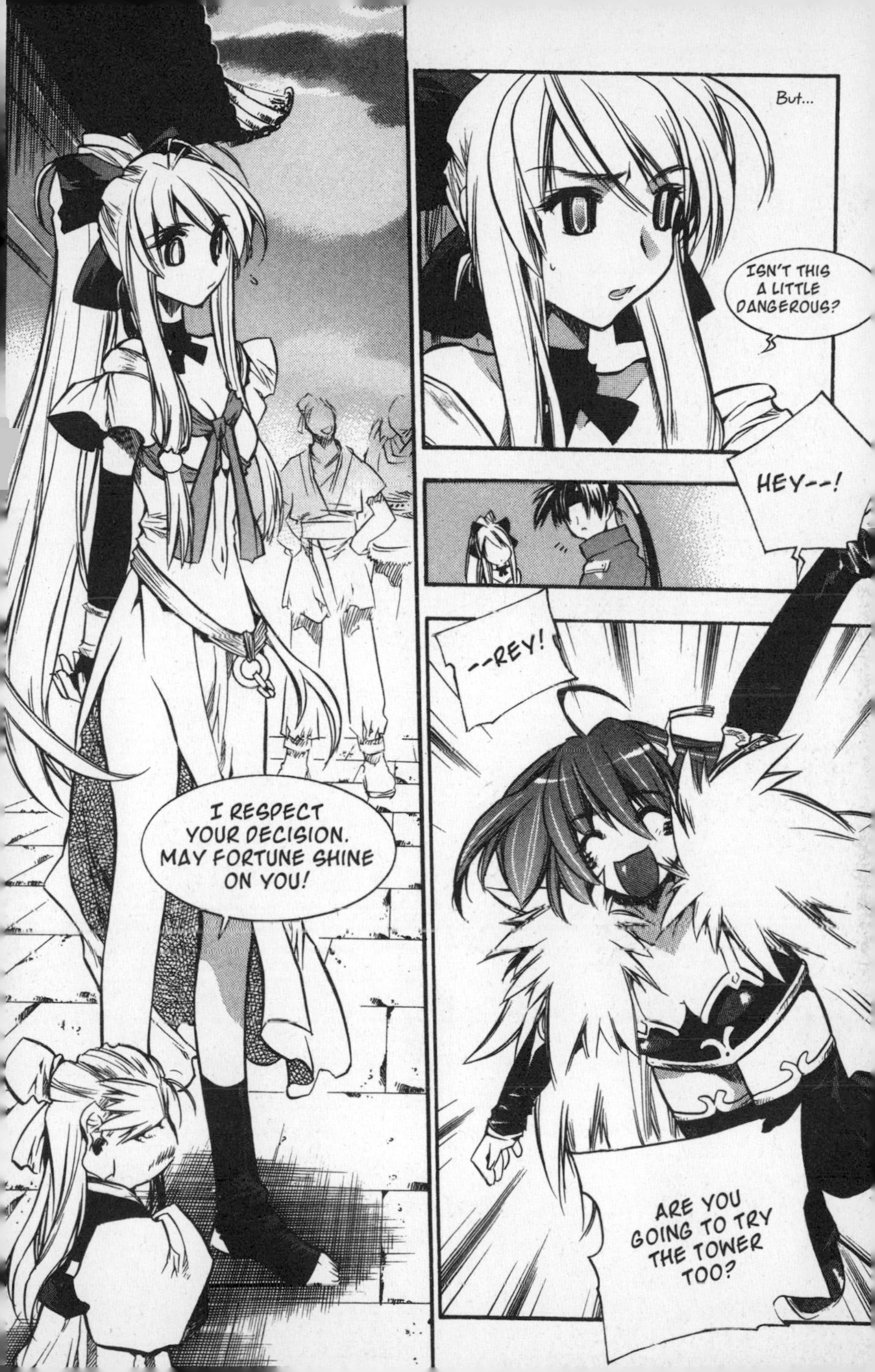
I RESPECT YOUR DECISION. MAY FORTUNE SHINE ON YOU!
But...
ISN'T THIS A LITTLE DANGEROUS?
HEY--!
--REY!
ARE YOU GOING TO TRY THE TOWER TOO?

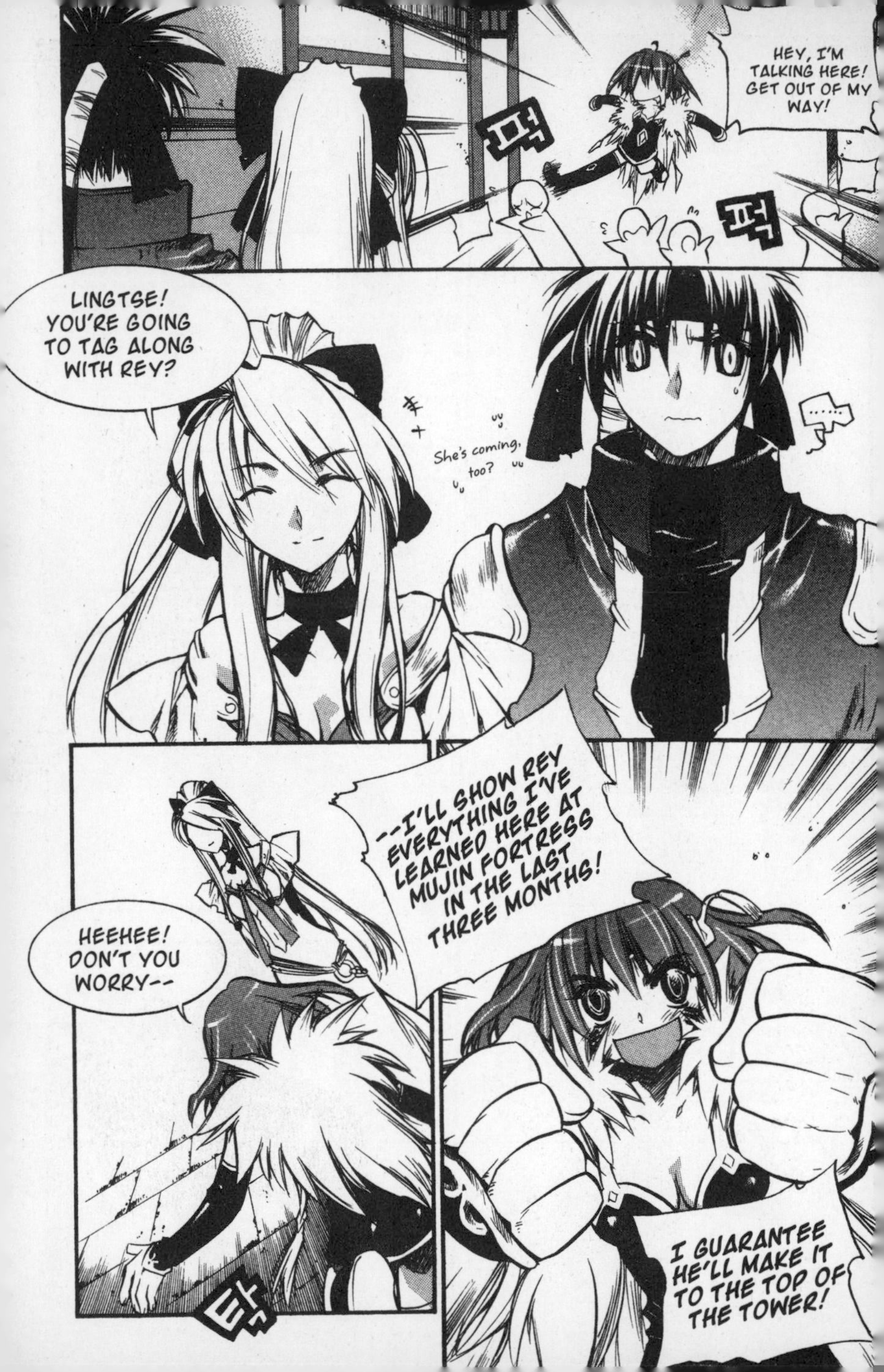

퍽
HEY, I'M TALKING HERE! GET OUT OF MY WAY!
퍽
LINGTSE! YOU'RE GOING TO TAG ALONG WITH REY?
She's coming, too?
......
HEEHEE! DON'T YOU WORRY--
--I'LL SHOW REY EVERYTHING I'VE LEARNED HERE AT MUJIN FORTRESS IN THE LAST THREE MONTHS!
탁
I GUARANTEE HE'LL MAKE IT TO THE TOP OF THE TOWER!

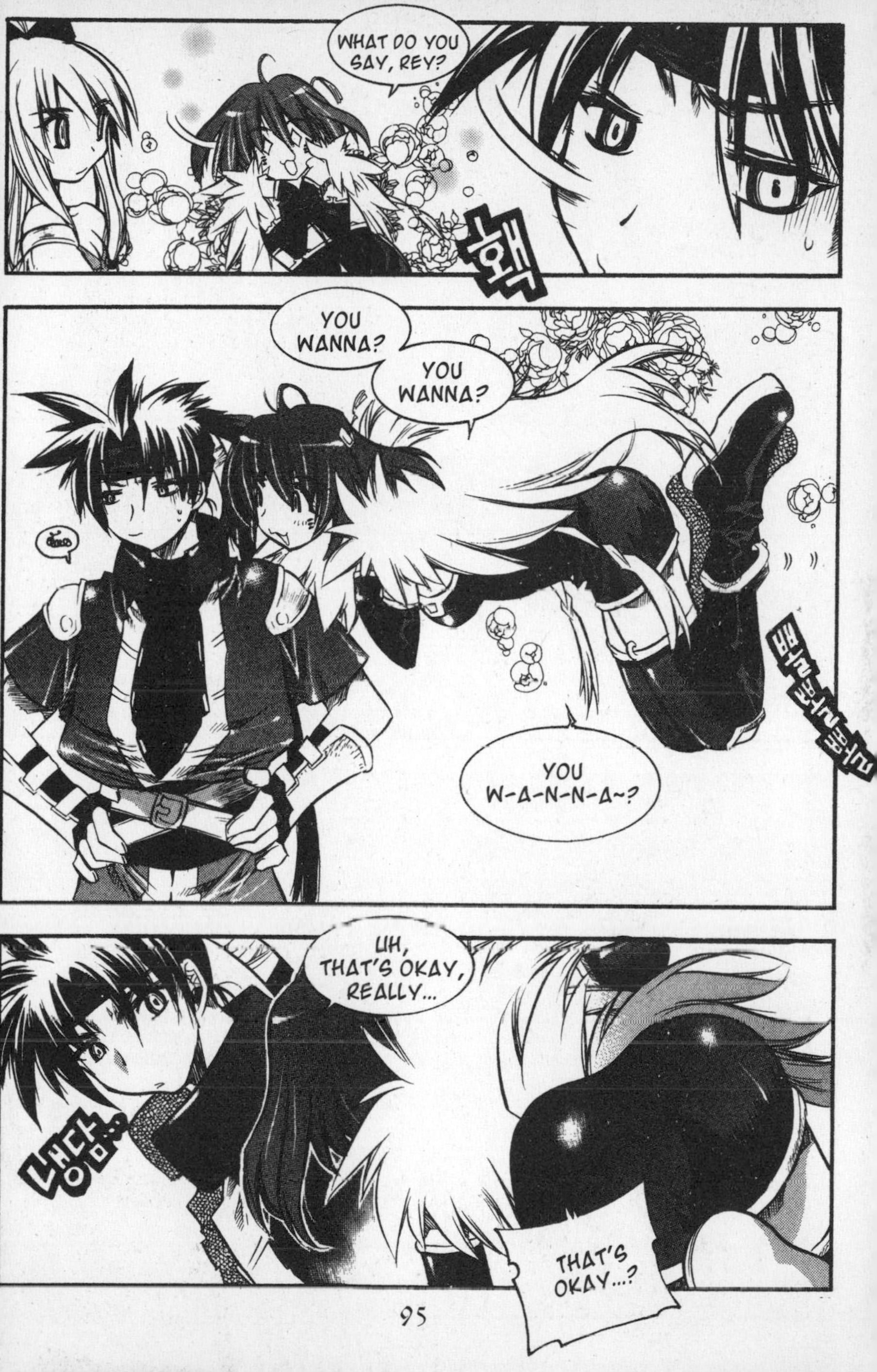
WHAT DO YOU SAY, REY?
홱
YOU WANNA?
YOU WANNA?
YOU W-A-N-N-A~?
UH, THAT'S OKAY, REALLY...
THAT'S OKAY...?

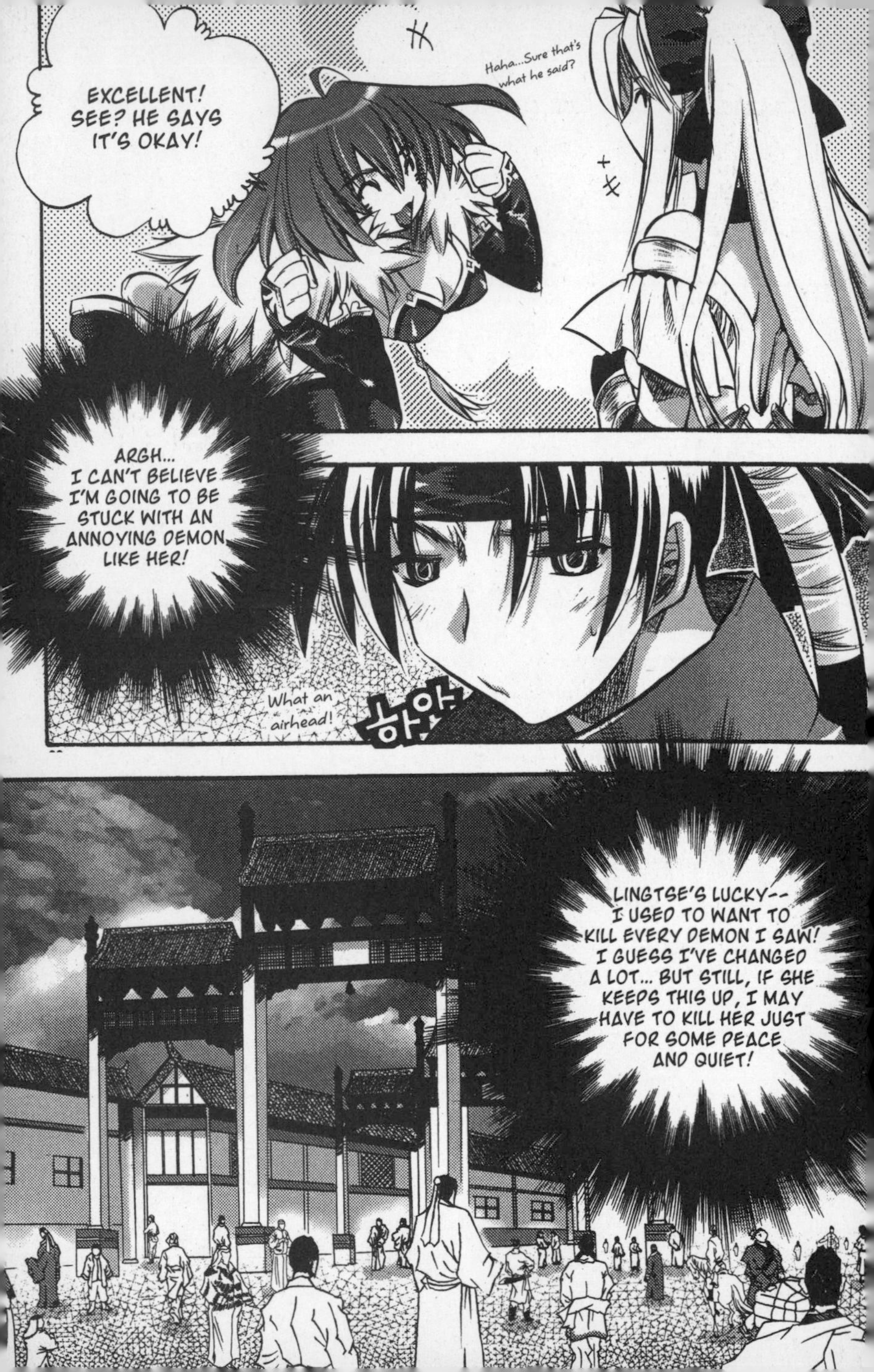
EXCELLENT! SEE? HE SAYS IT'S OKAY!
Haha...Sure that's what he said?
ARGH... I CAN'T BELIEVE I'M GOING TO BE STUCK WITH AN ANNOYING DEMON LIKE HER!
What an airhead!
하아
LINGTSE'S LUCKY-- I USED TO WANT TO KILL EVERY DEMON I SAW! I GUESS I'VE CHANGED A LOT... BUT STILL, IF SHE KEEPS THIS UP, I MAY HAVE TO KILL HER JUST FOR SOME PEACE AND QUIET!

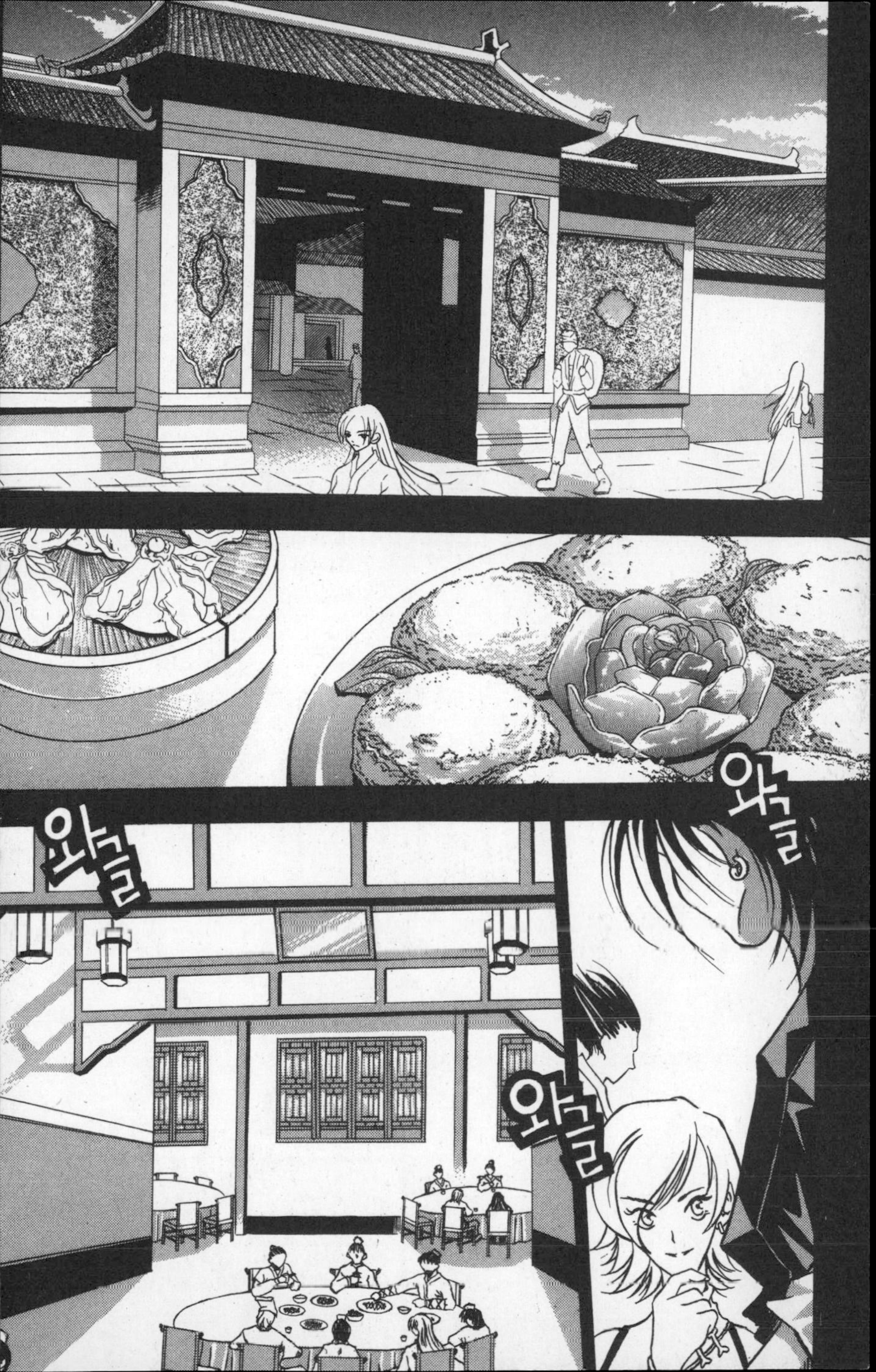
와글
와글
와글

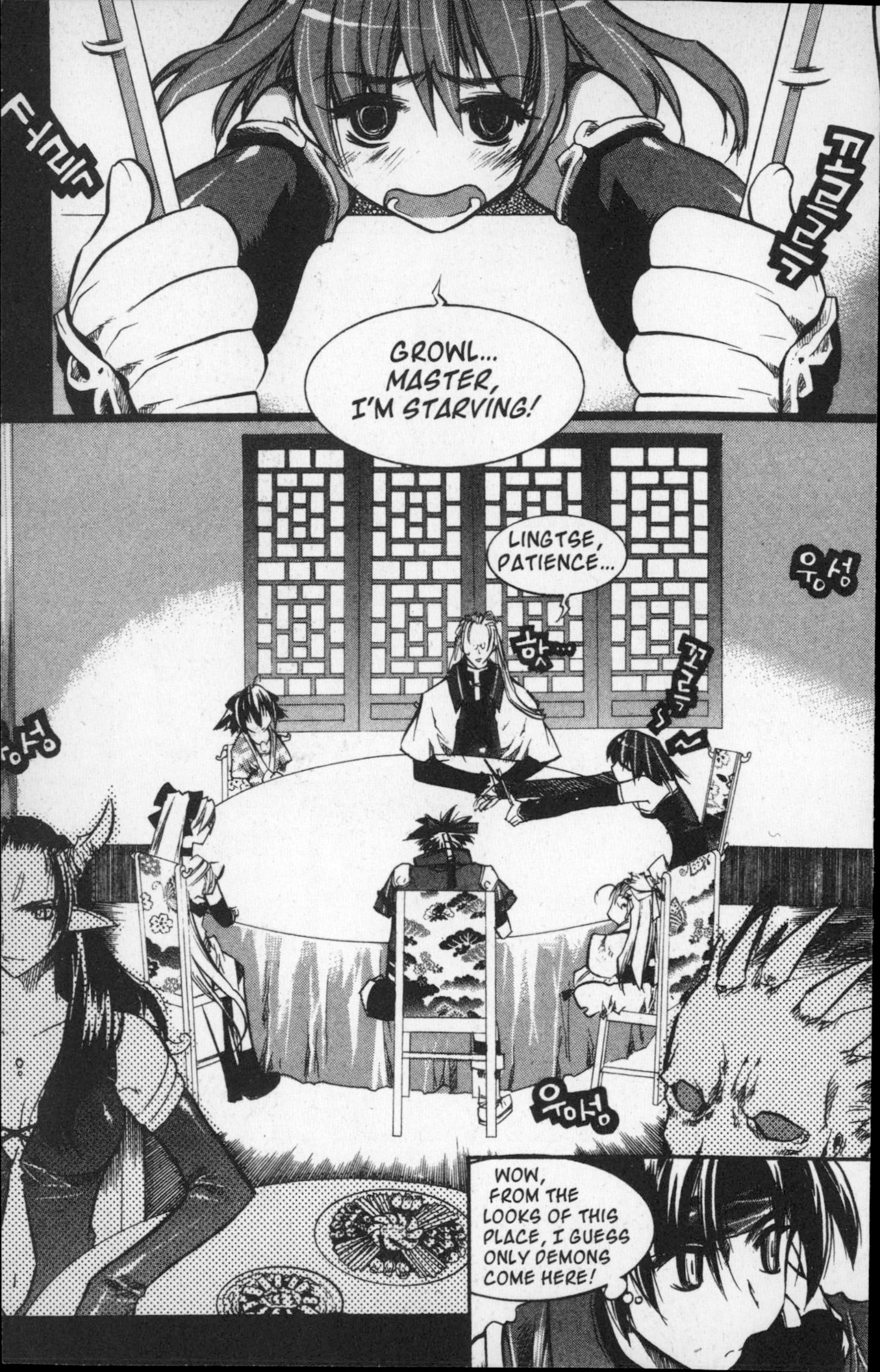
GROWL... MASTER, I'M STARVING!
LINGTSE, PATIENCE...
WOW, FROM THE LOOKS OF THIS PLACE, I GUESS ONLY DEMONS COME HERE!

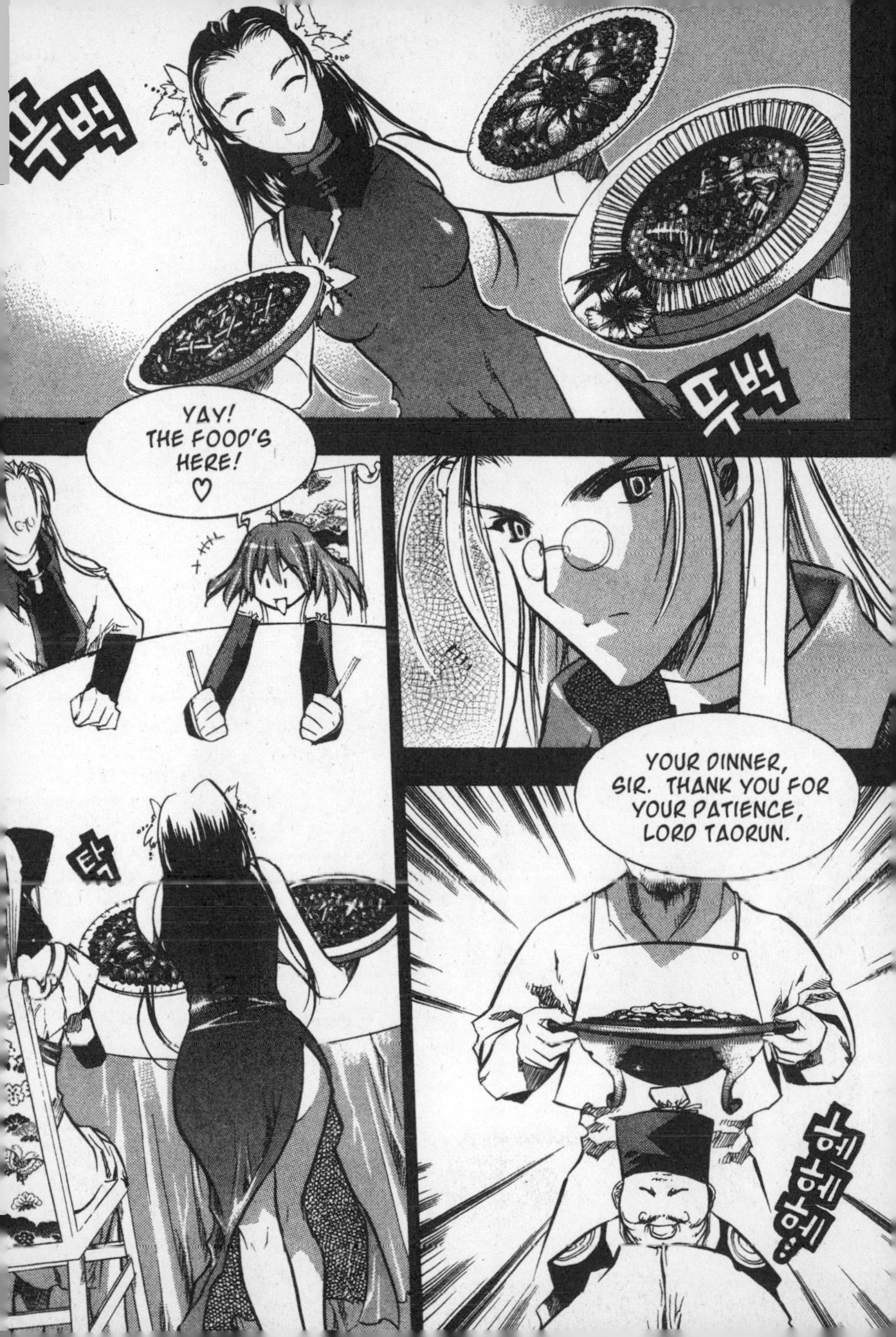
YAY! THE FOOD'S HERE! ♡
탁
YOUR DINNER, SIR. THANK YOU FOR YOUR PATIENCE, LORD TAORUN.

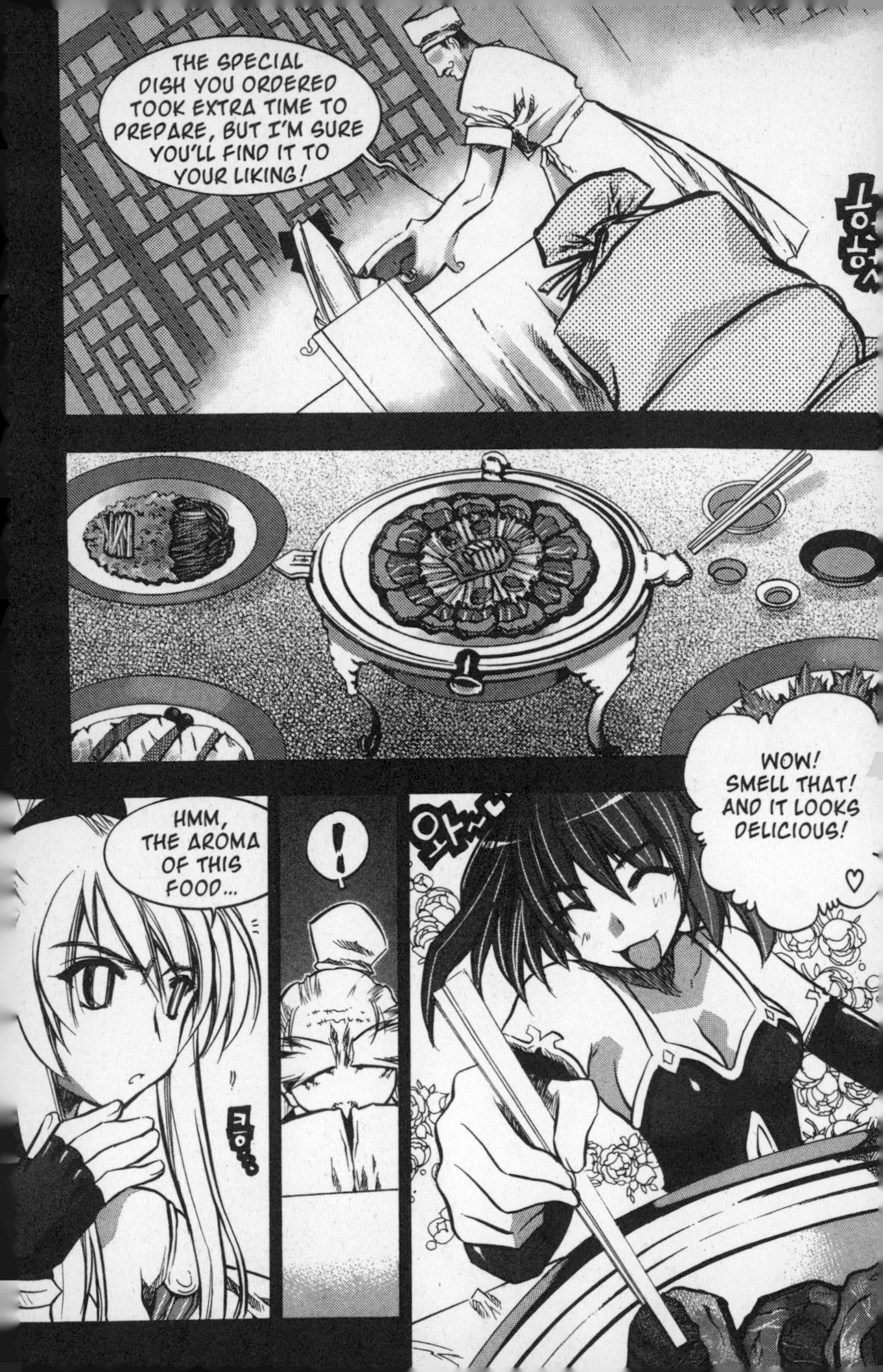
THE SPECIAL DISH YOU ORDERED TOOK EXTRA TIME TO PREPARE, BUT I'M SURE YOU'LL FIND IT TO YOUR LIKING!
HMM, THE AROMA OF THIS FOOD...
!
WOW! SMELL THAT! AND IT LOOKS DELICIOUS! ♡

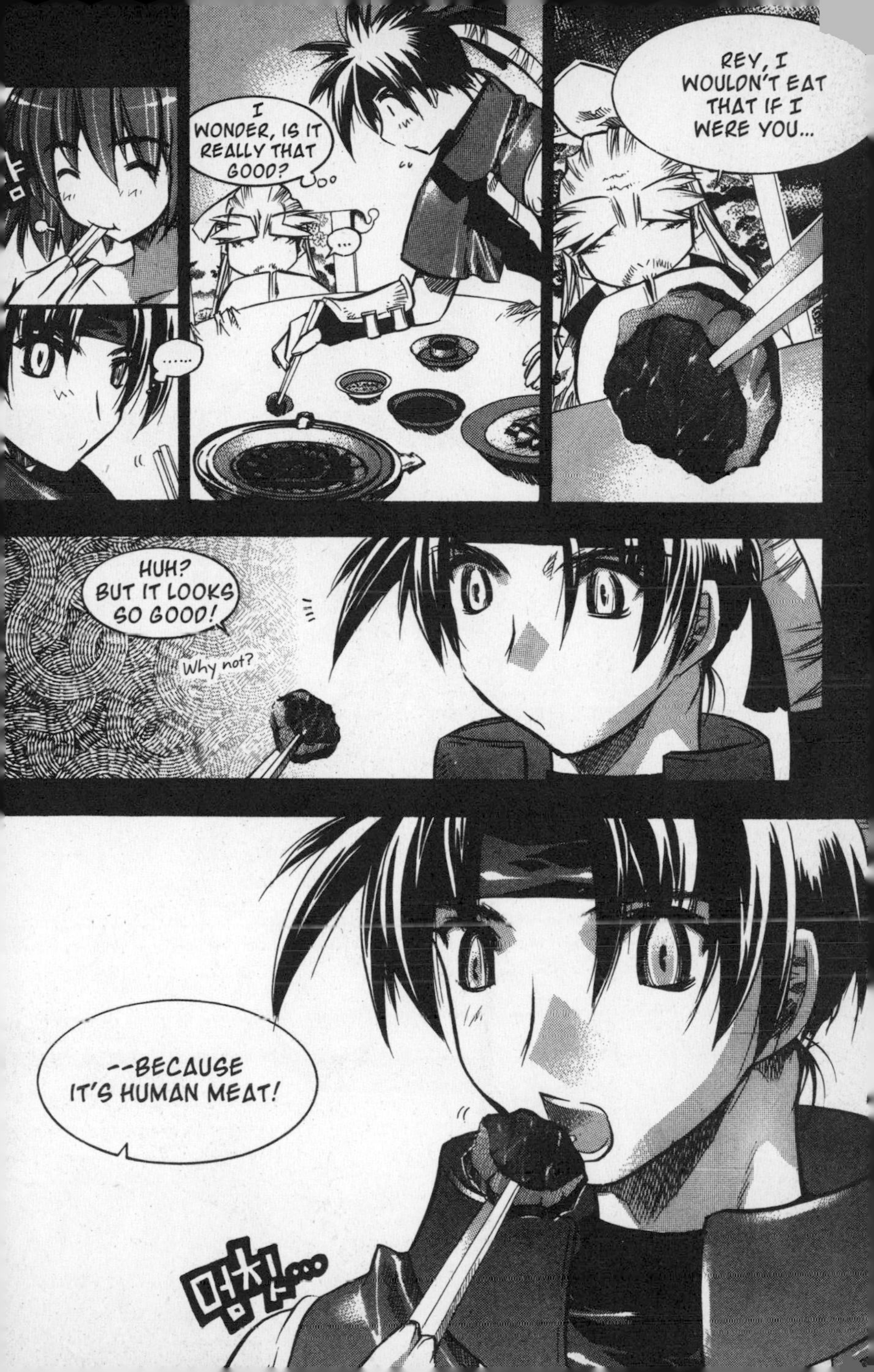
......
I WONDER, IS IT REALLY THAT GOOD?
...
REY, I WOULDN'T EAT THAT IF I WERE YOU...
HUH? BUT IT LOOKS SO GOOD!
Why not?
--BECAUSE IT'S HUMAN MEAT!

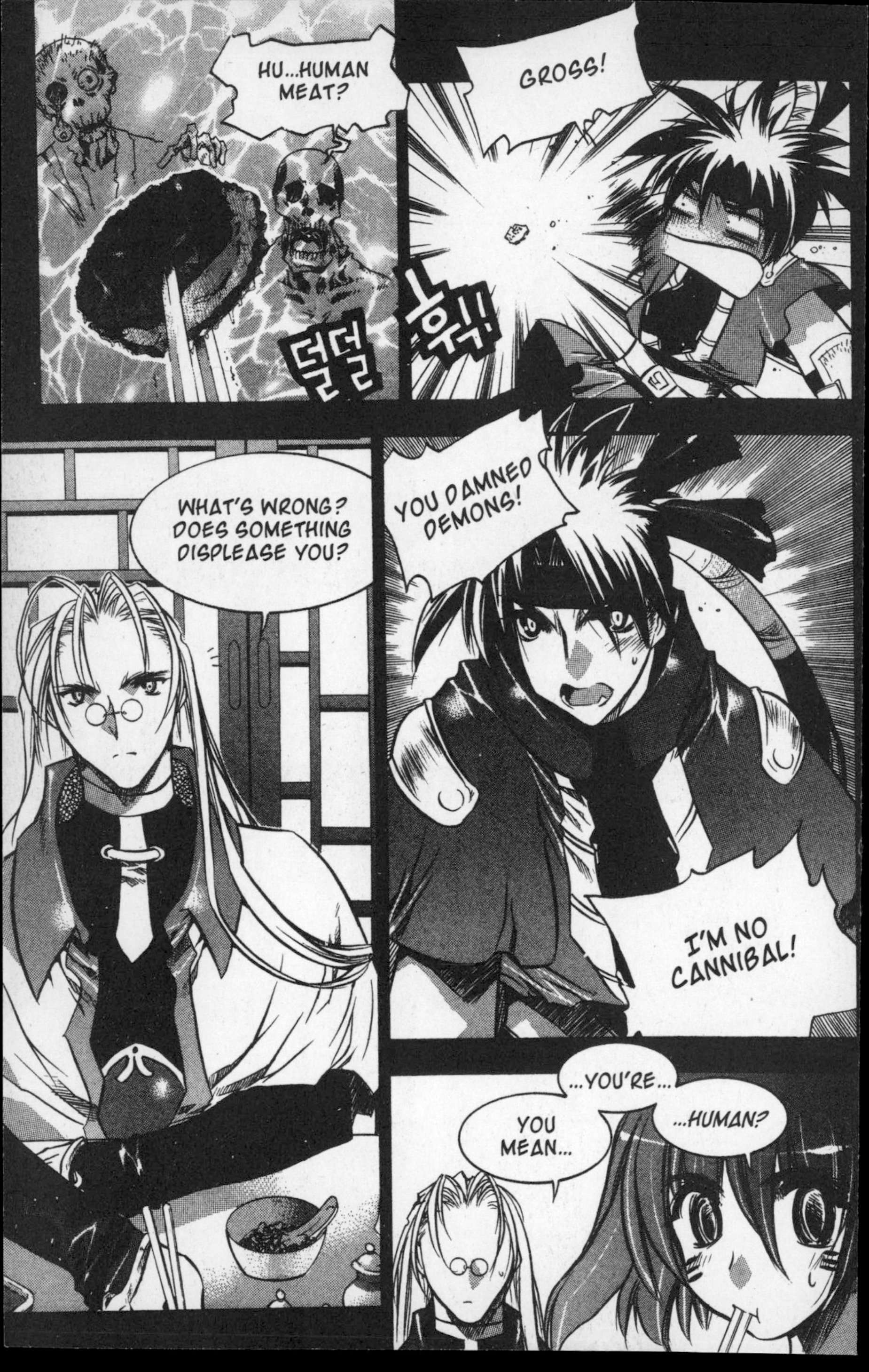
HU...HUMAN MEAT?
덜덜
GROSS!
WHAT'S WRONG? DOES SOMETHING DISPLEASE YOU?
YOU DAMNED DEMONS!
I'M NO CANNIBAL!
YOU MEAN...
...YOU'RE...
...HUMAN?

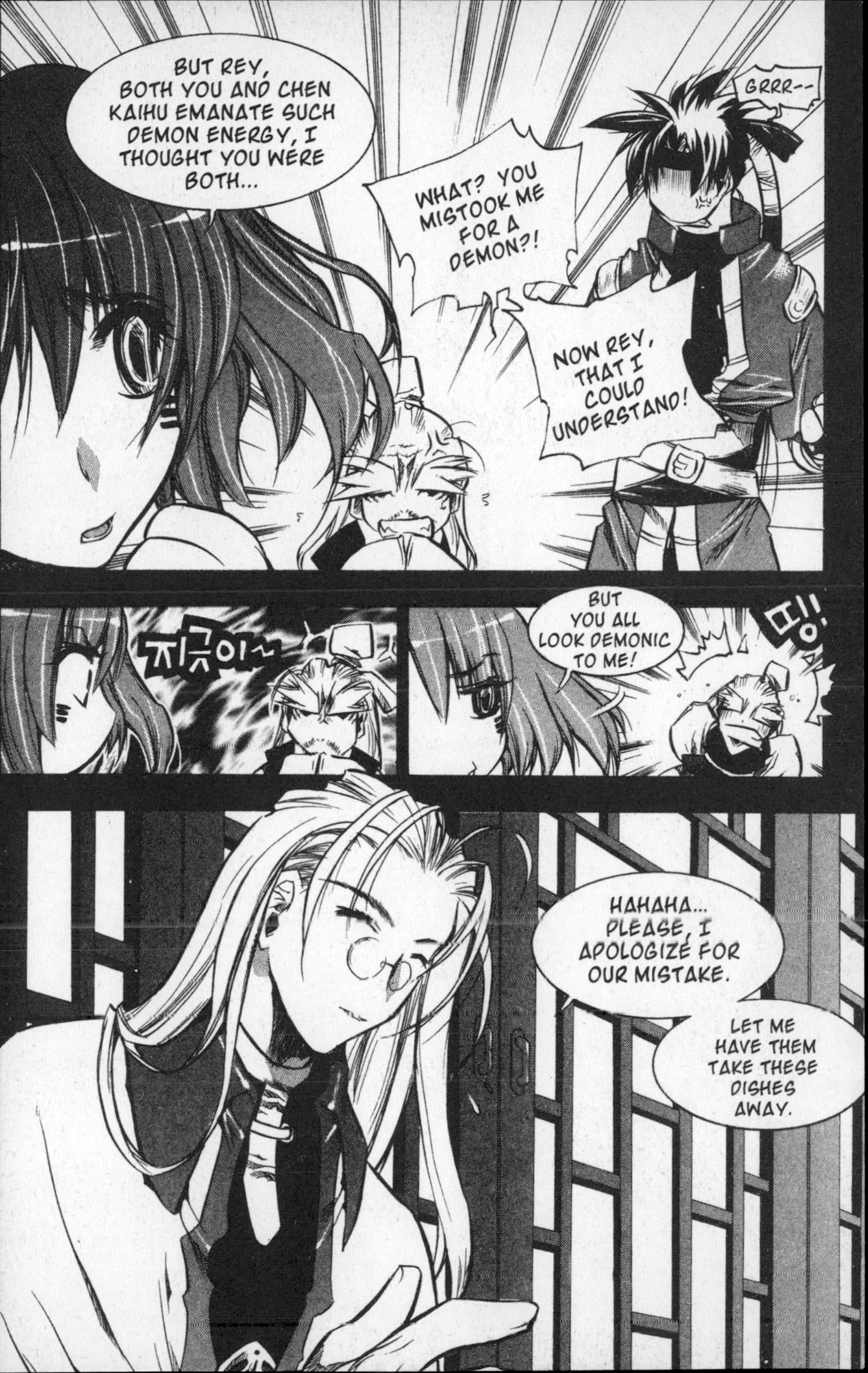
BUT REY, BOTH YOU AND CHEN KAIHU EMANATE SUCH DEMON ENERGY, I THOUGHT YOU WERE BOTH...
WHAT? YOU MISTOOK ME FOR A DEMON?!
GRRR--
NOW REY, THAT I COULD UNDERSTAND!
지긋이~
BUT YOU ALL LOOK DEMONIC TO ME!
띵!!
HAHAHA... PLEASE, I APOLOGIZE FOR OUR MISTAKE.
LET ME HAVE THEM TAKE THESE DISHES AWAY.

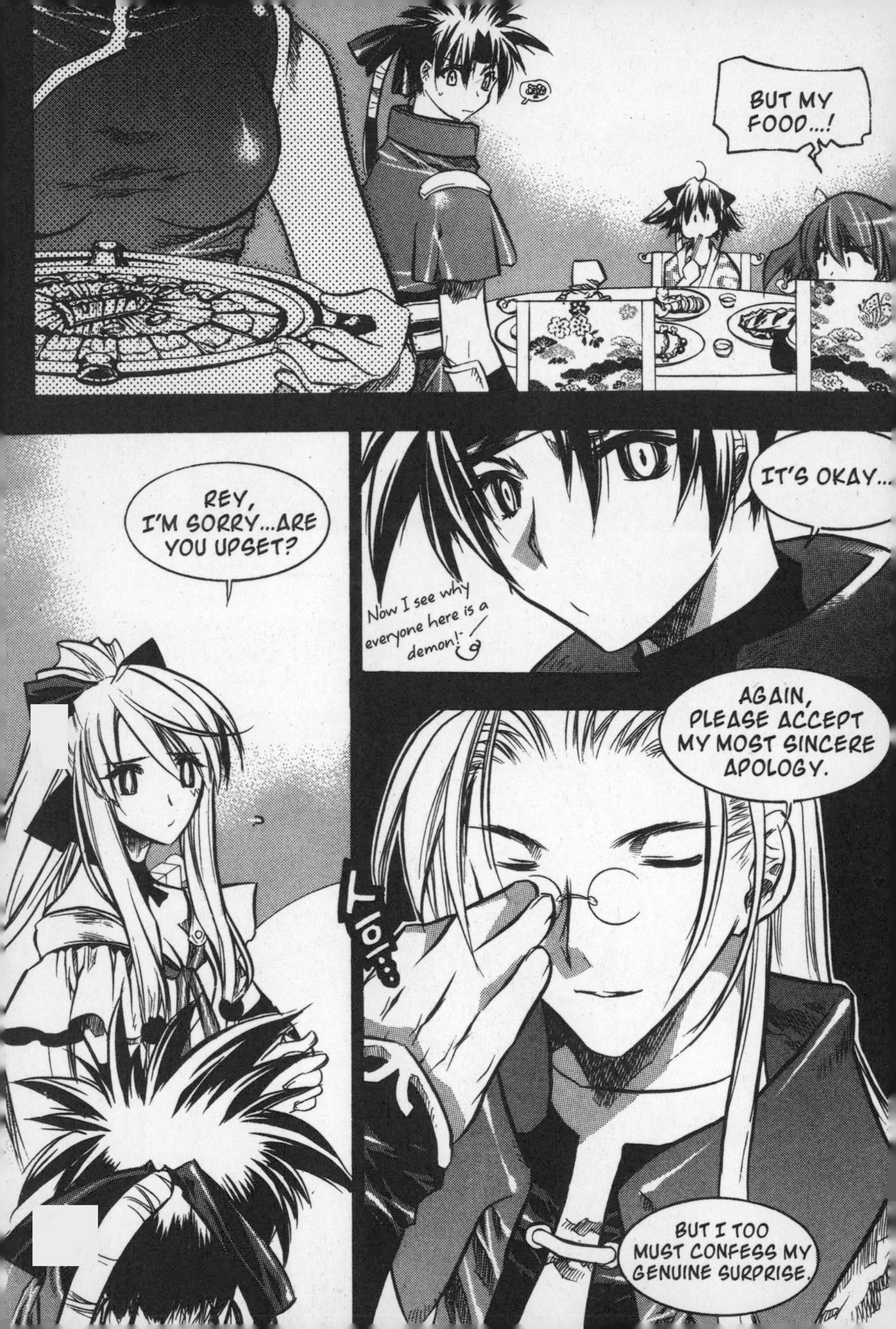
BUT MY FOOD...!
REY, I'M SORRY...ARE YOU UPSET?
IT'S OKAY...
Now I see why everyone here is a demon!
AGAIN, PLEASE ACCEPT MY MOST SINCERE APOLOGY.
BUT I TOO MUST CONFESS MY GENUINE SURPRISE.

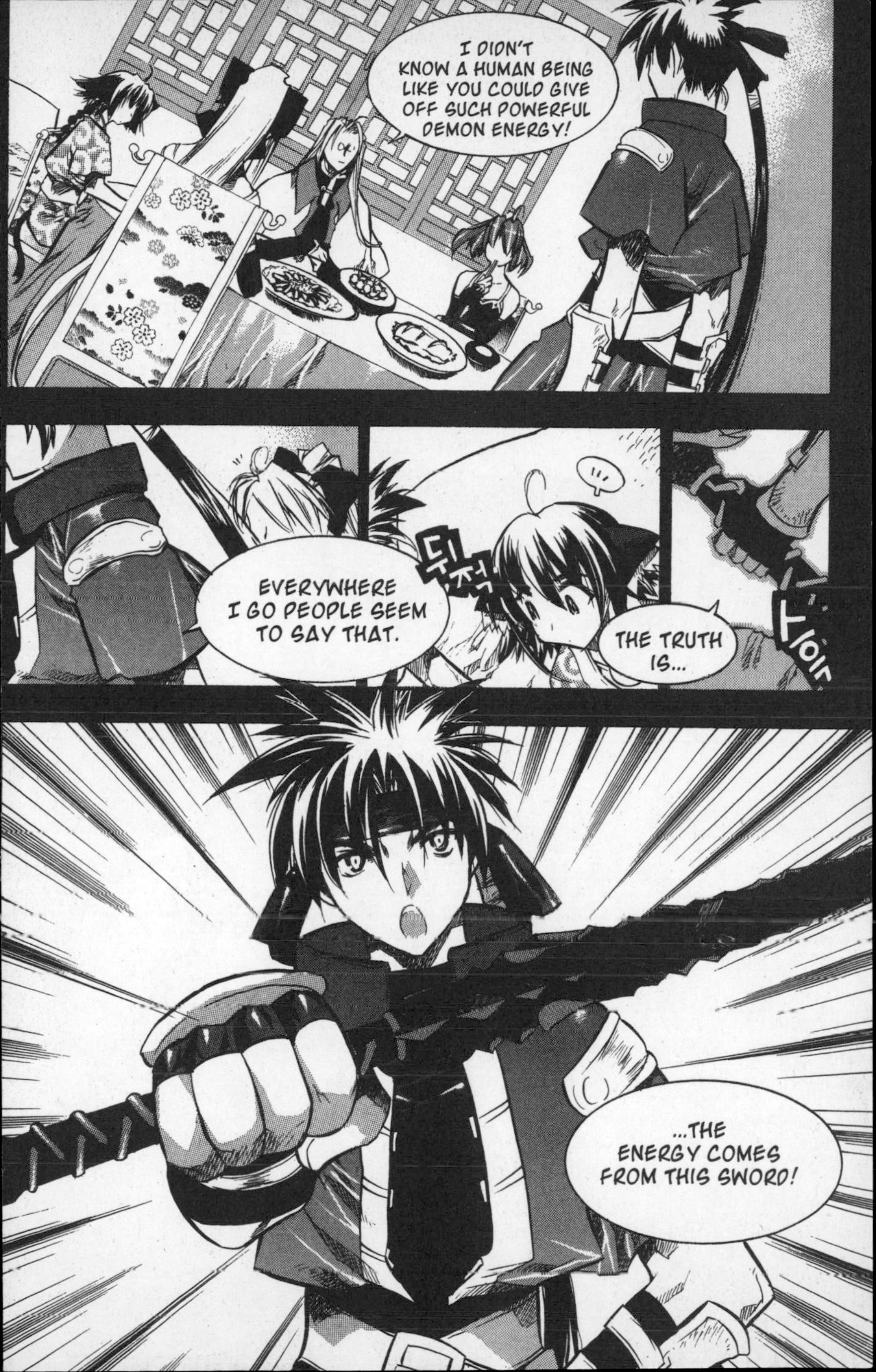
I DIDN'T KNOW A HUMAN BEING LIKE YOU COULD GIVE OFF SUCH POWERFUL DEMON ENERGY!
EVERYWHERE I GO PEOPLE SEEM TO SAY THAT.
뒤적
THE TRUTH IS...
...THE ENERGY COMES FROM THIS SWORD!

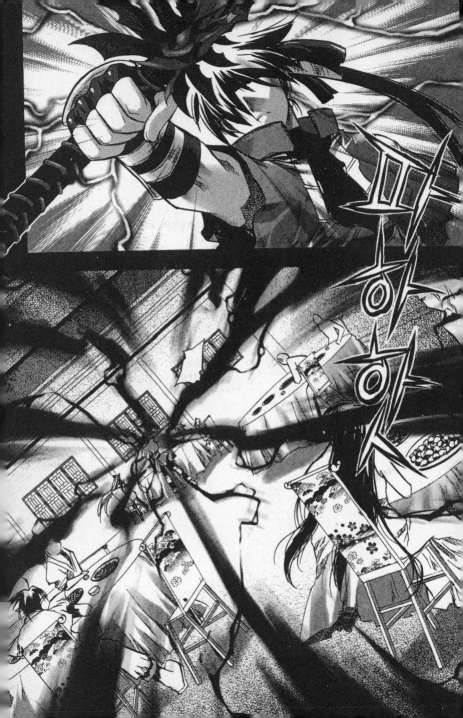

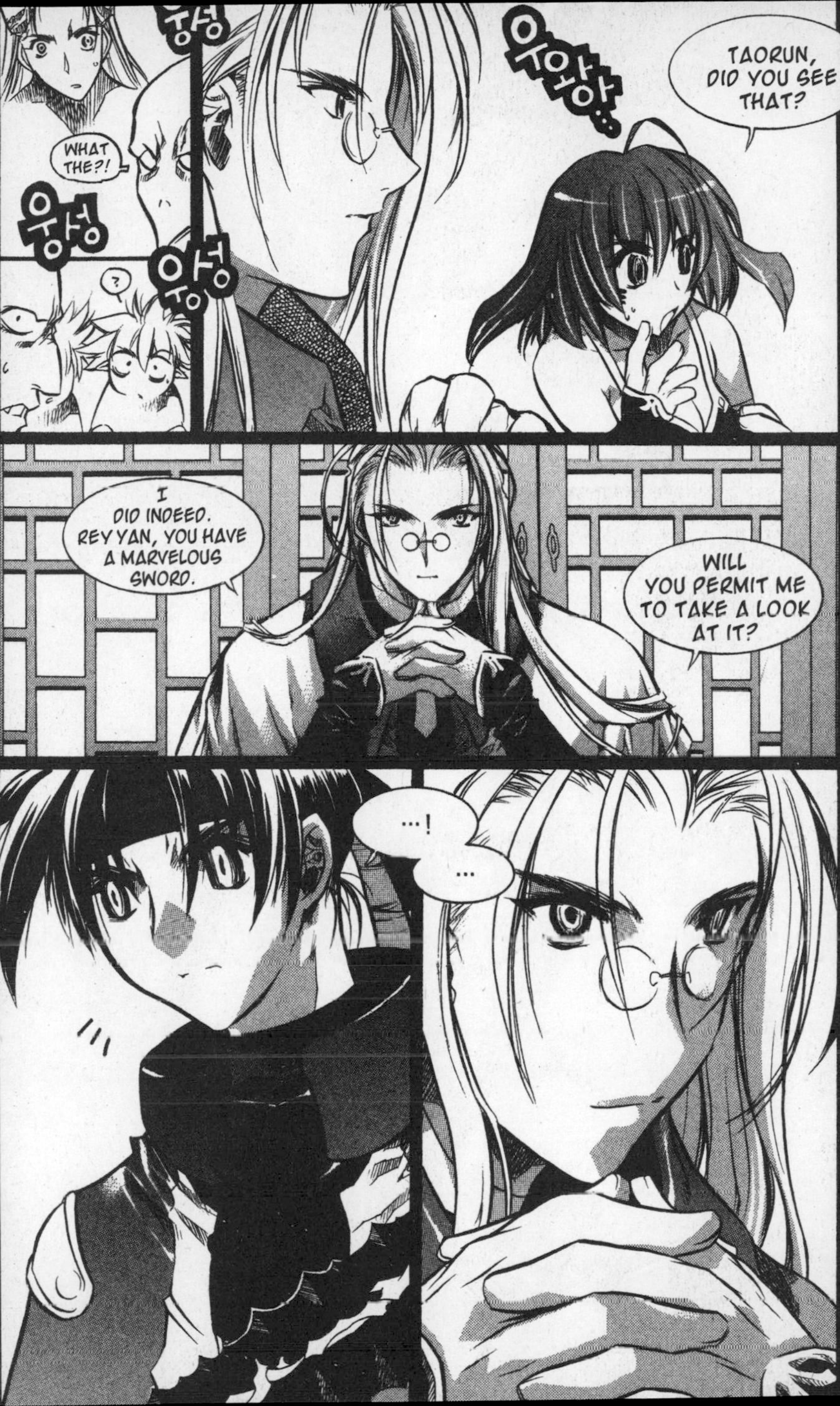
WHAT THE?!
?
TAORUN, DID YOU SEE THAT?
I DID INDEED. REY YAN, YOU HAVE A MARVELOUS SWORD.
WILL YOU PERMIT ME TO TAKE A LOOK AT IT?
...!
...

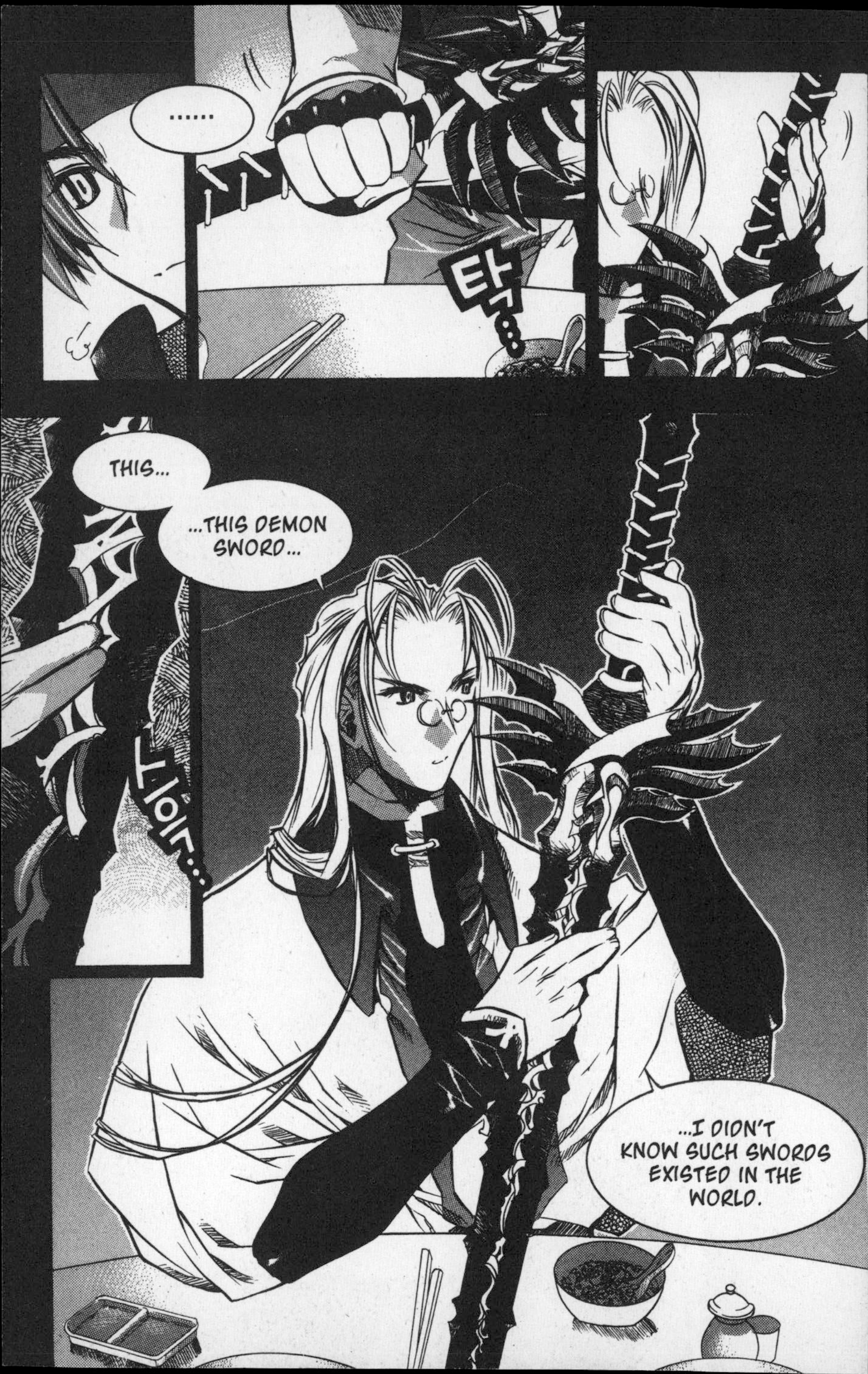
......
타...
THIS...
...THIS DEMON SWORD...
...I DIDN'T KNOW SUCH SWORDS EXISTED IN THE WORLD.

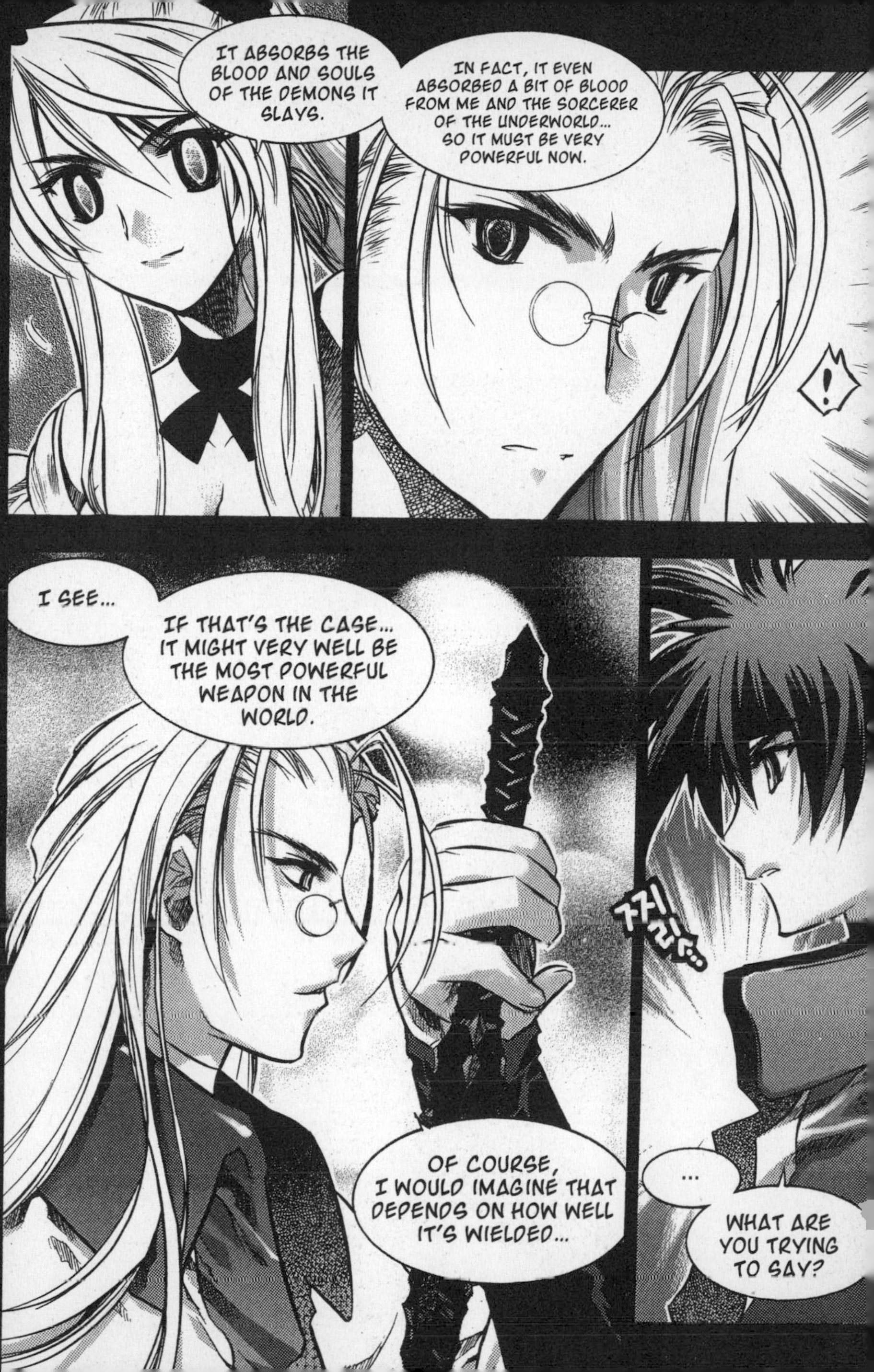
IT ABSORBS THE BLOOD AND SOULS OF THE DEMONS IT SLAYS.
IN FACT, IT EVEN ABSORBED A BIT OF BLOOD FROM ME AND THE SORCERER OF THE UNDERWORLD... SO IT MUST BE VERY POWERFUL NOW.
!
I SEE...
IF THAT'S THE CASE... IT MIGHT VERY WELL BE THE MOST POWERFUL WEAPON IN THE WORLD.
OF COURSE, I WOULD IMAGINE THAT DEPENDS ON HOW WELL IT'S WIELDED...
...
WHAT ARE YOU TRYING TO SAY?

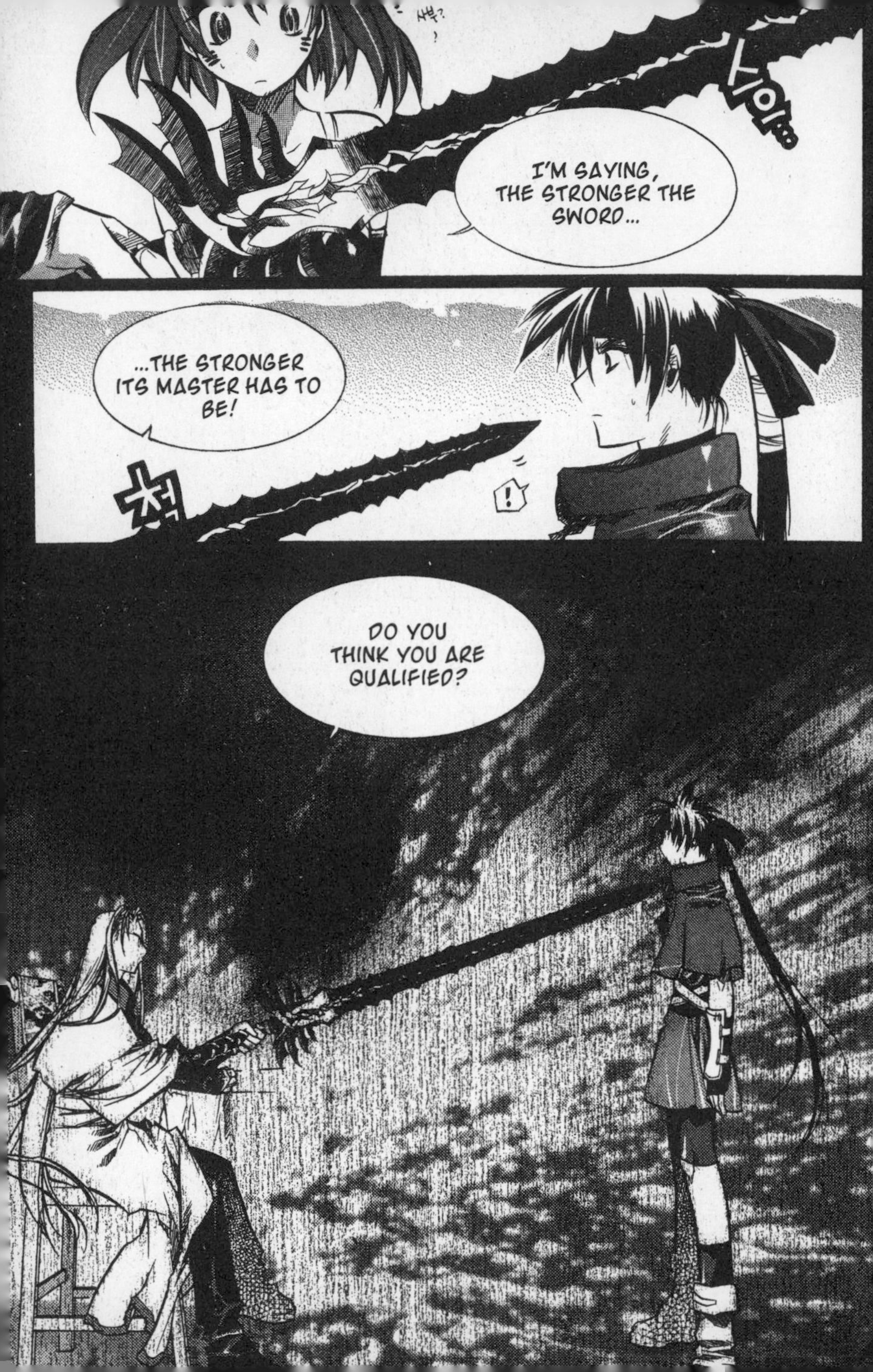
I'M SAYING, THE STRONGER THE SWORD...
...THE STRONGER ITS MASTER HAS TO BE!
척
DO YOU THINK YOU ARE QUALIFIED?

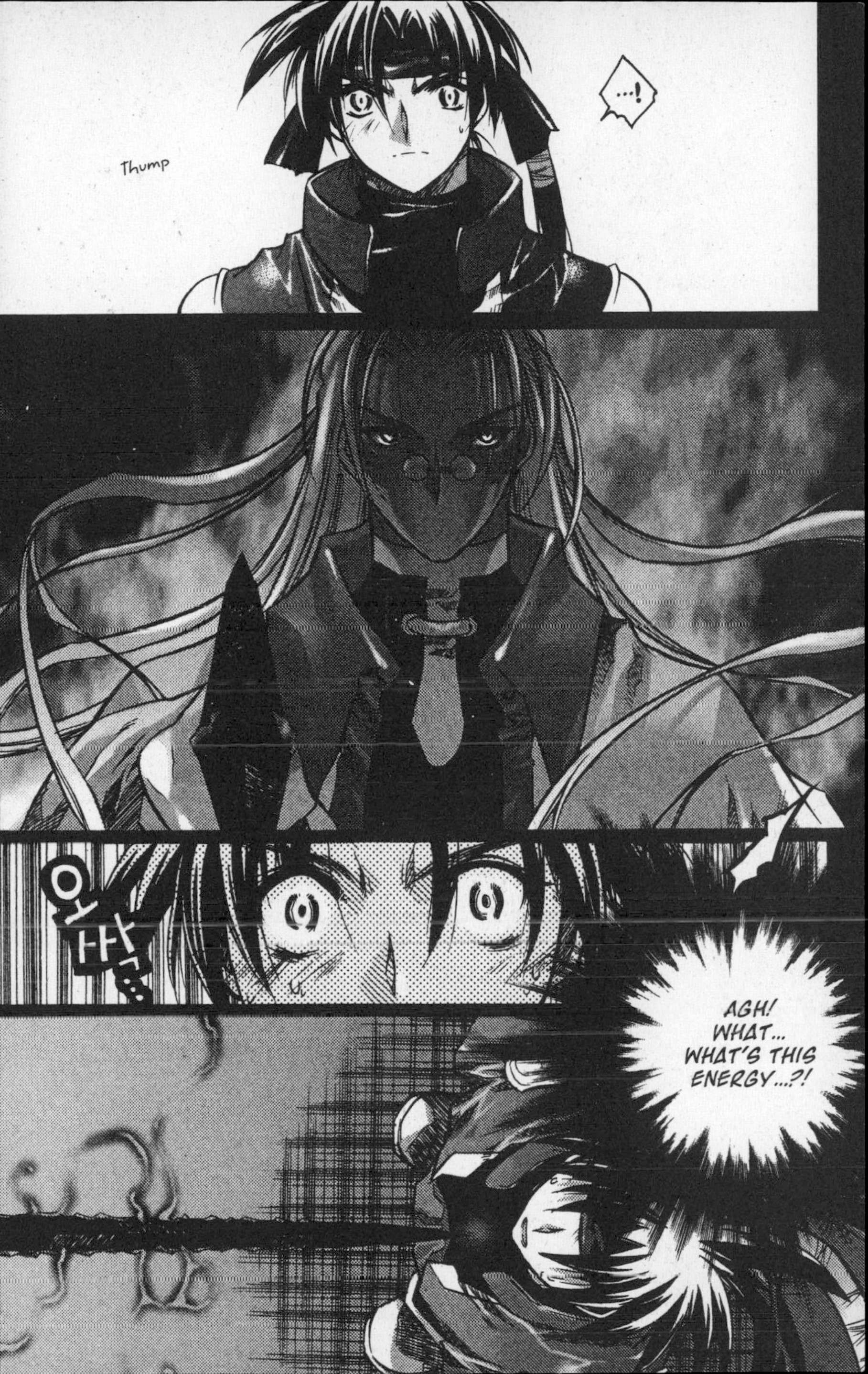
...!
Thump
오싹...
AGH! WHAT... WHAT'S THIS ENERGY...?!

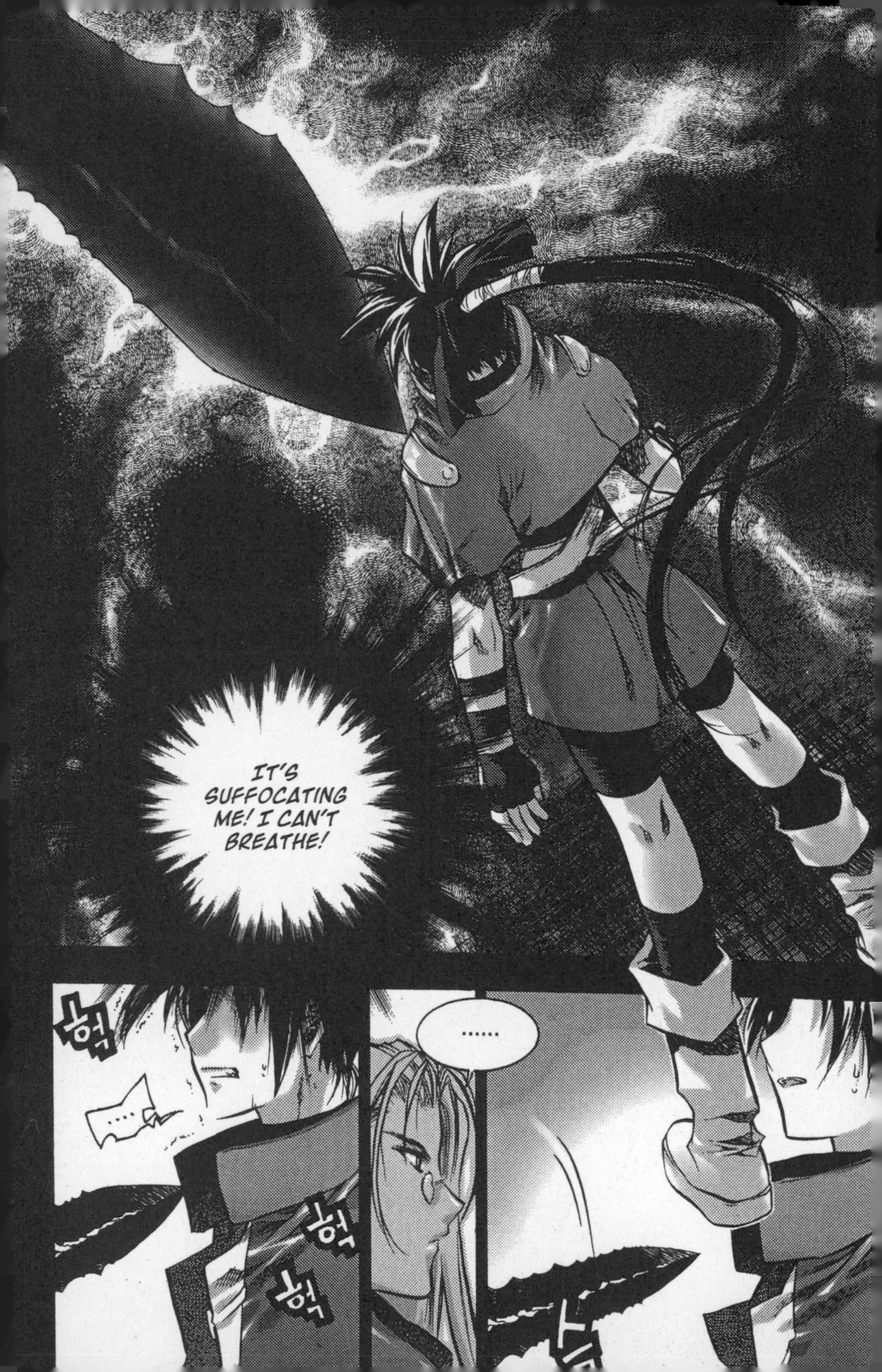
IT'S SUFFOCATING ME! I CAN'T BREATHE!
헉
....
헉
헉
......

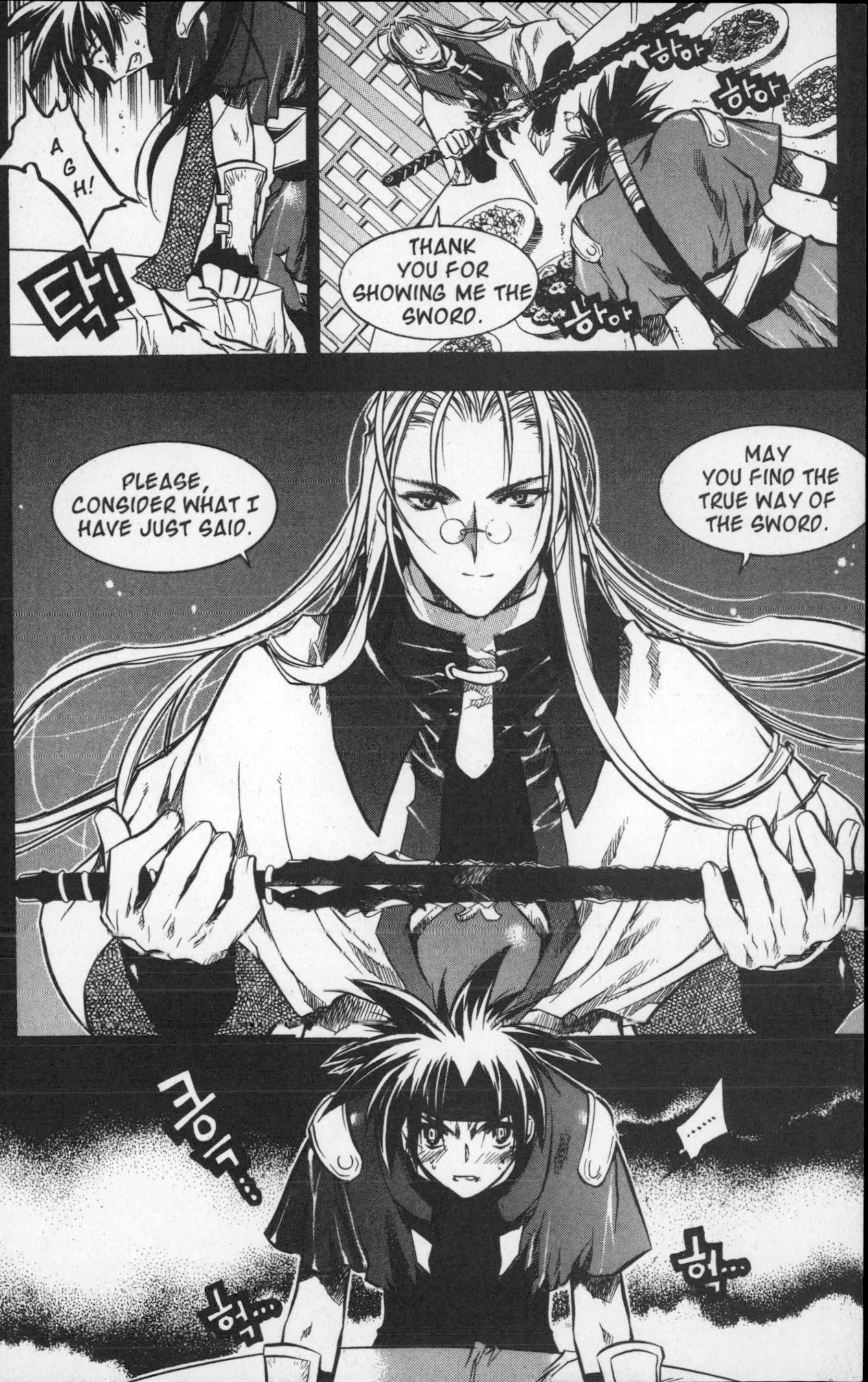

AGH!
탁!
하아
하아
THANK YOU FOR SHOWING ME THE SWORD.
하아
PLEASE, CONSIDER WHAT I HAVE JUST SAID.
MAY YOU FIND THE TRUE WAY OF THE SWORD.
......
헉...
헉...

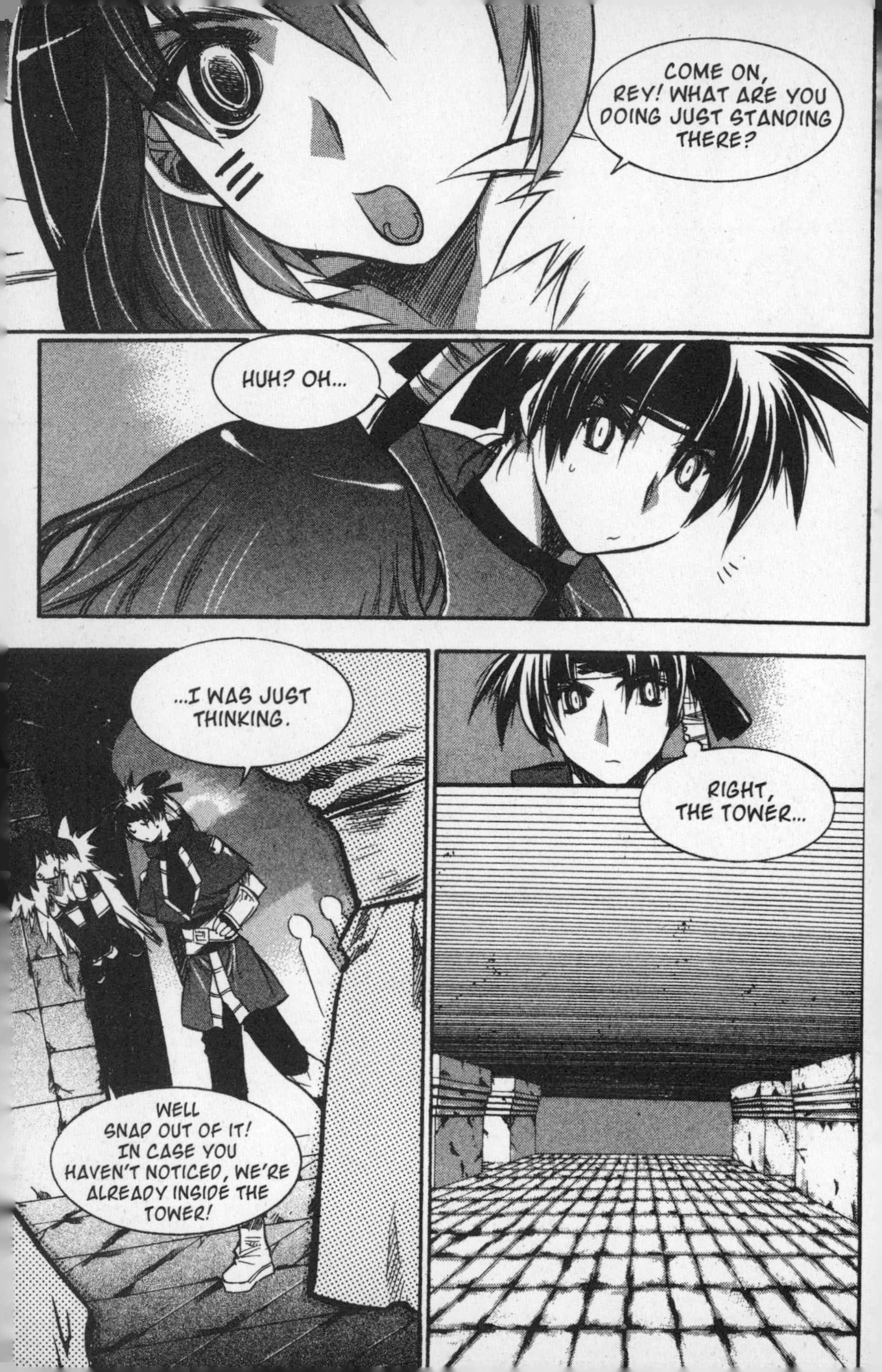
COME ON, REY! WHAT ARE YOU DOING JUST STANDING THERE?
HUH? OH...
...I WAS JUST THINKING.
WELL SNAP OUT OF IT! IN CASE YOU HAVEN'T NOTICED, WE'RE ALREADY INSIDE THE TOWER!
RIGHT, THE TOWER...

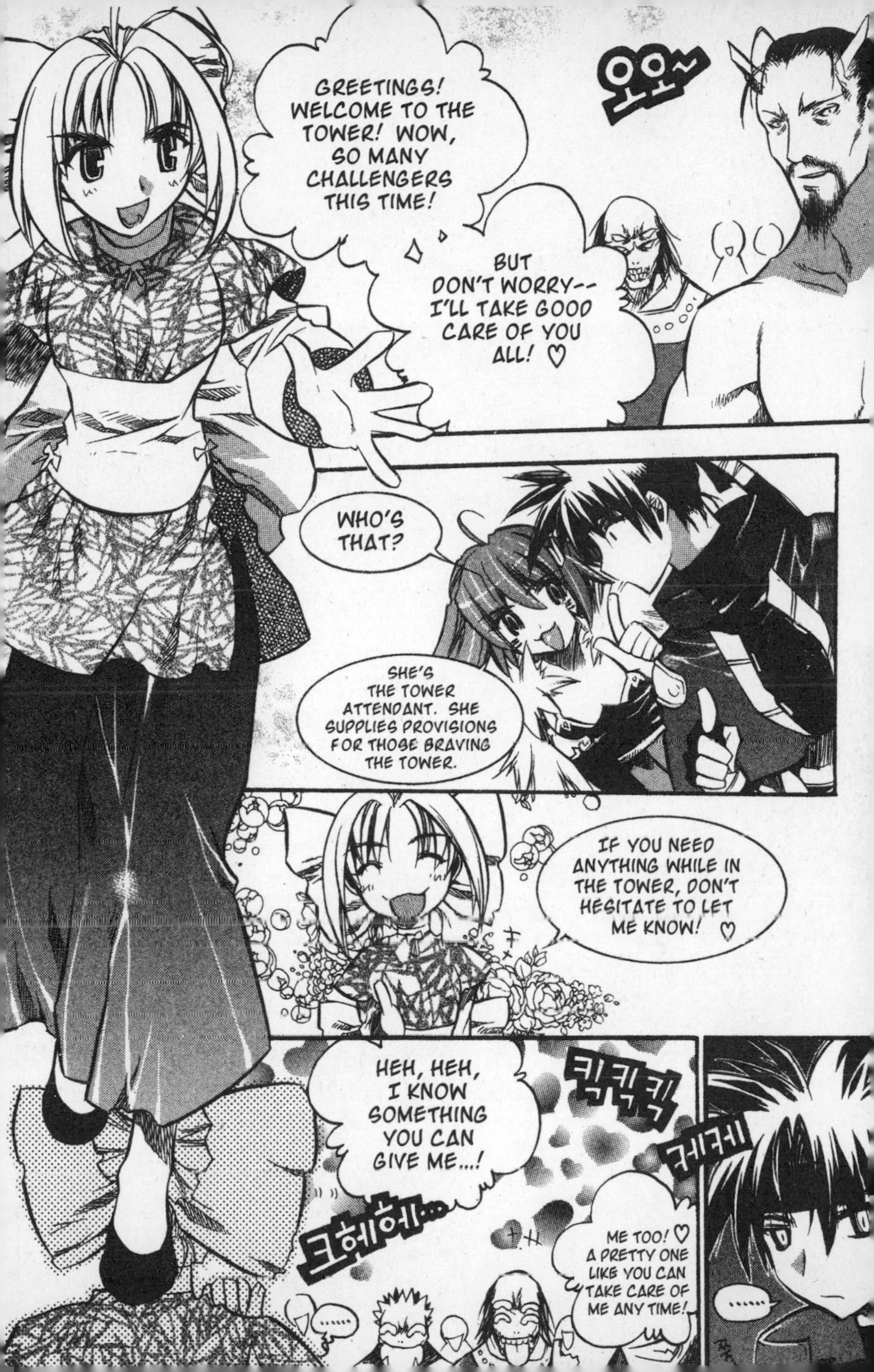
GREETINGS! WELCOME TO THE TOWER! WOW, SO MANY CHALLENGERS THIS TIME!
오오~
BUT DON'T WORRY-- I'LL TAKE GOOD CARE OF YOU ALL! ♡
WHO'S THAT?
SHE'S THE TOWER ATTENDANT. SHE SUPPLIES PROVISIONS FOR THOSE BRAVING THE TOWER.
IF YOU NEED ANYTHING WHILE IN THE TOWER, DON'T HESITATE TO LET ME KNOW! ♡
HEH, HEH, I KNOW SOMETHING YOU CAN GIVE ME...!
킥킥킥
크헤헤...
......
궤궤
ME TOO! ♡ A PRETTY ONE LIKE YOU CAN TAKE CARE OF ME ANY TIME!
......

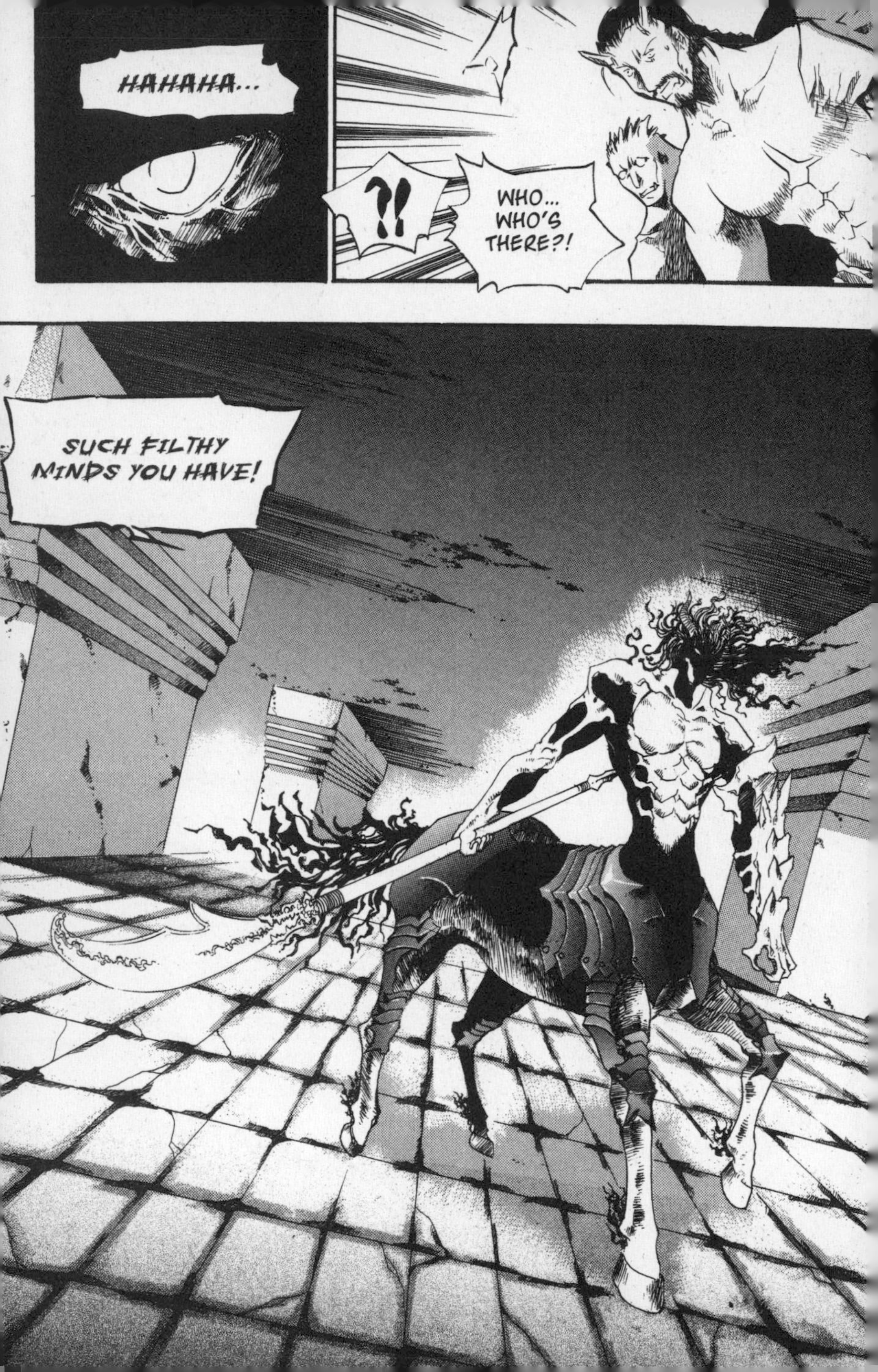
WHO... WHO'S THERE?!
?!
HAHAHA...
SUCH FILTHY MINDS YOU HAVE!

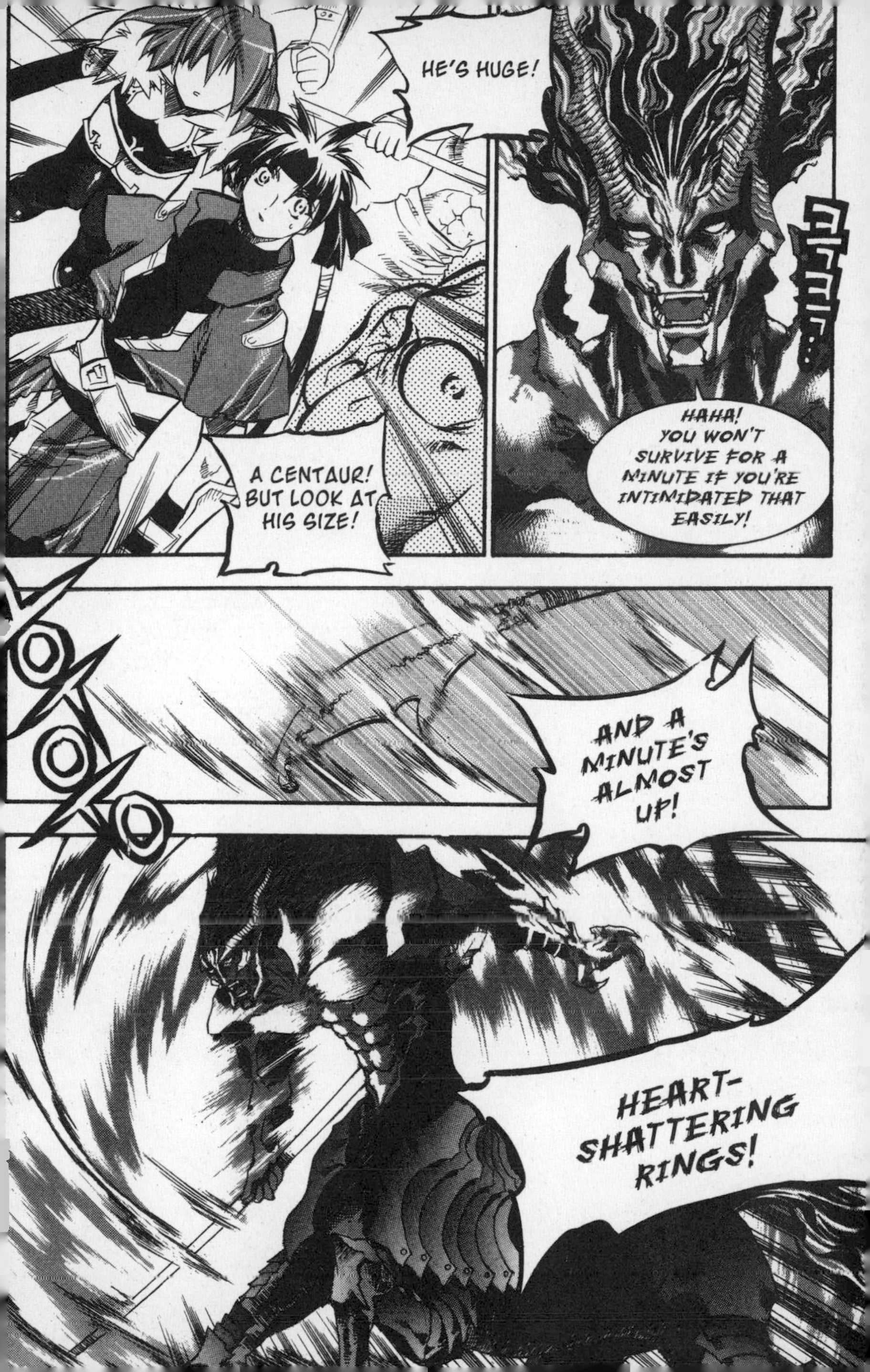
HE'S HUGE!
A CENTAUR! BUT LOOK AT HIS SIZE!
HAHA! YOU WON'T SURVIVE FOR A MINUTE IF YOU'RE INTIMIDATED THAT EASILY!
AND A MINUTE'S ALMOST UP!
HEART-SHATTERING RINGS!

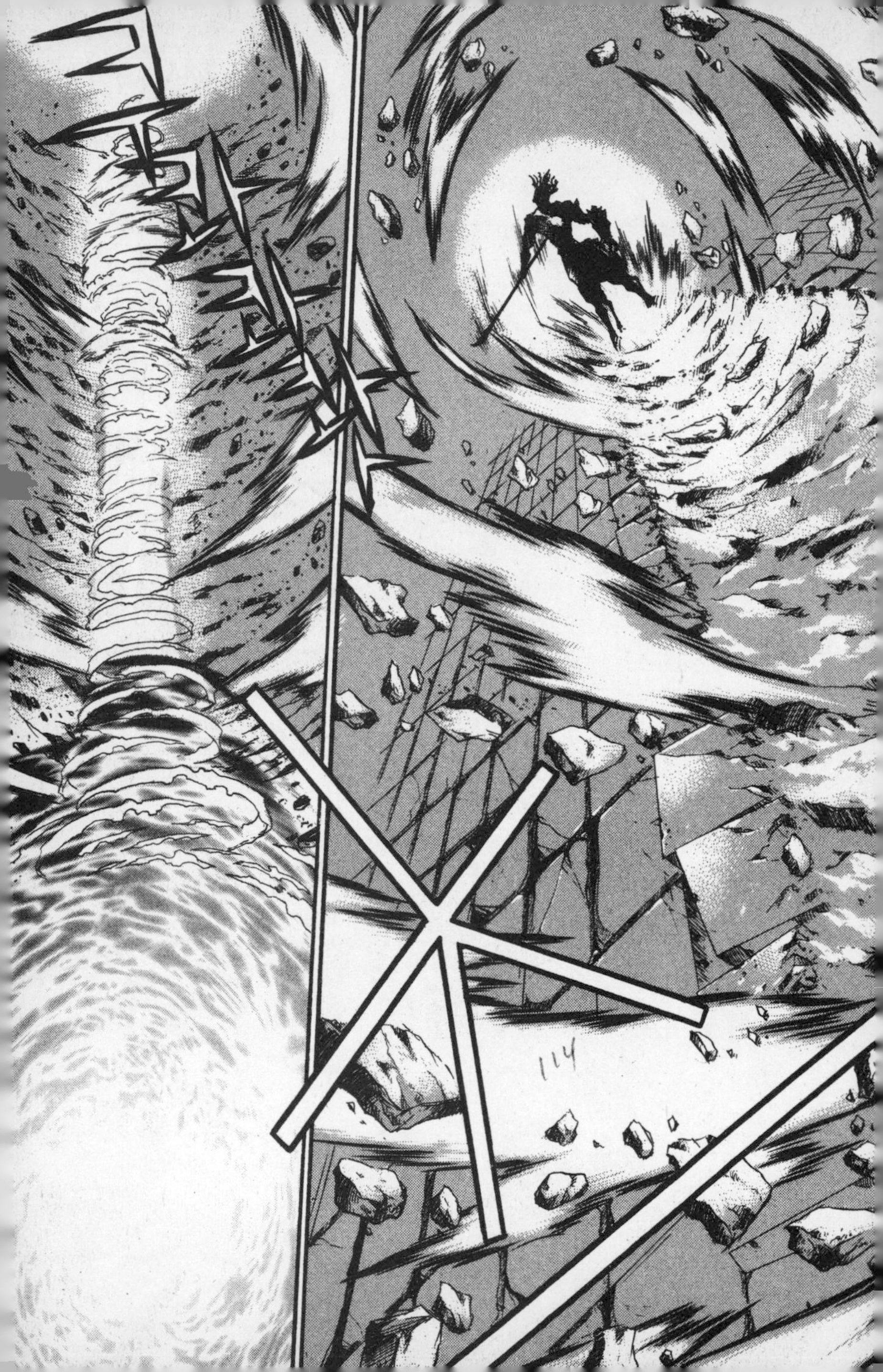

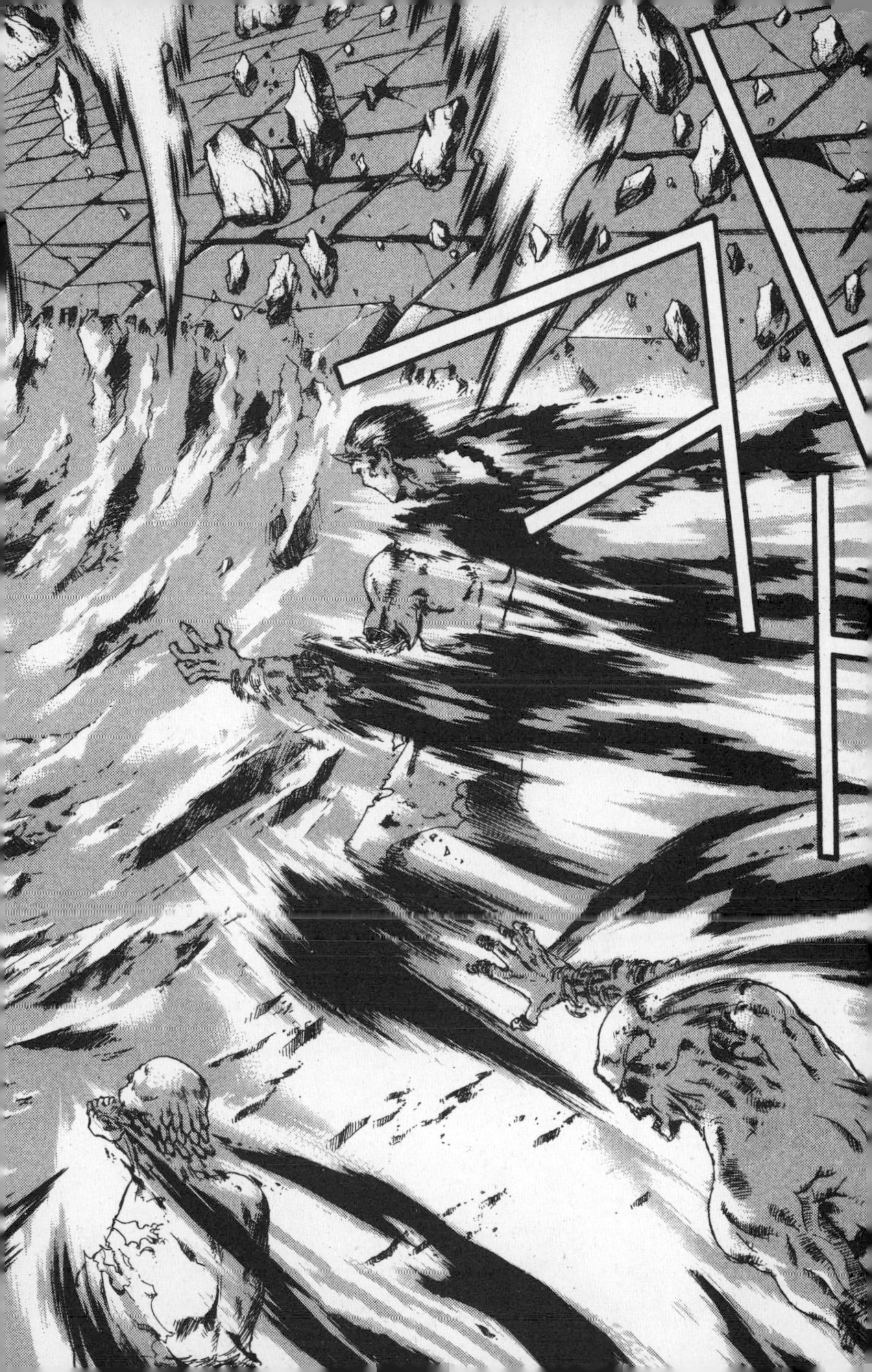

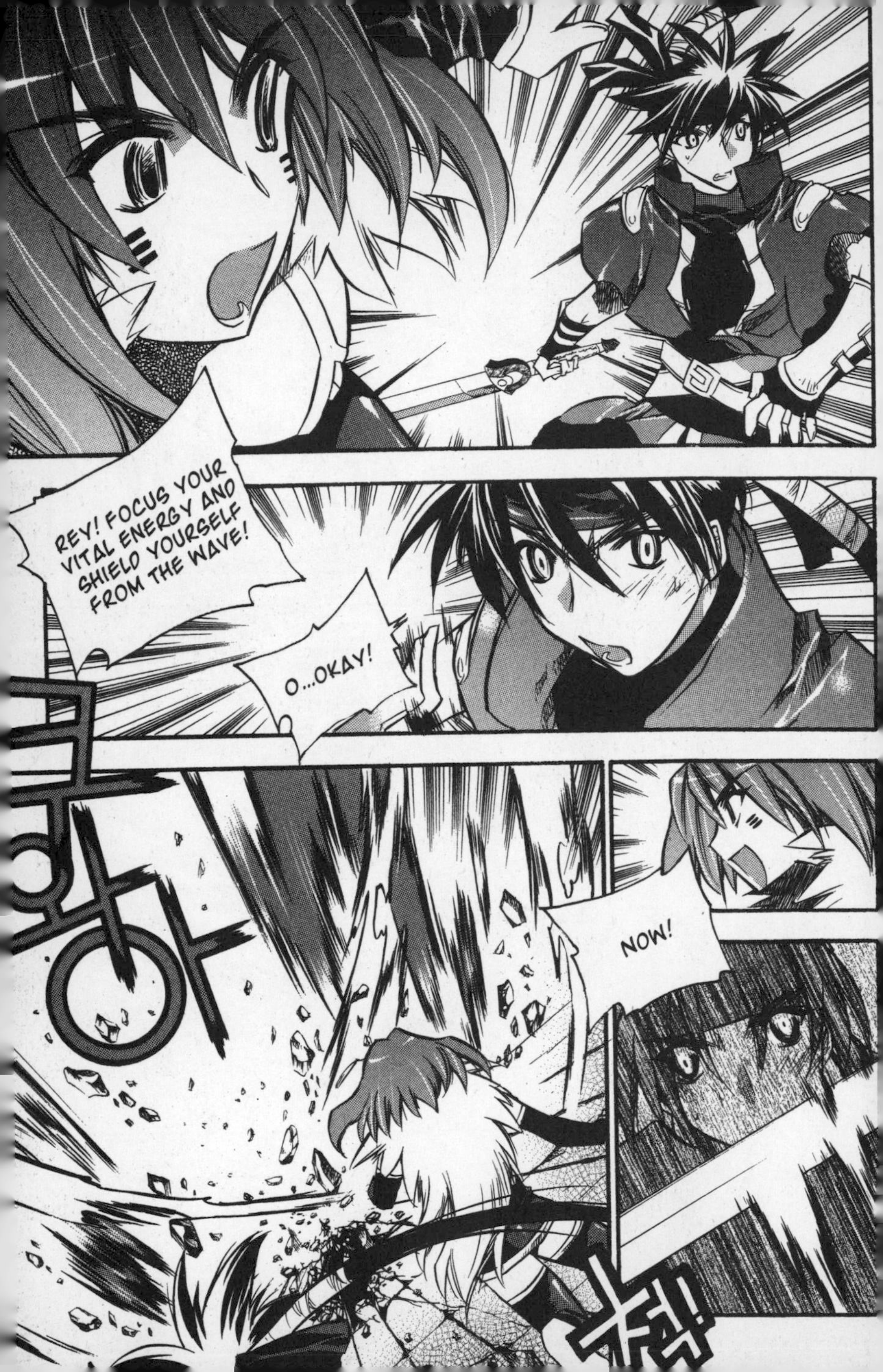
REY! FOCUS YOUR VITAL ENERGY AND SHIELD YOURSELF FROM THE WAVE!
O...OKAY!
NOW!

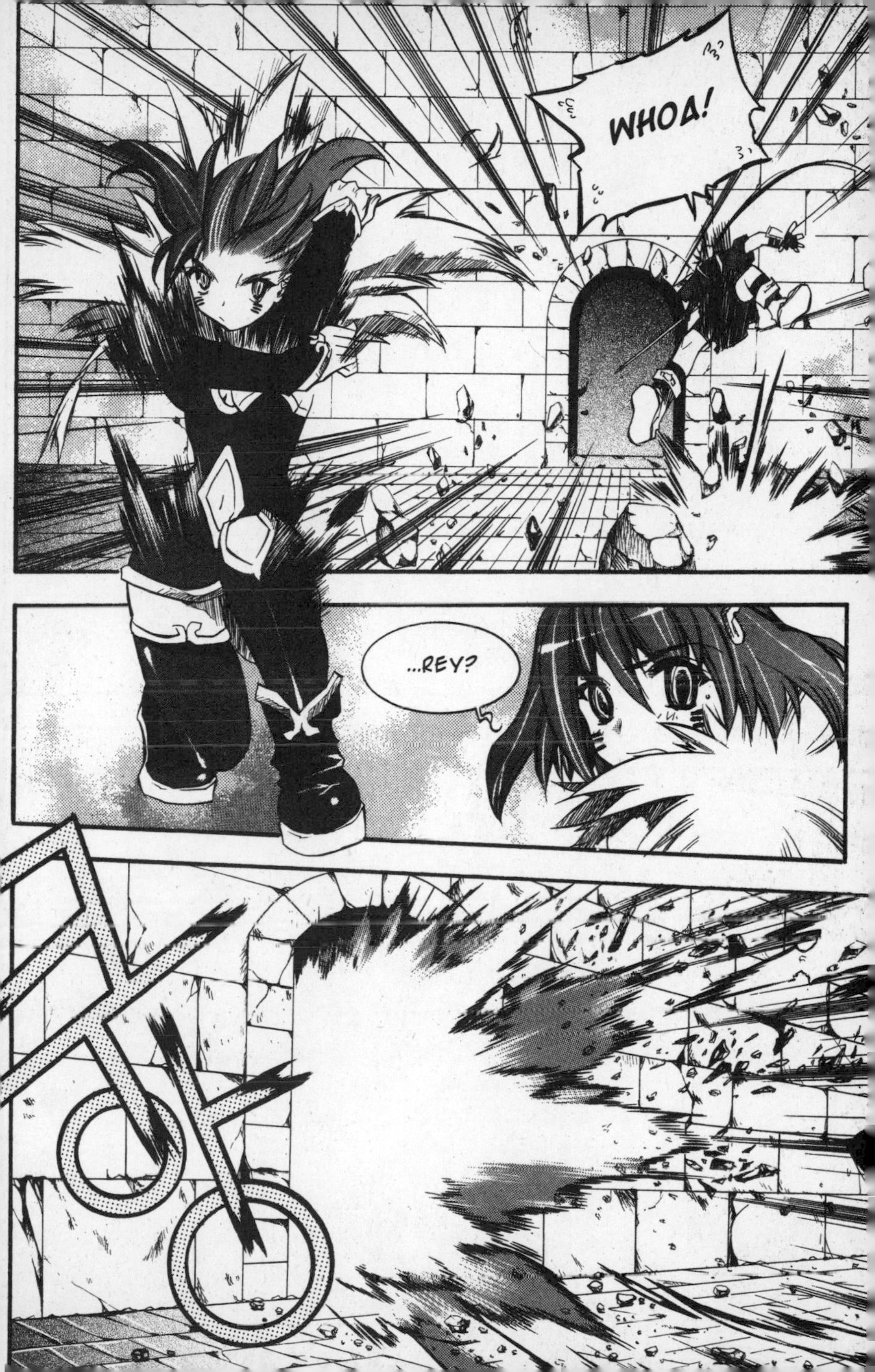
WHOA!
...REY?

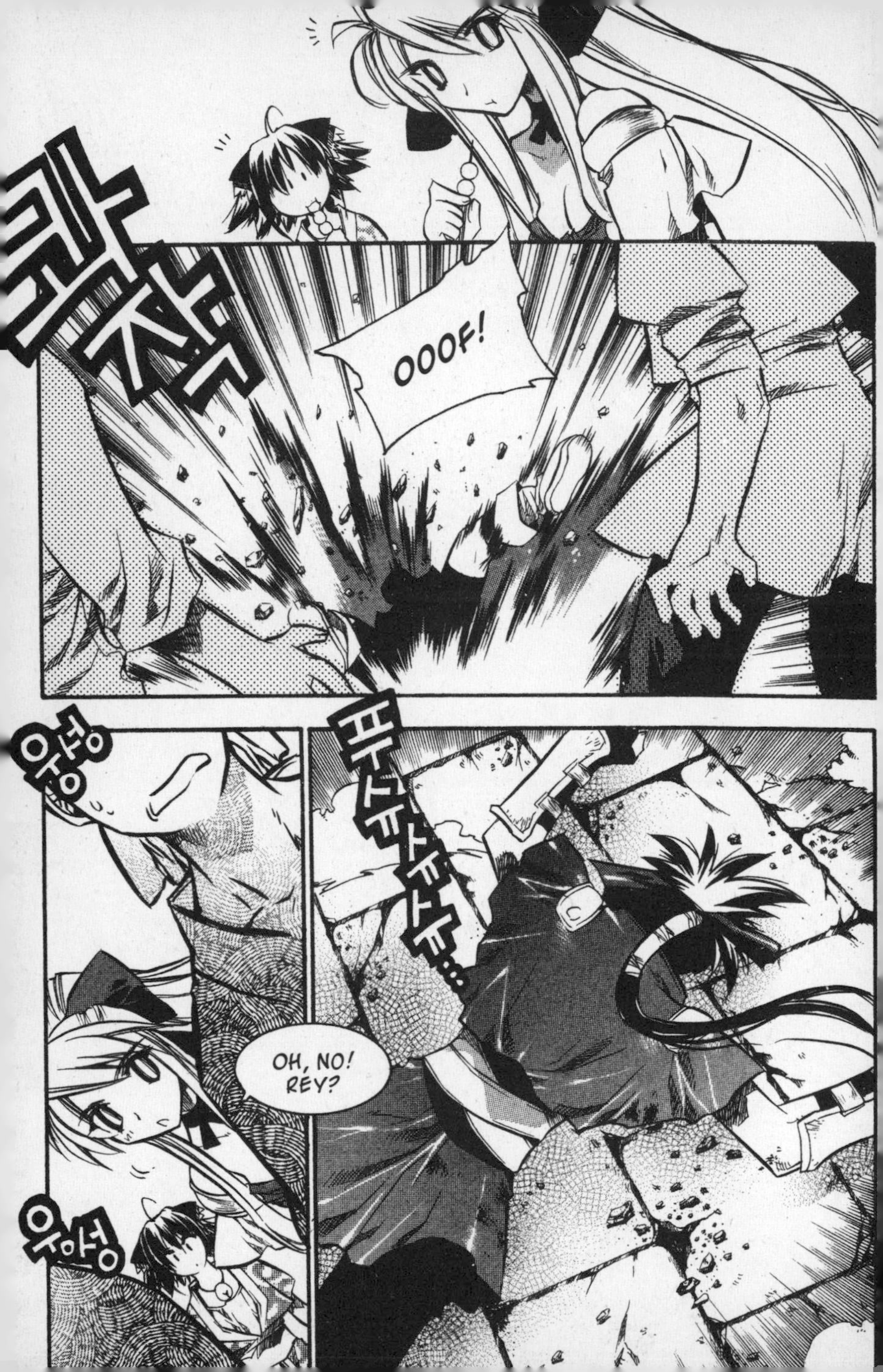
콰작
OOOF!
OH, NO! REY?

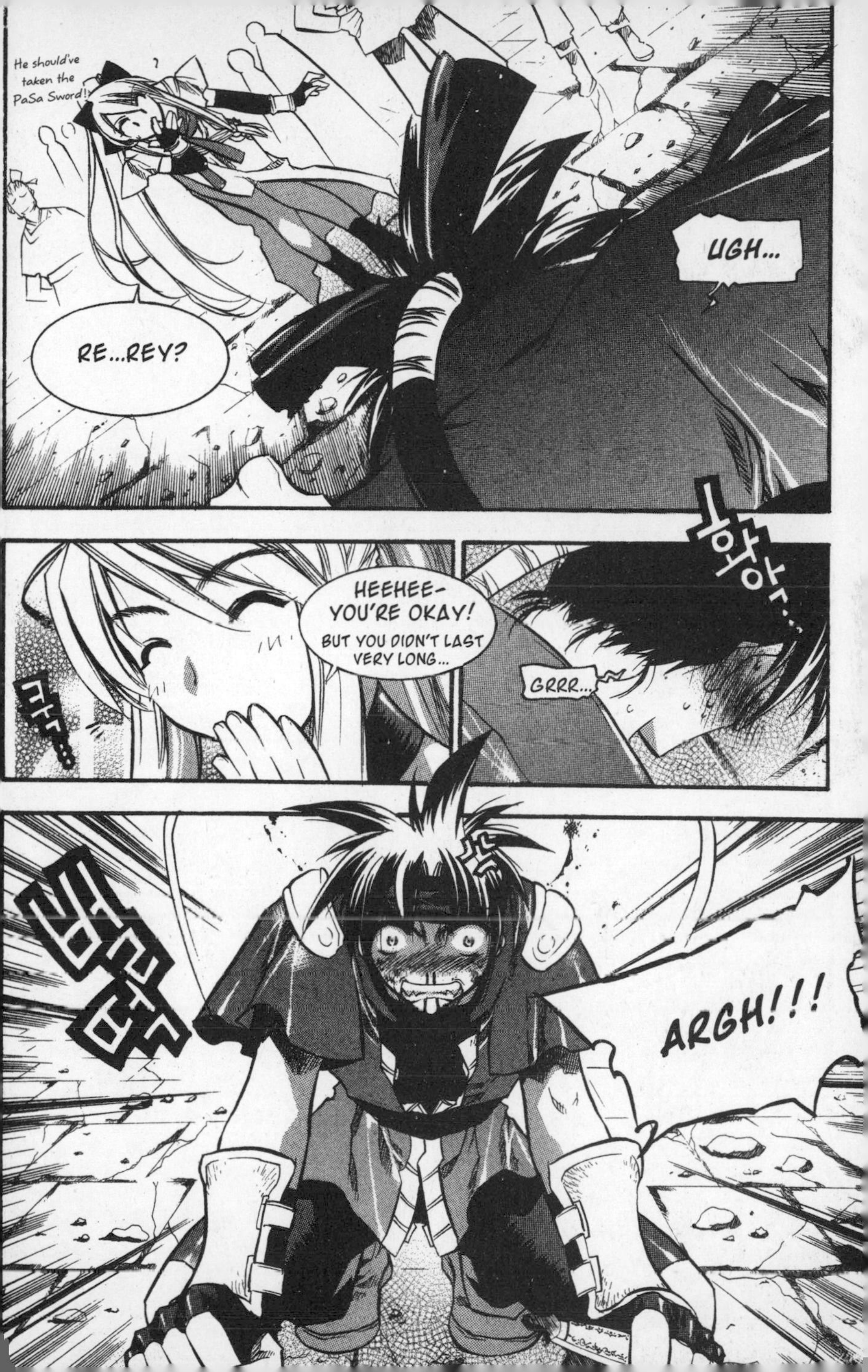
He should've taken the PaSa Sword!
RE...REY?
UGH...
HEEHEE- YOU'RE OKAY! BUT YOU DIDN'T LAST VERY LONG...
GRRR...
ARGH!!!

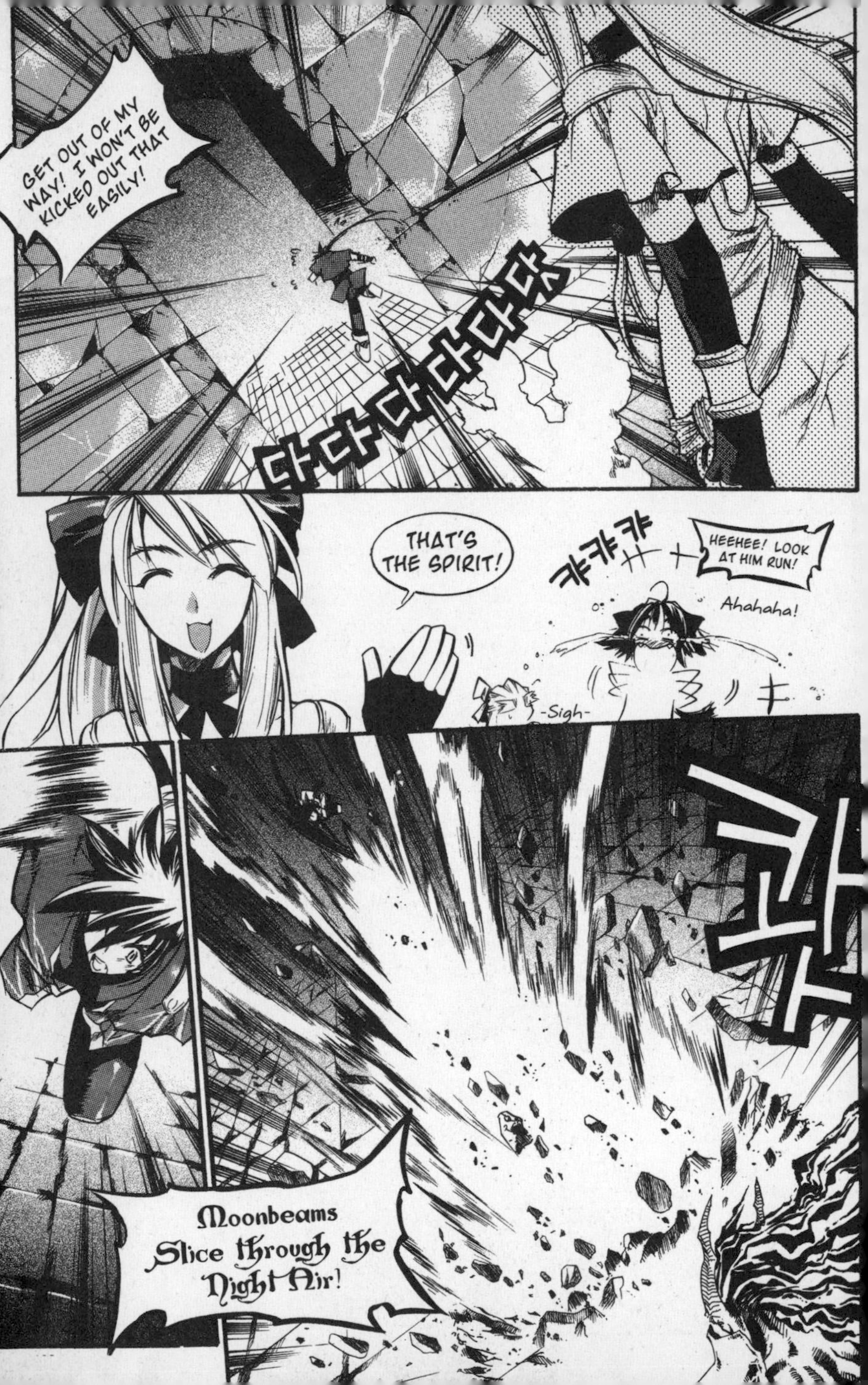
GET OUT OF MY WAY! I WON'T BE KICKED OUT THAT EASILY!
THAT'S THE SPIRIT!
HEEHEE! LOOK AT HIM RUN!
Ahahaha!
-Sigh-
Moonbeams Slice through the Night Air!

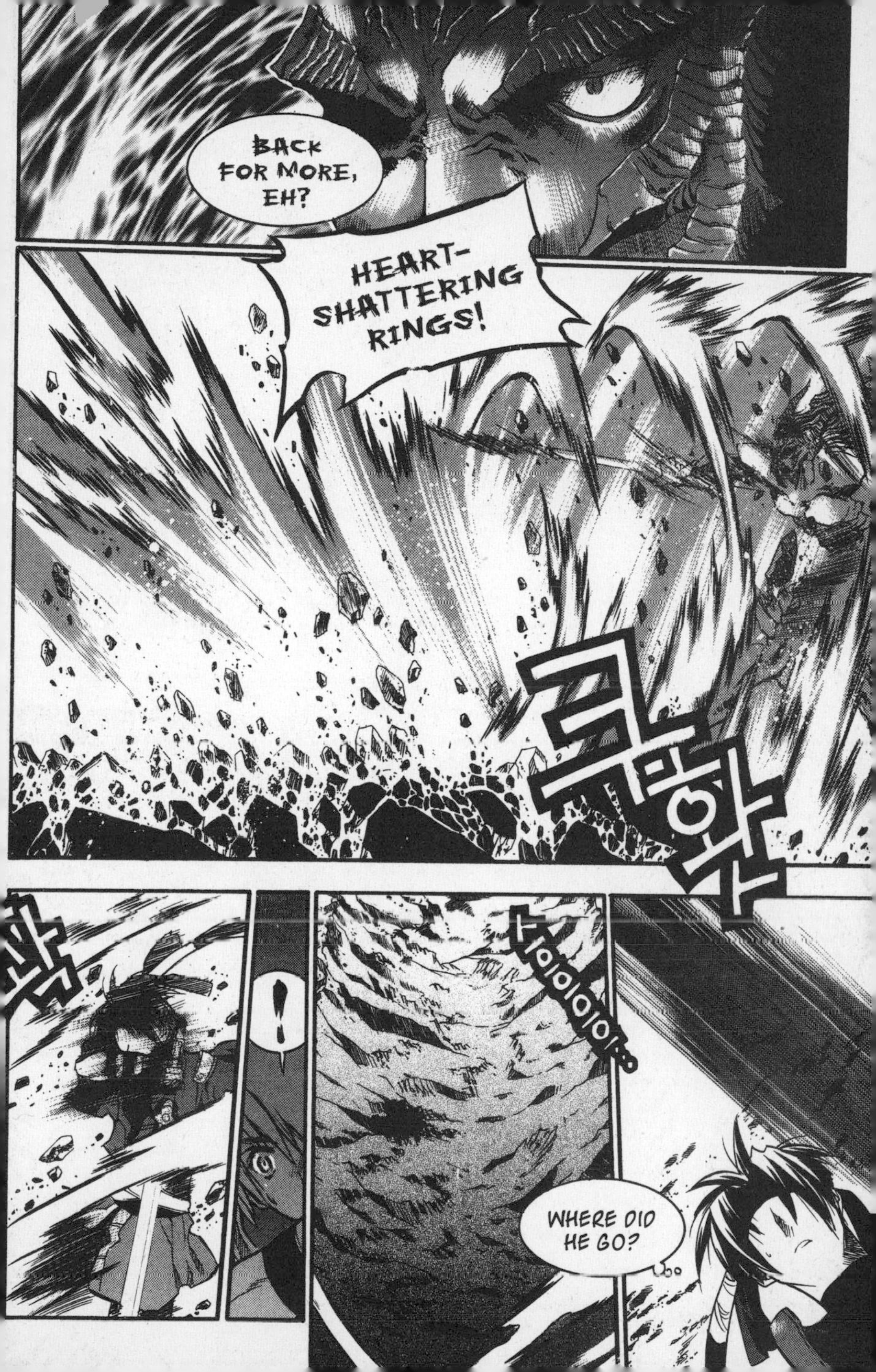
BACK FOR MORE, EH?
HEART-SHATTERING RINGS!
!
WHERE DID HE GO?

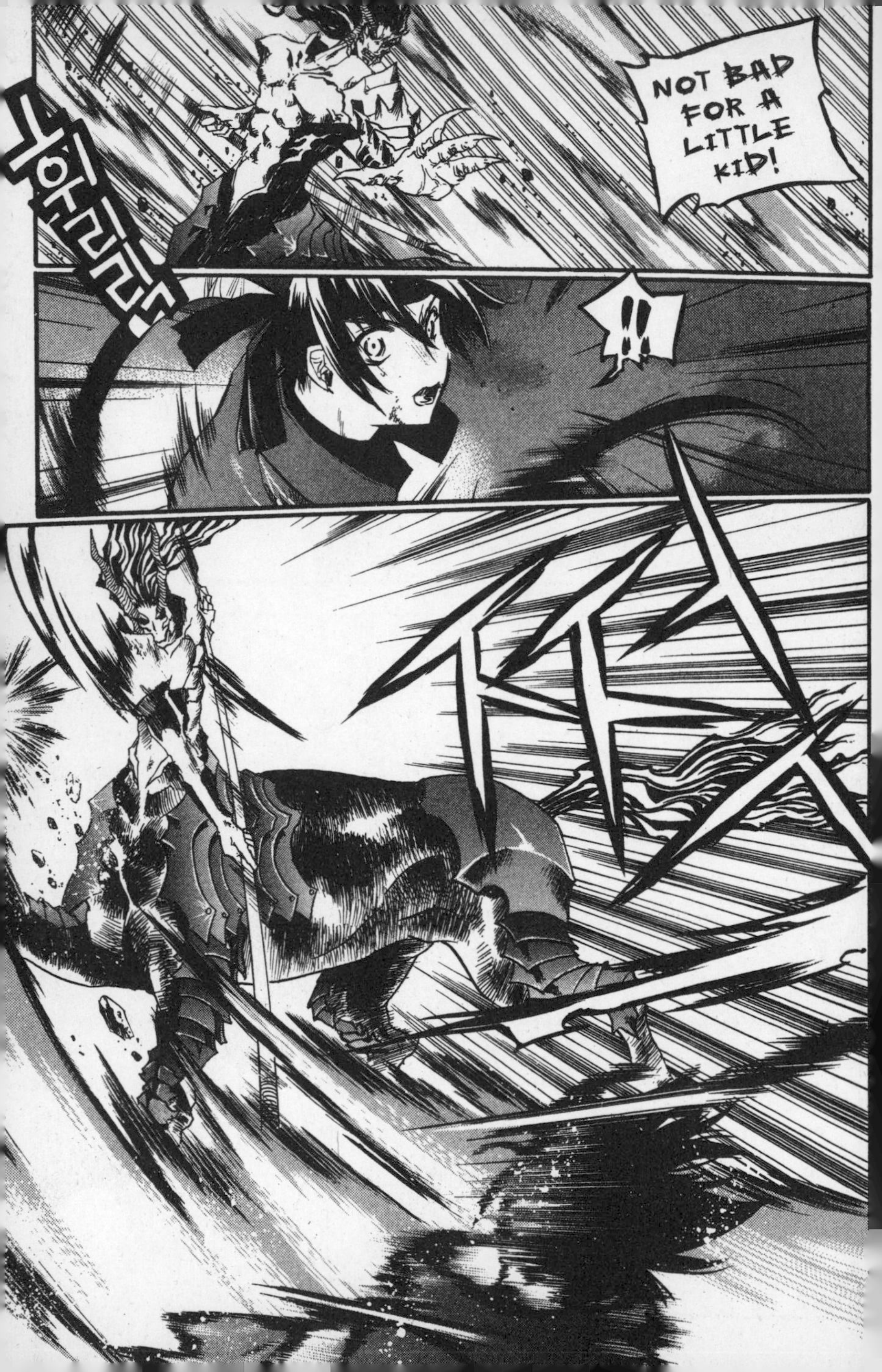
NOT BAD FOR A LITTLE KID!
!!

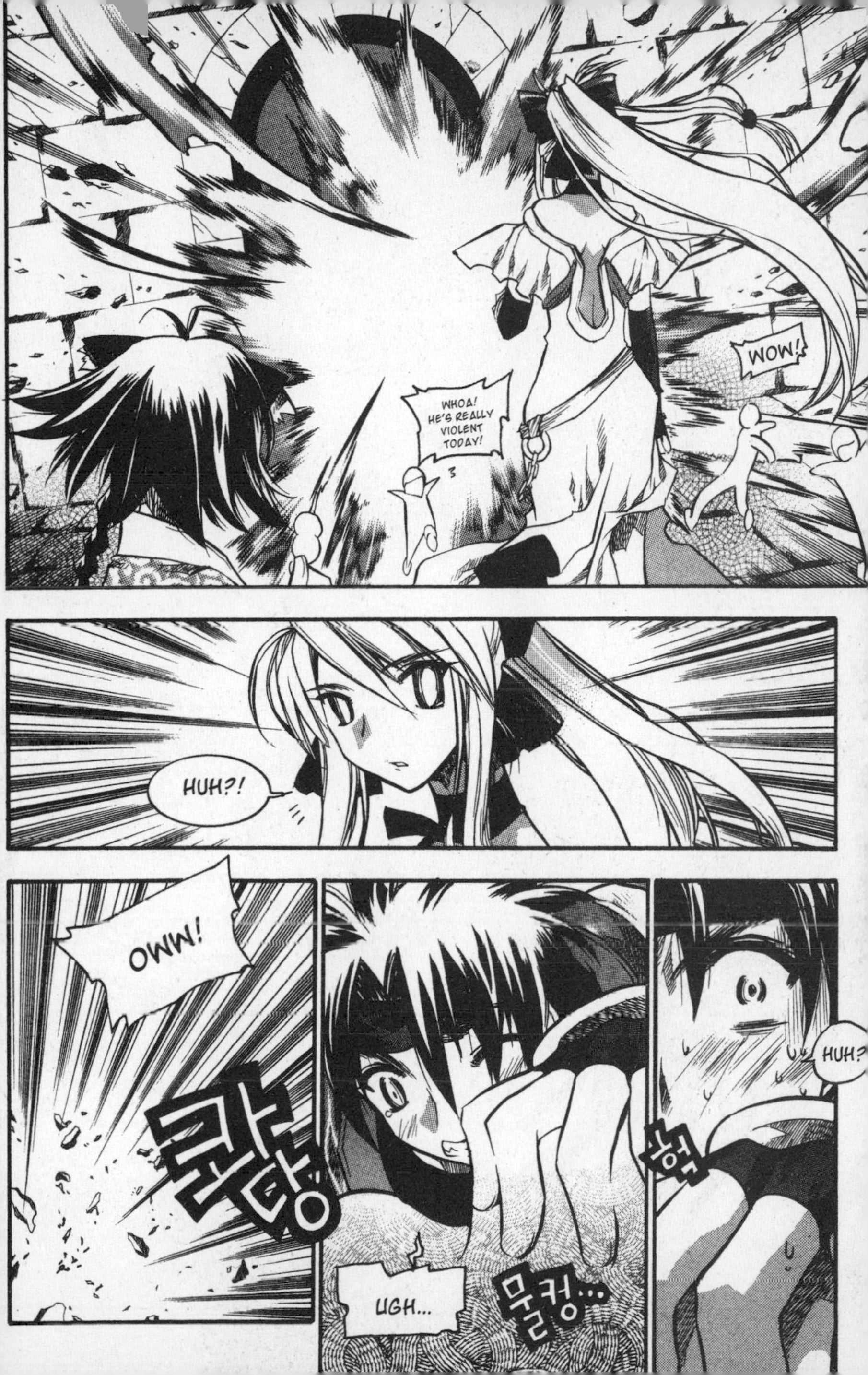
WHOA! HE'S REALLY VIOLENT TODAY!
WOW!
HUH?!
OWW!
콰당
UGH...
물컹...
헉
HUH?

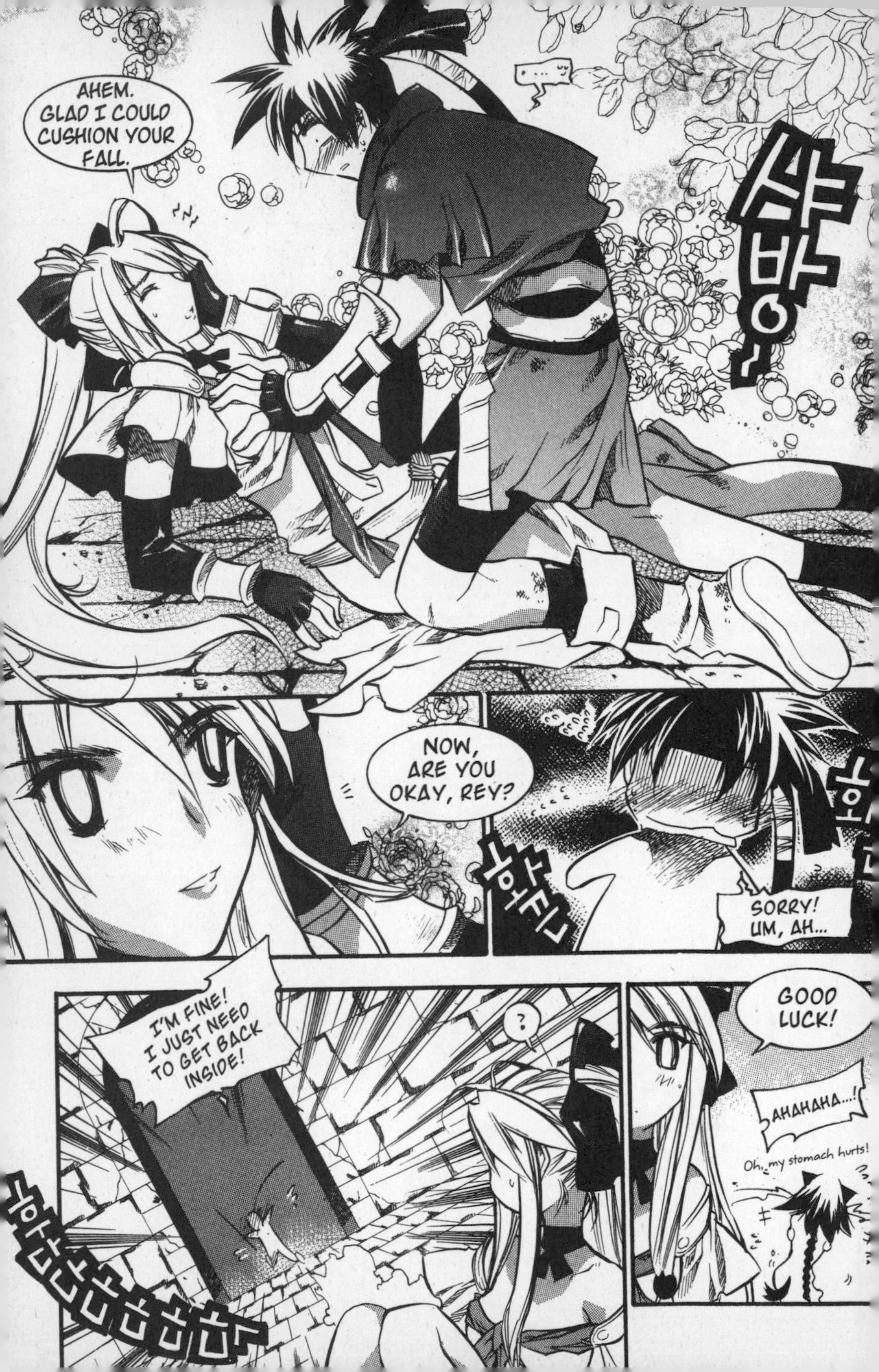
AHEM. GLAD I COULD CUSHION YOUR FALL.
NOW, ARE YOU OKAY, REY?
SORRY! UM, AH...
I'M FINE! I JUST NEED TO GET BACK INSIDE!
?
GOOD LUCK!
AHAHAHA...!
Oh, my stomach hurts!

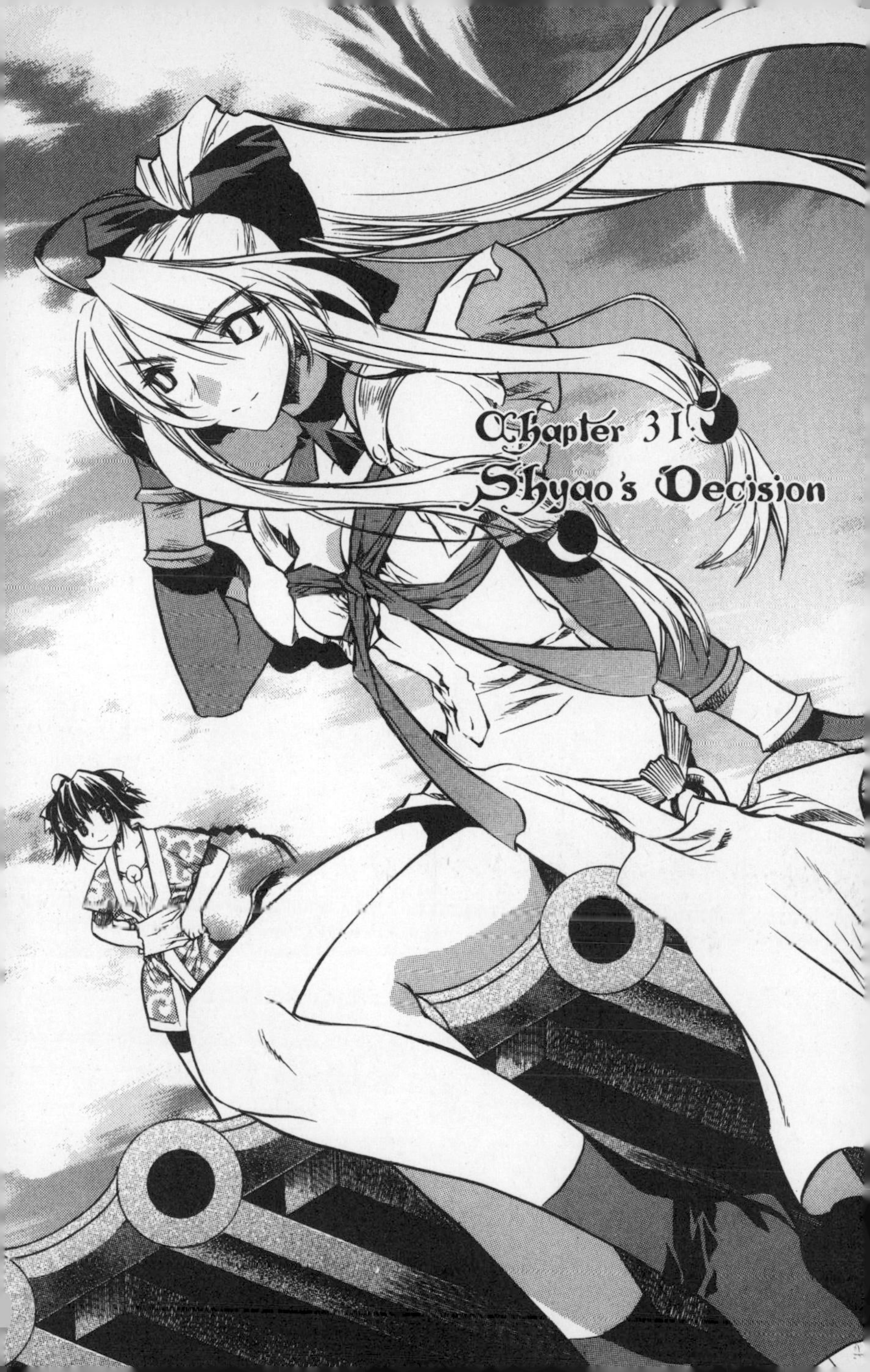
Chapter 31:
Shyao's Decision

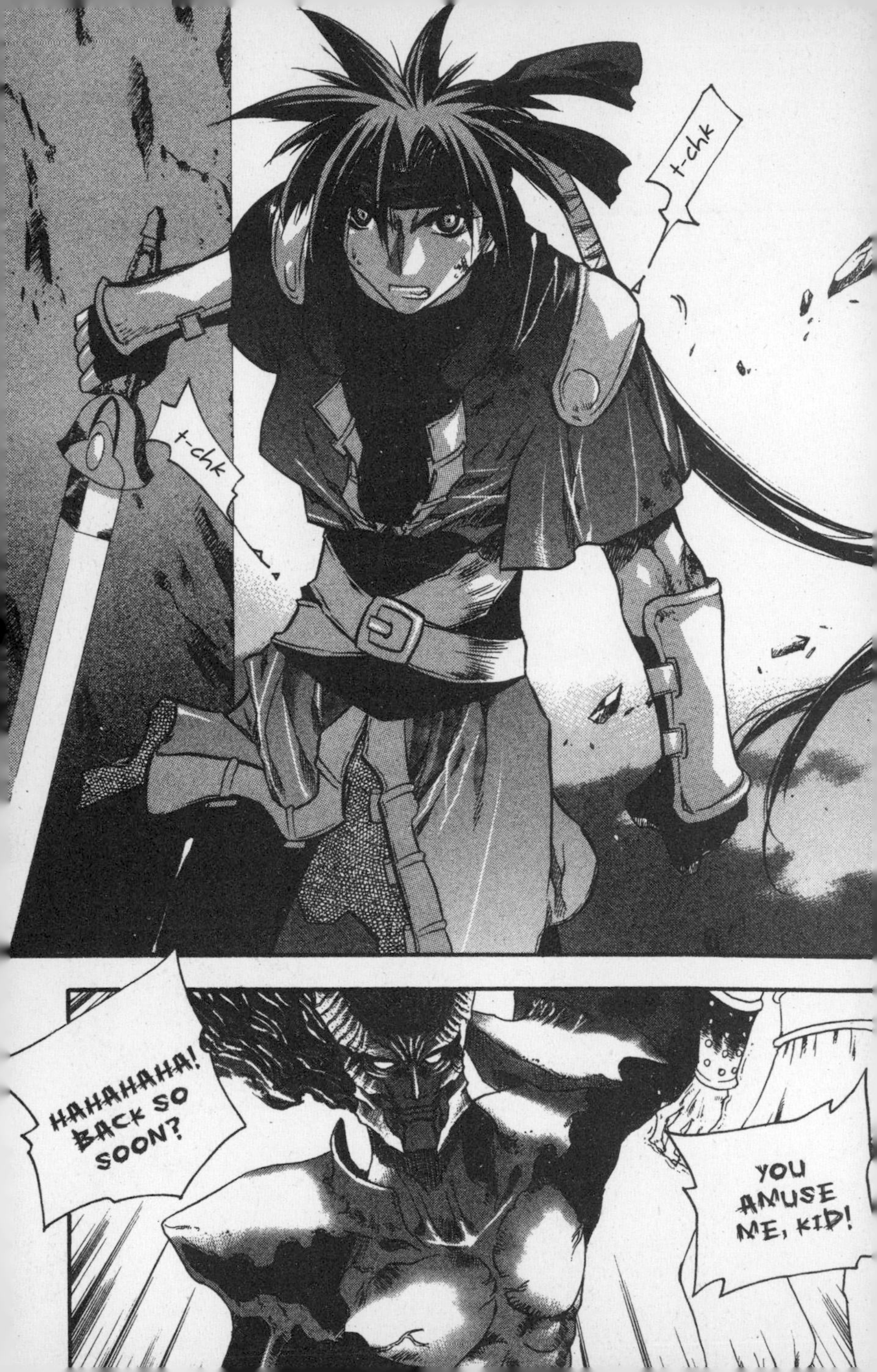
t-chk
t-chk
HAHAHAHA! BACK SO SOON?
YOU AMUSE ME, KID!

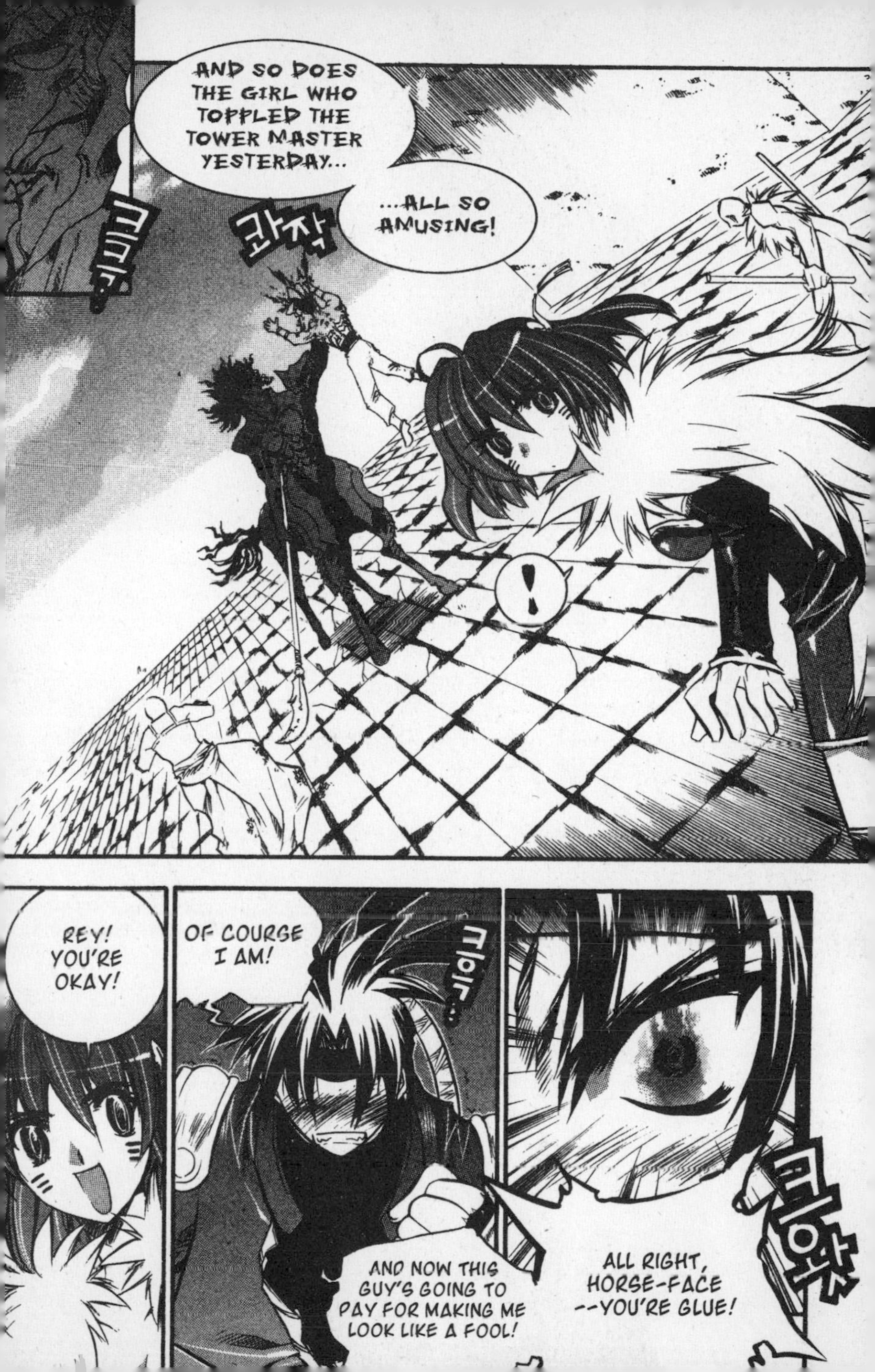
AND SO DOES THE GIRL WHO TOPPLED THE TOWER MASTER YESTERDAY...
콰작
...ALL SO AMUSING!
REY! YOU'RE OKAY!
OF COURSE I AM!
AND NOW THIS GUY'S GOING TO PAY FOR MAKING ME LOOK LIKE A FOOL!
ALL RIGHT, HORSE-FACE --YOU'RE GLUE!

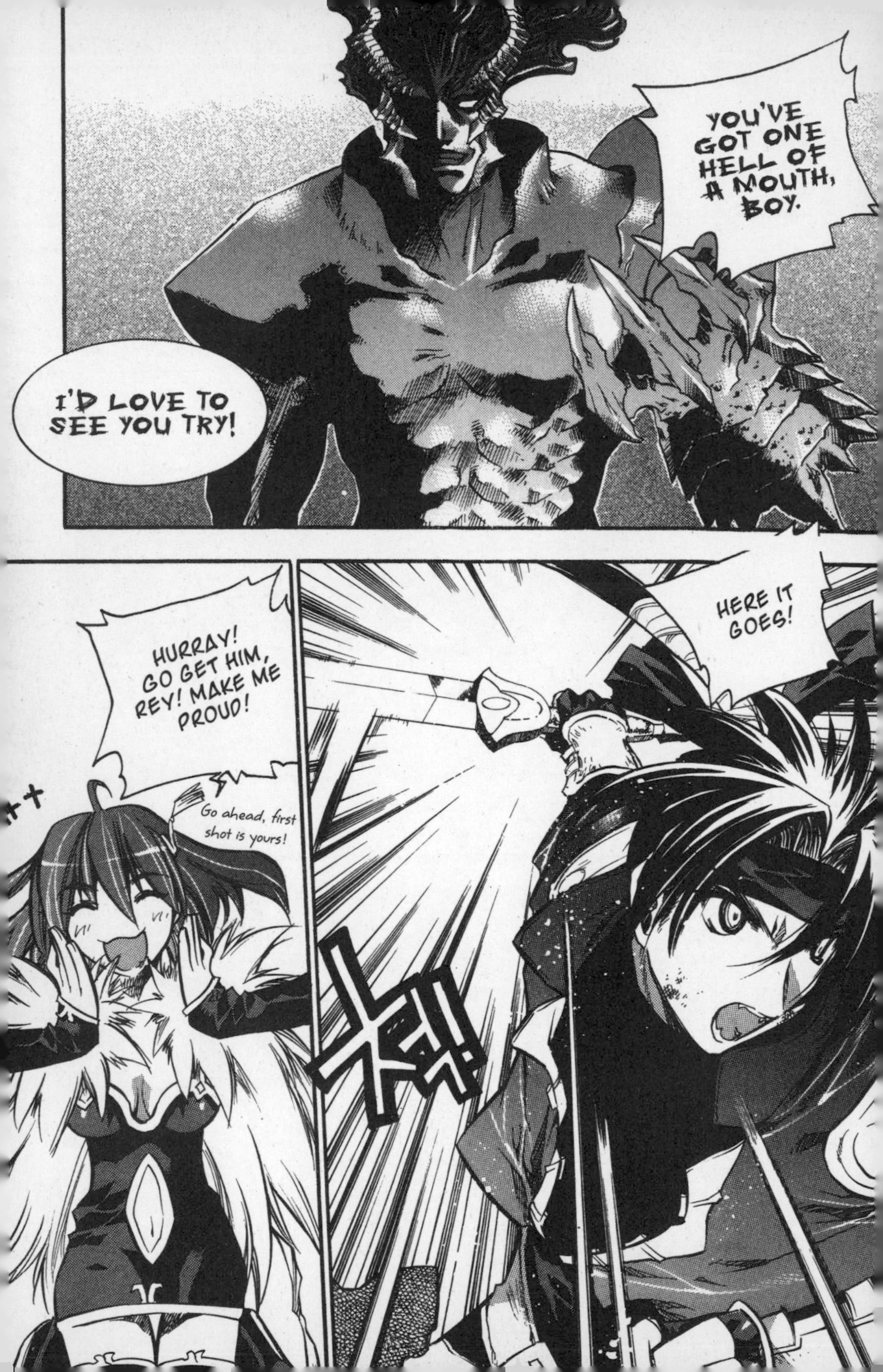
YOU'VE GOT ONE HELL OF A MOUTH, BOY.
I'D LOVE TO SEE YOU TRY!
HURRAY! GO GET HIM, REY! MAKE ME PROUD!
Go ahead, first shot is yours!
HERE IT GOES!

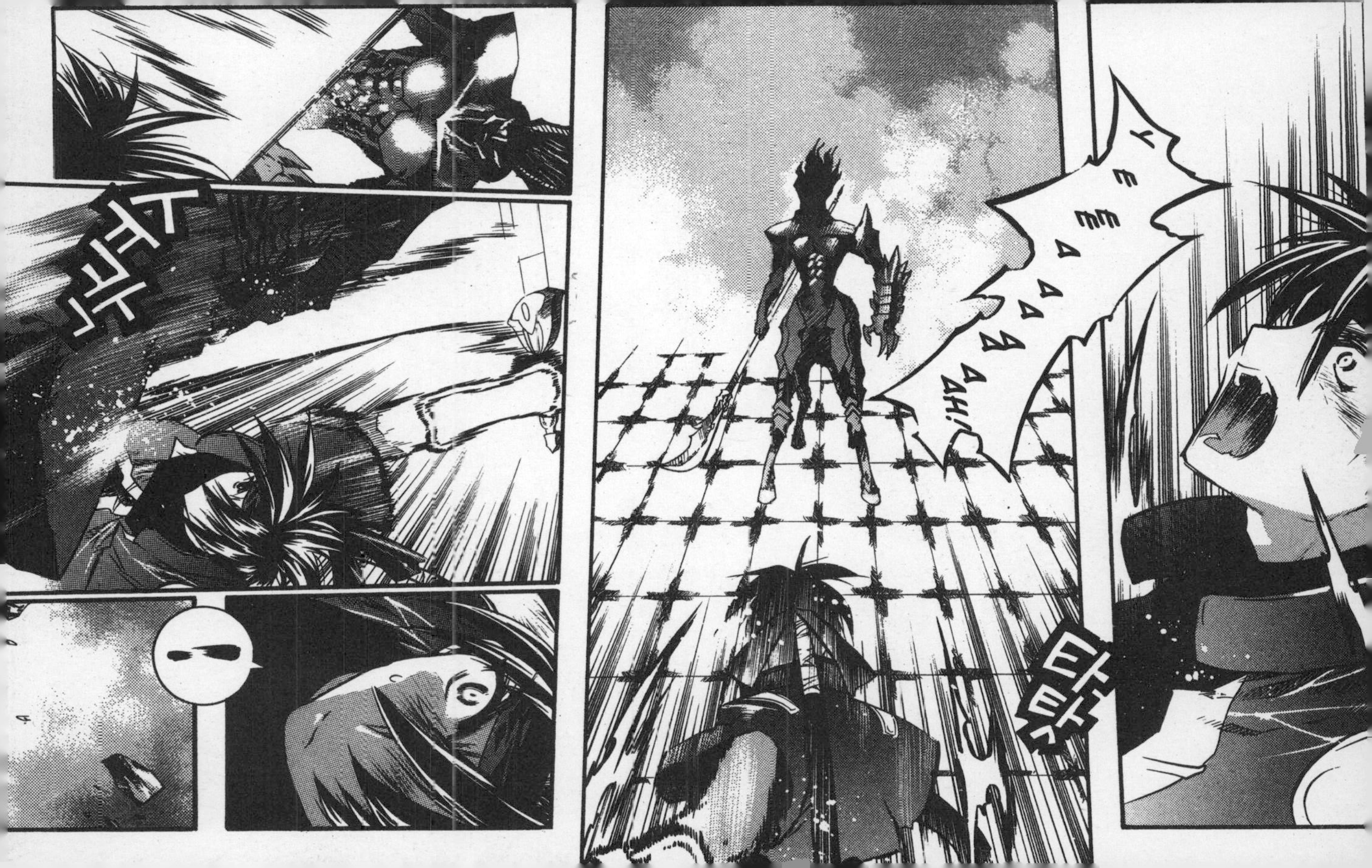
!
YEEEAAAAAAH!
타탓

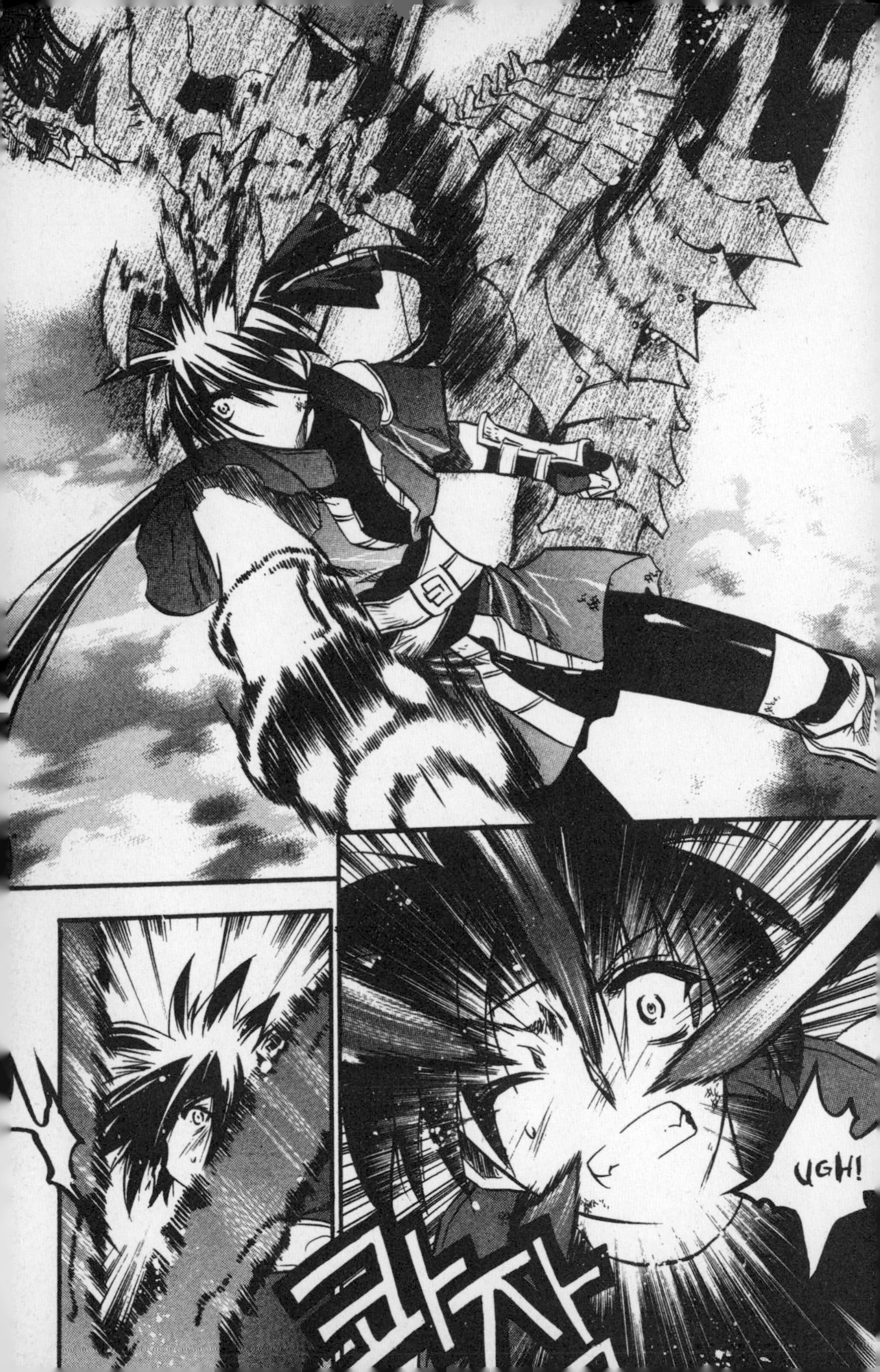
UGH!
콰직

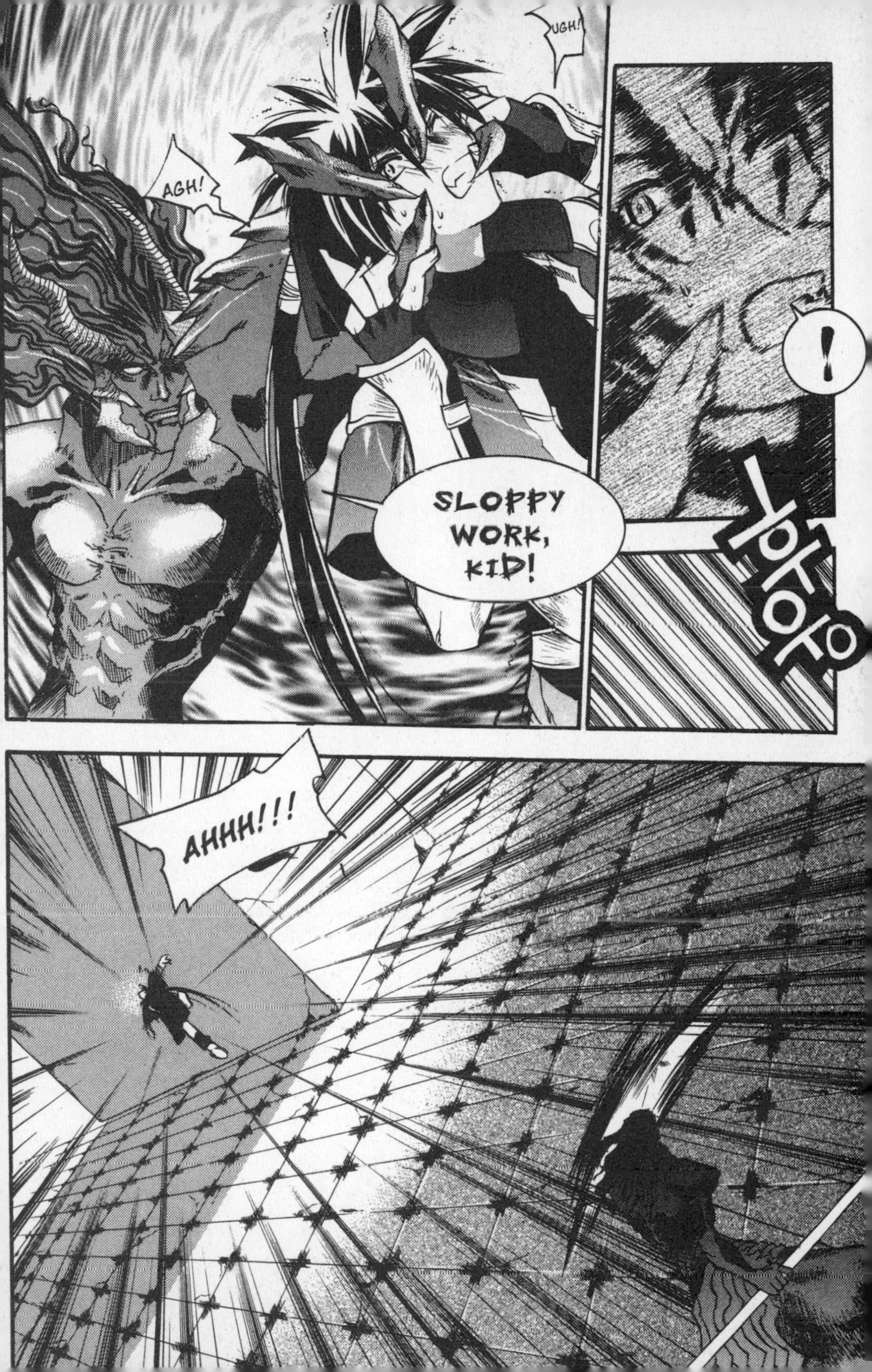
UGH!
AGH!
SLOPPY WORK, KID!
!
AHHH!!!

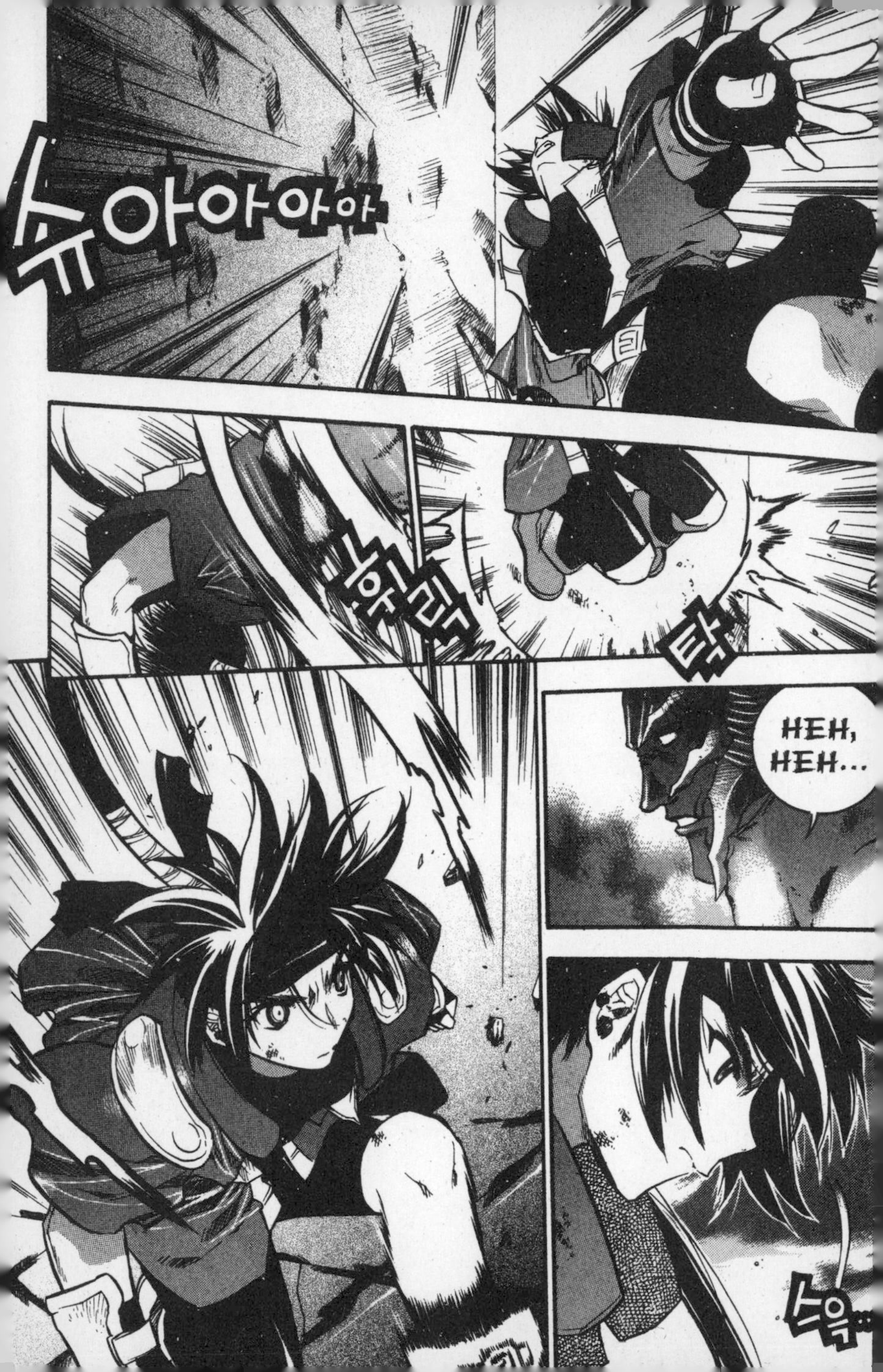
슈아아아아아
탁
HEH, HEH...
스윽...

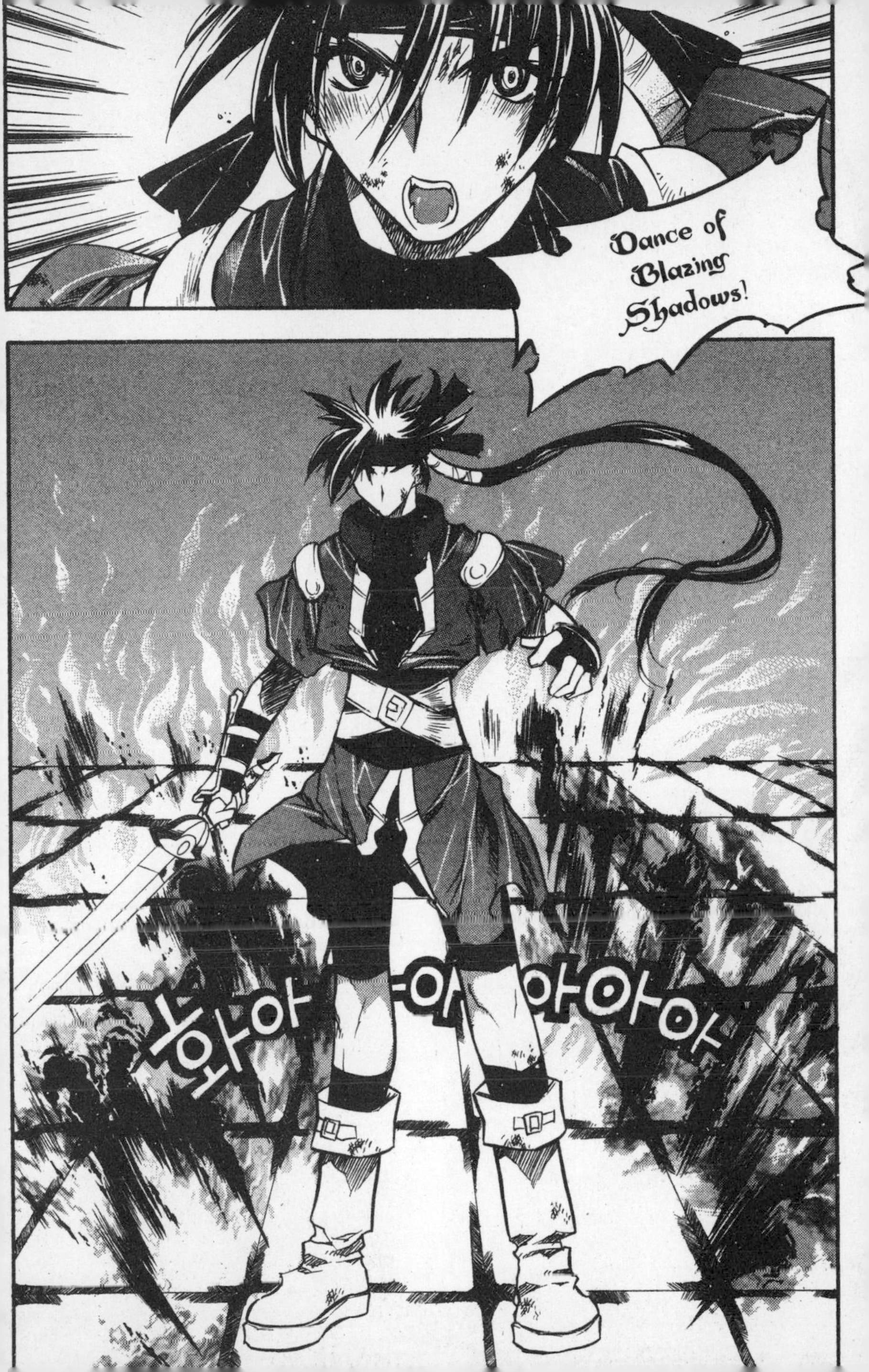
Dance of Blazing Shadows!

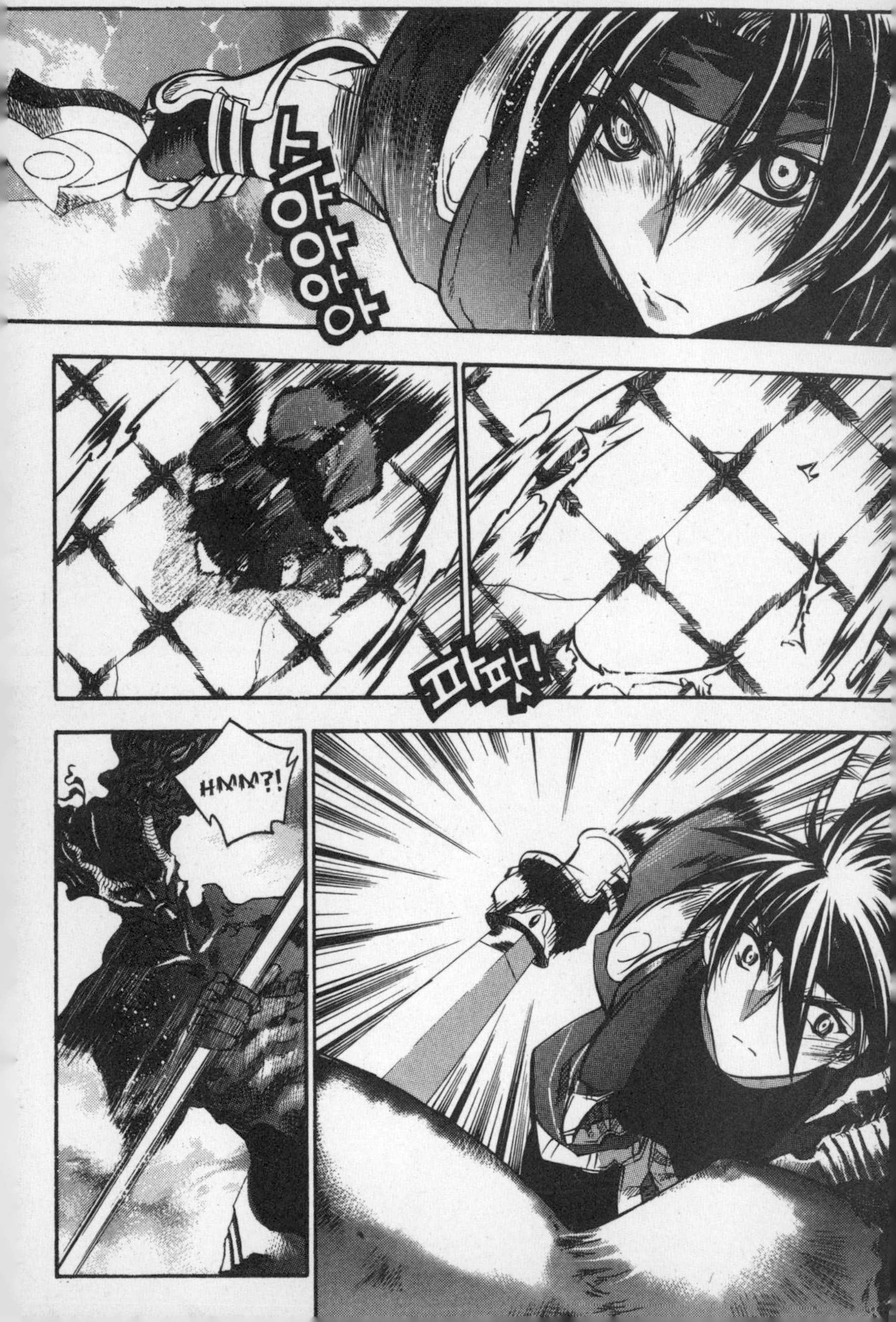
사아아아아
파팟!
HMM?!

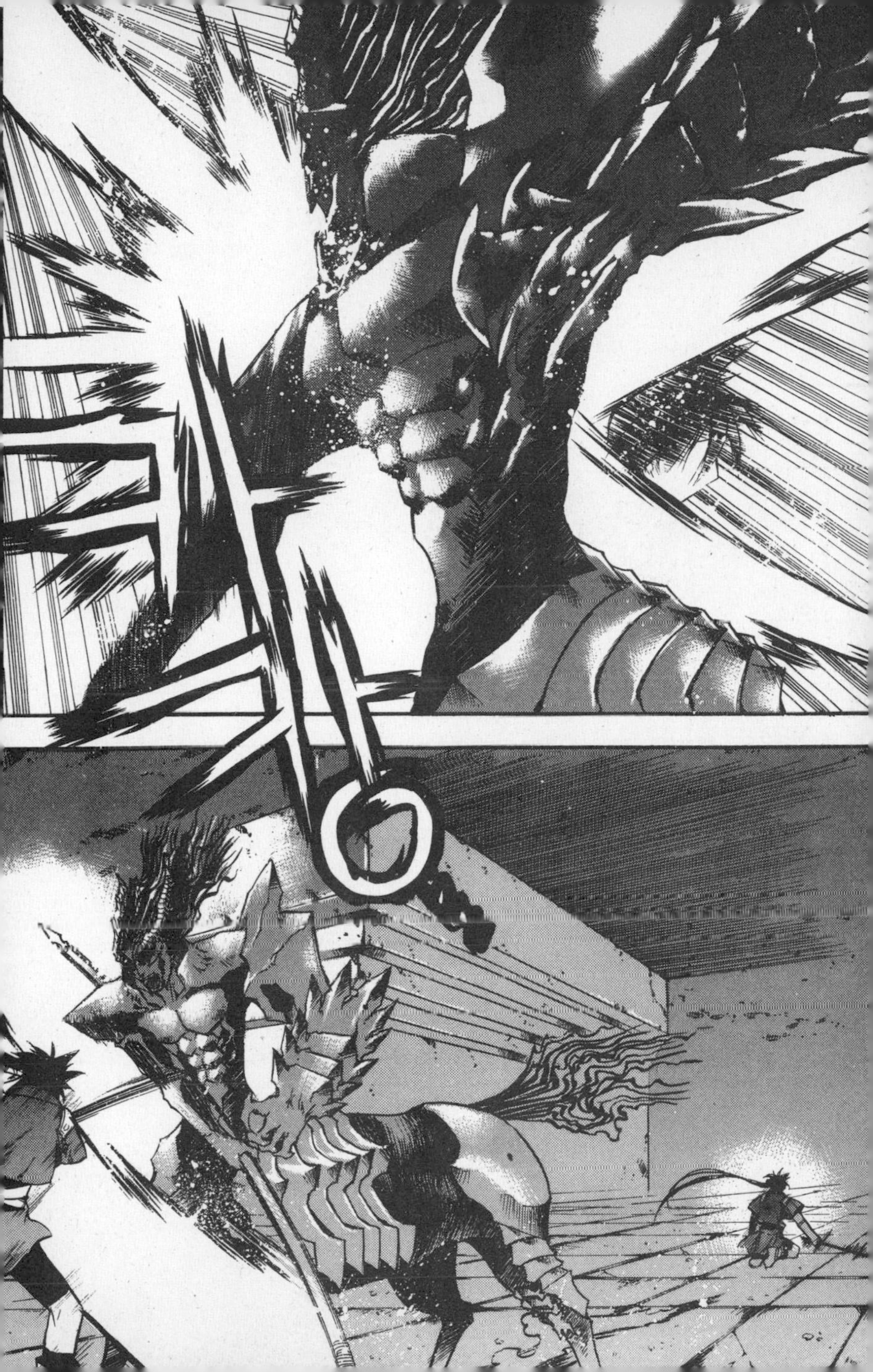

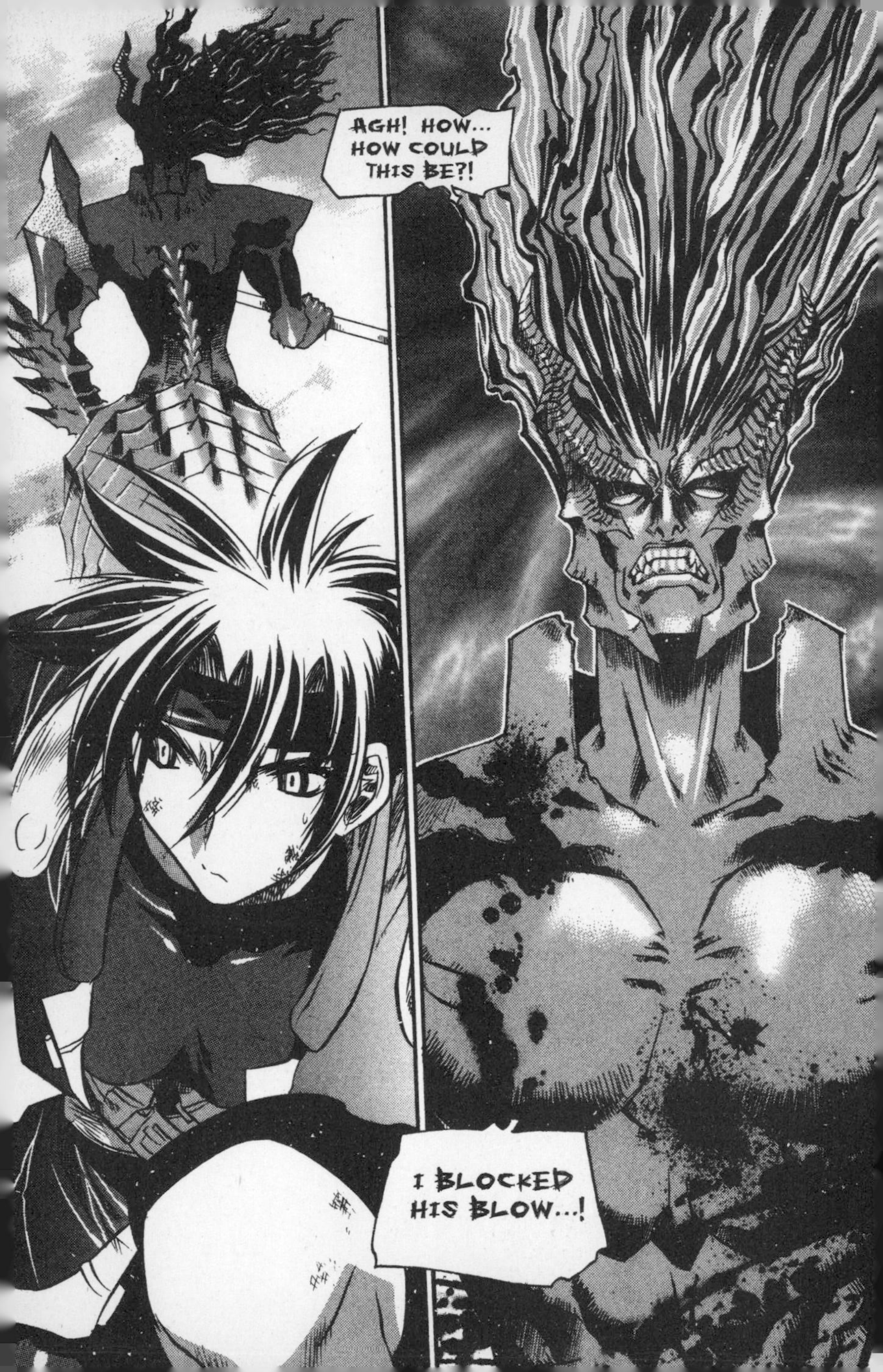
AGH! HOW... HOW COULD THIS BE?!
I BLOCKED HIS BLOW...!

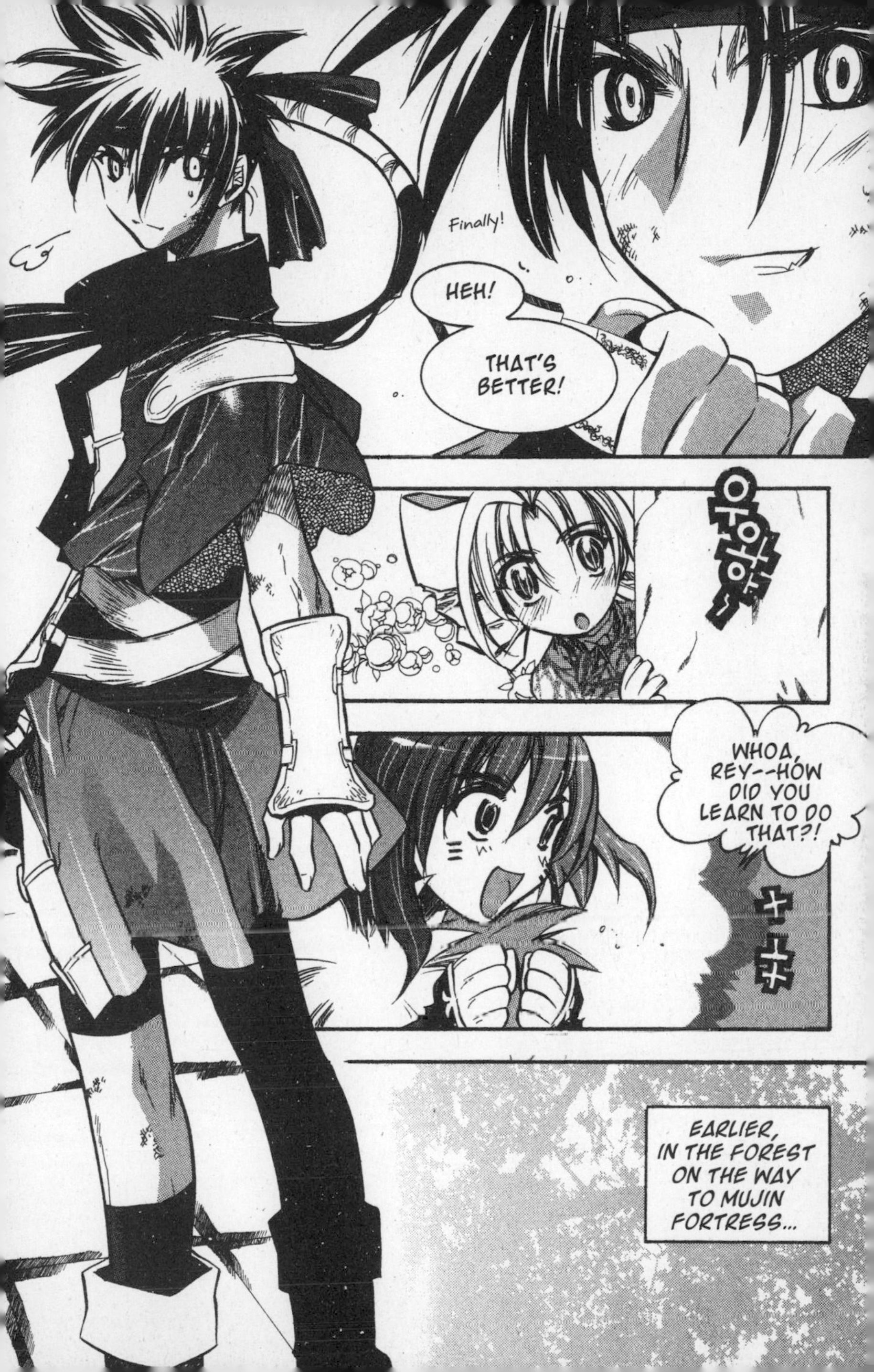
Finally!
HEH!
THAT'S BETTER!
WHOA, REY--HOW DID YOU LEARN TO DO THAT?!
EARLIER, IN THE FOREST ON THE WAY TO MUJIN FORTRESS...

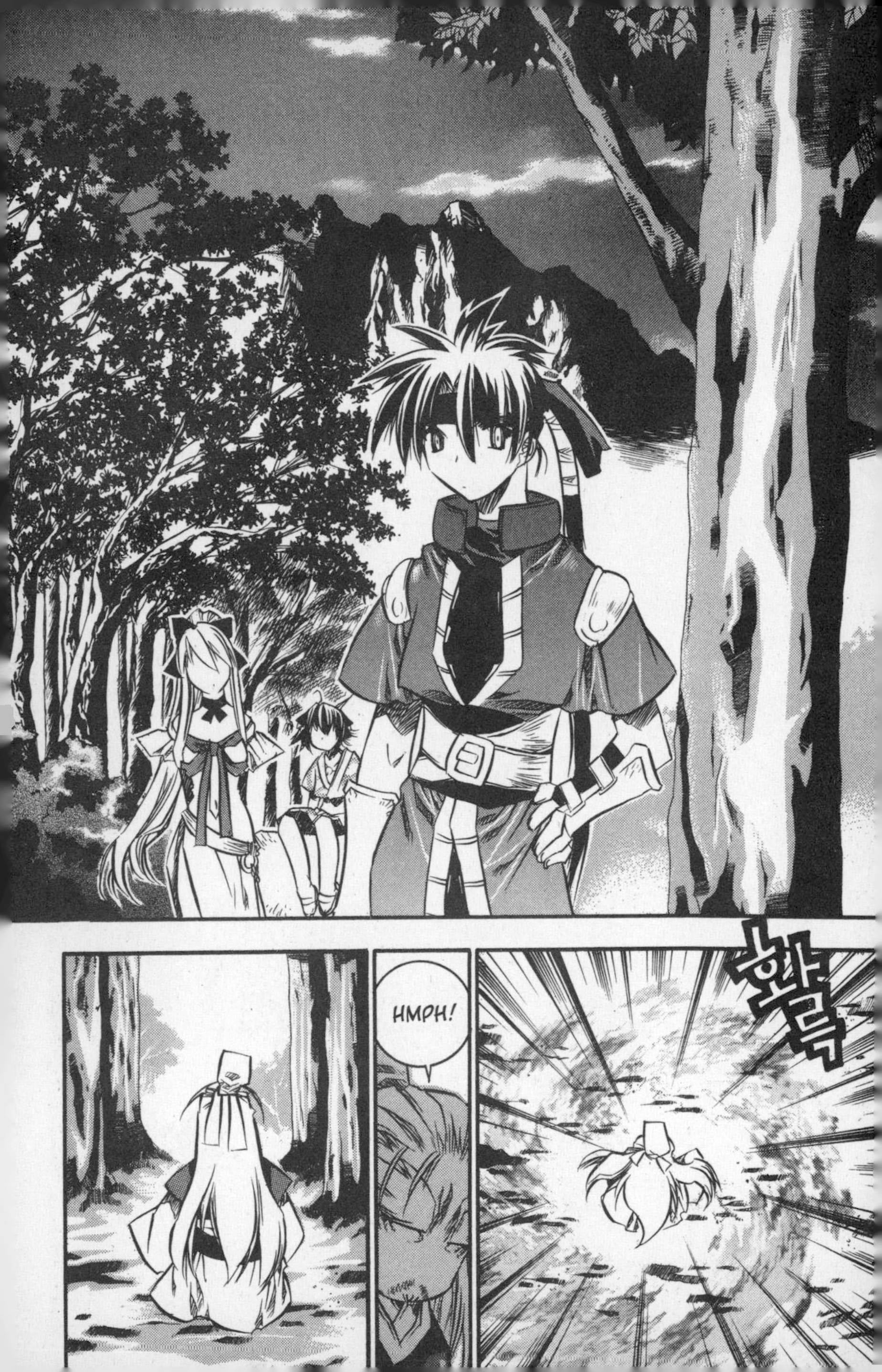
HMPH!
화륵

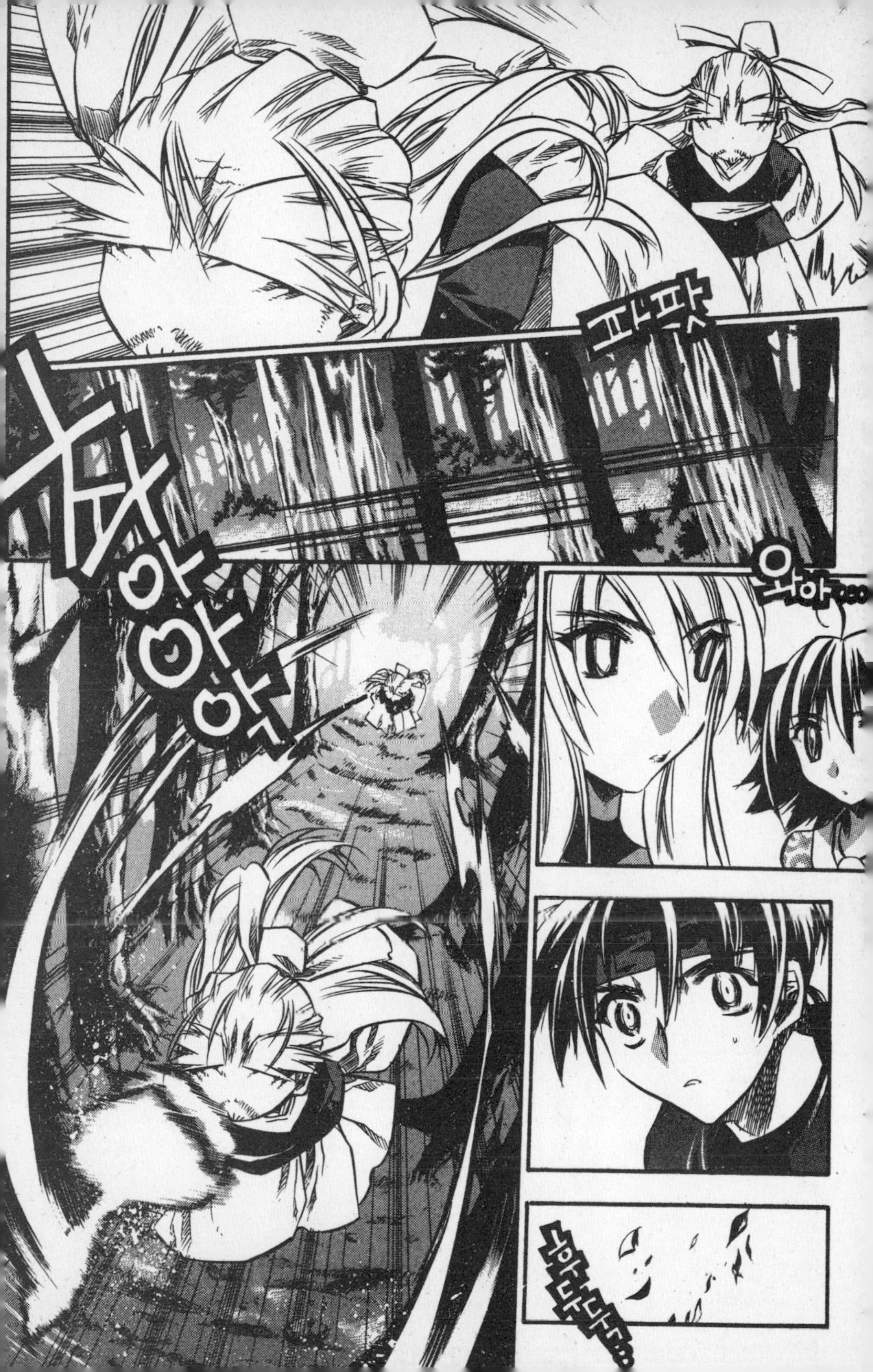
파팟
쏴아아아
와아…
후다닥…

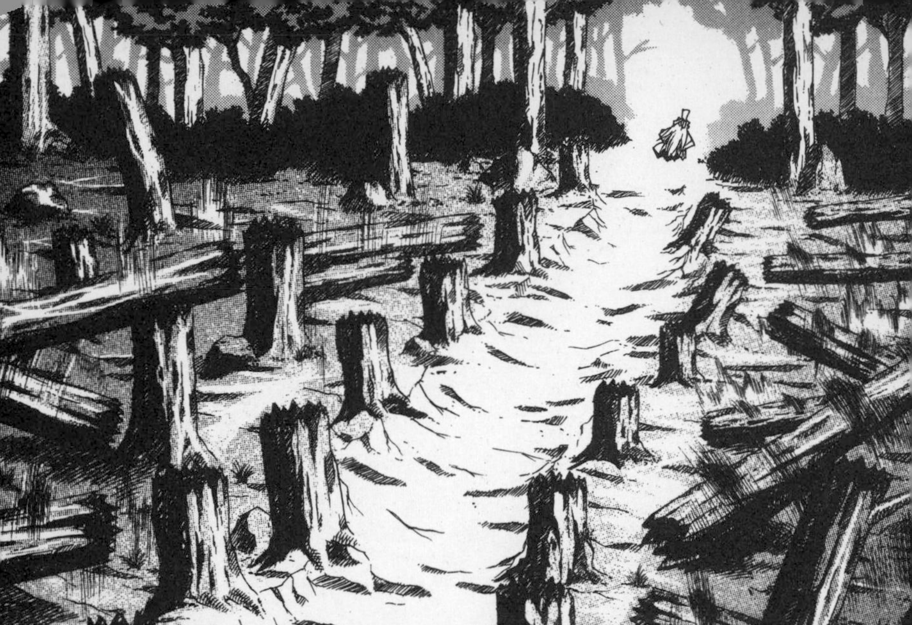
콰당
쿵

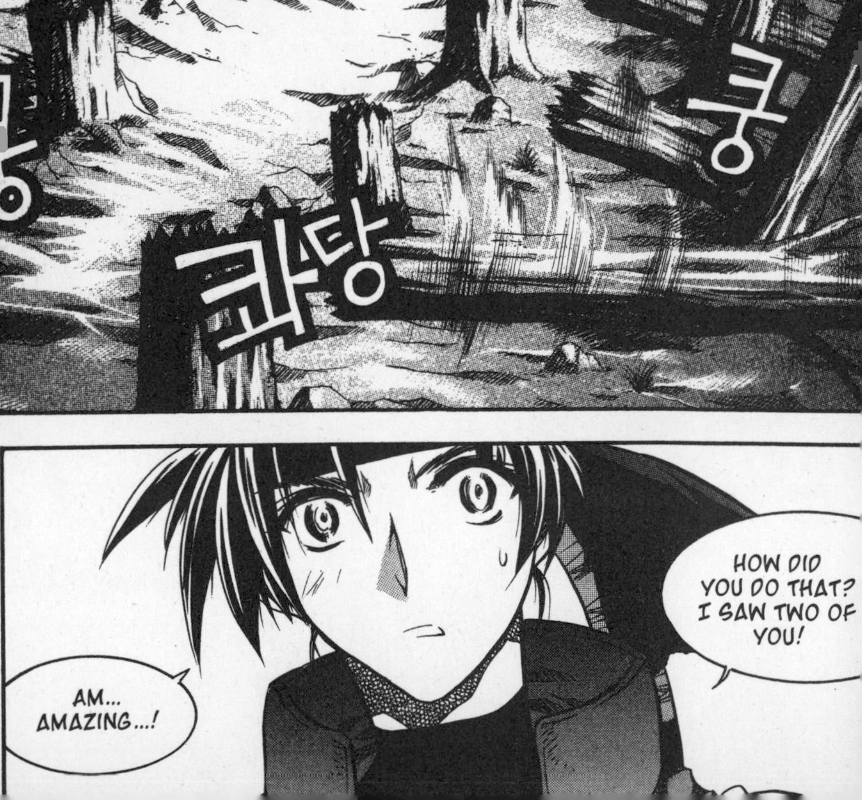
HOW DID YOU DO THAT? I SAW TWO OF YOU!
AM... AMAZING...!

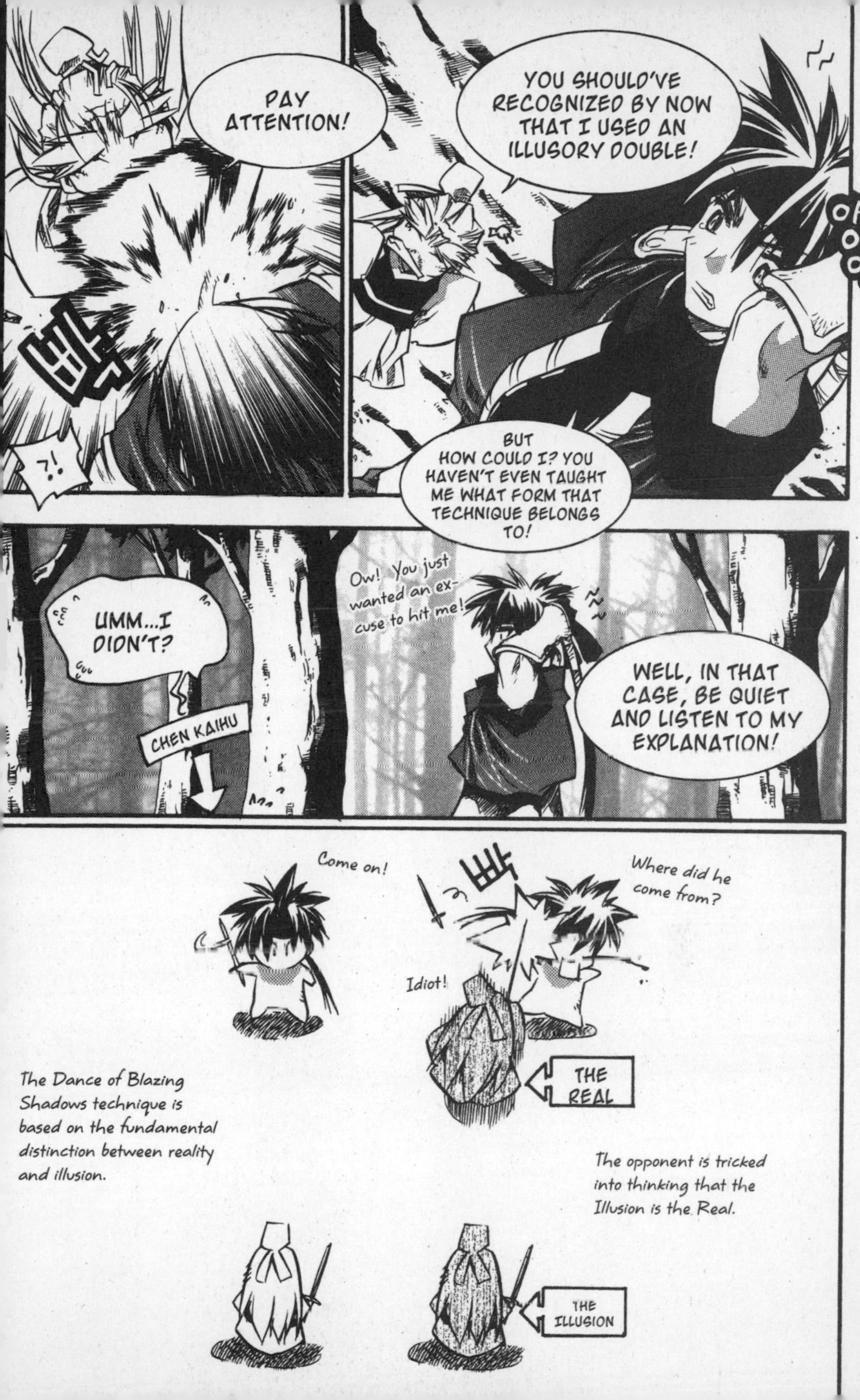
PAY ATTENTION!
빡
?!
YOU SHOULD'VE RECOGNIZED BY NOW THAT I USED AN ILLUSORY DOUBLE!
아야야
BUT HOW COULD I? YOU HAVEN'T EVEN TAUGHT ME WHAT FORM THAT TECHNIQUE BELONGS TO!
UMM...I DIDN'T?
CHEN KAIHU
Ow! You just wanted an excuse to hit me!
WELL, IN THAT CASE, BE QUIET AND LISTEN TO MY EXPLANATION!
Come on!
빡
Where did he come from?
Idiot!
The Dance of Blazing Shadows technique is based on the fundamental distinction between reality and illusion.
THE REAL
The opponent is tricked into thinking that the Illusion is the Real.
THE ILLUSION

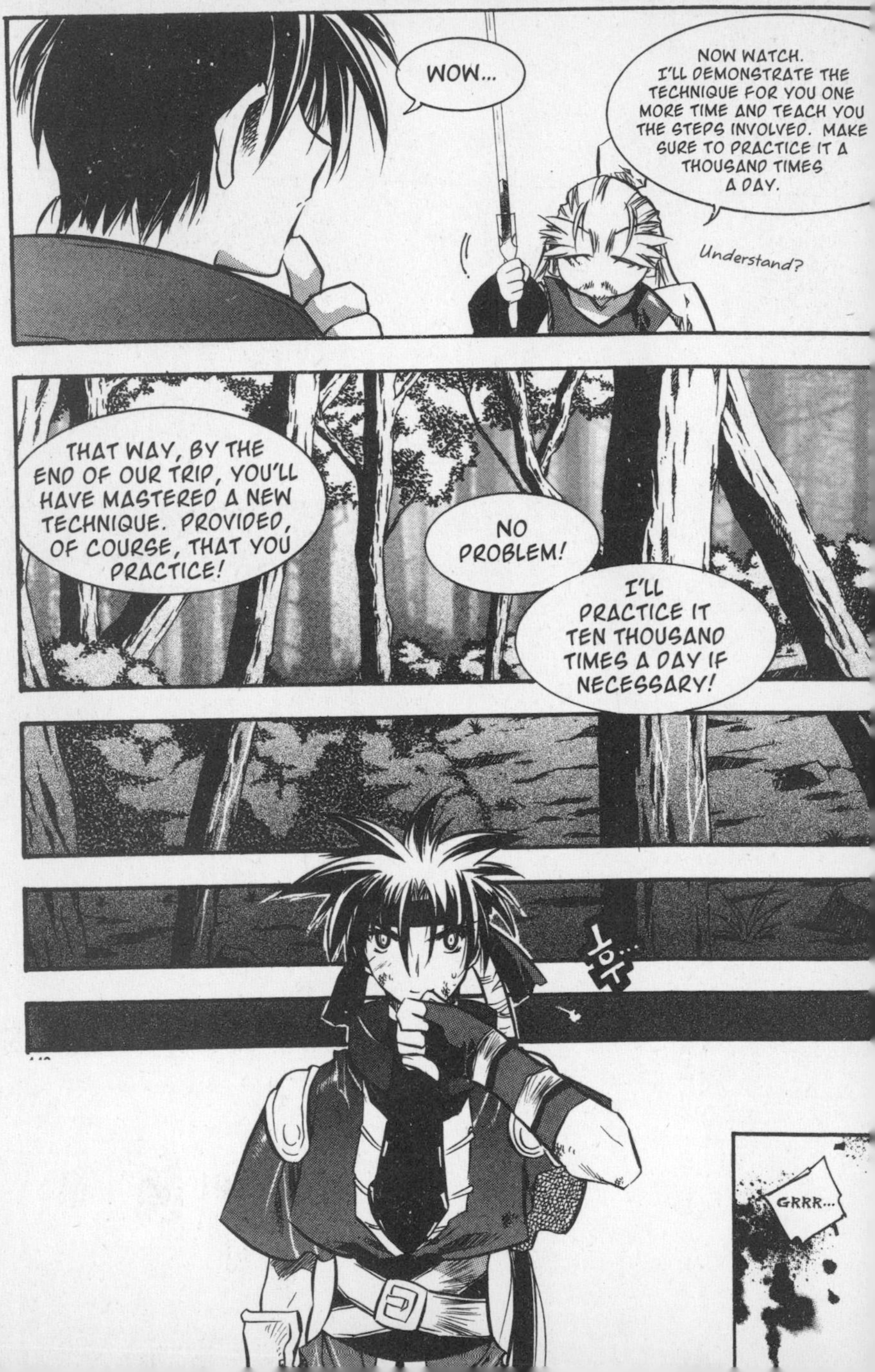
WOW...
NOW WATCH. I'LL DEMONSTRATE THE TECHNIQUE FOR YOU ONE MORE TIME AND TEACH YOU THE STEPS INVOLVED. MAKE SURE TO PRACTICE IT A THOUSAND TIMES A DAY.
Understand?
THAT WAY, BY THE END OF OUR TRIP, YOU'LL HAVE MASTERED A NEW TECHNIQUE. PROVIDED, OF COURSE, THAT YOU PRACTICE!
NO PROBLEM!
I'LL PRACTICE IT TEN THOUSAND TIMES A DAY IF NECESSARY!
GRRR...

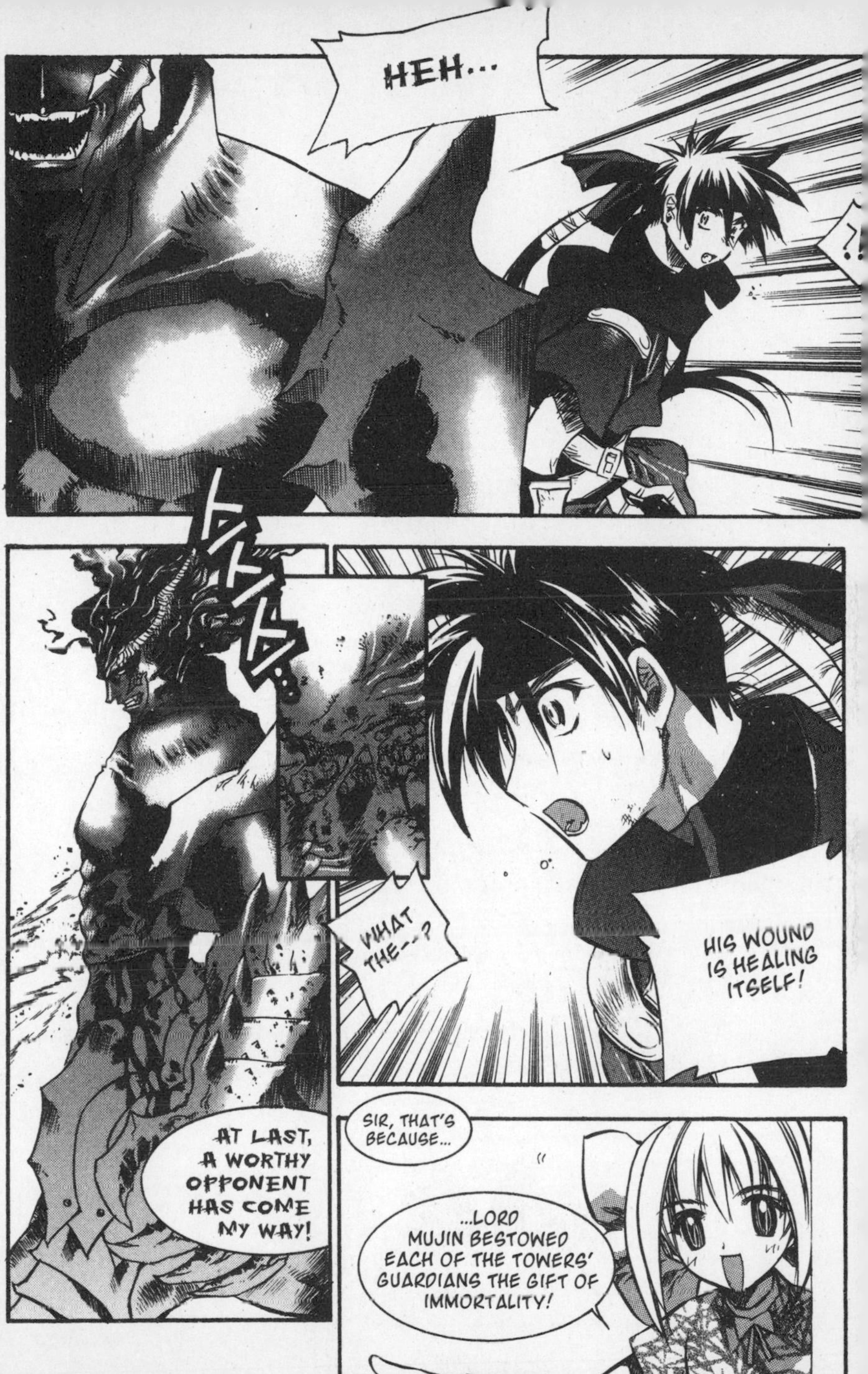
HEH...
?!
AT LAST, A WORTHY OPPONENT HAS COME MY WAY!
WHAT THE--?
HIS WOUND IS HEALING ITSELF!
SIR, THAT'S BECAUSE...
...LORD MUJIN BESTOWED EACH OF THE TOWERS' GUARDIANS THE GIFT OF IMMORTALITY!

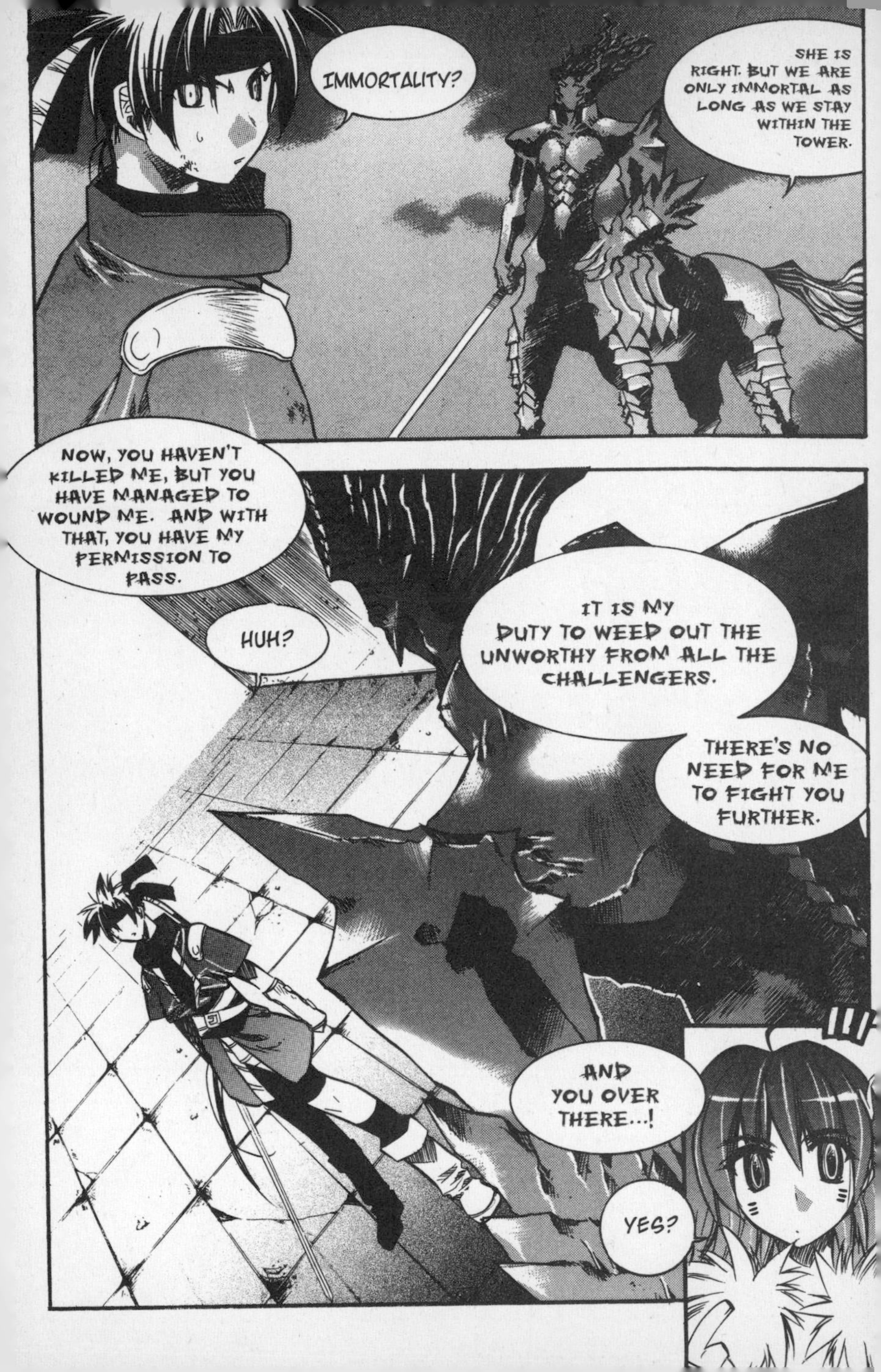
IMMORTALITY?
SHE IS RIGHT. BUT WE ARE ONLY IMMORTAL AS LONG AS WE STAY WITHIN THE TOWER.
NOW, YOU HAVEN'T KILLED ME, BUT YOU HAVE MANAGED TO WOUND ME. AND WITH THAT, YOU HAVE MY PERMISSION TO PASS.
HUH?
IT IS MY DUTY TO WEED OUT THE UNWORTHY FROM ALL THE CHALLENGERS.
THERE'S NO NEED FOR ME TO FIGHT YOU FURTHER.
AND YOU OVER THERE...!
YES?

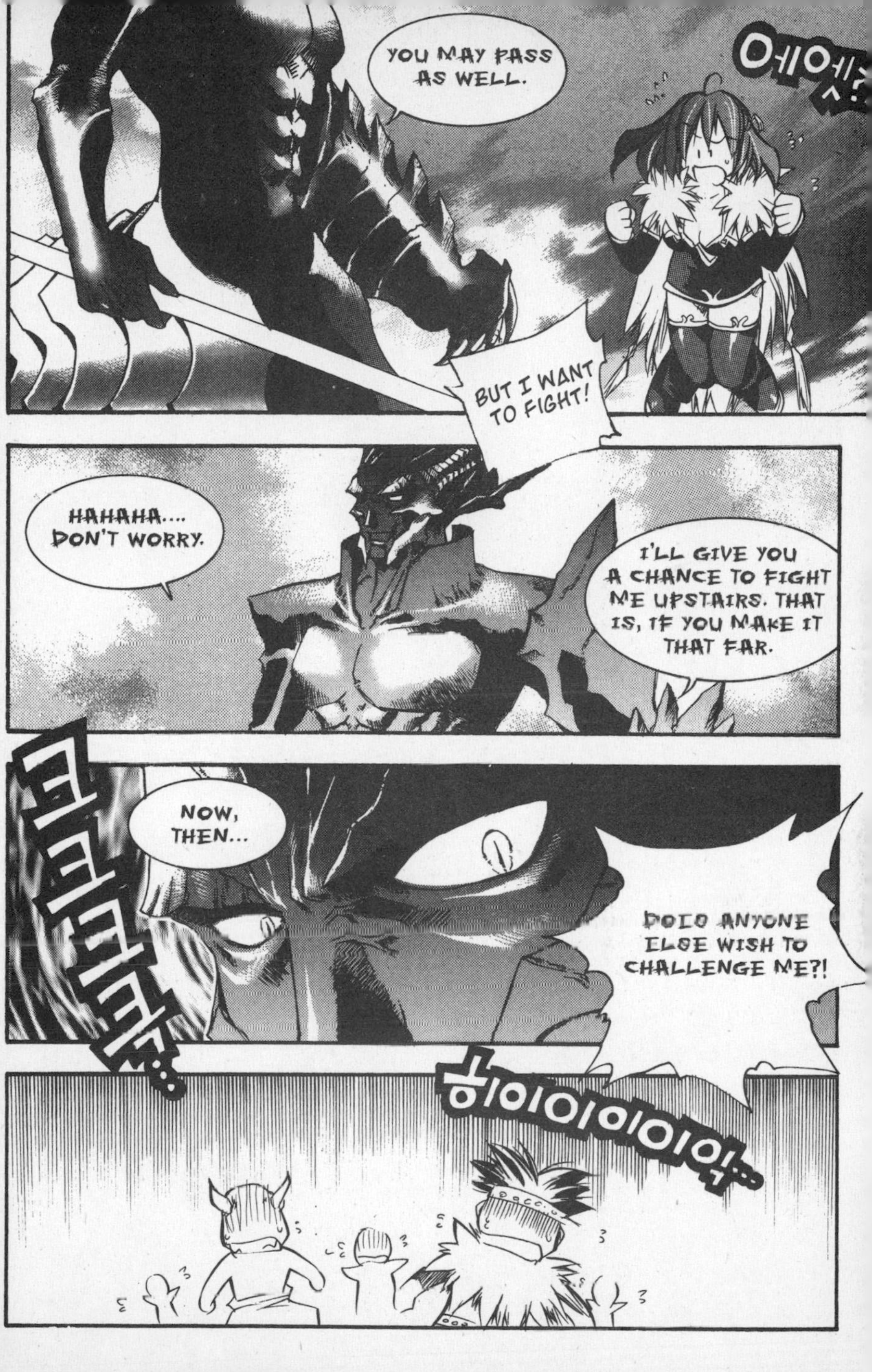
YOU MAY PASS AS WELL.
에에엣?!
BUT I WANT TO FIGHT!
HAHAHA.... DON'T WORRY.
I'LL GIVE YOU A CHANCE TO FIGHT ME UPSTAIRS. THAT IS, IF YOU MAKE IT THAT FAR.
NOW, THEN...
DOES ANYONE ELSE WISH TO CHALLENGE ME?!

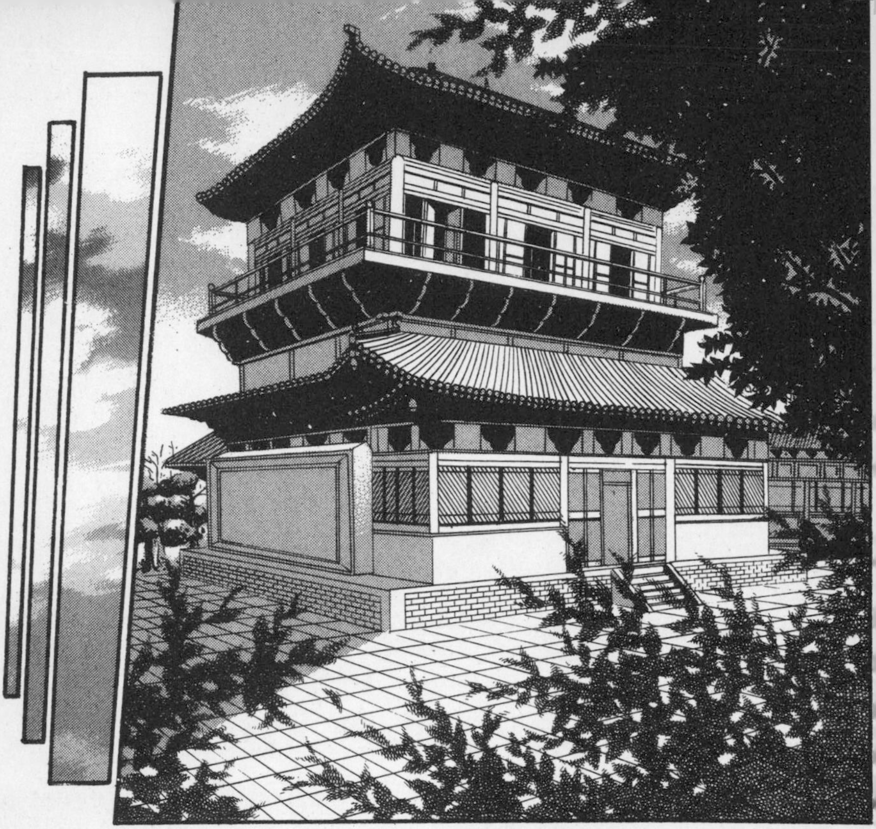

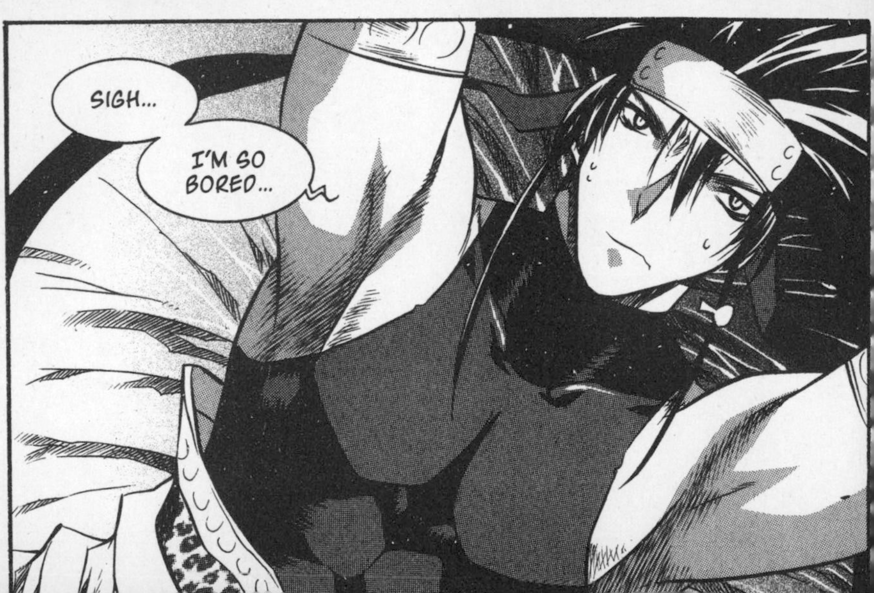
SIGH...
I'M SO BORED...

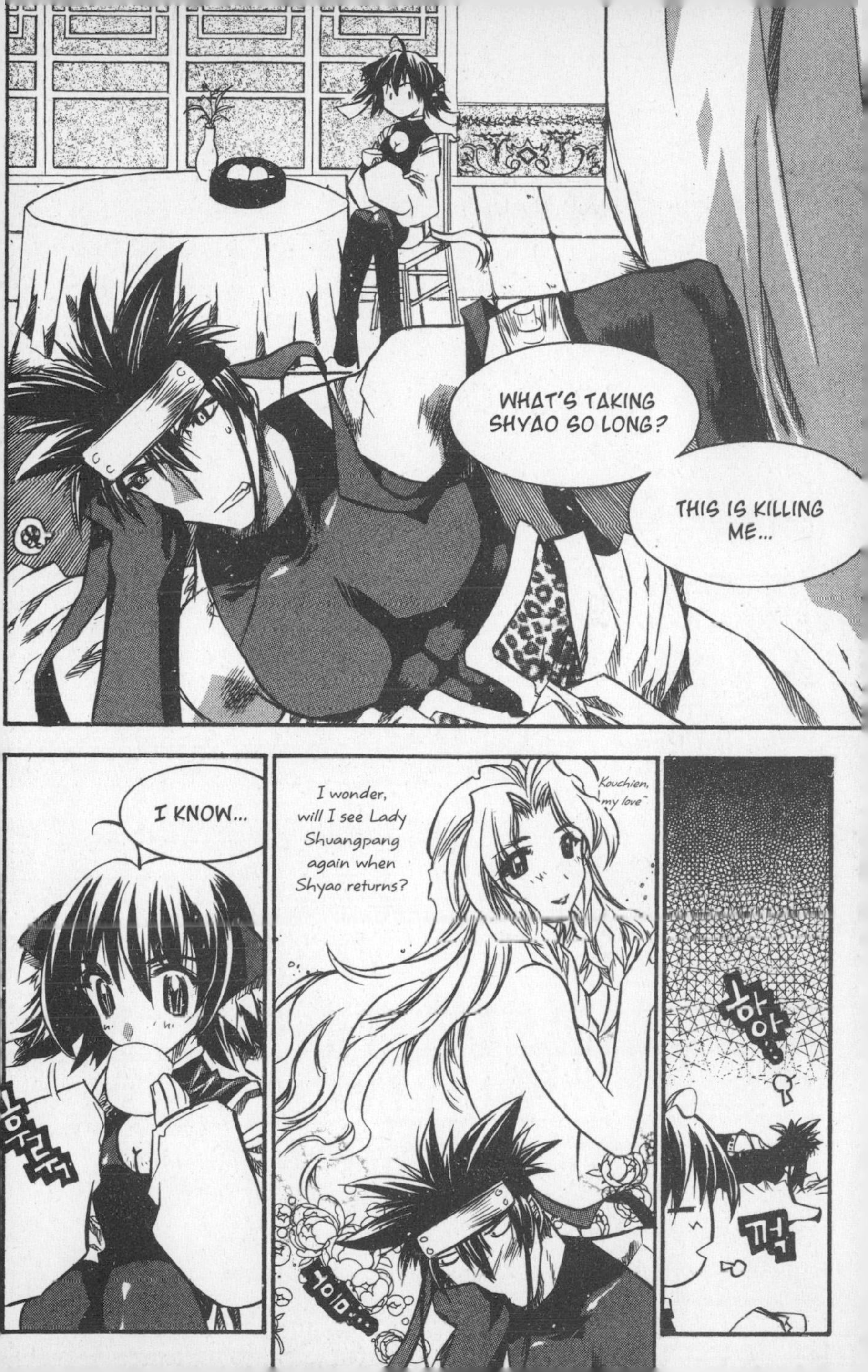
WHAT'S TAKING SHYAO SO LONG?
THIS IS KILLING ME...
I KNOW...
I wonder, will I see Lady Shuangpang again when Shyao returns?
Kouchien, my love~

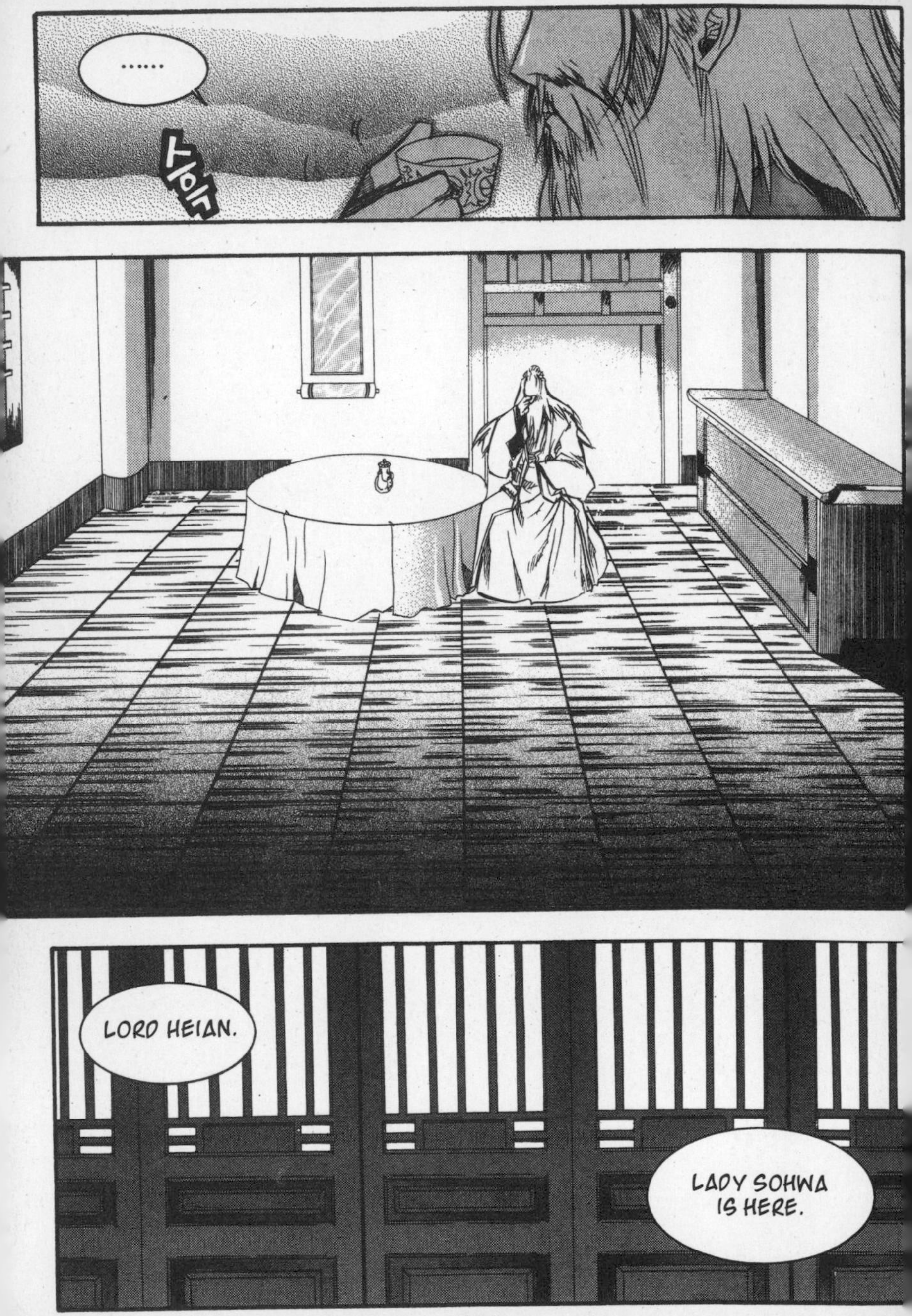
......
LORD HEIAN.
LADY SOHWA IS HERE.

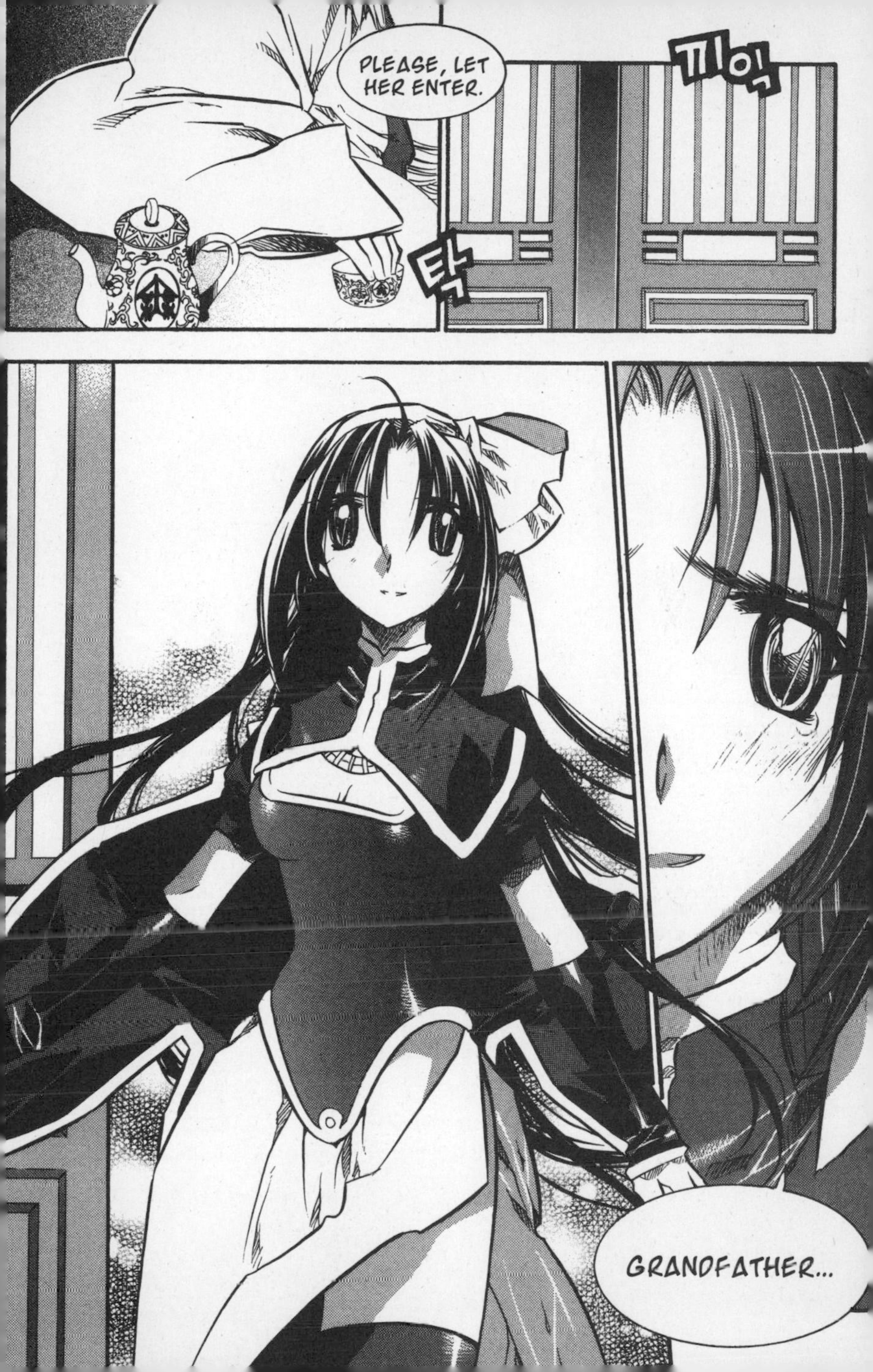
PLEASE, LET HER ENTER.
탁
끼익
GRANDFATHER...

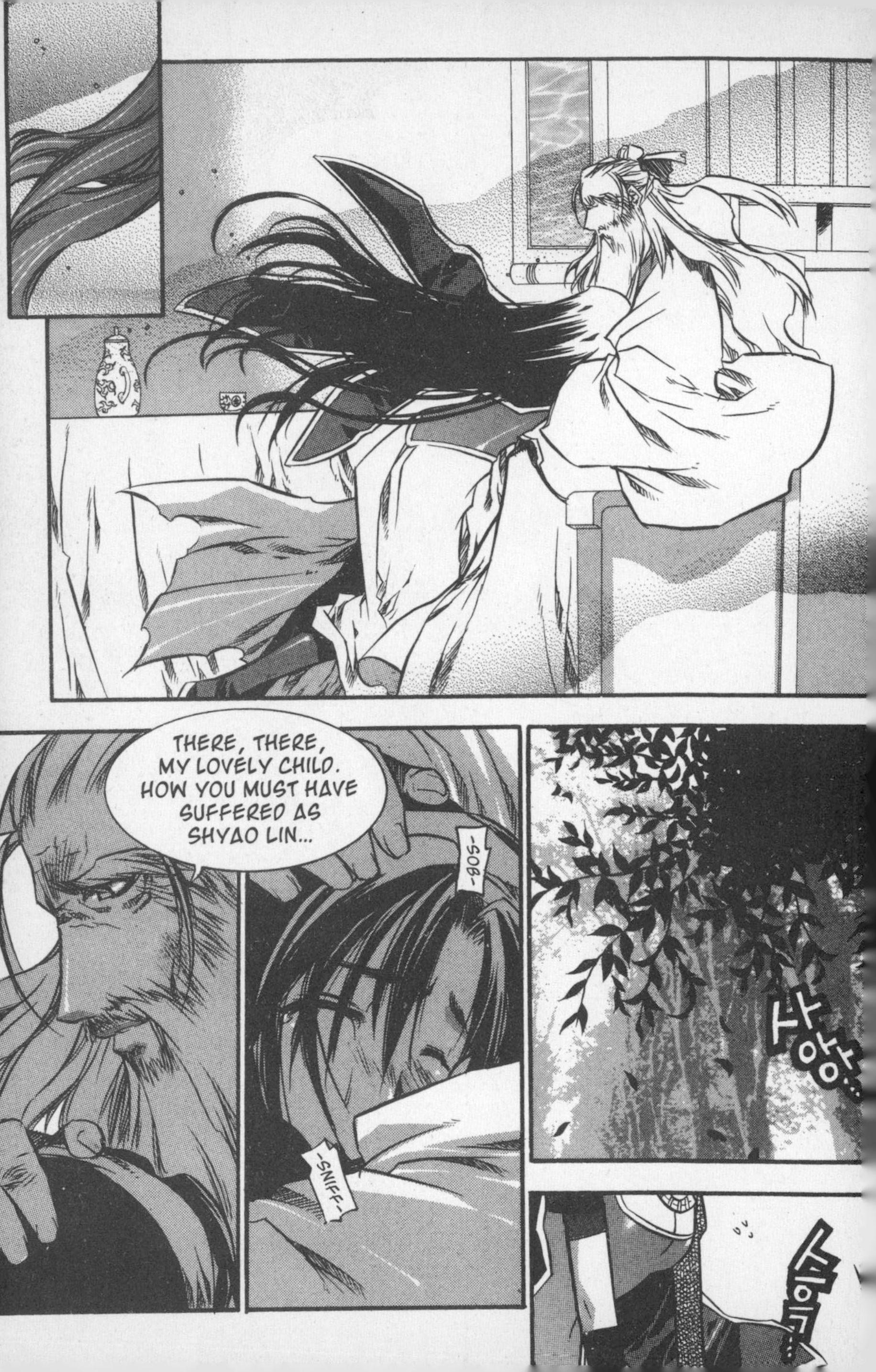
THERE, THERE, MY LOVELY CHILD. HOW YOU MUST HAVE SUFFERED AS SHYAO LIN...
-SOB-
-SNIFF-
사아앙...
스이익...

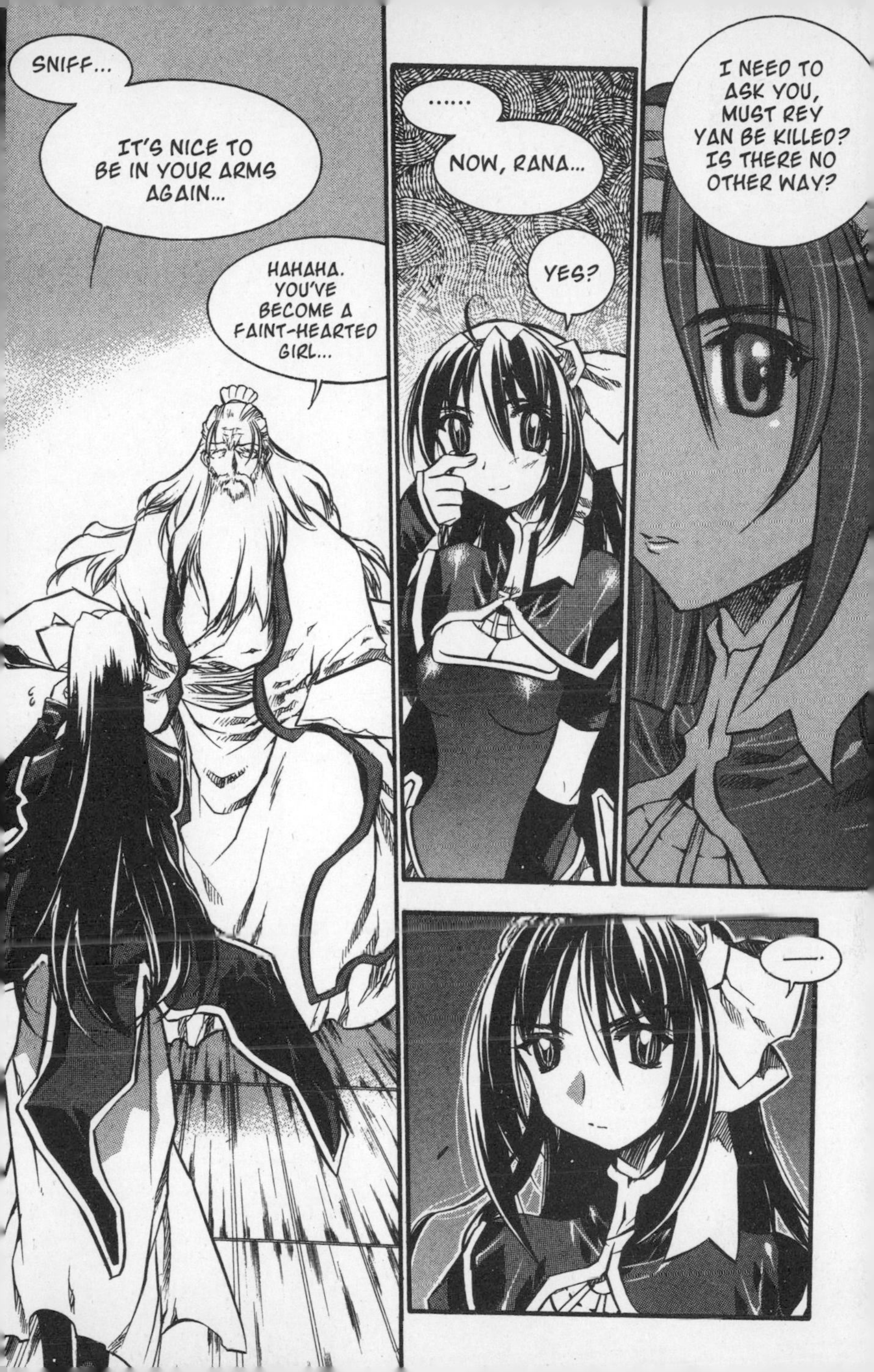
SNIFF...
IT'S NICE TO BE IN YOUR ARMS AGAIN...
HAHAHA. YOU'VE BECOME A FAINT-HEARTED GIRL...
......
NOW, RANA...
YES?
I NEED TO ASK YOU, MUST REY YAN BE KILLED? IS THERE NO OTHER WAY?
——.

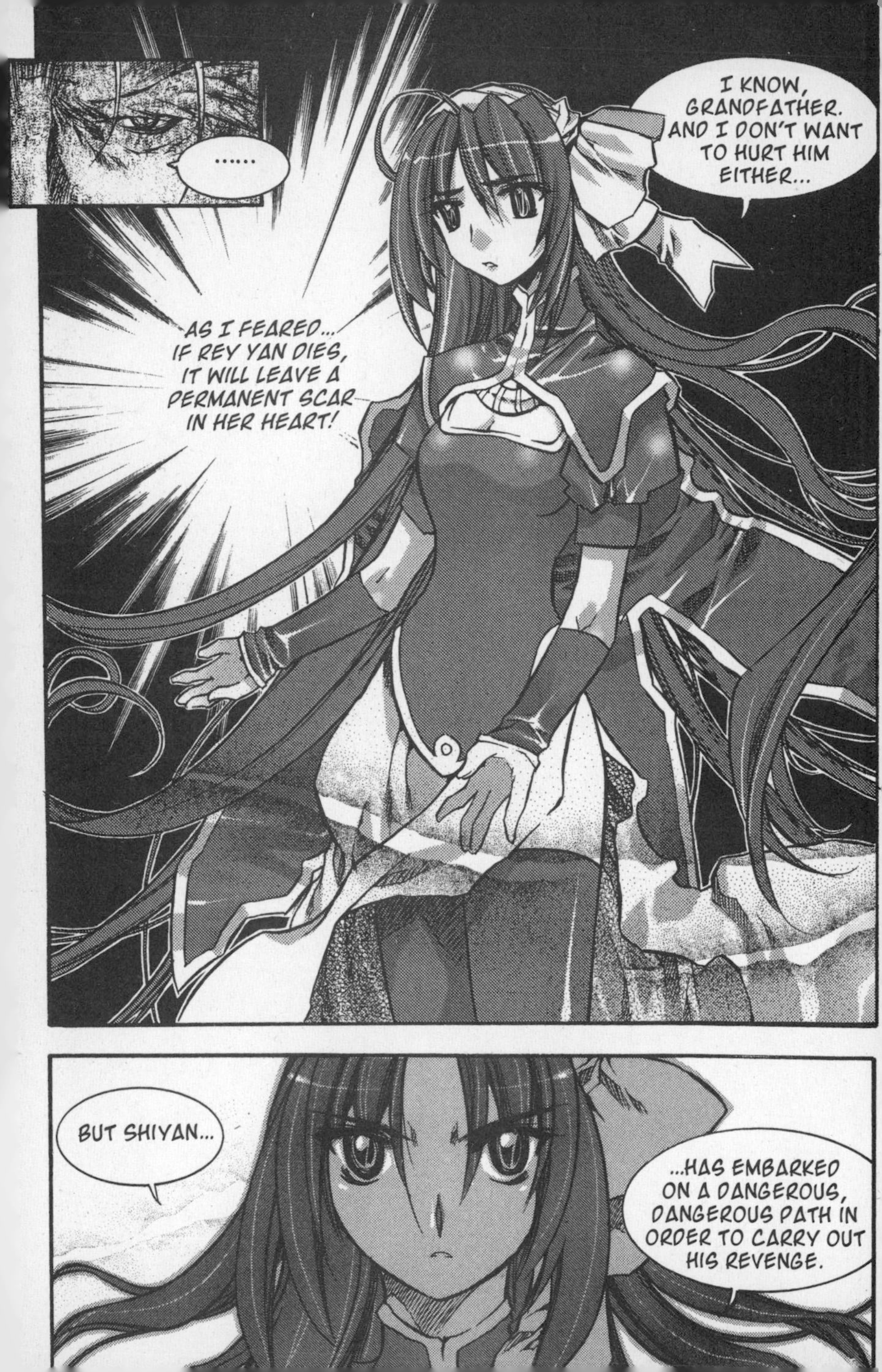
......
I KNOW, GRANDFATHER. AND I DON'T WANT TO HURT HIM EITHER...
AS I FEARED... IF REY YAN DIES, IT WILL LEAVE A PERMANENT SCAR IN HER HEART!
BUT SHIYAN...
...HAS EMBARKED ON A DANGEROUS, DANGEROUS PATH IN ORDER TO CARRY OUT HIS REVENGE.

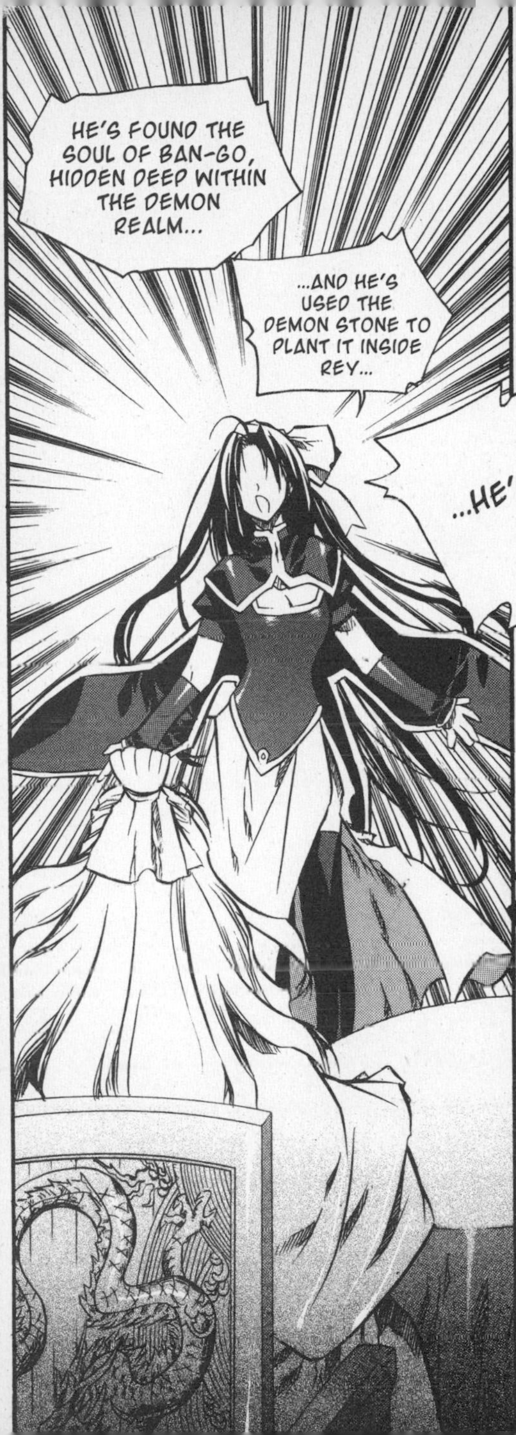
HE'S FOUND THE SOUL OF BAN-GO, HIDDEN DEEP WITHIN THE DEMON REALM...
...AND HE'S USED THE DEMON STONE TO PLANT IT INSIDE REY...
...HE'S MAD!

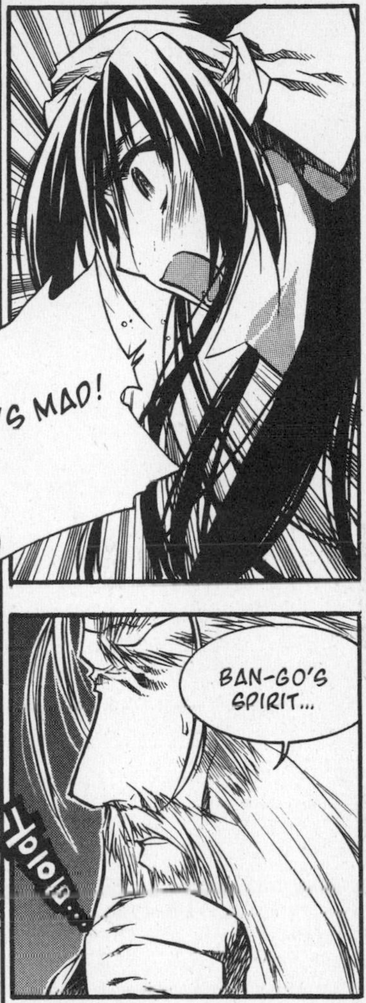
BAN-GO'S SPIRIT...

BAN-GO:
IN MYTHOLOGY, BAN-GO WAS THE DIVINITY BORN OF PRIMORDIAL CHAOS. DIVIDING THE COSMOS INTO YIN (HEAVEN) AND YANG (EARTH), BAN-GO HAULED THE HEAVEN UPON HIS SHOULDERS AND PRESSED DOWN ON THE EARTH TO SEPARATE THE TWO REALMS. UPON HIS DEATH, HE TRANSFORMED PARTS OF HIS COLOSSAL BODY INTO THE ELEMENTS: HIS BREATH INTO THE WIND AND CLOUDS; HIS VOICE INTO THUNDER; HIS LEFT EYE INTO THE MOON; HIS RIGHT EYE INTO THE SUN; HIS BLOOD INTO RIVERS; HIS MUSCLES INTO MOUNTAIN RANGES; HIS FLESH INTO THE FIELDS. HIS HAIR AND BEARD BECAME THE STARS; HIS SKIN AND BODY HAIR BECAME THE GRASS AND TREES; AND HIS TEETH AND BONES BECAME METAL ORES AND ROCKS.

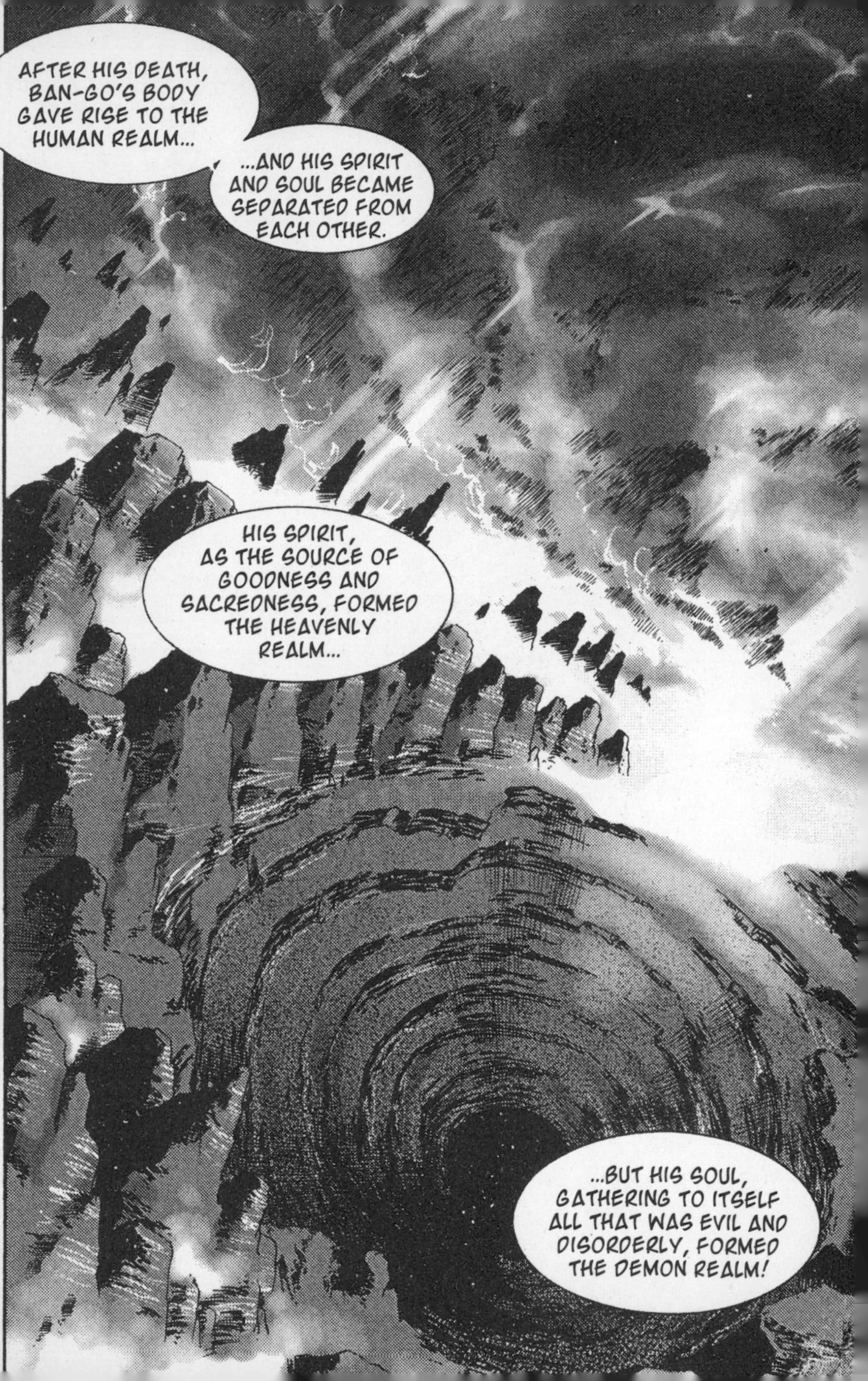
AFTER HIS DEATH, BAN-GO'S BODY GAVE RISE TO THE HUMAN REALM...
...AND HIS SPIRIT AND SOUL BECAME SEPARATED FROM EACH OTHER.
HIS SPIRIT, AS THE SOURCE OF GOODNESS AND SACREDNESS, FORMED THE HEAVENLY REALM...
...BUT HIS SOUL, GATHERING TO ITSELF ALL THAT WAS EVIL AND DISORDERLY, FORMED THE DEMON REALM!

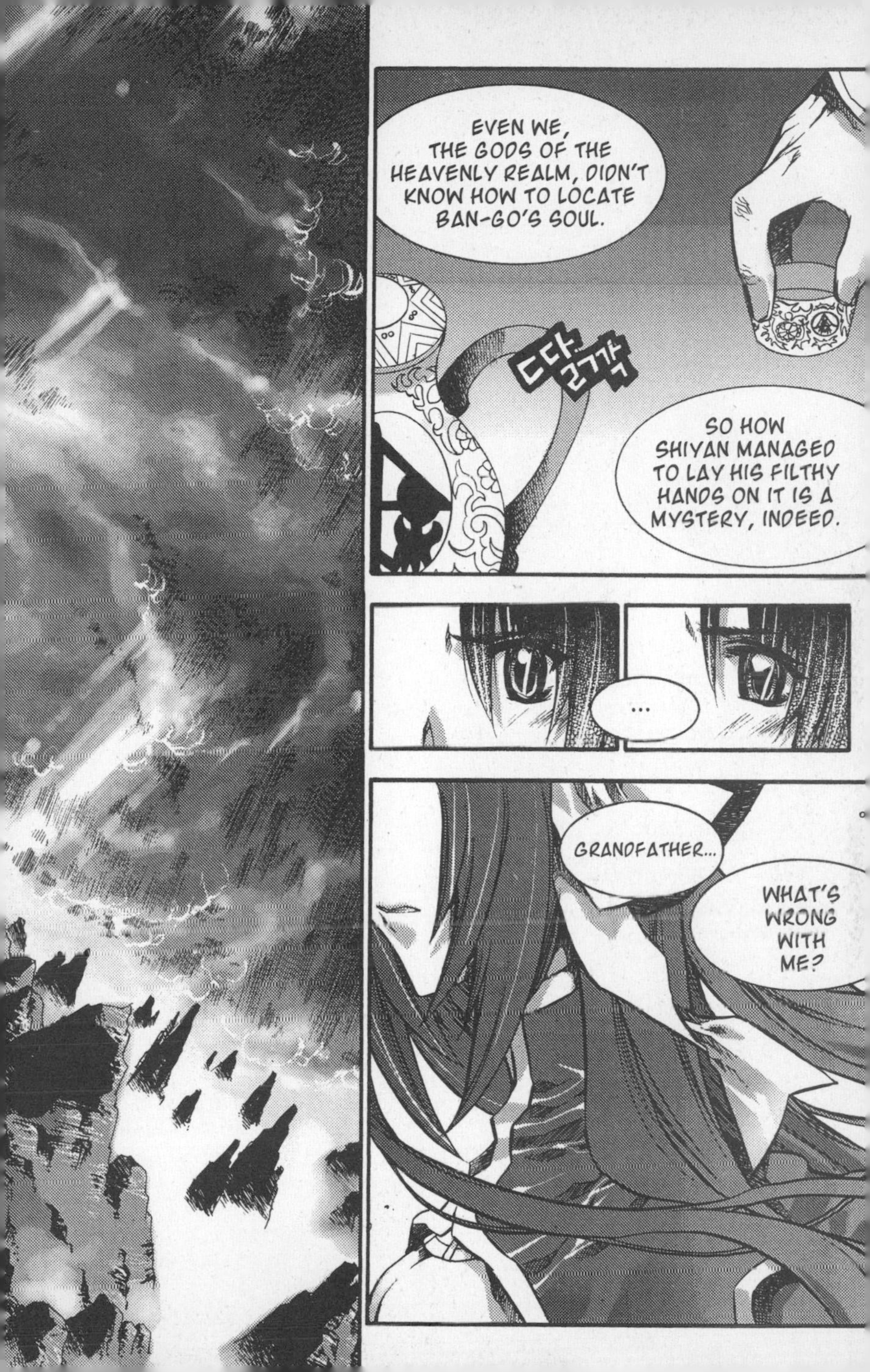
EVEN WE, THE GODS OF THE HEAVENLY REALM, DIDN'T KNOW HOW TO LOCATE BAN-GO'S SOUL.
SO HOW SHIYAN MANAGED TO LAY HIS FILTHY HANDS ON IT IS A MYSTERY, INDEED.
...
GRANDFATHER...
WHAT'S WRONG WITH ME?

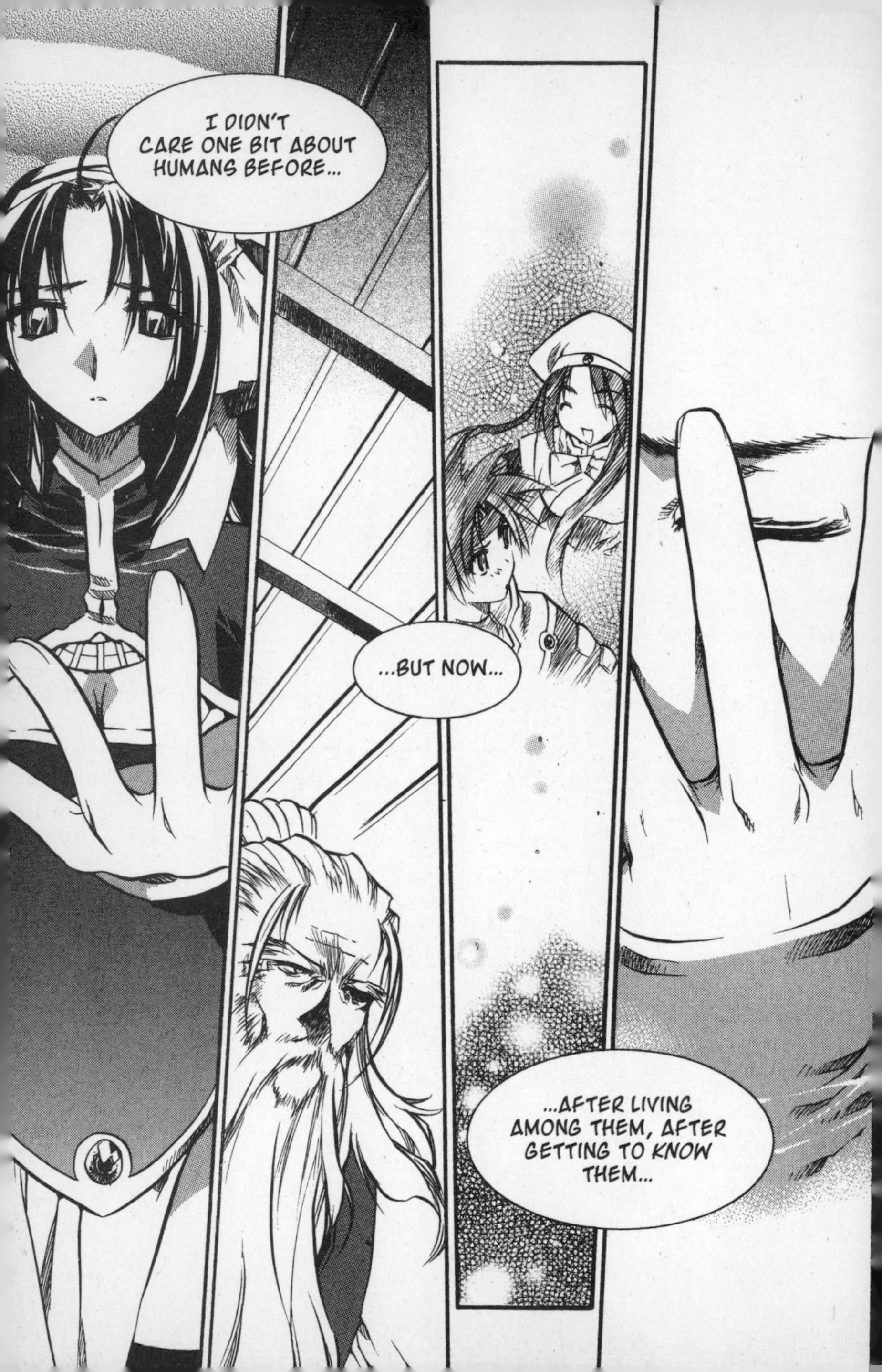
I DIDN'T CARE ONE BIT ABOUT HUMANS BEFORE...
...BUT NOW...
...AFTER LIVING AMONG THEM, AFTER GETTING TO KNOW THEM...

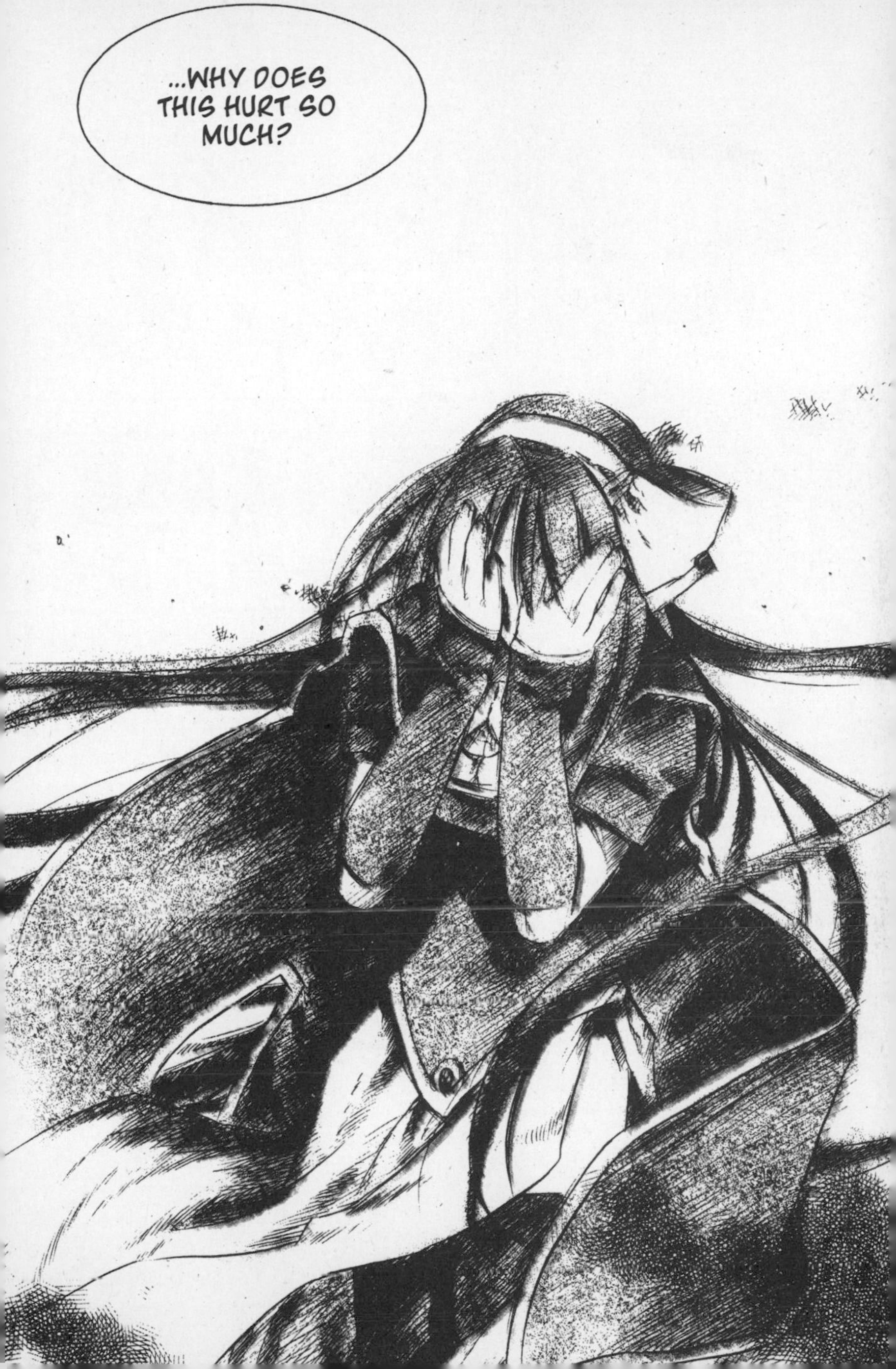
...WHY DOES THIS HURT SO MUCH?

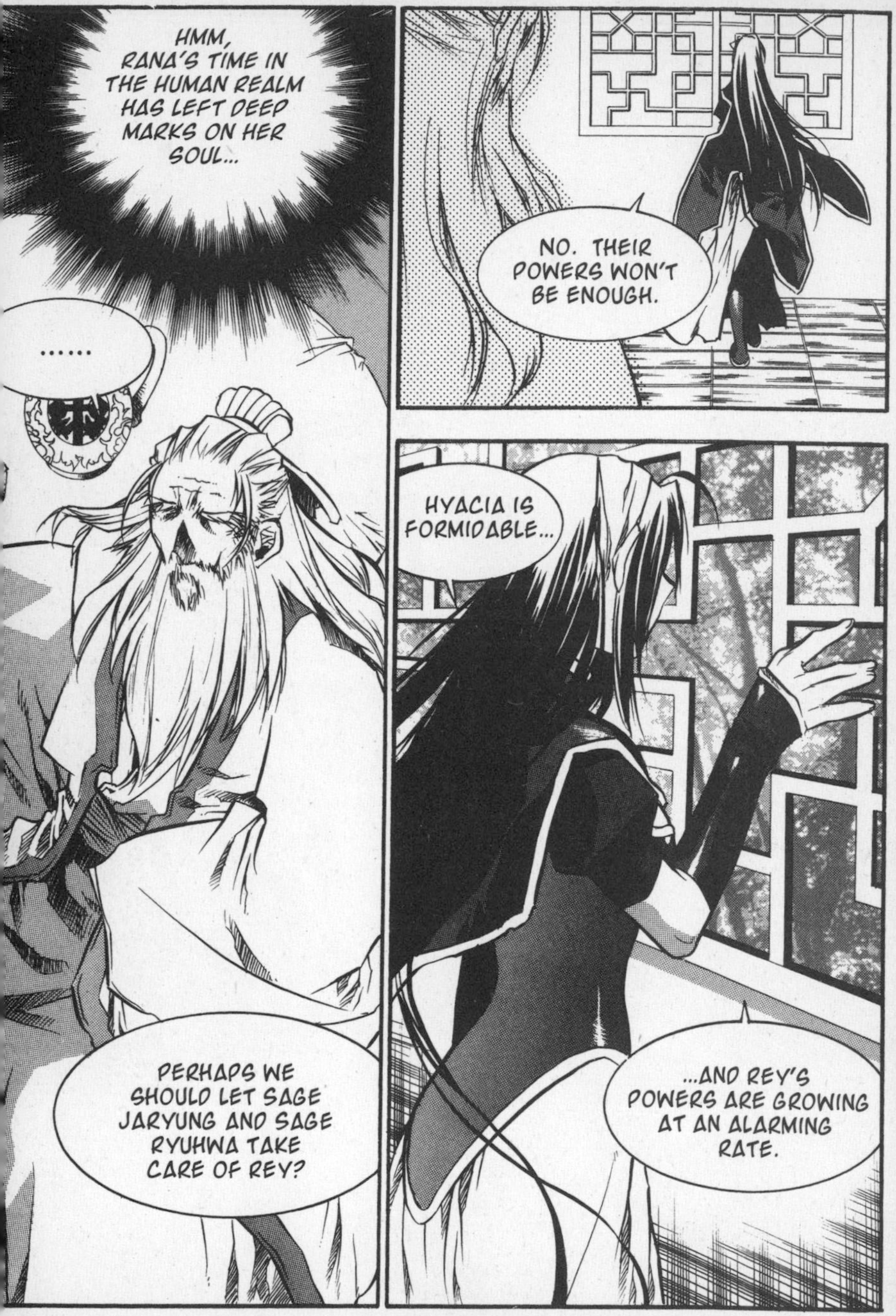
HMM, RANA'S TIME IN THE HUMAN REALM HAS LEFT DEEP MARKS ON HER SOUL...
......
PERHAPS WE SHOULD LET SAGE JARYUNG AND SAGE RYUHWA TAKE CARE OF REY?
NO. THEIR POWERS WON'T BE ENOUGH.
HYACIA IS FORMIDABLE...
...AND REY'S POWERS ARE GROWING AT AN ALARMING RATE.

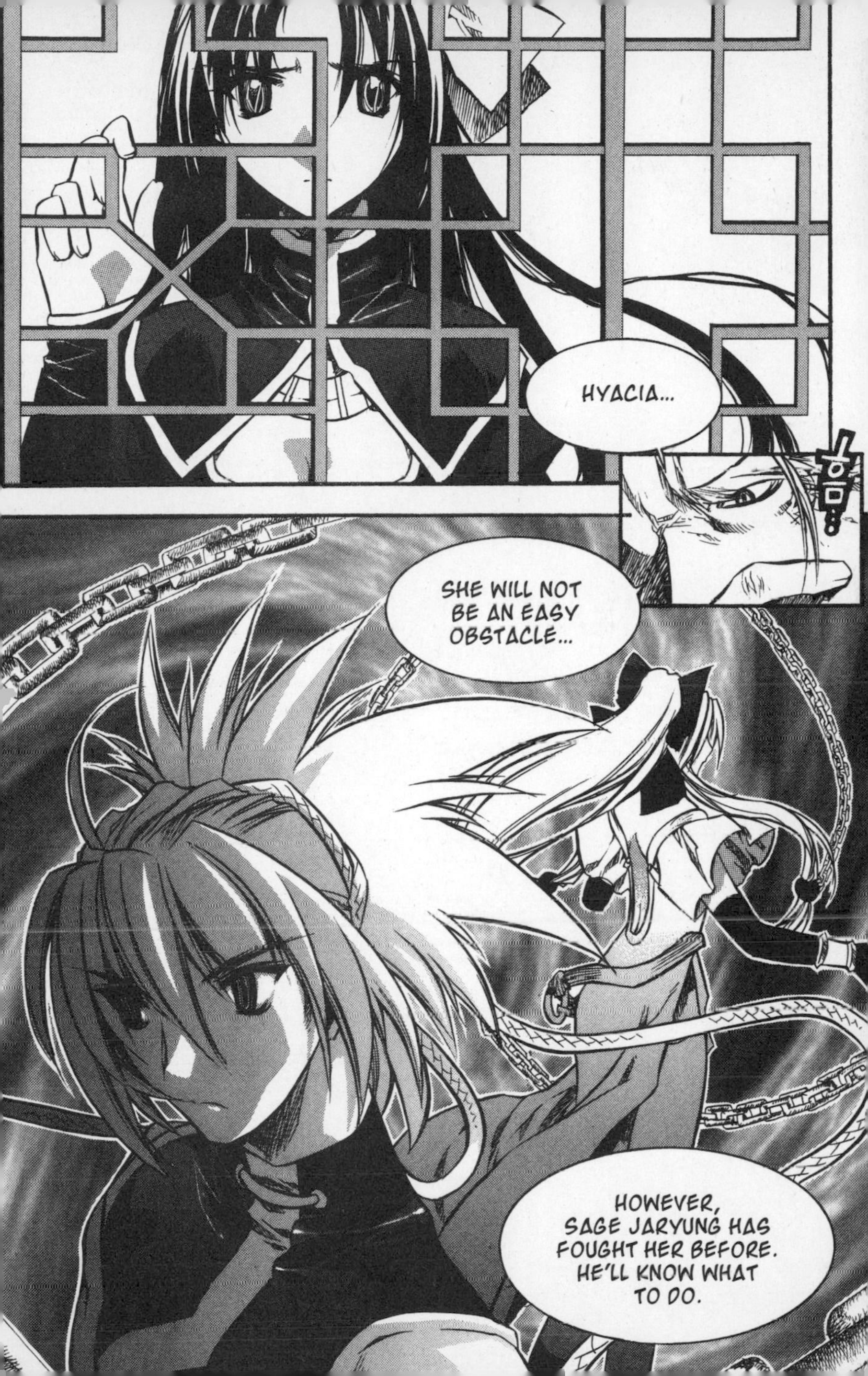
HYACIA...
흠
SHE WILL NOT BE AN EASY OBSTACLE...
HOWEVER, SAGE JARYUNG HAS FOUGHT HER BEFORE. HE'LL KNOW WHAT TO DO.

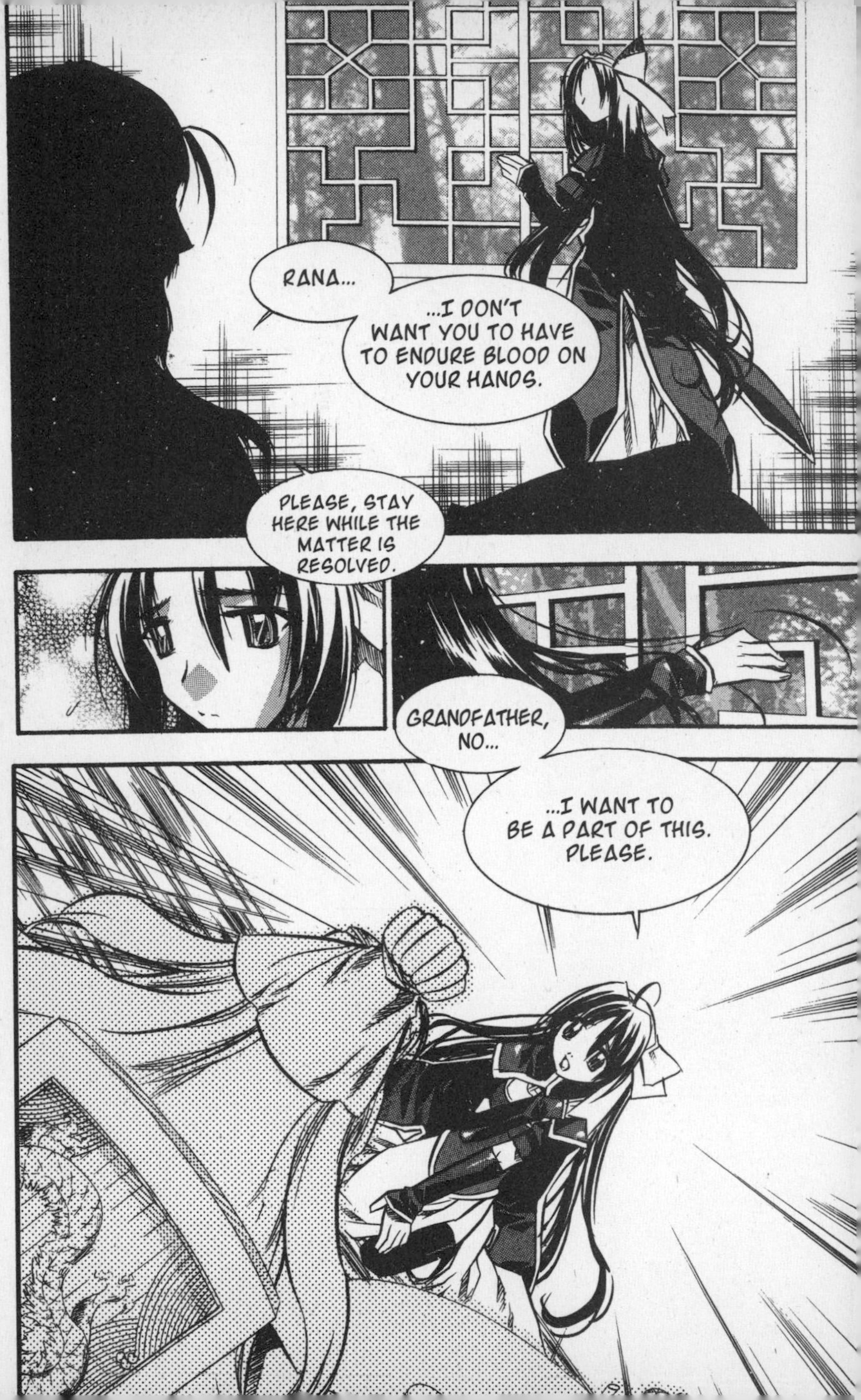
RANA...
...I DON'T WANT YOU TO HAVE TO ENDURE BLOOD ON YOUR HANDS.
PLEASE, STAY HERE WHILE THE MATTER IS RESOLVED.
GRANDFATHER, NO...
...I WANT TO BE A PART OF THIS. PLEASE.

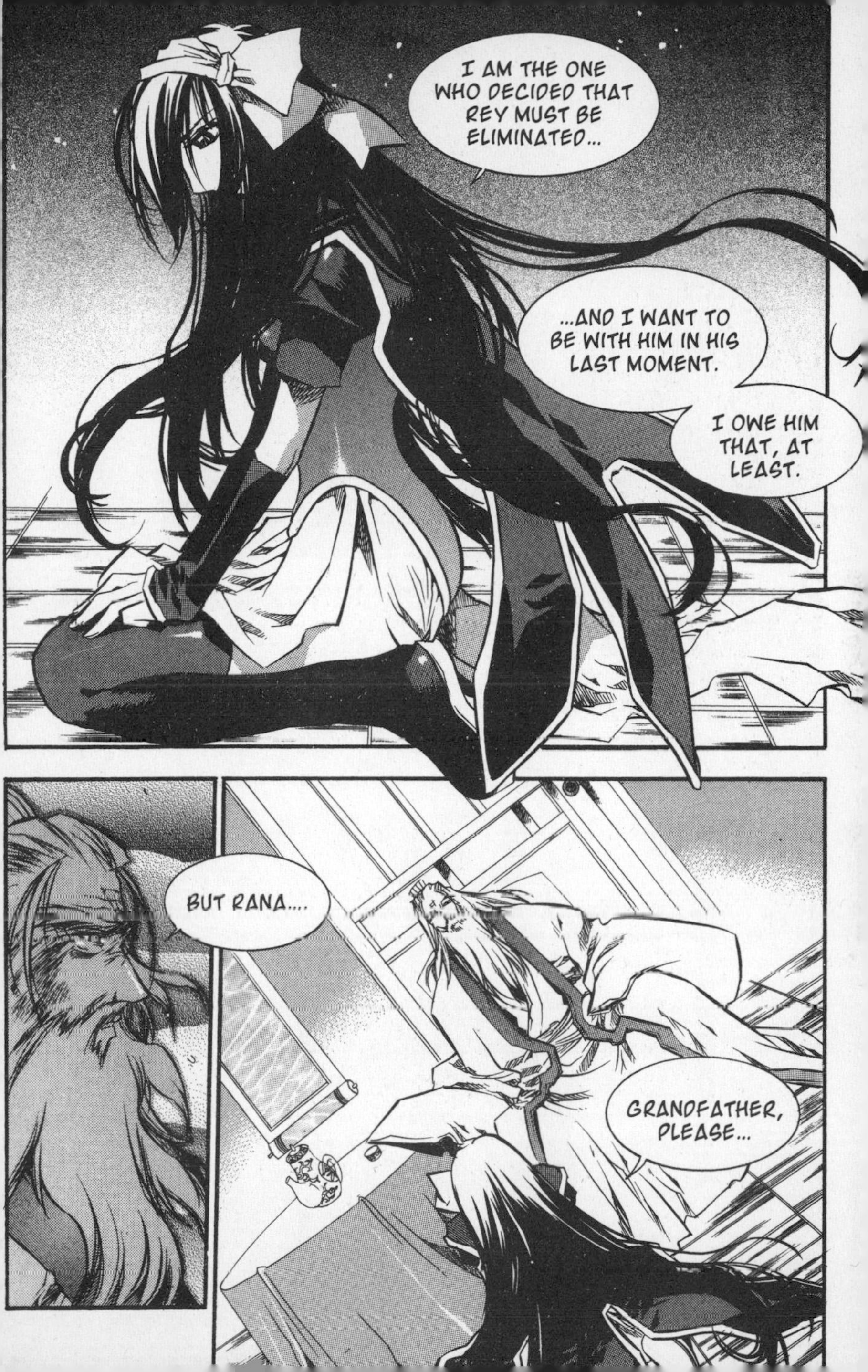
I AM THE ONE WHO DECIDED THAT REY MUST BE ELIMINATED...
...AND I WANT TO BE WITH HIM IN HIS LAST MOMENT.
I OWE HIM THAT, AT LEAST.
BUT RANA....
GRANDFATHER, PLEASE...

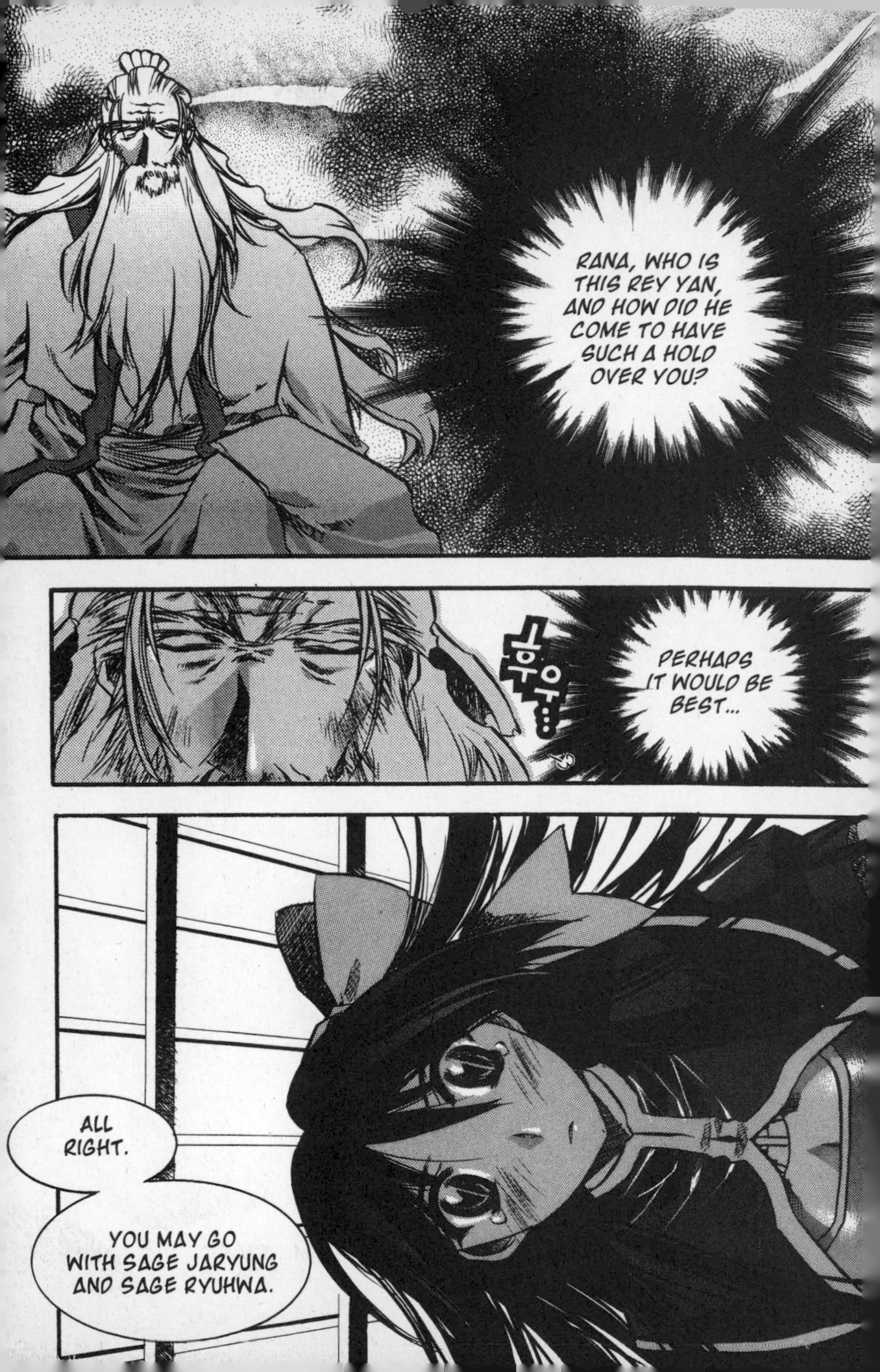
RANA, WHO IS THIS REY YAN, AND HOW DID HE COME TO HAVE SUCH A HOLD OVER YOU?
후우...
PERHAPS IT WOULD BE BEST...
ALL RIGHT.
YOU MAY GO WITH SAGE JARYUNG AND SAGE RYUHWA.

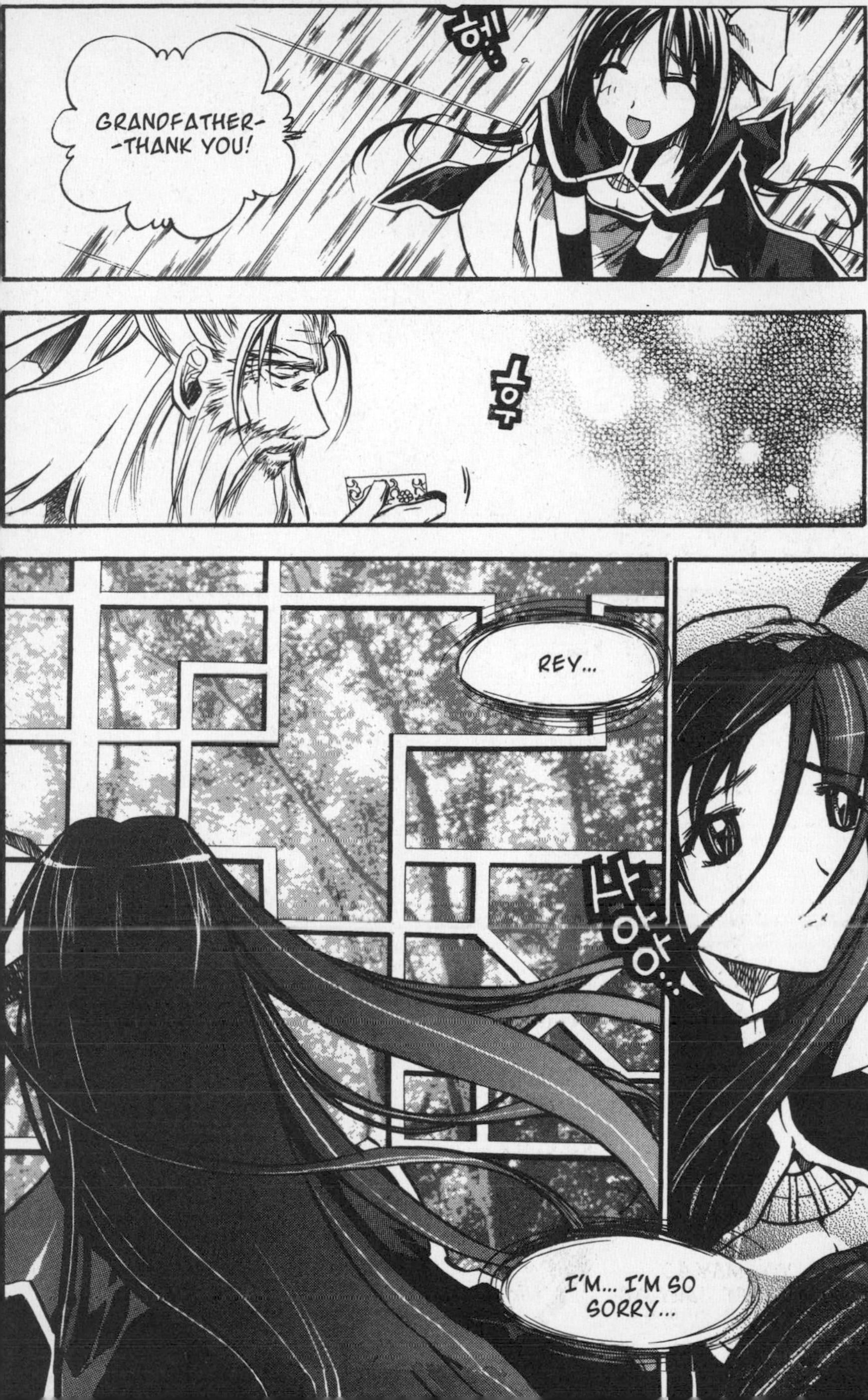
GRANDFATHER-
-THANK YOU!
헤
후
REY...
따아아...
I'M... I'M SO SORRY...

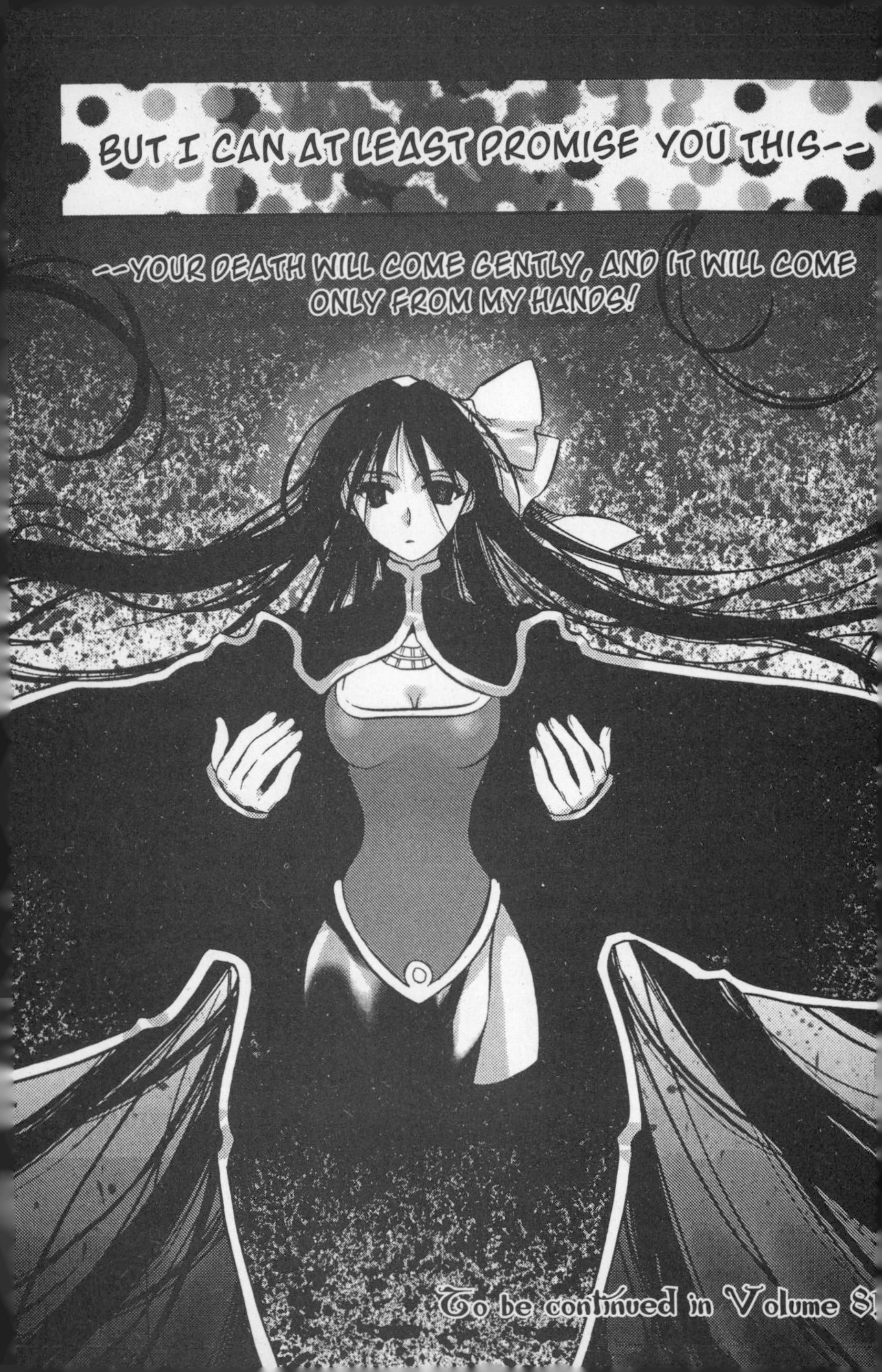
BUT I CAN AT LEAST PROMISE YOU THIS--
--YOUR DEATH WILL COME GENTLY, AND IT WILL COME ONLY FROM MY HANDS!
To be continued in Volume 8!

CHRONICLES OF THE
CURSED SWORD

As Rey continues to prove himself a mighty warrior within the Mujin Fortress, he is paid a visit from his dear friend, Shyao. But with her recently discovered true identity and a deadly new agenda, it may not be the warm reunion Rey had been hoping for. And as if that weren't bad enough, his "good buddy," Jaryoon is hot on his trail...and out for his blood!

Chronicles of the Cursed Sword Vol. 8
Available September, 2004

AUTHOR: YEO BEOP-RYONG
ILLUSTRATOR: PARK HUI-JIN

8

ALSO AVAILABLE FROM

MANGA

.HACK//LEGEND OF THE TWILIGHT
@LARGE
ABENOBASHI: MAGICAL SHOPPING ARCADE
A.I. LOVE YOU
AI YORI AOSHI
ANGELIC LAYER
ARM OF KANNON
BABY BIRTH
BATTLE ROYALE
BATTLE VIXENS
BRAIN POWERED
BRIGADOON
B'TX
CANDIDATE FOR GODDESS, THE
CARDCAPTOR SAKURA
CARDCAPTOR SAKURA - MASTER OF THE CLOW
CHOBITS
CHRONICLES OF THE CURSED SWORD
CLAMP SCHOOL DETECTIVES
CLOVER
COMIC PARTY
CONFIDENTIAL CONFESSIONS
CORRECTOR YUI
COWBOY BEBOP
COWBOY BEBOP: SHOOTING STAR
CRAZY LOVE STORY
CRESCENT MOON
CROSS
CULDCEPT
CYBORG 009
D•N•ANGEL
DEMON DIARY
DEMON ORORON, THE
DEUS VITAE
DIABOLO
DIGIMON
DIGIMON TAMERS
DIGIMON ZERO TWO
DOLL
DRAGON HUNTER
DRAGON KNIGHTS
DRAGON VOICE
DREAM SAGA
DUKLYON: CLAMP SCHOOL DEFENDERS
EERIE QUEERIE!
ERICA SAKURAZAWA: COLLECTED WORKS
ET CETERA
ETERNITY
EVIL'S RETURN
FAERIES' LANDING
FAKE
FLCL
FLOWER OF THE DEEP SLEEP
FORBIDDEN DANCE
FRUITS BASKET
G GUNDAM

GATEKEEPERS
GETBACKERS
GIRL GOT GAME
GIRLS' EDUCATIONAL CHARTER
GRAVITATION
GTO
GUNDAM BLUE DESTINY
GUNDAM SEED ASTRAY
GUNDAM WING
GUNDAM WING: BATTLEFIELD OF PACIFISTS
GUNDAM WING: ENDLESS WALTZ
GUNDAM WING: THE LAST OUTPOST (G-UNIT)
GUYS' GUIDE TO GIRLS
HANDS OFF!
HAPPY MANIA
HARLEM BEAT
I.N.V.U.
IMMORTAL RAIN
INITIAL D
INSTANT TEEN: JUST ADD NUTS
ISLAND
JING: KING OF BANDITS
JING: KING OF BANDITS - TWILIGHT TALES
JULINE
KARE KANO
KILL ME, KISS ME
KINDAICHI CASE FILES, THE
KING OF HELL
KODOCHA: SANA'S STAGE
LAMENT OF THE LAMB
LEGAL DRUG
LEGEND OF CHUN HYANG, THE
LES BIJOUX
LOVE HINA
LUPIN III
LUPIN III: WORLD'S MOST WANTED
MAGIC KNIGHT RAYEARTH I
MAGIC KNIGHT RAYEARTH II
MAHOROMATIC: AUTOMATIC MAIDEN
MAN OF MANY FACES
MARMALADE BOY
MARS
MARS: HORSE WITH NO NAME
MINK
MIRACLE GIRLS
MIYUKI-CHAN IN WONDERLAND
MODEL
MY LOVE
NECK AND NECK
ONE
ONE I LOVE, THE
PARADISE KISS
PARASYTE
PASSION FRUIT
PEACH GIRL
PEACH GIRL: CHANGE OF HEART
PET SHOP OF HORRORS
PITA-TEN

ALSO AVAILABLE FROM TOKYOPOP®

PLANET LADDER
PLANETES
PRIEST
PRINCESS AI
PSYCHIC ACADEMY
QUEEN'S KNIGHT, THE
RAGNAROK
RAVE MASTER
REALITY CHECK
REBIRTH
REBOUND
REMOTE
RISING STARS OF MANGA
SABER MARIONETTE J
SAILOR MOON
SAINT TAIL
SAIYUKI
SAMURAI DEEPER KYO
SAMURAI GIRL REAL BOUT HIGH SCHOOL
SCRYED
SEIKAI TRILOGY, THE
SGT. FROG
SHAOLIN SISTERS
SHIRAHIME-SYO: SNOW GODDESS TALES
SHUTTERBOX
SKULL MAN, THE
SNOW DROP
SORCERER HUNTERS
STONE
SUIKODEN III
SUKI
THREADS OF TIME
TOKYO BABYLON
TOKYO MEW MEW
TOKYO TRIBES
TRAMPS LIKE US
UNDER THE GLASS MOON
VAMPIRE GAME
VISION OF ESCAFLOWNE, THE
WARRIORS OF TAO
WILD ACT
WISH
WORLD OF HARTZ
X-DAY
ZODIAC P.I.

NOVELS

CLAMP SCHOOL PARANORMAL INVESTIGATORS
KARMA CLUB
SAILOR MOON
SLAYERS

ART BOOKS

ART OF CARDCAPTOR SAKURA
ART OF MAGIC KNIGHT RAYEARTH, THE
PEACH: MIWA UEDA ILLUSTRATIONS

ANIME GUIDES

COWBOY BEBOP
GUNDAM TECHNICAL MANUALS
SAILOR MOON SCOUT GUIDES

TOKYOPOP KIDS

STRAY SHEEP

CINE-MANGA™

ALADDIN
CARDCAPTORS
DUEL MASTERS
FAIRLY ODDPARENTS, THE
FAMILY GUY
FINDING NEMO
G.I. JOE SPY TROOPS
GREATEST STARS OF THE NBA
JACKIE CHAN ADVENTURES
JIMMY NEUTRON: BOY GENIUS, THE ADVENTURES OF
KIM POSSIBLE
LILO & STITCH: THE SERIES
LIZZIE MCGUIRE
LIZZIE MCGUIRE MOVIE, THE
MALCOLM IN THE MIDDLE
POWER RANGERS: DINO THUNDER
POWER RANGERS: NINJA STORM
PRINCESS DIARIES 2
RAVE MASTER
SHREK 2
SIMPLE LIFE, THE
SPONGEBOB SQUAREPANTS
SPY KIDS 2
SPY KIDS 3-D: GAME OVER
THAT'S SO RAVEN
TOTALLY SPIES
TRANSFORMERS: ARMADA
TRANSFORMERS: ENERGON
VAN HELSING

**You want it? We got it!
A full range of TOKYOPOP
products are available now at:
www.TOKYOPOP.com/shop**

04.23.04T

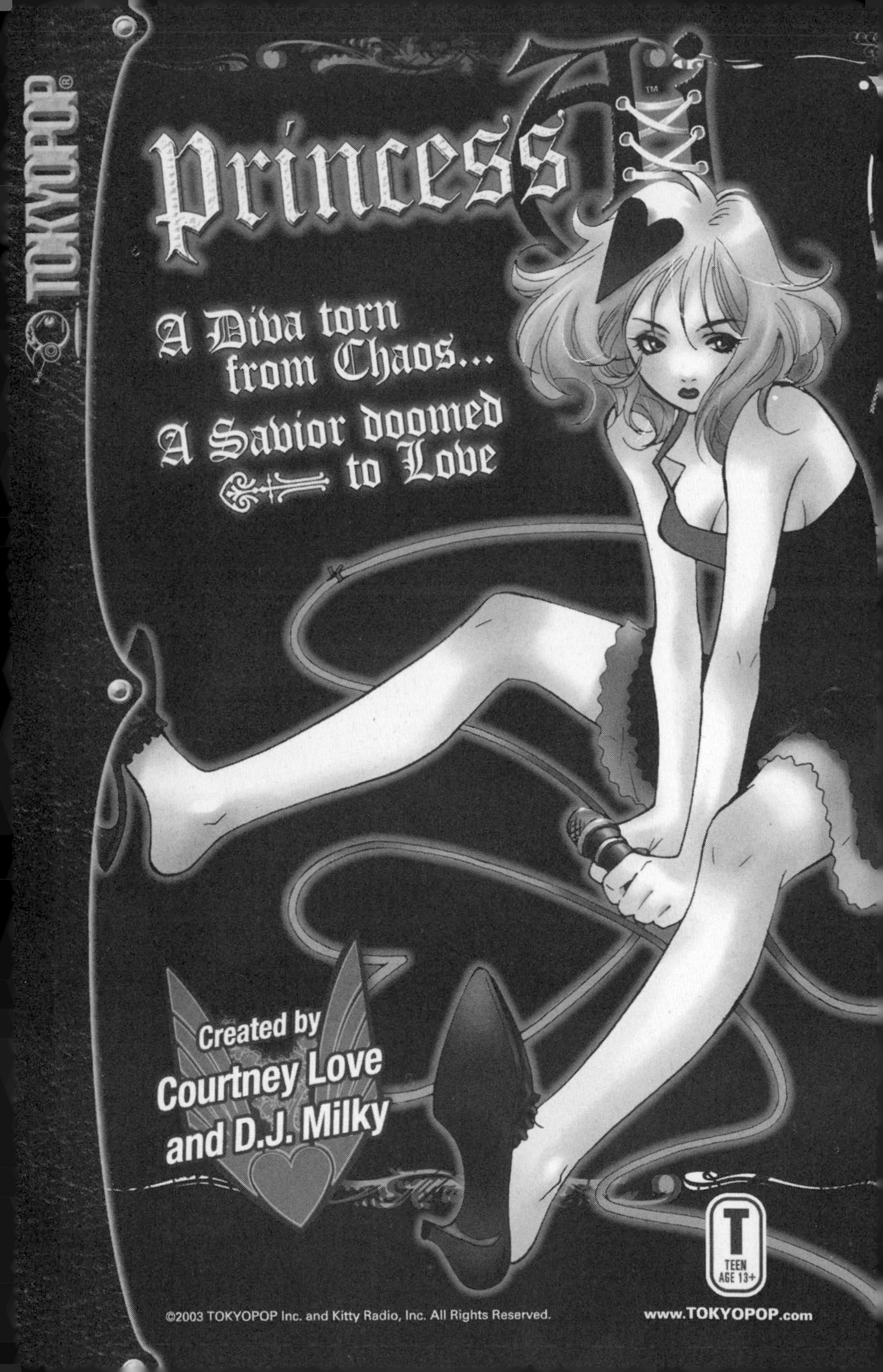

TOKYOPOP
Princess Ai™
A Diva torn from Chaos...
A Savior doomed to Love
Created by
Courtney Love
and D.J. Milky
T TEEN AGE 13+
©2003 TOKYOPOP Inc. and Kitty Radio, Inc. All Rights Reserved.
www.TOKYOPOP.com

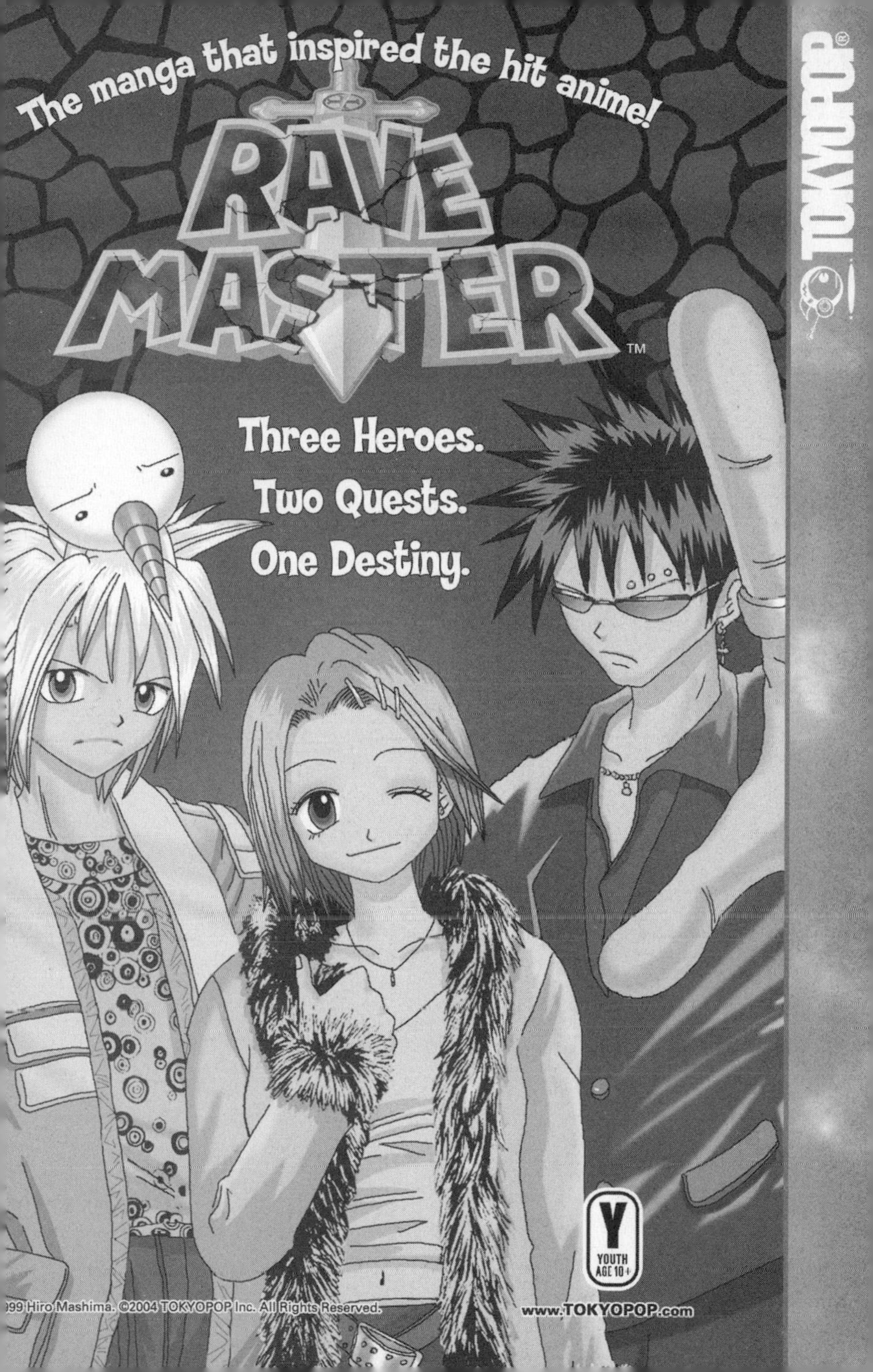
The manga that inspired the hit anime!
RAVE MASTER™
Three Heroes.
Two Quests.
One Destiny.
Y
YOUTH
AGE 10+
99 Hiro Mashima. ©2004 TOKYOPOP Inc. All Rights Reserved.
www.TOKYOPOP.com
TOKYOPOP

Suikoden

幻想水滸伝

III

A legendary hero.
A war with no future.
An epic for today.

TOKYOPOP®